U.S.-CHINESE RELATIONS

U.S.-CHINESE RELATIONS
Perilous Past, Pragmatic Present

Robert G. Sutter

ROWMAN & LITTLEFIELD PUBLISHERS, INC.

Lanham • Boulder • New York • Toronto • Plymouth, UK

Published by Rowman & Littlefield Publishers, Inc.
A wholly owned subsidiary of The Rowman & Littlefield Publishing Group, Inc.
4501 Forbes Boulevard, Suite 200, Lanham, Maryland 20706
http://www.rowmanlittlefield.com

Estover Road, Plymouth PL6 7PY, United Kingdom

British Library Cataloguing in Publication Information Available

Library of Congress Cataloging-in-Publication Data
Sutter, Robert G.
  U.S.-Chinese relations : perilous past, pragmatic present / Robert G. Sutter.
     p. cm.
  Spine title: United States-Chinese relations
  Includes bibliographical references and index.
  ISBN 978-0-7425-6841-9 (cloth : alk. paper) — ISBN 978-0-7425-6842-6 (pbk. : alk.
paper) — ISBN 978-0-7425-6843-3 (electronic)
  1. United States—Foreign relations—China. 2. China—Foreign relations—United
States. I. Title. II. Title: United States-Chinese relations.
  E183.8.C5S893 2010
  327.73051—dc22

                                                                        2010003928

∞™ The paper used in this publication meets the minimum requirements of
American National Standard for Information Sciences—Permanence of Paper for Printed
Library Materials, ANSI/NISO Z39.48-1992.

Printed in the United States of America

Contents

1

Introduction and Overview

RELATIONS BETWEEN THE UNITED STATES AND CHINA emerged as the most important bilateral relationship in the twenty-first century. China's global economic importance and rising political and military power came in a world order where the United States faced many challenges but still exerted broad leadership reflecting its superpower status. Whether the two powers will support international peace and development and pursue more cooperative ties, will become antagonistic as their interests compete, or will pursue some other path in world affairs, remains the subject of ongoing debate among specialists and policy makers in both countries.[1]

Recent Positive Relations and Converging Interests

Publicly, officials in China and the United States emphasize the positive aspects of the relationship. These include ever closer trade and investment ties leading to deepening economic interdependence of the United States and China. Converging security interests involve dealing with international terrorism, North Korea's nuclear weapons program, UN peacekeeping, and other issues involving sensitive situations in Asia and the world. China has come far in the post-Mao Zedong (d. 1976) period in adopting norms of free-market economic behavior supported by the United States and essential to China's success in dealing with the conditions of economic globalization of the current era. China also has substantially changed policies on proliferation of weapons of mass destruction to conform more to U.S.-backed international

norms. U.S.-China collaboration on climate change and environmental issues has grown in the recent period, and bilateral discussion on human rights
continues amid mixed reviews on progress in China toward accepting U.S.-
backed international norms. U.S.-China differences over Taiwan have subsided with the coming to power in 2008 of Taiwan President Ma Ying-jeou,
who has sharply shifted Taiwan toward a more cooperative stance in relations
with China. In broad terms and with some reservations, the U.S. government
accepts and supports the Chinese Communist administration as a leading
actor in world affairs; the Chinese administration has moved to accept, at least
for now, the existing international order in which the United States exerts
leading power in Asian and world affairs.[2]

The Chinese and American administrations have strong reasons to emphasize the positive aspects of their relationship and to minimize public discussion of negative aspects. As explained in chapter 7, doing the latter—that is,
publicly calling attention to negative aspects of the relationship—tends to run
against their interests in promoting stability, security, and development in their
respective countries and in the broader international order. Sino-American
differences are dealt with mainly through private channels of diplomacy called
dialogues. There are over sixty such dialogues between the governments of
Presidents Barack Obama and Hu Jintao. The most important is the U.S.-China
strategic and economic dialogue which held its first meeting in July 2009.

Students and other readers inexperienced with the complicated background
and context of Sino-American relations could be misled by the benign image
of U.S.-China relations which flows from recent public discourse of U.S. and
Chinese officials. Adding to the mix is the point of view of some commentators, particularly in the United States, emphasizing the convergence of interests between the United States and China. Some argue for an international
order determined chiefly by cooperation between the two governments, what
is called a "G-2" world order for the twenty-first century.[3]

This book associates more with the wide range of scholarly and other assessments in the United States, China, and elsewhere that are noted in the
source citations and bibliography of this book which view Sino-American
relations as more complicated and conflicted than recent official discourse
and arguments by commentators in favor of a Sino-American international
condominium would lead us to expect. The review offered here endeavors to
synthesize and analyze the views of various assessments regarding the background, issues, and trends in Sino-American relations. It shows enormous
changes over time, with patterns of confrontation, conflict, and suspicion
much more prevalent than patterns of accommodation and cooperation.
The past four decades have featured sometimes remarkable improvements
in relations as leaders on both sides have pursued practical benefits through

pragmatic means. That the base of cooperation is often incomplete, thin, and dependent on changeable circumstances at home and abroad is evident as the societies and governments more often than not show salient differences over a variety of critical issues involving security, values, and economics. Getting below the surface of recent positive official discussion, the review in this book also shows officials, elites, and public opinion on both sides demonstrating suspicion and wariness of the other country and its possible negative intentions or implications affecting Sino-American relations.

The purpose of the book is not to argue against the recent positive trajectory seen in the public assessments by U.S. and Chinese officials regarding Sino-American relations. The recent positive approach of both the Chinese and American governments is seen as reasonable and good. It is based on common interests of both countries in seeking greater cooperation. Nevertheless, experienced policy makers and observers on both sides understand that the positive official discourse and improvements in Sino-American relations involve only part of a complicated Sino-American relationship. This book seeks to assess more fully the complexity of the relationship so the prevailing positive official view between the two nations is placed in proper context.

Turning Points and Determinants

The most dramatic turn in Sino-American relations came under the leadership of President Richard Nixon (1969–74) and Chairman Mao Zedong. The Sino-American opening surprised even some of the most sophisticated international observers because the U.S. and Chinese administrations, and the broader American and Chinese societies, had spent much of the Cold War in overt confrontation and conflict over a broad range of issues regarding security, economics, politics, and values. The interests and values of both governments and societies were very different and usually in conflict. Both Nixon and Mao pragmatically pursued better relations with one another on account of their respective acute crises and weaknesses brought on by international and domestic pressures and circumstances. The expanding power of the Soviet Union loomed large in the calculus of both countries, and provided one of the few common points in the Shanghai Communiqué marking Nixon's landmark visit to China in 1972. The rest of the communiqué was full of differences registered by the two governments over salient issues in Asian and world affairs. More broadly, free market and democratic America and Maoist China slowly emerging from its most xenophobic, rigidly ideological, and brutally totalitarian phase put aside their enormous differences for pragmatic reasons of realpolitik.

Since the Nixon-Mao opening, the pattern of the U.S. and Chinese leaders pragmatically seeking cooperation for practical reasons having to do with international and domestic circumstances has been the key determinant in developing cooperative Sino-American relations. Common opposition to the threat and expansion of Soviet power in the latter decades of the Cold War was the foundation of Sino-American cooperation in the 1970s and 1980s. Post-Mao China shifted economic policy and integrated China increasingly with the countries of the developed world, building a new foundation for Sino-American cooperation. The ideological rigidity and autarchy of Mao's later years was replaced by political reform and openness to international engagement.

However, progress in relations came to an abrupt halt at the end of the 1980s. The brutal crackdown on student-led demonstrations in Tiananmen Square in 1989 had a negative impact on American public opinion, as well as on the attitudes of the American media, the Congress, and a variety of U.S. non-government interest groups, that endures into the twenty-first century. The collapse of communism in Europe and much of the rest of the world led to the end of the Soviet Union in 1991, ending the strategic foundation of improving Sino-American relations. Without a strategic rationale for cooperating with China and grossly offended by China's blunt use of force at Tiananmen, Americans in Congress, the media, and among a wide range of interest groups gave free rein to criticizing China over the wide range of political, security, economic, and cultural differences existing between the two governments and societies. Those differences and the conflicting interests and values that lay behind them had received infrequent and secondary attention for twenty years on account of pragmatic American pursuit of strategic and other interests through improved relations with China.

The U.S. government endeavored with mixed success to sustain key economic and other ties with China amid this barrage of American criticism of China. Chinese leaders and popular opinion reacted very negatively to the American onslaught, though Chinese leaders were more able and willing than their American counterparts to control government and public attention to Sino-American differences as they sought to sustain important ties with the United States.

U.S. threats to condition or end normal trade relations with China were turned aside as U.S. business interests seeking to benefit from the newly burgeoning Chinese market mobilized and lobbied effectively to sustain these ties important to their interests. President Clinton bowed to congressional and media pressure in allowing Taiwan's president to visit the United States in 1995. China's reaction in the form of provocative military exercises in the Taiwan area was so strong that the Clinton government became much more attentive in seeking to manage differences with China in ways that would not cause crises and would lead to greater U.S.-China engagement.

President Clinton's pragmatic search for greater engagement with China did not still the vigorous criticism of China and Clinton's newly moderate policy toward China on the part of many in Congress as well as U.S. media and various interest groups. President George W. Bush (2001–2009) had an initially tougher stance toward China more in line with congressional, media, and other American critics. Chinese officials endeavored to moderate the U.S. administration's tough stance and succeeded through various concessions in easing Sino-American tensions and building areas of cooperation. By 2003, concerns over North Korea's nuclear weapons development and broader problems in the U.S. campaign against terrorism and the war in Iraq saw the U.S. president shift toward the emphasis on common ground with China that prevailed in the latter years of his government and that characterized the stance of the incoming administration of President Barack Obama. The Chinese administration welcomed the moderation of the U.S. presidents as it endeavored to maintain a positive and cooperative posture toward the United States, seen as supportive of broader Chinese goals emphasizing development and seeking national wealth and power.

Enduring Differences; Diverging Interests and Values

The major turning points and determinants of U.S.-China relations over the last forty years show that without powerful, practical reasons for pragmatic accommodation and cooperation, strong and often deeply rooted and enduring differences between the two governments and the broader societies are likely to emerge. Even in the best of times, those differences tend to obstruct progress and improvement in Sino-American relations. The differences between the United States and China in recent years can be summarized.

China. China's many disagreements with the United States can be grouped into four general categories of disputes, which have complicated U.S.-China relations for years. Chinese leaders were quite vocal about their differences with the United States in reaction to the waves of U.S. criticism of China in the 1990s. China came to moderate its public opposition to U.S. policies and practices beginning at the start of this decade, thereby reducing the salience of some of these issues, but they remained important and were reflected in Chinese policies and actions. The risk-adverse Hu Jintao leadership appeared to have little incentive to accommodate the United States on these sensitive questions; a dramatic Chinese change in favor of the United States on these questions might open the leadership to attack from within the leadership and/or from segments of China's elite and public opinion.

Based on recent Chinese statements and commentary in official Chinese media, the four categories in priority order are: opposition to U.S. support for Taiwan and involvement with other sensitive sovereignty issues, notably Tibet; opposition to U.S. efforts to change China's political system; opposition to the United States playing the dominant strategic role along China's periphery in Asia; and opposition to many aspects of U.S. leadership in world affairs. Some specific issues in the latter two categories include U.S. policy in Iraq, Iran, and the broader Middle East; aspects of the U.S.-backed security presence in the Asia-Pacific; U.S. and allied ballistic missile defenses; U.S. pressure on such governments as Myanmar (Burma), North Korea, Sudan, Zimbabwe, Cuba, and Venezuela; U.S. pressure tactics in the United Nations and other international forums, and the U.S. position on global climate change.[4]

United States. U.S. differences with China continue to involve clusters of often contentious economic, security, political, sovereignty, and foreign policy issues. Economic issues center on inequities in the U.S. economic relationship with China that include a massive trade deficit, Chinese currency policies and practices, U.S. dependence on Chinese financing U.S. government budget deficits, and Chinese enforcement of intellectual property rights. Security issues focus on the buildup of Chinese military forces and the threat they pose to U.S. interests in Taiwan and the broader Asia-Pacific. Political issues include China's controversial record on human rights, democracy, religious freedom, and family planning practices. Sovereignty questions involve disputes over the status of Taiwan, Tibet, Xinjiang, and Hong Kong. Foreign policy disputes focus on China's support for such "rogue" states as Sudan, Myanmar (Burma), Iran, Cuba, Zimbabwe, and Venezuela; and Chinese trade, investment, and aid to resource rich and poorly governed states in Africa that undermines Western sanctions and other measures designed to pressure these governments to reform.[5]

As discussed in the chapters below, these differences reflect conflicting interests and values. For example, in the security area, the United States has a developed a strong strategic interest in sustaining free military access to the Pacific rim in Asia and in fostering a favorable balance of power in the East Asian region. China has long opposed large powers developing and sustaining military power along China's periphery. As China's military power rises in conjunction with its economic power and political influence, it is widely seen to challenge the core American security interests in Asia's Pacific Rim, notably endeavoring to restrict American military access along key areas of China's periphery.

China's need for a free flow of resources such as oil from the Middle East and other developing countries puts a premium on secure lines of communication that remain heavily influenced by the global reach of the U.S. Navy. Pragmatic adjustment to U.S. dominance has been China's recent position, but debate in China foreshadows stronger Chinese efforts to control with their own forces those critically important routes once the Chinese military develops global reach of its own. This challenge to existing U.S. interests in sustaining dominance in such global commons is mirrored in Chinese efforts to improve abilities in space warfare and cyber warfare, among others.

In the area of state sovereignty, China has long regarded U.S. support for the administration in Taiwan separate from China's control as a gross violation of Chinese sovereignty. The United States judges that it has a longstanding commitment to Taiwan that, if not sustained, will undermine American credibility with Japan and other key allies. U.S. values support promotion of democracy abroad; Taiwan's vibrant democracy adds to reasons for the United States to support Taiwan in the face of pressure from the authoritarian Communist Party administration of China, which is viewed negatively by a majority of the American people.

American commitment to human rights and the promotion of democratic governance prompts interventions in support for Tibetan and other ethnic groups and Chinese political dissidents who come under sometimes brutal suppression by the Chinese authorities. Chinese nationalists influential in the Communist Party's administration and broad segments of public opinion in China see such American actions as thinly disguised efforts, reminiscent of imperialist efforts directed at China in the past, to split Tibet and other parts of China from Chinese control, and to promote political change in China that would end the country's communist rule, which the current Chinese leadership sees as their key interest to preserve.

The Americans tend to have more complaints than the Chinese about economic relations as both sides seek to protect their interests in development from being undermined by perceived selfish and exploitative actions of the other. American differences focus on Chinese unfair trading practices, currency manipulation, intellectual property piracy, and other actions that are seen to grossly disadvantage the United States as China speeds toward rapid development while sustaining massive trade surpluses in trade with the United States and accumulating the world's largest foreign exchange reserves. Chinese complaints center on U.S. handling of international economic regulation and the fate of China's over $1 trillion investment in U.S. government affiliated securities.

With the end of the George W. Bush administration's stance at odds with the climate change agenda of much of the rest of the world, the United

States is moving to undertake concrete commitments to reduce green house gas emissions and improve the outlook for the international environment. China's interests in continued rapid economic growth argue against China taking concrete measures in this area that would prove costly to Chinese development. How the two sides will deal with these often conflicting interests remains a key uncertainty at the outset of the Barack Obama administration's interaction with China.

Lessons of History

The differences between the United States and China reflect interests and values of the states and societies that are often deeply rooted in historical experience. In the past four decades of generally improved Sino-American relations, the differences often have been offset and overridden by converging American and Chinese interests dealing with important common strategic, economic, or other interests, but they persist and continue to complicate forward movement in U.S.-China relations. The recent record shows they have the potential to seriously disrupt and upset Sino-American relations, should leaders on either side choose to focus on them rather than continuing improvement in Sino-American ties. A major finding of this study is that the positive equilibrium that prevails in relations between the China and America today is a fragile one on account of the array of differences that continue to divide the two governments and societies.

The endurance of Sino-American differences is not surprising given the historical experience between the United States and China. The development of Sino-American relations since the opening under Nixon and Mao was preceded by two hundred years of interaction. Some American and Chinese politicians and commentators choose to focus on the positive aspects of those many years of interaction. They focus on longstanding U.S. support for the "open door" to China and the territorial integrity of the country in the face of imperialist threats from other powers in the nineteenth and twentieth centuries. The United States did not join Western powers using military force to attack China in order to gain greater diplomatic or economic advantage in nineteenth century China. U.S.-China military cooperation against Japanese aggression in World War II is a prime example of Sino-American cooperation. The role of U.S. businesses and missionaries in helping to advance the Chinese economy, educate Chinese students, and improve conditions in the country also receive prominent play.

Unfortunately, such accounts of Sino-American cooperation are partial and misleading. An effort to review the record in greater depth in the following chapters leads to a much more mixed and on the whole negative assessment of Sino-American relations, underlying reasons for distrust and wariness that continue to characterize the relationship up to the present.

1783–1941. Initial American traders and missionaries had no choice but to accommodate the restrictions and sometimes capricious practices of Chinese regulation of trade and other foreign interaction at Canton in southeastern China. While doing no fighting, the U.S. government benefitted fully as Great Britain, France, and other powers used wars to compel the declining Qing dynasty (1644–1912) to meet foreign demands and grant privileges to foreigners. Americans took full advantage of the resulting Treaty System, which gave foreigners extraterritoriality, the right to reside in China under foreign laws and jurisdiction. The series of foreign treaties imposed on China in the nineteenth century and the early twentieth century opened Chinese ports to foreign commerce and residence; established equal diplomatic relations between the foreign powers and China, with foreign diplomats stationed in the Chinese capital, Peking; allowed foreign missionaries and others to live and work throughout China; provided for concessions of land and development rights that made parts of China, like Shanghai, into foreign-ruled enclaves; and allowed foreign military forces to patrol Chinese coastal and inland waterways and eventually to deploy ground forces in China to secure their interests. The treaties also marked the loss of substantial pieces of Chinese territory to foreign ownership.

American diplomats, merchants, and missionaries reacted with concern as European powers and later Japan began at the end of the nineteenth century to carve up Chinese territory into exclusive spheres of influence. However, U.S. government actions in response were mainly symbolic, using diplomatic notes, agreements, and other non-binding measures to support the principles of free access to China and Chinese territorial integrity. U.S. importance in China also grew by default as previously active European powers withdrew forces and resources during World War I. Imperial Japan used military and other means of coercion to solidify Japanese control in parts of China, notably Manchuria.

Though there often was strenuous U.S. debate, the prevailing U.S. official position was that limited U.S. capabilities and interests in China argued against the United States confronting increasingly dominant Japanese power in East Asia. U.S. officials endeavored to use international agreements and political measures to persuade Japanese officials to preserve Chinese integrity and free international access to China. The U.S. efforts were seriously complicated by political disorder in China and by U.S. leaders' later preoccupation with the consequences of the Great Depression. In the 1930s, Japan created a puppet state in Manchuria and continued encroachments in northern China.

The United States did little apart from symbolic political posturing in response to the Japanese aggression and expansion.

The American-Chinese experience in this more than century-long period saw the emergence of patterns of behavior that influenced U.S. and Chinese attitudes and policies toward one another. American officials and elite and popular opinion tended to emphasize what they saw as a uniquely positive role the United States played as a supporter of Chinese national interests and the well-being of the Chinese people, with some commentators seeing the emergence of a U.S. special relationship with China. Chinese officials and elites, including a rising group of Chinese patriots in the late nineteenth and early twentieth centuries, tended to see American policies and practices as less aggressive than other powers but of little substantive help in China's struggle for national preservation and development. Chinese officials often endeavored to manipulate American diplomacy to serve Chinese interests, but they usually were disappointed with the results. American government policies and practices were seen at bottom to serve narrow U.S. interests, with little meaningful concern for China. Gross American discrimination and persecution of Chinese residents and Chinese immigrants in the United States underlined a perceived hypocrisy in American declarations of special concern for China.

1941–1969. With the Japanese attack on Pearl Harbor, the United States emerged as the most important foreign power in China. However, waging war in China and dealing with complications there, notably the bitter rivalry between Chiang Kai-shek's Nationalist forces and the Communist forces under the direction of Mao Zedong, received secondary attention. The turning tide of the war with Japan caused U.S. planners to look beyond generalities about China's leading role as a partner of the United States in postwar Asia to the realities of preparations for civil war in China possibly involving the United States and Soviet Union on opposite sides. This problem eventually led to U.S. arrangements with the Soviet Union, notably those negotiated at the Yalta conference of February 1945, and continued American support for Chiang's Nationalist government. U.S. actions and policy choices reinforced existing American proclivities to back Chiang Kai-shek's Nationalists, who continued to enjoy broad political support in the United States. Though some American officials pushed for a more balanced U.S. approach that dealt constructively with the Chinese Communists, others were suspicious of the Communists on ideological grounds and because of their ties to the USSR. There also was skepticism about the strength and prospects of the Communist forces. The drift and bias in U.S. policy foreshadowed the U.S. failure in China once the Communists defeated the Chinese Nationalists on mainland China in 1949 and moved in early 1950 to align with the Soviet Union against the United States in the Cold War.

For their part, the Chinese Communists for a period appeared deeply concerned that America would align closely with the Chinese Nationalists after the defeat of Japan in China. Over time, they showed more confidence in their growing strength as well as support from the Soviet Union. Their longstanding prejudice against U.S. "imperialism" was reinforced by American policy and behavior in China during the 1940s that supported their enemy, Chiang Kai-shek, and appeared to marginalize their interests.

Mao Zedong and his Communist Party-led fighters faced daunting challenges as they endeavored to consolidate their rule after defeating Chiang Kai-shek's Nationalist forces in the Chinese Civil War and establishing the People's Republic of China on the Chinese mainland in 1949. Seeking needed technical and economic backing as well as guarantees and support for China's national security, the Maoist leadership endeavored to consolidate relations with the Soviet Union and strengthened its opposition to the United States.

The record of the Maoist period shows a complicated mix of revolutionary imperatives and more conventional imperatives of security and nation-building driving Chinese decision making. Adding to the mix was the emergence of the dominant role of Mao Zedong and how his strong-man rule came to determine Chinese decision making regarding Chinese foreign relations in particular, notably relations with the United States. One consequence was the ability and the actual tendency of China to shift direction dramatically in foreign affairs, seen notably in China's strong alignment with the Soviet Union in 1950 and break with Moscow ten years later.

At the start of the Cold War, Asia seemed secondary in U.S. strategy. The United States demobilized rapidly after World War II. When the Korean War broke out unexpectedly, the United States abruptly reversed recent practice and began what became massive commitments of military power and related assistance to stop the spread of perceived communist expansion in Asia. The strategic U.S. concerns with shoring up the regional balance of influence against communist expansion in Asia dominated the U.S. foreign policy calculus toward China and other East Asian countries. Strong efforts by the U.S. government to mobilize domestic American support for the costs and risks associated with U.S. leadership of the containment effort overshadowed private calculations of American leaders and strategists that appeared to favor a more nuanced and flexible American approach toward China. U.S. elites and supporting groups began to chafe publicly in the 1960s at what they saw as a counterproductive U.S. attempt to isolate China. Their efforts to encourage greater U.S. flexibility toward China failed in the face of strident Chinese opposition to the United States at the start of China's Cultural Revolution and concurrent large increases in U.S. combat forces fighting Chinese-backed Communist forces in Vietnam.

Assessment:

Key features of U.S. and Chinese interests and values are explained in the following chapters dealing with this historical experience. They appear to have a lasting and on the whole negative impact of Sino-American relations today.
On the U.S. side:

- U.S. policy and practice demonstrates the strong rationale to seek change in China in directions favored by the United States. This values-based American approach often clashes with the realities in U.S.-China relations arguing for greater U.S. policy pragmatism.
- U.S. government and non-government opinion shows wariness and unacceptance of China until and unless it accommodates satisfactorily to U.S. values and norms.
- U.S. exceptionalism—as U.S. policymakers backed by broader American opinion often see their actions in morally correct terms, they have a tendency to play down or ignore the negative implications of their actions for China and Chinese interests.
- Non-government actors play a strong role in influencing policy, reinforcing the need for U.S. government policy to deal with domestic U.S. determinants in relations with China as well as the international aspects of those relations. These non-government actors tend to reinforce the three above noted elements of a U.S. values-based approach to China less accommodating to Chinese policies and practices at odds with U.S. norms.
- The longstanding U.S. strategic interest in China saw a prolonged reluctance to undertake the risks, costs, and commitments of leadership in relations with China until forced to do so by Pearl Harbor. This period disappointed those in China seeking help from the United States. Since then, U.S. leadership and resolve generally has continued amid often great sacrifice and trauma, caused in particular by repeated, sometimes very costly and often unpredicted shifts in China. The resulting distrust in Sino-American relations seems strong.

On the China side:

- A longstanding dark view of foreign affairs compels China to sustain and advance national power and independence in order to protect its interests in the face of acquisitive and often duplicitous world powers, notably the United States.
- China shows particular worry about the leading world power (usually the United States) and how it will use its presence and influence along China's periphery, broader international influence, and involvement in

Chinese internal affairs to enhance its own power and influence at the expense of Chinese interests and influence.

- As China rises in international power and influence, the leading power (the United States) is seen to be inclined to constrain and thwart the rise in order to preserve its dominant position.
- Chinese suspicions and wariness toward the United States and toward foreign affairs generally are reinforced by strong currents of nationalism and Chinese domestic politics sensitive to perceived foreign pressures or impositions.

Differences amid Recent Dynamics

Against this largely negative historical background and amid the erratic trajectory of Sino-American relations over the past four decades leading to the positive but still fragile equilibrium that prevails in recent years are a few more recent experiences that reinforce suspicion, wariness, and negativism in Sino-American relations.

- Taiwan: Private and until recently secret Nixon administration interaction with China shows U.S. leaders at the outset giving assurances to China about Taiwan that appeared to open the way to unification on terms agreeable to China. Subsequently, Chinese leaders were repeatedly confronted with U.S. actions at odds with the earlier U.S. promises and impeding Chinese ambitions regarding Taiwan. Chinese distrust of U.S. policy, especially regarding Taiwan, became deep and long-lasting, and continues today.
- Secrecy: Beginning with Nixon, various U.S. administrations determined to hide U.S. concessions on Taiwan and other sensitive issues through secret diplomacy with China in order to keep Congress as well as U.S. media and other interested Americans in the dark on these sensitive questions. One result was repeated backlash from these forces against U.S. administration China policy. Such backlash was seen in congressional action drafting the Taiwan Relations Act of 1979 and congressional and media reaction to the George H. W. Bush handling of the China policy after the Tiananmen incident. The perceived duplicity of U.S. administration on sensitive issues of China policy has led to continued suspicion among congressional officials, the media, and other U.S. opinion leaders regarding the purpose and implications of sensitive U.S. policies toward China. The U.S. domestic backlash and suspicion poses a significant drag on U.S. administration efforts to move forward on sensitive issues in U.S.-China relations.

- Respective costs and benefits: Debate in the United States and China repeatedly centers on whether one side or the other is gaining disproportionately in the relationship while the other side defers and makes concessions. The Chinese administration, given its authoritarian system, has done a better job than the United States in keeping such debate from spilling over publicly to affect policy in negative ways. Nonetheless, the tendency of both sides to be wary of being taken advantage of by the other remains strong.
- Non-government actors: Elites in the Chinese and U.S. administrations have been the key decision makers in Sino-American relations. However, foreign policy in the United States, and particularly U.S. policy toward China, has a long history of American non-government forces influencing policy. These groups and individuals have been especially important when broader international and domestic circumstances do not support a particular elite-led policy toward China. Thus, they were particularly important in the years after the Tiananmen incident and the end of the Cold War. Chinese leaders for their part say they are constrained by nationalistic public opinion in China, which they aver is adverse to Chinese compromises on Taiwan or other sensitive issues in the interests of fostering better U.S.-China relations.

Purpose and Scope of This Book

This book assesses determinants—historical and contemporary—that explain the fragile positive equilibrium prevailing today between areas of convergence and areas of divergence in contemporary U.S.-China relations. It also thoroughly examines those issues (i.e., areas of convergence and divergence) and offers a likely forecast for U.S.-China relations.

Chapter 1 introduces the subject, explains the purpose and scope of the book, and provides an overview of the main findings of the study. Chapters 2 through 7 treat the historical development and status of U.S.-China relations with an eye toward discerning historical determinants relevant to contemporary U.S.-China relations. Chapters 8 through 11 examine four major issue-areas in contemporary U.S.-China relations, endeavoring to discern determinants relevant to the status and outlook of the relationship. Chapter 12 concludes the study with an outlook for Sino-American relations.

2

Patterns of American-Chinese Relations Prior to World War II

Throughout much of the nineteenth century, the United States played a limited role in Chinese affairs. Initial American traders and missionaries had no choice but to accommodate the restrictive and sometimes capricious practices of Chinese regulation of trade and other foreign interaction at Canton in southeastern China, part of the Chinese administration's broad Tribute System restricting and regulating Chinese interaction with foreigners.[1]

As noted previously, the U.S. government followed the lead of Great Britain, France, and other powers that used wars to compel the declining Qing dynasty (1644–1912) to meet foreign demands and grant privileges to foreigners, including Americans who did not take part in the fighting. Americans in China supported and benefited from the resulting Treaty System. The emerging new order gave foreigners extraterritoriality, the right to reside in China under foreign laws and jurisdiction. The series of foreign treaties imposed on China in the nineteenth and early twentieth century opened Chinese ports to foreign commerce and residence; established equal diplomatic relations between the foreign powers and China, with foreign diplomats stationed in the Chinese capital, Peking; allowed foreign missionaries and others to live and work throughout China; provided for concessions of land and development rights that made parts of China, like Shanghai, into foreign-ruled enclaves; and allowed foreign military forces to patrol Chinese coastal and inland waterways and eventually to deploy ground forces in China to secure their interests. The treaties also marked the loss of substantial pieces of Chinese territory to foreign ownership.[2]

A few American companies made significant profits in China trade, but the scope of U.S. trade and investment there remained very small. Christian missionaries comprised the largest and most influential group of Americans in China until the start of World War II, but for much of the period they numbered only in the hundreds.[3]

American diplomats, merchants, and missionaries reacted with concern as European powers and later Japan began at the end of the nineteenth century to carve up Chinese territory into exclusive spheres of influence. However, U.S. government actions in response were mainly symbolic, using non-binding measures such as diplomatic notes and agreements to support the principles of free access to China and Chinese territorial integrity. U.S. importance in China also grew by default as previously active European powers withdrew forces and resources during World War I. Imperial Japan used military and other coercion to solidify Japanese control in parts of China, notably Manchuria.[4]

Though there often was strenuous U.S. debate, the prevailing U.S. official position was that limited U.S. capabilities and interests in China argued against the United States confronting increasingly dominant Japanese power in East Asia. U.S. officials endeavored to use international agreements and political measures to persuade Japanese officials to preserve Chinese integrity and free international access to China. The U.S. efforts were seriously complicated by political disorder in China and by U.S. leaders' later preoccupation with the consequences of the Great Depression. In the 1930s, Japan created a puppet state in Manchuria and continued encroachments in northern China. The United States did little apart from symbolic political posturing in response to the Japanese aggression and expansion.[5]

As summarized in Chapter 1, the American-Chinese experience in this more than century-long period saw the emergence of patterns of behavior that influenced U.S. and Chinese attitudes and policies toward one another. American officials and elite and popular opinion tended to emphasize what they saw as a uniquely positive role the United States played as a supporter of Chinese national interests and the well-being of the Chinese people, with some commentators seeing the emergence of a U.S. special relationship with China. Chinese officials and elites, including a rising group of Chinese patriots in the late nineteenth and early twentieth centuries, tended to see American policies and practices as less aggressive than other powers but of little substantive help in China's struggle for national preservation and development. Chinese officials often endeavored to manipulate American diplomacy to serve Chinese interests, but they usually were disappointed with the results. American government policies and practices were seen at bottom to serve narrow U.S. interests, with little meaningful concern for China. Gross

American discrimination against and persecution of Chinese residents and Chinese immigrants in the United States underlined a perceived hypocrisy in American declarations of special concern for China.[6]

U.S. Interests, Actions, and Perceptions

Beginning in the late eighteenth century, new American freedom from British rule brought American loss of access to previous British-controlled trade partners. This prompted an American search for new trading opportunities in China. Though actual U.S. trade with China remained relatively small, the China market often loomed large in the American political and business imagination. Meanwhile, U.S. officials sometimes sought to channel U.S. investment in ways that would preserve American commercial opportunities in China in the face of foreign powers seeking exclusive privileges and spheres of influence.[7]

Americans also were in the vanguard of Protestant missionaries sent to China in the nineteenth century. U.S. missionaries came in groups and as individuals to work in the treaty ports and eventually grew to many hundreds working throughout China to spread the gospel and to carry out relief, education, medical, and other works of benefit to Chinese people. Part of a well-organized network of church groups that reached deep into the United States for prayers and material support, American missionaries explained Chinese conditions to interested Americans, fostering a sense of special bond between the United States and China. They also served as advisers to U.S. officials dealing with China, and sometimes became official U.S. representatives in China. Their core interest remained unobstructed access to Chinese people for purposes of evangelization and good works carried out by the American missionaries and their foreign and Chinese colleagues.[8]

Though commercial and missionary interests remained at the center of U.S. priorities in China well into the twentieth century, a related strategic interest also had deep roots. In 1835, several years before the first U.S. treaty with China in 1844, the United States organized the Asiatic Squadron. This U.S. Navy group began in 1842 to maintain a regular presence along the China coast. It later was called the Asiatic Fleet. Initially two or three vessels, it grew to thirty-one vessels by 1860 before forces were recalled on account of the American Civil War. It varied in size after the Civil War, but was sufficiently strong to easily destroy the Spanish forces in Manila harbor during the Spanish-American War in 1898. It protected American lives and commerce in China and throughout maritime East and South Asia and reinforced American diplomacy in the region.[9]

Strong American interest in commercial, missionary, and strategic access to China seemed to contrast with only episodic American diplomatic interest in China. The U.S. government occasionally gave high-level attention to the appointment of envoys or the reception of Chinese delegations. Caleb Cushing, Anson Burlingame, and some other nineteenth-century U.S. envoys to China were well connected politically. Some U.S. envoys endeavored to use their actions in China to influence broader U.S. policy or to advance their own political or other ambitions. U.S. envoys sometimes came from the missionary community in China. On the other hand, the post of U.S. minister in China often was vacant, with an interim official placed in charge in an acting capacity. Generally speaking, whenever nineteenth-century U.S. envoys pushed for more assertive U.S. policies that involved the chance of significant expenditure of U.S. resources or political risk, Washington decision makers reflected the realities of limited U.S. government interests in the situation in China and responded unenthusiastically. This broad pattern continued into the twentieth century, though U.S. officials from time to time took the lead in low-risk political and diplomatic efforts in support of U.S. interests in unimpeded commercial and other access to China.[10]

Not surprisingly, the Americans with an interest in China tended to emphasize the positive features of U.S. policy and behavior. Thus, the United States was seen to have behaved benignly toward China, especially when compared with Japan and the European powers that repeatedly coerced and attacked China militarily. The U.S. government repeatedly voiced support of China's territorial and national integrity. Through missionary and other activities, including education activities that brought tens of thousands of Chinese students for higher education in the United States by the 1940s, Americans also showed strong sympathy and support for the broader welfare of the Chinese people.[11]

U.S. officials, opinion leaders, and commentators tended to ignore or soft-pedal negative features of U.S. relations with China. Most notable was the so-called exclusion movement that grossly discriminated against and often violently persecuted Chinese immigrants to the United States. The movement took hold in U.S. politics beginning in the 1870s and lasted for almost a hundred years. At first centered in western states with some significant concentrations of Chinese workers, the exclusion movement reflected widespread American prejudice and fear of Chinese workers amid sometimes difficult economic times in the United States. American elites and common people took legal and illegal actions, including riots and the murder of hundreds of Chinese in the United States, to stop Chinese immigration to the United States and drive away those Chinese already in the United States. Various state governments and the national government passed an array of laws and the

U.S. courts made a variety of decisions that singled out Chinese immigrants for negative treatment and curbed the legal rights of Chinese residents and Chinese citizens of the United States. The movement eventually broadened to include all Asians. The National Origins Act of 1924 barred all new Asian immigration. U.S. mistreatment of Chinese people in the United States became a major issue for the Chinese government, which complained repeatedly against unjust U.S. actions, but with little effect. It was the target of a Chinese anti-American boycott in 1905.[12]

Chinese Interests, Actions, and Perceptions

The Chinese side of the American-Chinese relationship during the more than century-long experience prior to World War II saw Chinese officials and elite opinion in the nineteenth and early twentieth centuries remain preoccupied with massive internal rebellions and disruptions. In this context, the United States figured secondarily in Chinese government and elite concerns. The opinion of the Chinese populace was less important in China-U.S. relations until the anti-Christian and anti-missionary riots later in the nineteenth century and grassroots nationalistic actions like the anti-American boycott reacting to the U.S. mistreatment of Chinese immigrants in 1905.[13]

Qing dynasty officials often were too weak to confront foreign aggression and military pressure in the nineteenth and early twentieth centuries. Their diplomacy frequently amounted to versions of appeasement. Forced to give ground to foreign demands, the Qing officials gave special emphasis to capitalizing on real or perceived differences among the foreign powers, hoping to use some foreign powers to fend off others. Chinese officials repeatedly tried to elicit U.S. actions that would assist Chinese interests against other generally more aggressive and demanding powers. Although U.S. envoys in China often would be caught up in these Chinese schemes and argue for U.S. positions at odds with other powers in China, Washington decision makers tended to adhere to a low-risk approach that offered little of substance to support the Chinese efforts.[14]

Qing dynasty initiatives endeavoring to use possible U.S. support against other foreign powers did not blind Chinese government officials to U.S. interests in China that worked against Chinese government concerns. The spread of foreign missionaries throughout China as a result of treaties reached in 1860 meant that these foreign elites soon ran up against strong resistance from local Chinese elites. The local Chinese elites, the so-called gentry class, often fomented popular outbursts and riots against the foreigners and their

Chinese Christian adherents. The American missionaries sought the support of their official representatives in China who backed their demands to the Chinese government for protection, punishment of Chinese malefactors, and compensation with strong diplomacy and frequent use of gunboats. This posed a very difficult dilemma for Qing officials, who needed to deal with the threats from the Americans and other foreign officials pressing for protection of missionaries and punishment of offending Chinese elites, while sustaining the support of local Chinese elites who provided key elements of Chinese governance at the local levels.[15]

Meanwhile, American government officials were seen by Chinese officials and other elites as transparently hypocritical in demanding protection of special rights for American missionaries and other U.S. citizens in China, while U.S. officials and people were carrying out repeated and often violent infringements on the rights and basic safety of Chinese workers in the United States. In this context, Chinese officials tended to be sympathetic with the merchant-led and student-encouraged anti-American boycott that took hold in Chinese coastal cities in 1905 and that focused on Chinese anger over U.S. discrimination against Chinese in immigration to the United State and poor treatment of Chinese in the United States.[16]

With the withdrawal of the European powers to fight World War I, the United States loomed larger in the strategies of the weak Chinese governments following the end of the Qing dynasty in 1912. However, the United States remained unwilling to take substantial risks of confrontation with the now dominant power in China, imperial Japan. The U.S. reaction to the gross Japanese infringements on Chinese sovereignty in the so-called Twenty-One Demands of 1915 elicited statements on non-recognition and not much else from the United States. President Woodrow Wilson gravely disappointed Chinese patriots by accepting Japan's continued control of the former German lease hold in China's Shantung province at the Versailles Peace Treaty ending World War I.[17]

The Nine Power Treaty at the U.S.-convened Washington Conference of 1921–1922 pledged to respect Chinese territorial integrity, but when Japan took over Manchuria, creating a puppet state in the early 1930s, the U.S. government offered little more than words of disapproval. Given this experience, Chinese patriots were not persuaded by the protestations of some American commentators that the United States had developed a special relationship with China based on concern for the well-being of the Chinese people and preservation of China's sovereignty and integrity. When Japan, after occupying Manchuria, moved in 1937 to launch an all-out war against China and the United States did little in response, Chinese patriots became even more cynical about American intentions and policies.[18]

Nineteenth-Century Encounters

American traders and seamen were the first from the United States to interact with China. When American traders went to China prior to the Opium War of 1839–1842, Chinese regulations under the Tribute System in foreign affairs confined them, along with most other foreign maritime traders, to Canton, in southeastern China. There, local officials supervised and taxed foreign trade, foreigners were required to live and work in a designated area of Canton during the trading season, and foreign interaction with Chinese was kept to a minimum; certain Chinese merchants were designated to deal with foreign merchants.[19]

Chinese foreign relations under the Tribute System were unequal; they emphasized the superiority of China, its system of governance, and the emperor. The foreigners were expected to abide by Chinese laws and regulations and to accord with Chinese instructions. As a result, although American and other foreign merchants and their foreign employees benefited from the trading opportunities at Canton, they were subject to interventions from Chinese authority that appeared unjust from a Western perspective and dangerous to those concerned.

A graphic illustration of the vulnerability of foreigners in China was the case of Francesco Terranova. A Sicilian-born sailor on an American ship trading at Canton in 1821, Terranova was accused of the murder of a boatwoman selling fruit to the ship. He and his shipmates denied the charge. A standoff resulted, with Chinese authorities cutting off American trade until Terranova was handed over. The American merchants and shipowners gave in; Terranova was handed over, tried in secret under Chinese procedures with no American present, convicted, and executed. American-Chinese trade resumed.[20]

Like their British colleagues, American merchants brought opium into China, balancing their purchases of tea and other Chinese commodities. The burgeoning trade in illegal opium entering China in the period before the Opium War was carried out mainly by British merchants, though American merchants carried Turkish opium to China and held about 10 percent of the Chinese opium market. American opium along with British opium was confiscated and destroyed by Chinese authorities in Canton in 1839, leading to Great Britain going to war. The U.S. government took no part in the fighting.[21]

After the British in 1842 negotiated the Treaty of Nanjing ending the Opium War and opening five Chinese treaty ports for foreign residency and trade, the United States appointed Caleb Cushing as commissioner to China to negotiate a U.S. treaty with China. He negotiated the Treaty of Wang-hsia in 1844, obtaining the rights and privileges Britain had gained by force of arms. Chinese negotiator Ch'i-ying followed a general policy of trying to appease foreign demands, and the U.S. treaty included language to the effect that Chinese concessions made to other foreign nations would apply to the United States as well. American merchants, missionaries, and others were free to settle in the five treaty ports; and Americans, like other foreigners in China, had the right of extraterritoriality. This legal system meant that foreigners and their activities in China remained governed by their own law and not Chinese law.[22]

Emblematic of the wide-ranging influence some American missionaries exerted over the course of U.S. policy toward China at this time was the role of Peter Parker (1804–1888). Parker was a medical missionary in Canton in the 1830s. He assisted Caleb Cushing in negotiating the Treaty of Wang-hsia. He was an interpreter and also helped to facilitate the talks by being on good terms with the chief Chinese government negotiator and his aides. Parker eventually became U.S. commissioner in China in 1856. Faced with a harder Chinese line at that time toward foreign demands for broader commercial and missionary privileges, Parker favored Britain's approach emphasizing firmness and appropriate use of force to advance foreign interests. When Chinese forts in Canton in 1856 fired on U.S. warships under the command of Commodore James Armstrong, Parker backed Armstrong's destruction of the forts. Parker later had ambitions for the United States to gain a foothold in Taiwan and to have a more active U.S. naval presence in China, but these initiatives were not supported by the U.S. government.[23]

The upsurge of the massive Taiping Rebellion beginning in 1850 caught Chinese authorities and American and foreign observers by surprise as the rebel movement came to dominate southeastern China and most of the Yangtze River valley. Some Americans at first were attracted by Taiping leader Hung Hsiu-ch'uan's avowed Christian beliefs. Hung came to his own unique views of Christianity, though he had three months of study in 1837 with an American missionary in Canton, Issachar Roberts. As the Taiping leader's warped views of Christianity became clearer to Americans, they added to reasons Americans and other foreigners shied away from the radical rebel leader and his destructive activities.[24]

Though seeing U.S. interests resting with continued Qing dynasty rule, American officials nonetheless were ready to join with Great Britain, France, and others in pressing for treaty revisions that would open more treaty ports, allow for missionary activities outside the treaty ports, and establish foreign legations in the Chinese capital. Britain and France used military force to back up their demands, and in 1858 the Chinese government signed treaties with them and also with the Americans, who did no fighting. When British and French envoys returned in 1859 to exchange ratification, they refused Chinese ratification instructions and a battle resulted in which the Chinese drove off the foreigners. During the battle, the U.S. commodore accompanying the American envoy (Minister John Ward) had his forces, with Ward's approval, join with the British in fighting the Chinese. Ward nonetheless followed the Chinese instructions for treaty ratification and managed to exchange ratification. The British and French returned in force in 1860 and marched to Peking before setting forth new conditions in the treaties of 1860 that also benefited the United States.[25]

U.S. policy in China supported stronger Chinese government efforts after 1860 that worked within the confines of the Treaty System and accepted Western norms while strengthening the Chinese government, economy, and military. American Frederick Townsend Ward had led a foreign mercenary force paid by Chinese merchants to protect Shanghai during the Taiping Rebellion, and he later worked with Chinese authorities in leading a Chinese force that helped to crush the rebellion. Americans supported the newly established Chinese Imperial Maritime Customs Service. This foreign-managed customs service had its roots in Shanghai in the 1850s during the years of threat posed by the Taiping Rebellion; it emerged as a unique Chinese-foreign enterprise (over four hundred foreign employees in 1875) that preserved the Chinese administration's access to an important and reliable source of revenue. The U.S. government saw its interests well served by cooperating amicably with Britain and France as they worked collaboratively with a newly reformist Chinese administration seeking to strengthen China along Western lines. The American Civil War weakened American military presence in China and prompted U.S. policy to place a premium on avoiding disputes with Britain and France that might lead the European powers to be more inclined to support the secessionist south.[26]

Anson Burlingame, U.S. minister to China 1861–1867, symbolized American collaboration with other foreign powers and with China in promoting Chinese reforms and greater outreach to advanced Western countries. After leaving his position as minister, Burlingame accepted a Chinese offer to lead a Chinese delegation to observe and have talks with leaders of the West. The trip was moderately successful, meeting acceptance notably in America and England. The so-called Burlingame Treaty was signed during the delegation's visit to the United States in 1868. Among other provisions in the treaty, the United States said it would not interfere in the internal development of China, China recognized the right of its people to emigrate, and the United States gave Chinese immigrants the right to enter the United States. At the time, there were more than 100,000 Chinese in the United States. Many had come with the support of American business interests and their national and local U.S. government backers seeking reliable labor for the rapid development of the American West.[27]

Unfortunately, American society showed deep prejudice against Chinese that eventually spread to other immigrants from Asia. Ironically, this came at a time when a wide range of elements in the United States generally welcomed the hundreds of thousands of immigrants coming annually to the United States from Europe. There emerged in the 1870s a broadly based exclusion movement in the United States that was a dominant feature in U.S. relations with China for decades to come. This widespread U.S. movement was grounded in prejudice and fear of Chinese workers amid sometimes difficult economic times in the United States. Showing blatant racism against Chinese, Americans took legal and illegal actions, including riots and the murder of hundreds of Chinese in the United States, to stop Chinese immigration to the United States. In September 1885, mobs of white workers attacked Chinese in Rock Springs, Wyoming, killing twenty-eight in an outburst of burning, looting, and mayhem. The state governments and the national government passed an array of laws and the U.S. courts made a variety of decisions that singled out Chinese immigrants for negative treatment and curbed the legal rights of Chinese residents and Chinese citizens in the United States. In 1888, the Scott Act restricted Chinese laborers entry and denied them reentry into the United States. In 1892, the Geary Act stripped Chinese in the United States, whether citizens or not, of substantial legal rights, requiring them to obtain and carry at all times a certificate showing their right to reside in the United States. Without such proof, the punishment was hard labor and deportation. The movement broadened to include all Asians. The National Origins Act of 1924 barred new Asian immigration.[28]

Chinese officials in the Chinese legation in Washington protested U.S. discrimination and persecution of Chinese and endeavored to reach agreements with the U.S. government that would assure basic protection of Chinese rights. They repeatedly found U.S. actions in violation of treaty obligations and other agreements. U.S. violations seriously undermined diplomatic relations between the two countries in the 1890s. U.S. mistreatment of Chinese people in the United States also prompted patriotic merchants, students, and others to organize anti-American movements. A boycott closed several coastal Chinese cities to U.S. goods for several months in 1905. Nevertheless, the U.S. exclusion movement persisted and grew.

Adding to the friction in Sino-American official relations at this time were the tensions caused by expanding U.S. and other foreign missionary activities in China and the resulting anti-foreign backlash in China. Attacks against Chinese Christians and their missionary leaders became common occurrences in the later part of the nineteenth century, prompting American and other Western governments to press the Chinese administration for strong remedial actions, and prompting foreign officials to take actions on their own, including the use of foreign gunboats, in order to protect their interests and citizens. The Chinese authorities repeatedly found themselves caught between competing pressures. On the one hand were the strong American and other foreign pressures to protect missionaries and Chinese Christians. On the other hand was the strong need to preserve the support of local Chinese elites (the so-called gentry class), whose cooperation was essential for the maintenance of local governance in the minimally staffed Chinese administration at the grassroots level. The gentry often tended to see the foreign missionaries as posing social, political, and ideological challenges to the Chinese elite, and they frequently took steps to foster anti-foreign sentiment against them by the broader Chinese society. [29]

Illustrating the marked shift toward the negative in official U.S. attitudes toward China from the comparatively benign and somewhat paternalistic views of Anson Burlingame was the shift in approach of Charles Denby, who served as American minister in China from 1885–1898. A loyal Democrat appointed by the first Grover Cleveland administration, Denby stayed as U.S. minister through the end of the second Cleveland administration. Initially favoring a temperate position in seeking cooperation with Chinese officials seen as moving toward reform, Denby came later to the view that Chinese government incompetence and weakness endangered American and other missionaries and opened China to unchecked ambitions by outside powers. He saw little alternative to the United States' joining coercive foreign powers in order to protect U.S. interests. [30]

Chinese official disappointment and frustration with the United States were reflected in the experience of Li Hung-chang (Li Hongzhang) (1823–1901). Dominating Chinese foreign policy in the last third of the nineteenth century, this senior regional and national leader and commissioner of trade in northern China repeatedly employed the past practice of Chinese leaders in using initiatives toward the United States in an effort to offset pressures on China from other powers. And, as in those earlier episodes, he found the U.S. response wanting, and became increasingly cynical about the utility of appealing to the United States for support. [31]

As in the case of earlier episodes of Chinese efforts to use the United States against more aggressive foreign powers, Li's view was based on the judgment that the United States posed little threat to Chinese territories or tributary states, while its commitment to commerce provided common ground in U.S.-China relations that could be used by Chinese officials to win American support against more grasping and aggressive foreign powers. Li was forced to deal with the growing source of friction between the United States and China posed by U.S. immigration policy discriminating against Chinese. Initially, he endeavored to deal with this issue through negotiation.

Li sought U.S. assistance in dealing with Chinese difficulties with Japan over the Liu-ch'iu (Ryukyu) Islands in the 1870s. President Ulysses S. Grant favored a cooperative U.S. policy toward China and was a personal friend of Anson Burlingame, the prominent proponent of cooperative China-U.S. relations. After leaving office, Grant traveled to Asia in 1879 and was encouraged by Li to intercede with Japan on China's behalf regarding a dispute over the Liu-ch'iu (Ryukyu) Islands. Grant also received at this time a promise from the Chinese government to negotiate treaty restrictions on Chinese immigration into the United States. Li later sought U.S. endorsement of Chinese claims in Korea in the face of Japanese pressure there in the 1880s. He also sought U.S. mediation in a growing dispute with France over Vietnam in the 1880s. All of these initiatives achieved little of benefit to China. By July 1894, Li sought U.S. good offices to avoid a war with Japan over Korea only after exhausting other options. After that, Li endeavored to rely on Russia and other European powers to deal with Japanese demands after the Japanese defeated China in 1895. Unlike other Chinese officials, including his senior colleague Chang Chih-tung (Zhang Zhidong), Li did not emphasize the option of turning to the United States for meaningful assistance in the period of demands by Russia, Japan, and other imperial powers for major territorial and other concessions from China at the turn of the nineteenth century.[32]

U.S.-China Relations amid Foreign Domination, Internal Decline, and Revolution in China, 1895–1941

China's unexpected defeat by Japan in the Sino-Japanese War of 1894–1895 led European powers to join Japan in seeking exclusive spheres of influence and commercial and territorial rights in China. Alarmed that U.S. interests in free commercial access to China would be jeopardized, U.S. officials formulated a response that led to the so-called "Open Door Notes" of 1899 and 1900. The notes sought the powers' agreement that even if they established special spheres in China, they would not discriminate against foreign trade or interfere with customs collection. They underlined U.S. interests in preserving equal commercial access to China and the preservation of the integrity of the Chinese Customs Service, a crucial source of revenue for the struggling Chinese government.[33]

Though generally unenthusiastic about the U.S. initiatives, most concerned powers offered evasive and qualified responses, but all in effect endorsed the principles in the Open Door Notes. As the United States and other foreign powers dispatched troops to crush the Boxer Uprising and lift the siege of foreign legations in Beijing, the United States in July 1900 sent a second round of Open Door Notes which expressed concern for preserving Chinese sovereignty. The foreign powers went along with the notes.

U.S. policy makers repeatedly referred to the U.S. Open Door Policy following the issuing of the Open Door Notes. The William H. Taft administration in 1910 interpreted the policy to extend beyond equal trade opportunity to include equal opportunity for investment in China. The Wilson administration in 1915 reacted to the Japanese Twenty-One Demands against China by refusing to recognize such infringements of the Open Door policy. The related principles concerning U.S. support for the territorial integrity of China were featured prominently in the Nine Power Treaty of the Washington Conference in the Warren Harding administration in 1922, and in the non-recognition of Japanese aggression in Manchuria during the Hoover administration in 1932. The Harry Truman administration sought Soviet Union leader Joseph Stalin's promise that the Open Door policy would be observed in the Soviet-influenced areas of Manchuria following the Soviet military defeat of Japanese forces there in 1945. In general, American political leaders dealing with China throughout the twentieth century tended to refer to the Open Door policy in positive terms, as a U.S. attempt to prevent China from being carved up into commercially impenetrable foreign colonies. Chinese interpretations often emphasized that Americans were more concerned about maintaining their own commercial access and were prepared to do little in practice in supporting Chinese sovereignty. The historical record tends to support the Chinese interpretations.[34]

Most prominent in U.S. policy toward China in the tumultuous period of the Open Door Notes was John Hay. Secretary of State under President William McKinley and, after McKinley's assassination in 1901, President Theodore Roosevelt, Hay strove to preserve U.S. commercial access to China and other interests amid widespread foreign encroachment on the weakened Qing dynasty. Responding to the unexpected Japanese defeat of China in 1895 and European powers' extortion of leaseholds and concessions in the following three years, Hay used the work of State Department China expert William Rockhill and his British colleague from the Chinese Imperial Maritime Customs Service, Alfred Hippisley, as the basis for official U.S. messages sent to all foreign powers concerned with China in September 1899.[35]

The first Open Door Notes were followed by the crisis associated with the Boxer uprising. A grassroots anti-foreign insurrection in northern China, known as the Boxers, came to receive support from some Chinese officials, and by 1899 and 1900 it was carrying out widespread attacks against foreign missionaries and Chinese Christians. As the movement grew, it received the support of the Qing court, though regional leaders in most of China did not support the Boxers. The insurgents occupied Peking and Tientsin, besieging foreign legations and settlements. About twenty thousand foreign troops were mustered, including thousands of Americans, to end the siege and put down the insurgents. They ended the siege of Tientsin in July and Peking in August. Many troops stayed, carrying out punitive expeditions.[36]

As the United States and other foreign powers dispatched troops to crush the Boxer Uprising and lift the siege of foreign legations in Peking, Hay in July 1900 sent a second round of Open Door Notes in which he expressed concern for preserving Chinese sovereignty. He depicted local Chinese authorities as responsible for law and order and the safety of foreigners in China. This helped the United States and other powers continue to work constructively with regional Chinese leaders in central and southern China who were maintaining law and order, and focus their anti-Boxer suppression more narrowly, in northern China.

Though Hay tried to reduce the large size of the foreign indemnity demanded of China, the United States took its $25 million share of the $333 million indemnity China was required to pay the foreign powers under terms of the Boxer Protocol signed in September 1901 and stationed troops along with other powers in northern China under terms of the protocol. While continuing to work in support of China's territorial integrity and equal commercial access to China, Hay responded to U.S. pressures to obtain a coaling station in China by making a perfunctory and ultimately vain effort in December 1900 to acquire such a station on the China coast.[37]

Meanwhile, as Russia endeavored to consolidate its hold in Manchuria, and Japan and Great Britain worked together against it, and ultimately formed an alliance in 1902, Hay attempted to secure U.S. interests with a new Sino-American trade treaty and a request for opening two new treaty ports in Russian-dominated areas of Manchuria. Russia at first resisted Chinese acceptance of the U.S. request but decided to withdraw its opposition when it was clear to them that Americans or other foreigners, notably Japanese, would not settle in the ports.[38]

Though Li Hung-chang and his increasingly skeptical view of the utility of overtures to the United States for Chinese interests remained salient in Chinese foreign policy decision-making until his death in 1901, an important force often arguing for closer Chinese coordination with the United States at this time came from Chang Chih-tung (1837–1909). A powerful Chinese official, well entrenched as governor general in the provinces, Chang endeavored in the period after Japan's defeat of China in 1895 and subsequent European powers' extortion of concessions to cooperate with the United States as a power opposing seizure of Chinese territory. Though he supported China's reliance on Russia after the defeat by Japan in 1895, he came by 1898 to seek the support of Britain and the United States, viewing them as commercial powers with substantial interests in blocking seizures of Chinese territory by Japan, Russia, and others.[39]

That year, he entrusted an American consortium to build the Hankow-Canton railway. The U.S. business group was known as the American-China Development Company. Organized in 1895 and representing U.S. railway, banking, and investment interests, the company received from the Chinese government in 1898 a concession to build and operate a railway between the two Chinese cities. The company demanded and received better terms from the Chinese government in a supplementary agreement in 1900.[40]

Chang made initiatives to the United States during and after the Boxer Uprising seeking U.S. mediation with the foreign powers and U.S. assistance in moderating the foreign reaction to the crisis. Chang sought without much success U.S. help in limiting the size of the foreign indemnity and in dealing with Russian military occupation of Manchuria after the Boxer Uprising. He subsequently became disillusioned with the American consortium for the Hankow-Canton railroad. Some of the American shareholders sold interest in the company to a Belgian syndicate, which by 1904 controlled five of seven seats on the company's board of directors. Chang and the Chinese government then sought to buy back the concession; and the U.S. government encouraged efforts by American investors to restore American control to the company. In the end, American shareholders, having restored American ownership of the company, gained considerable profit by selling their interests in the railway concession back to the Chinese government in 1905.

Chang's frustration with the United States also was seen as he intervened at several points with the Chinese central government and the U.S. government emphasizing strong antipathy among Chinese patriots over the U.S. exclusion of Chinese in the late nineteenth century and the early twentieth century. During the anti-American boycott of 1905, prompted heavily by Chinese resentment over U.S. restrictions on Chinese immigration, Chang privately advised President Theodore Roosevelt to ease the U.S. restrictions.[41]

American officials also were active in the late nineteenth century and early twentieth centuries pressing the Chinese government to protect American and other missionaries and their converts subjected to frequent attacks often fomented by Chinese local elites. The Boxer Uprising in 1899–1900 added greatly to the anti-Christian attacks and implicated the Qing government in the violence. Hundreds of foreign missionaries and thousands of Chinese Christians were killed. The violence against missionaries subsided but did not end. The Lien-Chou massacre of 1905 represented the most serious incident in U.S.-China relations in the decade. The murder of five U.S. missionaries in this southern Chinese city prompted President Theodore Roosevelt to consider the use of force in Canton, and American forces began gathering in Canton harbor. Roosevelt already was strongly critical of the prolonged anti-American boycott underway in China at this time. Chinese officials ultimately took steps to punish those responsible for the massacre and to pay an indemnity.[42]

The Sino-American maneuvering over the Hankow-Canton railway was emblematic of an erratic pattern of American business and government interest in investment in China in railway and other development plans in the last fifteen years of Qing rule. Also reflected at this time was erratic Chinese interest in using such U.S. involvement in efforts to offset foreign encroachment. The focus of American-Chinese interest came to rest in Manchuria, where Russia and especially Japan were consolidating spheres of influence. Prominent figures on the Chinese side in this issue were Tang Shao-yi, a governor in Manchuria, and the regional and emerging national leader of China, Yuan Shih-kai, both of whom sought such U.S. support.[43]

A protégé of Li Hung-chang, Yuan emerged as the most important military and political leader in China in the early twentieth century until his death in 1916. His base of power was in northern China, and he was closely involved with efforts to stem the decline of Chinese influence and control in Manchuria in the face of Russian and Japanese advances. He supported approaches by Tang Shao-yi and others to the Theodore Roosevelt administration seeking U.S. support in order to counter Japanese expansion in Manchuria. Seeking good relations with the United States, he argued for suppression of the anti-American boycott in China in 1905.[44]

Tang had studied in the United States and worked with Yuan and others in encouraging the United States government and business to become more involved with railway building in Manchuria as a means to counter Japanese expansion there. Tang sought support from U.S. financial backers and officials in China. As U.S. consul general in Mukden, Manchuria, during the Theodore Roosevelt administration, Willard Straight attempted to work with Tang and other Chinese officials to use U.S. investments to counter Japanese domination in Manchuria. In 1908 Tang traveled to Washington, where he met with Secretary of State Elihu Root who underlined the Theodore Roosevelt administration's lack of interest in confronting Japan in Manchuria by sharing with Tang the yet-unpublished Root-Takahira Agreement. The latter was an exchange of notes between Root and Japanese Ambassador Takahira Kogoro that underlined U.S. commitment to the status quo in the Pacific region, including China; U.S. desire to maintain friendly relations with Japan; and lack of U.S. interest in considering any Chinese-inspired plan to challenge Japanese interests in Manchuria.[45]

U.S. government policy on supporting railway building as a means to challenge other powers' encroachment and support Chinese influence in

Manchuria shifted markedly for a time during the Taft administration, 1909–1913. The president and Secretary of State Philander Knox tried to use schemes involving U.S. investment in railways to prevent Russia and Japan from dominating Manchuria. A leading example of these plans was a proposed railway in Manchuria between the cities of Chinchow and Aigun. Willard Straight had left U.S. government service and was working with Chinese officials and U.S. and foreign backers to promote plans to build the railroad. Straight signed an agreement with Chinese authorities in Manchuria in October 1909 to have an American banking group finance the Chinchow-Aigun route. Before moving forward with the deal, the Chinese authorities in Peking awaited U.S. efforts to deal with expected Japanese and Russian anger over this challenge to their spheres of influence in Manchuria. In this regard, Secretary of State Knox proposed a bold plan to neutralize or internationalize all railway projects in Manchuria. Japan and Russia rejected Knox's plan and warned against the Chinchow-Aigun railway. Chinese central government authorities temporized, and U.S. investors showed little enthusiasm. The Taft administration's "dollar diplomacy" failed. The U.S. administration subsequently adopted a more moderate stance emphasizing U.S. cooperation with European powers, and ultimately Russia and Japan, in an international consortium dealing with loans to China. Ironically, Hsi-liang, the Chinese governor-general in Manchuria in the last years of the Qing dynasty, and his Qing dynasty colleagues chose this time to try to consolidate ties with the United States and to seek greater U.S. support against Russia and Japan in Manchuria. However, Chinese government emissaries found the Taft administration now maintained a low profile regarding Manchuria.[46]

The pattern of U.S. government policy on the one hand supporting an open door of international commercial access to China and Chinese territorial integrity, and on the other hand avoiding actions that would complicate U.S. relations with salient foreign powers expanding in China, continued with the fall of the Chinese empire. In the thirty years from the end of the Qing dynasty in early 1912 to the attack on Pearl Harbor in late 1941, U.S. policy and practice endeavored to stake out positions and formulate political measures designed to support Chinese sovereignty and integrity. But they did so while generally avoiding the risk of confrontation with imperial Japan, which emerged as the dominant power in East Asia after the pullback and weakening of European powers in the region with the start of World War I. U.S. policy makers also were challenged by revolutionary movements and violent anti-foreign sentiment sweeping China in the 1920s. They tended to adjust to these trends pragmatically, giving way to some of the Chinese demands and eventually establishing good working relations with the Nationalist Chinese administration of Chiang Kai-shek, the dominant leader of China by the late 1920s.

Japan moved quickly to consolidate its position in China with the start of World War I. Allied with Great Britain and siding with the Allies in World War I, Japan occupied German concessions in China's Shantung province in 1914. In January 1915, Japan presented the Chinese government with five sets of secret demands that became known as the Twenty-One Demands. The demands were leaked, which compelled Japan to defer the more outrageous ones, but they resulted in May 1915 in Sino-Japanese treaties and notes confirming Japan's dominant position in Shantung, southern Manchuria, and eastern Inner Mongolia and Japan's special interests in an industrial area in central China. U.S. officials debated how to respond. Secretary of State William Jennings Bryan at first reaffirmed U.S. support for China's territorial integrity and equal commercial access to China, but also acknowledged Japan's "special relations" with China. President Woodrow Wilson subsequently warned that the United States would not accept infringements on its rights, and Bryan said the United States would not recognize infringements on U.S. rights, Chinese sovereignty, or the Open Door policy. In a bid to expand U.S. leverage, Wilson then reversed an earlier decision and supported American banks lending money to China through an international consortium as a means to balance Japanese expansion in China.

Japan was not seriously deterred and maneuvered to see that its position in Shantung province was secured by the Versailles Peace Treaty ending World War I. Like Japan, the Chinese government had aligned with the victorious allied powers. U.S. and Chinese delegations worked closely at the peace conference to free China from restrictions on her sovereignty, and Chinese negotiators were particularly interested in regaining control of the former German concession in China's Shantung province. Nevertheless, Japan earlier signed secret agreements with European powers that bound them to support Japan's claims to the Shantung leasehold, and the Chinese government's position was weakened by having agreed as part of the Twenty-One Demands in 1915 to accept German-Japanese agreement on the concessions. Robert Lansing, a counselor at the State Department during the early years of the Wilson administration, argued against confrontation with Japan in defense of China's integrity at the time of Japan's Twenty-One Demands in 1915. As secretary of state in 1917, he negotiated and exchanged notes with Japanese envoy Ishii Kikujiro that acknowledged Japan's "special interests" in China, even though Japan privately agreed not to seek privileges at the expense of other friendly powers in China. The notes were used by Japan as evidence of tacit U.S. support for Japanese expansion in China. Though Lansing opposed President Wilson's decision at the Versailles Peace Conference in 1919 to accept Japanese claim to the German concessions in China's Shantung province, Wilson felt compelled to accept Japan's claim to the former German concessions. The president's action gravely disappointed Chinese patriots. The provision in the treaty was a catalyst for demonstration in Peking on May 4, 1919 that led to both intellectual reform campaigns and radical, anti-imperialist movements that spread throughout China in following years and became known collectively as the May Fourth Movement.[47]

The United States after World War I took the lead in calling a major conference to include powers with interests in the western Pacific, including China but not the Soviet Union, to deal with relevant security issues. The result was the Washington Conference of 1921–1922 that saw passage of a Nine Power Treaty supporting non-interference in Chinese internal affairs. U.S. delegates working with others also succeeded in getting Japan to agree to withdraw from Shantung under terms of agreements at the conference. Nonetheless, the treaty and the conference results disappointed Chinese patriots heavily influenced by the strong nationalistic fervor emerging in China at this time, as they had no enforcement mechanisms and did nothing to retrieve the rights of sovereignty China had been forced to give up to foreign powers over the previous eighty years.[48]

Meanwhile, U.S. policy makers were compelled to react to repeated acts of violence against Americans and other foreigners and their interests as revolutionary political and military movements swept through China during the 1920s. By 1925 the foreign treaty port rulers and collaborating Chinese provincial rulers seemed to an increasing share of the Chinese public to constitute an evil partnership of "imperialism" and warlords. The rising Chinese Nationalist Party under Sun Yat-sen (d. 1925) and his successor Chiang Kai-shek was receiving substantial military and financial support and training from the Soviet Union and the international Communist organization known as the Communist International or Comintern. Soviet-backed Communist agents were instrumental in assisting the establishment of the Chinese Communist Party, which was instructed to align with Sun and Chiang's much larger Chinese Nationalist Party. These movements were aligned in seeing the evils of imperialism and warlords as enemies of Chinese nationalism. Chinese industrialists had prospered with the withdrawal of competition from Western enterprises and the rise in foreign demand during World War I. They were more ready to take a stance against the foreigners in this period of revived foreign economic competition in China.[49]

In Shanghai early in 1925 union organizers were active and strikes increased, and at the same time merchants in the Chinese Chamber of Commerce protested against regulation and "taxation without representation" under the foreign-ruled Shanghai Municipal Council. An incident in Shanghai arising out of a strike against Japanese-owned textile mills led to an outburst of anti-imperialist and anti-foreign demonstrations and sentiment. British-officered police under the authority of the foreign-ruled Shanghai Municipal Council killed thirteen demonstrators on May 30, 1925. There ensued a nationwide multi-class movement of protests, demonstrations, strikes, boycotts, and militant anti-imperialism. This May Thirtieth movement dwarfed all previous anti-foreign demonstrations. In June a demonstration in Canton led to shooting between Nationalist Party cadets and Anglo-French troops, killing fifty-two Chinese. The resulting fifteen-month strike and boycott of Hong Kong crippled British trade with South China.[50]

In this revolutionary atmosphere, Chinese Communist Party organizations expanded membership rapidly. Consistent with guidance from the Stalin-dominated Comintern, the party remained in a wary united front with the larger Chinese Nationalists as Chiang Kai-shek consolidated his leadership and prepared to launch the Northern Expedition from the Nationalist base in Canton in 1926. The military campaign and attendant political agitation were designed to smash the power of the warlords, assert China's rights against imperialism, and reunify China. By 1927, the campaign had gained control of much of southern and central China.[51]

Advancing in Nanking in March 1927, some Nationalist forces attacked foreigners and foreign property in this city, including the American, British, and Japanese consulates. Several foreigners, including Americans, were killed. Looting and threats against foreigners did not stop until British and U.S. gunboats began to bombard the attackers. The Americans joined the other powers in demanding punishment, apology, and compensation from the Nationalist authorities. The Nationalist authorities at the time were in turmoil with a power struggle for leadership that saw Chiang Kai-shek's forces kill several hundred Communist Party and labor leaders in Shanghai the day after the Nanking incident, foreshadowing the start of a broader and violent Nationalist campaign against Communists and other perceived enemies. Maneuvering within the Nationalist leadership resulted in Chiang Kai-shek's emergence as dominant leader in January 1928. U.S. Secretary of State Frank Kellogg reacted with moderation and restraint to the violence and challenges to U.S. and foreign rights in China at this time. This helped to facilitate U.S. rapprochement with the Nationalist regime of Chiang Kai-shek once it consolidated power in 1928. In March 1928, Chiang's regime accepted American terms about the Nanking incident while the U.S. government expressed regret about the gunboat bombardment.[52]

Imperial Japan felt threatened by rising Chinese nationalism and endeavored to consolidate its hold in Manchuria. Japanese agents assassinated the Chinese warlord in Manchuria and eventually took control of the territory under the guise of an independent state, Manchukuo, created in 1932 and recognized among the major powers only by Japan. U.S. policy makers did not change their low-risk policy toward Japan despite Tokyo's blatant grab of Manchuria. Dealing with the disastrous consequences of the Great Depression, U.S. President Herbert Hoover was reluctant to respond forcefully to Japan's aggression in Manchuria and its breach of U.S.-backed security arrangements in the Nine Power Treaty of 1922 and the Kellogg-Briand Pact of 1928. With his secretary of state, Henry Stimson, in the lead, Hoover favored a moral stance of non-recognition of the changes brought by Japan's aggression. This so-called Hoover-Stimson doctrine failed in 1932 as Japanese forces expanded their military aggression in China to include attacks on Chinese forces in Shanghai. The Hoover administration formally protested, sent additional forces to China, and appealed to the world not to recognize the Japanese aggression. The Japanese halted the assault on Shanghai and the League of Nations adopted a resolution of non-recognition, but Japan created a puppet state of Manchukuo and withdrew from the League of Nations when it approved a report critical of Japan's actions.[53]

The Franklin Roosevelt administration continued a cautious stance in the face of Japanese aggression in China, though some administration officials showed sympathy and support for China. Harry Hopkins, a close adviser to President Roosevelt, was sympathetic to China's cause and provided a channel of communication between Chiang Kai-shek's administration and the U.S. president. Secretary of the Treasury Henry Morganthau endeavored to support the struggling Chinese Nationalist Party government against Japanese aggression. In 1934, the United States inaugurated, primarily for domestic reasons, a silver purchase program which caused great turmoil in the Chinese economy as massive amounts of silver left China by 1935. In response, Morganthau initiated a silver purchase program for Nationalist China, paying it hundreds of millions of dollars in gold and U.S. dollars for 500 million ounces of silver.[54]

Even when Japan engaged in all-out brutal war against China in 1937, Washington showed sympathy to China but offered little in the way of concrete support. Responding to Japanese aggression against China and other military expansion, President Franklin D. Roosevelt in a speech on October 5, 1937, called for a quarantine of an "epidemic of world lawlessness." No specific U.S. actions in Asia followed because the U.S. government was not prepared to stand against Japan as it ruthlessly advanced in China. Indeed, Japanese aircraft in December 1937 sank the U.S. gunboat *Panay* and machine-gunned its survivors in the Yangtze River. U.S. officials accepted Japan's apology and compensation, not choosing to make this an issue of confrontation with Japanese aggression in China.[55]

Stanley Hornbeck, a senior State Department specialist on China, played important roles in advising and implementing U.S. policy toward China during this period. A strong supporter of China, he also was realistic about Chinese weaknesses and capabilities in the face of Japanese power. He was involved in various efforts to provide U.S. support for the Chinese Nationalist Party government and to resist Japanese aggression without directly confronting Japan. Those U.S. efforts were slow in coming.[56]

As secretary of state in the Franklin D. Roosevelt administration in the years prior to World War II, Hornbeck's boss Cordell Hull shied away from support of China, then at war with Japan. He sought to avoid U.S. involvement in an Asian war at a time of heightened tensions and war in Europe. Hull disapproved a plan supported by Treasury Secretary Henry Morgenthau to provide China $25 million in credits to purchase supplies in the United States, but President Roosevelt approved the plan while Hull was out of the country in December 1938. Hull resisted efforts to impose sanctions on Japan, but eventually the State Department in January 1940 announced that the United States would not renew a 1911 commercial treaty with Japan. This step allowed the United States subsequently to impose selective embargoes on the sale of strategic materials to Japan, leading to a U.S. oil embargo in 1941.[57]

By this time, with the support of Treasury Secretary Morganthau and others, President Roosevelt approved the formation of the American Volunteer Group, also known as the "Flying Tigers," to support the beleaguered Chinese Nationalist administration in the face of Japanese aggression. The group arose from plans by retired U.S. General Claire Chennault and others that resulted in a secret presidential order allowing U.S. pilots to resign their commissions and sign contracts with a firm whose operating funds came from the lend-lease air program, for the purpose of flying fighter planes transferred to the Chinese government under lend-lease. The lend-lease program was proposed by the president and approved by Congress in early 1941 and China became eligible to receive lend-lease aid on May 6, 1941. The Flying Tigers helped to protect airspace over the Chinese Nationalist capital in China's interior city of Chungking and other Chinese Nationalist holdings against attacks by Japanese warplanes.[58]

Nongovernmental American interaction with China continued to focus on economic exchange and missionary-related activities, although educational exchange separate from missionary activities grew in importance. U.S. trade with China increased to $290 million in 1929, worth almost half of the $692 million value of U.S.-Japanese trade that year. As world trade contracted sharply with the Great Depression, the importance of U.S. exports to Japan relative to U.S. exports to China increased. In 1936, the year prior to the start of the Sino-Japanese War, U.S. exports to China were valued at $47 million, while U.S. exports to Japan were valued at $204 million. The balance of U.S. economic interests appeared to reinforce continued strong isolationist tendencies in the United States to avoid involvement on the side of China in opposition to increasingly apparent aggression by Imperial Japan.[59]

Japanese atrocities in the war against China beginning in 1937 and Imperial Japan's subsequent alignment with Nazi Germany in 1940 hardened American public attitudes as well as those of U.S. officials against Japan. Individual Americans with close ties to both the Chiang Kai-shek and Roosevelt administrations and a number of organizations such as the Committee for Non-Participation in Japanese Aggression advocated giving U.S. aid to China. Thomas Corcoran, formerly a White House lawyer close to President Roosevelt, was among the group of several former federal officials paid by Chiang Kai-shek agents to insure stronger U.S. support for the Nationalist government. Henry Luce, the child of Christian missionaries in China, created a powerful media enterprise in the United States centered on *Time* and *Life* magazines. Luce used these widely read publications to strongly support Chiang Kai-shek and his American-educated wife, Soong Mayling, hailing the nation-building struggles of the Nationalist Party government and its protracted resistance to Japanese aggression. The Committee to Defend America by Aiding the Allies and other groups and individuals worked against those in American politics who continued to adhere to a non-interventionist stance. The latter included The Women's International League for Peace and Freedom and the National Council for Prevention of War. The non-interventionist stance was buttressed by widespread feeling in the United States in the 1930s that the United States had mistakenly intervened in World War I on behalf of the privileges of a few, prompting peace activists to work to prevent repetition of such errors.[60]

The missionary response to China's problems in the early twentieth century went well beyond evangelical matters. Expanding from about a thousand American missionaries representing twenty-eight societies in China in 1900, the respective numbers increased by 1930 to more than three thousand missionaries representing sixty societies. Adjusting to the rise of nationalism in China, the emphasis now focused on making the Christian church in China indigenous, led by Chinese and at least partially self-supporting, with Americans assisting and advising. The YMCA had an emphasis on programs for literacy and social work and proved to be attractive to younger Chinese leaders. The North China famine of 1920–1921 saw the creation of the China International Famine Relief Commission that by 1936 used over $50 million in foreign donations to promote basics in rural development. An interdenominational Protestant conference in 1922 organized the National Christian Council that set to work on social issues in urban and rural China. James Yen, educated at Yale University and with the YMCA, used support from the

Rockefeller Foundation to begin to spread literacy and practical education to rural China.[61]

American reformist ideas and influence were notable among the more moderate elements of the Chinese intelligentsia at this time. The latter tended to be foreign-trained and to work in academic and scientific institutions. The dozen Christian colleges were coming under more Chinese control and relied on Chinese sources for more than half of their income, though a majority of their faculties were foreign-trained. The big national universities also had staffs largely trained abroad, mostly in the United States. Such American influence also was evident in the various research institutes of the central government and the big Rockefeller-supported Peking Union Medical College. Supporting these trends, 2,400 Chinese students entered American universities between 1900 and 1920; and 5,500 did so between 1920 and 1940. They studied in 370 institutions and tended to major in such practical subjects as engineering and business. They returned to China as a new elite in Chinese business, academic, and government circles.[62]

3

Relations during
World War II, Civil War, Cold War

U.S.-China Relations during World War II and China's Civil War

U.S. Interests, Actions, and Perceptions

THE JAPANESE ATTACK ON PEARL HARBOR thrust the United States into a leadership position in China and in global affairs. American debates over international involvement and the longstanding U.S. reluctance to assume costs and risks of leadership were put aside. President Franklin D. Roosevelt and his war cabinet enjoyed broad domestic support as they mobilized millions of American combatants and enormous contributions of equipment and treasure in working with and leading Allied powers in the largest war the world has ever seen. The coalition eventually defeated the Axis powers. U.S. leaders and interests focused on effectively fighting the massive worldwide conflict and dealing with issues that would determine the postwar international order.

The United States emerged as the most important foreign power in China. However, waging war in China and dealing with complications there, notably the bitter rivalry between Chiang Kai-shek's Nationalist forces and the Communist forces under the direction of Mao Zedong, received secondary attention. Circumstances in China contrary to American plans and expectations also repeatedly forced U.S. leaders to adjust strategies.[1]

Early American assessments that China would provide strong forces and reliable bases for the defeat of Japan proved unrealistic given the many weaknesses of Chiang Kai-shek's Nationalist armies, the inability of the

United States to supply and train large numbers of Chinese forces on account of Japan's control of the main surface routes of supply, and the primacy Chiang's Nationalists and Mao's Communists gave to their struggle with one another. The United States shifted focus to defeating Japan by advancing through the Pacific Islands; it strove to keep China in the war as a means to tie down the one million Japanese soldiers deployed to the country.[2]

The turning tide of the war with Japan caused U.S. planners to look beyond generalities about China's leading role as a partner of the United States in postwar Asia to the realities of preparations for civil war in China possibly involving the United States and Soviet Union on opposite sides. Debate among U.S. officials about how to deal with the Chinese Nationalists and the Chinese Communists and the postwar order in China eventually led to direct U.S. arrangements with the Soviet Union, notably those negotiated at the Yalta conference of February 1945, and continued American support for Chiang's Nationalist government. In this context, U.S. leaders encouraged negotiations and mediated between the Chinese Nationalists and Chinese Communists in order to avoid civil war and shore up China's position as a power in Asia friendly to the United States.[3]

Though they were repeatedly and deeply disappointed with the weaknesses and corruption of the Nationalist Chinese administration, American officials tended to follow paths of least resistance when dealing with the dispute between the Chinese Nationalists (KMT) and the Chinese Communists (CCP). U.S. actions and policy choices reinforced existing American proclivities to back Chiang Kai-shek's Nationalists, who continued to enjoy broad political support in the United States. They avoided the difficult U.S. policy reevaluation that would have been required for U.S. leaders to position the United States in a more balanced posture in order to deal constructively with the Chinese Communists as well as the Chinese Nationalists. Though some American officials pushed for a more balanced U.S. approach, others were suspicious of the Communists on ideological grounds and because of their ties to the USSR. There also was skepticism about the strength and prospects of the Communist forces. In the end, it appeared that moving American policy from support for Chiang Kai-shek's Nationalists would be too costly for American interest in shoring up a postwar Chinese administration friendly to the United States. The drift and bias in U.S. policy, strengthened by interventions of important U.S. officials such as U.S. presidential envoy and ambassador to China Patrick Hurley, foreshadowed the U.S. failure in China once the Communists defeated the Chinese Nationalists on mainland China in 1949 and moved in early 1950 to align with the Soviet Union against the United States in the Cold War.[4]

Chinese Interests, Actions, and Perceptions

Having survived with enormous cost and deprivation four years of war with Japan, Chiang Kai-shek and his Nationalist administration were relieved as the United States entered the war with Japan in 1941. The eventual defeat and collapse of the Japanese empire seemed likely. The Nationalist administration was prepared to cooperate with its new U.S. ally in the war effort against Japan, but repeatedly it showed greater interest in using U.S. supplies and support in order to prepare to deal with the opposing Communist forces and securing Nationalist leadership in postwar China. Chiang Kai-shek and his lieutenants sought to maximize the material, training, financial, and political support from the United States, while fending off repeated U.S. requests for greater contributions by Nationalist armies in the war effort against Japan. When U.S. officials in China repeatedly became frustrated with the lackluster support of the war effort from what was often seen as a corrupt, repressive, and narrowly self-serving Nationalist Chinese administration, Chiang and his allies tried to outmaneuver them through such means as appeals to top U.S. leaders and special U.S. envoys sent to China, lobbying in Washington, and thinly veiled warnings that the Nationalists might seek accommodation with Japan.[5]

The Nationalists also resisted efforts by U.S. officials in China to open direct American communication with and possible support for the Chinese Communist forces. Furthermore, Chiang and his administration fended off repeated U.S. calls for greater reform and accountability in the Chinese Nationalist administration. They accommodated U.S. mediation efforts to bridge the divide between the Nationalists and Communists. They found strong common ground with U.S. mediator Patrick Hurley. U.S. mediator George Marshall was much more critical of Chiang Kai-shek and Nationalist policies and actions. The Nationalists appeared to have little choice but grudgingly to go along with the humiliating arrangements imposed on them as a result of U.S.-Soviet negotiations at Yalta. Their future depended on preserving U.S. support. They strove to continue this support without conditions that would compromise the goal of a Nationalist-ruled China in postwar Asia.[6]

The Chinese Communists under the leadership of Mao Zedong had strong and well-developed ideological and foreign policy leanings opposed to U.S. policy in China and U.S. leadership in world affairs. Their connections with the Soviet Union and the influence of the USSR on their approach to the United States also were significant. They endorsed the twists and turns of Soviet maneuvers in the early years of the war, and they followed Moscow's lead in an overall positive approach to the United States as it entered the war in 1941.[7]

Probably more important in Chinese Communist calculations were the realities of power in China. Like Chiang Kai-shek's Nationalists, the Communists under Mao foresaw the eventual defeat of Japan at the hands of the United States. The United States rapidly became the predominant power in East Asia, and in China it brought its power, influence, and aid to bear solely on the side of Chiang Kai-shek's Nationalists, who were determined to subordinate and suppress the Communists. For CCP leaders, there was a serious likelihood that the United States, because of growing association with Chiang Kai-shek, might use its enormous power against the CCP during the anticipated Chinese civil war following Japan's defeat.[8]

To counter this prospect, the Communists had the option of looking to their Soviet ally for support. But Moscow at that time was showing little interest in defending CCP interests against a challenge by U.S.-backed Nationalist forces. The Communists saw that only at great risk could they ignore the change that had taken place in the balance of forces in China. Seeking to keep the United States from becoming closely aligned with Chiang Kai-shek against CCP interests, the Communists decided to take steps on their own to ensure that Washington would adopt a more even-handed position. They strove to put aside historical difficulties with the United States and soft-pedaled ideological positions that might alienate Washington as they sought talks with U.S. officials in order to arrive at a power arrangement that would better serve CCP interests in China.[9]

The United States chose to rebuff the Communist initiatives, leaving the CCP facing the likelihood of confrontation with a strong U.S.-backed KMT army at the end of the Pacific war. Fortunately for the CCP, Moscow built its strength in East Asia during the final months of the war and the period following Japan's defeat, and the United States rapidly withdrew its forces from East Asia at the war's end. Later in the 1940s, the Communists obtained more support from the USSR, leading eventually to the Sino-Soviet alliance of 1950. Meanwhile, the Communist forces grew in strength while the larger Nationalist forces suffered from significant weaknesses including poor leadership and morale, paving the way to Communist victory against the U.S.-supported Nationalists in 1949.[10]

Encounters and Interaction in the 1940s

It is hard to imagine a decade of more consequence for modern China and its relations with the United States than the 1940s. The U.S. entry into World War II marked the beginning of the end of Japanese aggression in China and the Asia-Pacific. The stalemate between Japanese forces occupying the more well-developed eastern regions of China and the Chinese Nationalists and Chinese Communist forces holding out in China's interior eventually broke and ended under the pressure of the U.S.-led war effort against imperial Japan. The end of the Japanese occupation of China opened the way to Chinese civil war and resolution of the decades-long conflict between Chinese Nationalist and Chinese Communist forces. As the leading foreign power in China, the United States wielded its influence in ways seen to accord with U.S. interests and goals. At bottom, the U.S. actions and policies did not mesh well with realities in China. The result by the end of the decade was a massive failure of U.S. efforts to establish a strong China, friendly to the United States, in postwar Asia.[11]

The China theater was a secondary concern in the overall war effort as the United States first focused on defeating Adolf Hitler and the Nazi-led forces in Europe. Initial expectations that China could be built up and play an active strategic role in the war effort, with Chinese armies under Chiang Kai-shek's leadership pushing back the Japanese and allowing China to become a staging area for attack on Japan, proved unrealistic. Chiang's Nationalist armies were weak, and the Americans were unable to provide large amounts of military equipment because Japan cut off surface routes to Nationalist-held areas of China. U.S. strategists turned to an approach of island-hopping in the Pacific, with U.S.-led forces coming from the south and east of Japan, taking island positions in step-by-step progress toward the Japanese home islands. The role for the Chinese armies in this strategy mainly was to stay in the war and keep the many hundreds of thousands of Japanese forces in China tied down and unable to reinforce Japanese positions elsewhere.[12]

The United States recognized Chiang Kai-shek and the Chinese Nationalist government as China's representative in war deliberations and insisted that Chiang's China would be one of the great powers that would lead world affairs in the postwar era. President Roosevelt strongly supported China's leading role and met with Chiang Kai-shek and British Prime Minister Winston Churchill at an Allied conference in Cairo in 1943 which determined, among other things, that territories Japan had taken from China would be restored to China. U.S. aid in China flowed exclusively to Chiang and his officials. The commanding American general in the China theater, Joseph Stilwell, was appointed as Chiang Kai-shek's chief of staff. American contact with and understanding of the rival Chinese Communists were minimal. Mao Zedong's forces were cut off from American and other contact by a blockade maintained by Nationalist Chinese forces. There were American contacts with the Chinese Communist liaison office allowed in the Chinese wartime capital of Chungking.[13]

Chiang Kai-shek welcomed American support but constantly complained that it was insufficient. General Stilwell and many other U.S. officials in China were appalled by what they saw as corrupt, repressive, and self-serving Chinese Nationalist leadership, and the unwillingness of Chiang and his lieutenants to use U.S. assistance against Japan as they focused on building capabilities to deal with the Chinese Communists. Stilwell and his American staff were interested in establishing relations with the Chinese Communist forces who seemed more willing to fight Japan. Chiang resisted these American leanings.[14]

Despite widespread dissatisfaction with Chiang Kai-shek and the Chinese Nationalist administration on the part of many American officials as well as media and other nongovernment American observers in China, Chiang Kai-shek maintained a positive public image in the United States. Publicists such as Henry Luce using *Time* and *Life* magazines continued to laud the leadership of the courageous leader of China in the face of Japanese aggression. President Roosevelt's personal emissary to China, Lauchlin Currie, traveled to China in 1941 and again in 1942. He advised the U.S. president to follow policies of strong support for Chiang Kai-shek and the Chinese Nationalists. The Chungking government should be treated as a "great power"; Chiang should be given greater economic and military support and should be encouraged to reform. In Currie's view and the view of other U.S. officials in Washington, close U.S. cooperation with Chiang would promote cooperation within China and ensure a more effective struggle against Japan. While President Roosevelt's private calculations regarding Chiang Kai-shek and the situation in China remain subject to interpretation, his actions and statements generally adhered to this kind of positive American orientation toward Nationalist China.[15]

Emblematic of broader support for the Chiang administration in the United States was the positive reception given to Madame Chiang Kai-shek when she toured the United States from November 1942 to May 1943. In February 1943 she delivered a stirring speech to the U.S. Congress. She appealed for more American aid and higher U.S. priority to the war effort in China. Roosevelt and his war planners were unwilling to change their focus on defeating Germany first, but the U.S. Congress took steps to redress the grossly discriminatory U.S. immigration policies against China. In 1943, it acknowledged China as an ally and amended exclusion provisions to permit 105 Chinese to immigrate annually. Initial steps also were taken to amend the various treaty provisions between the United States and China providing for unequal relations that were offensive to Chinese nationalism. In 1943, the administration signed a treaty surrendering American extraterritorial rights in China, and the Senate readily agreed.[16]

Some influential U.S. military leaders, notably General Claire Chennault of the American Volunteer Group ("Flying Tigers") and the Army Air Force, were much more sympathetic to Chiang Kai-shek than Stilwell and his supporters. Chennault pressed for U.S. military efforts that were supported by Chiang but opposed by Stilwell and his staff. He collaborated with and won Chiang's support for plans involving U.S. use of Chinese Nationalist-defended air bases in China to attack Japanese positions and shipping with U.S. bombers. Stilwell opposed the plans that diverted U.S. supplies from his efforts to build Chinese armies in order to open ground supply routes to occupied China and for other use against Japan. Stilwell warned that once the U.S. bombing attacks from Chinese air bases rose in Japan's war calculus as a result of Chennault's plan, the bases would be subject to Japanese ground attack and might be overrun because of weak Chinese Nationalist defenses for the bases. Indeed, presumably prompted at least in part by the U.S. air attacks, Japanese forces in 1944 overran the weakly defended air bases and expanded more deeply into Nationalist-held areas, provoking a major crisis between Chiang and Stilwell and between the United States and its Nationalist allies.[17]

The Chinese Communists, for their part, took advantage of limited interaction with U.S. officials, media, and nongovernment representatives in Chungking in order to build on the image they had already established through their brief encounters with American and other Western news personnel at the Communist base in Yenan in north China in the 1930s. Consistent with their approach to Edgar Snow and other American visitors in that period, the Communists emphasized the image of a relatively democratic and honest political administration, positive public support received by the Yenan leadership, and the CCP's reasonably benign attitude at that time toward free enterprise. In this way, they attempted to appeal to American ideals. At the same time, the Communist spokespersons tried to drive a wedge between Americans and Chinese Nationalists by criticizing what they viewed as the corrupt, oppressive, and totalitarian rule of the nationalist government. In line with their approach toward Snow and other visitors in the 1930s, the Communist officials did not disavow the CCP's ultimate Marxist-Leninist goals regarding the future of China but indicated that such objectives were to be achieved at the end of a long "democratic" period. They thus revealed to American officials and other representatives the image of a Chinese party worthy of U.S. support, willing to compromise with Washington, and deserving of a share of power in China. In this context, heavy stress was placed on the Nationalists' unwillingness to share power as the prime cause for continuing Communist-Nationalist confrontation in China.[18]

The central role in CCP policy toward and interaction with the United States was played by senior Communist leader Zhou Enlai, the chief Communist representative in Chungking during World War II. In his frequent contacts with American officials and other U.S. representatives, Zhou demonstrated repeatedly a preference for realistic exchange, unencumbered by ideological constraints or bitterness over past Chinese affronts at the hands of U.S. "imperialism." He initiated a CCP proposal for the establishment of an American liaison mission to Yenan, cast doubt on Nationalist willingness to pursue the war against Japan, and attacked Chungking's legitimacy as the regime best serving the interests of the Chinese people. Zhou, along with visiting senior Communist military leader Lin Biao, who was visiting Chungking for negotiations with the Chinese Nationalists, appealed for U.S. supplies so that the Communists could go on the offensive against Japan. They also promised close intelligence sharing with the United States regarding enemy activities near the Communist base areas. They condemned the Nationalists' passivity in the war effort while the Chiang Kai-shek forces reinforced their military blockade against the Communists.

Zhou Enlai's initiatives and subsequent interaction with American officials visiting Yenan on the part of Mao Zedong and other senior CCP leaders reflected pragmatic actions to deal with potentially adverse circumstances. The American entry into the war against Japan strengthened the position of the Communists' adversary, Chiang Kai-shek, and raised the strong possibility that the United States would continue to side firmly with Chiang following the defeat of Japan and the establishment of a new Chinese administration. The relatively weak strategic position of the Chinese Communist forces in China at this time and the low probability that the Soviet Union would take decisive actions to protect the Chinese Communists from U.S.-backed pressure from Chiang Kai-shek's Nationalists, added to incentives for the CCP to appeal to the United States for closer relations and support.[19]

The depth of the American-Chinese Nationalist alignment meant that the Communists could have little hope of undermining the American Nationalist relationship. But by opening formal contacts with Americans though a U.S. liaison mission in Yenan or other means, the Communists would at least have the opportunity to encourage the Americans to move away from Chungking over the critical issue of the Chinese civil dispute. In particular, a formal American mission in the Communist base area would allow CCP leaders to present their case to the highest levels in Washington; it would enable Mao and his group to scotch many ill-founded Nationalist allegations concerning the Communist leaders and policies, which had heretofore enjoyed credibility with U.S. policy makers. Further, formal ties with Washington would enhance the Communists' ability to solicit U.S. military supplies. The Communist leaders also seemed confident and proud of the economic, political, and military situation in their base area; if their administrative achievements could be shown to American officials, they would compare favorably with the deteriorating situation in nationalist-held areas.[20]

In early 1944, there was a formal U.S. presidential request to Chiang Kai-shek for the establishment of an American military observer mission in the

Communist-held areas of China. The proposal was grudgingly approved by Chiang Kai-shek during the visit to China of American Vice President Henry Wallace in June 1944. Amid the crisis caused by Japanese forces overrunning U.S. air bases in China and penetrating deep into previously Nationalist-controlled territory, Chiang was in a weak position to resist the U.S. request.[21]

American officials were not only interested in shoring up Chinese resistance to Japanese aggression and improving military coordination against Japan with the Chinese Communists. By this time U.S. officials were deeply involved in plans for dealing with previously unanticipated divisions weakening China and posing the danger of Chinese civil war once Japan was defeated. There was concern that the Chinese Nationalists might draw in the United States on their side of the conflict and that the Chinese Communists might draw in the Soviet Union on their side of the conflict. To deal with this potentially dire situation warranted closer American interaction with and understanding of the policies and intentions of the Chinese Communist forces through the establishment of the U.S. military observer mission to Yenan.[22]

Responding to Vice President Wallace's expressions of concern over the Chinese war effort and the Nationalist government's loss of public support, Chiang focused on American and especially Stilwell's responsibility. Chiang impressed the American visitor with his determination to remove Stilwell or to have the United States send a personal representative from Roosevelt to control Stilwell and give Chiang regular access to the president free from the interference of the Departments of War and State, which were seen as influenced by Stilwell and his supporters in the U.S. embassy.[23]

Patrick Hurley, a prominent Republican who served as President Herbert Hoover's secretary of war, was a key figure in U.S. policy toward the Chinese Nationalist Party and the Chinese Communist Party in 1944–1945. His strong support for the Chinese Nationalists and accusations against opponents within the United States government had lasting impacts on U.S. relations with China. Hurley was sent as a special envoy by President Franklin D. Roosevelt to China in September 1944. Dealing with the major disputes then causing a crisis between Chiang Kai-shek and General Joseph Stilwell, Hurley sided with Chiang. Roosevelt recalled Stilwell in October 1944, appointing General Albert Wedemeyer as his replacement. Hurley was appointed as ambassador to replace Clarence Gauss, who shared Stilwell's negative opinions about Chiang and the Nationalists.[24]

In November 1944, Hurley traveled to Yenan and negotiated a Five-Point Agreement with Mao Zedong and his senior colleagues. Among other things, the agreement summarized Hurley's promises of equal treatment and U.S. aid to the Communists in a coalition with the Nationalists. Returning to Chungking, he switched and sided strongly with Chiang Kai-shek in his demand that

Communist forces be disbanded before the Communists could be brought in to a Nationalist-led Chinese coalition administration. Much of the U.S. embassy staff in Chungking rebelled against Hurley by sending a collective message to Washington in early 1945 warning of the dire consequences of Hurley's alienation of the Communists and bias toward Chiang's Nationalists. The ambassador disputed the charges in a meeting with President Roosevelt, who supported Hurley, leading to transfers of dissident U.S. staff from Chungking.[25]

As U.S. ambassador, Hurley supported the Nationalist-Communist peace talks in Chungking in September 1945. Chiang Kai-shek, backed by Hurley and the Harry Truman administration, demanded the Communists surrender their forces and territory as a precondition for joining a coalition. Fighting spread in China, and the talks collapsed. Hurley, unsuccessful in urging a full U.S. commitment to Chiang's cause, abruptly resigned as ambassador in November 1945, blaming pro-Chinese Communists in the State Department for thwarting U.S. policy. After the Communist victory in China and the Chinese intervention in the Korean War, Hurley's charges provided a leading wedge for congressional investigators seeking to purge alleged pro-Communists and other security risks from among the ranks of the Chinese affairs specialists in the State Department and other agencies.[26]

U.S. leaders worried about conditions in China and how they would affect the final stages of the war against Japan. They foresaw the inability of weak Chinese Nationalist forces to defeat the hundreds of thousands of Japanese forces in China as the war in the Pacific moved toward an end, and the danger of a Nationalist-Communist civil war in China that would drag in the United States and the Soviet Union on opposite sides. In the end, as a result of the so-called Far Eastern Agreement of the Allied powers at Yalta in February 1945, Soviet forces, not Chinese forces, would take on the main task of defeating Japanese armies concentrated in Manchuria and northern China. In compensation, Russian territory taken by Japan would be restored; Russian interests in Manchuria, including a naval base, would be restored; and Outer Mongolia would remain independent. The United States promised to obtain the concurrence of China's Nationalist government to provisions regarding Manchuria and Mongolia, which were claimed by China. The Soviet Union also expressed willingness to negotiate a friendship and alliance treaty with China's Nationalist government. The Far Eastern Agreement had negative implications for the Chinese Nationalist government, which was not consulted on the territorial concessions to the Soviet Union, and for the Chinese Communists, who appeared to be isolated from the Soviet Union.[27]

The broad outlines of U.S. policy toward China prevalent in early 1945 persisted as Harry Truman became president upon the death of Franklin Roosevelt in April 1945, and as the war in the Pacific came to an unexpectedly quick end with Japan's surrender after the U.S. atomic bomb attacks in August 1945. U.S. policy strongly supported Chiang Kai-shek's Nationalist forces. U.S. airplanes and other means were used to transport Nationalist forces to various parts of China to take the surrender of Japanese forces. The U.S. government provided hundreds of millions of dollars of military equipment and other assistance. The rival Communists were urged to participate in peace talks and come to terms in a united Chinese administration under Chiang's overall leadership. President Truman commanded that Japanese-controlled forces in China surrender their positions and arms to Chiang Kai-shek's representatives, not to Communist forces.[28]

The Soviet army entered the war in China and defeated Japanese armies. The Soviet Union signed a friendship treaty with Chiang Kai-shek's Nationalist government, as noted in the Far Eastern Agreement at Yalta. Seemingly isolated, the Chinese Communists agreed to join peace talks in Chungking in September where Chiang, backed by U.S. Ambassador Hurley and the Truman administration, demanded the Communists surrender their armed forces and territory as a precondition for joining a coalition government under Chiang's leadership.

There was little consideration at high levels of U.S. policy for a more evenhanded U.S. approach to the Nationalist-Communist rivalry in China, though some American officials warned of the danger of civil war and were uncertain how the Chinese Nationalists, weakened by years of warfare and led by often corrupt and inept officials, would fare. As the peace talks deadlocked and Communist-Nationalist armed conflict spread in northern China in late 1945, it became clear to U.S. planners that Chiang's forces would not defeat the Chinese Communists without a substantial commitment of U.S. military forces. It was against this background that Ambassador Hurley pushed for an open-ended U.S. commitment to Chiang Kai-shek, but Washington decision makers demurred and Hurley resigned.[29]

President Truman appointed General George Marshall as his personal representative to salvage the deteriorating situation in China. Marshall managed a few months of shaky peace, but they were followed by frequent fighting in Manchuria as Nationalist and Communist forces vied to take control as Soviet occupiers retreated. U.S. aid continued to go exclusively to Nationalist-held areas and increased markedly in mid-1946. On July 1, 1946, Chiang Kai-shek ordered a nationwide offensive against the Communists. Marshall intervened, got Truman to stop U.S. arms aid to Chiang, and Chiang agreed to U.S.-Nationalist-Communist truce teams to prevent fighting in northern China. The fighting still spread, however, and soon became a full-scale war.[30]

The failure to avoid civil war in China did not lead to fundamental change in the broad framework of U.S. policy in China. Even though the Nationalists appeared increasingly weak and inept, and seemed headed for defeat on the mainland by 1948, the Truman administration continued support for them and took no significant steps to reach out to the Chinese Communists. In 1948, the administration supported the China Aid Act providing $125 million for the failing Nationalist government in China. This was done in large measure to avoid resistance from many pro–Chiang Kai-shek congressional members regarding the administration's requests for funding the Marshall Plan for Europe and Japan. Prospects for positive U.S. relations with the Chinese Communists were soured by years of one-sided U.S. support for the Chinese Nationalists.[31]

Given what were seen by Truman administration officials as continued strong U.S. congressional and other domestic constraints against abandoning Chiang Kai-shek and opening U.S. contacts with Chiang's enemy, the Chinese Communists, the Truman administration officials allowed developments in China to settle the civil war in favor of the Chinese Communists. Over time, they hoped to find constructive ways for the United States to deal with the new Chinese Communist regime. There was strong debate in the administration as to whether the United States should allow Taiwan, the island off the Chinese coast where Chiang and his Nationalist forces retreated after their defeat on the mainland in 1949, to fall to the Communists. The policy decided upon was one of no intervention to protect Taiwan.[32]

U.S. Secretary of State Dean Acheson was known for his efforts to end U.S. support for Chiang Kai-shek and his Nationalist Party regime. He sought publication of the famed "China White Paper." This lengthy (over a thousand pages) document was issued by the U.S. State Department in August 1949. It was critical of Chiang Kai-shek and his administration for corruption and other failings as they lost the Chinese Civil War with the Chinese Communist forces. The report served to support the Truman's administration's efforts to cut support for Chiang's Nationalists. It also deflected attention from U.S. policy oversights and mistakes. The report was attacked by Chiang's Nationalists, Mao's Communists, and many U.S. supporters of Chiang Kai-shek.[33]

Also during the last months of the Chinese Civil War on the Chinese mainland, Acheson instructed the U.S. ambassador to Nanjing, Leighton Stuart, to seek contacts with the Communist forces advancing on the Nationalist capital. Stuart stayed in the city after Nationalist forces retreated. He made contact with Huang Hua, a former student of his who was sent by the Communist leaders to investigate U.S. intentions. Stuart was invited to meet Communist leaders setting up their new capital in Beijing, but President Truman was unwilling to support a plan to have the ambassador travel to Beijing for talks with the Communist rulers.[34]

The Chinese Communists, meanwhile, reinforced their victory in the civil war with the announcement that they would side with the Soviet Union in the emerging Cold War struggle with the United States and its non-Communist allies. Amid these grim developments for U.S. interests in China, the administration endeavored to adopt a lower profile regarding China. U.S. leaders anticipated Communist victory over Chiang's forces holding out in Taiwan and a subsequent long process of the United States working to build some semblance of workable ties with the new regime in China. The U.S. military position in the region was weak as a result of the rapid U.S. demobilization and withdrawal of forces following World War II. While the United States had shown strong military and political resolve following Pearl Harbor in defeating Japanese aggression and that of the Axis coalition, U.S. leaders were only gradually coming to the realization of a need for continued strong military preparations and presence in Asia in order to deter new sources of expansion and aggression.[35]

Conflict and Containment

Chinese Interests, Actions, and Perceptions

Mao Zedong and his Communist Party–led fighters faced daunting challenges as they endeavored to consolidate their rule after defeating Chiang Kai-shek's Nationalist forces in the Chinese Civil War and establishing the People's Republic of China on the Chinese mainland in 1949. China had been war-ravaged for decades and arguably had been without effective governance for over a century. The Communists were a rural-based movement with decades of experience in guerrilla war and supporting administrative efforts in the Chinese countryside, but little experience in managing the complicated affairs of China's cities, its urban economy, or its national administration. Seeking needed technical and economic backing as well as guarantees and support for China's national security, the Maoist leadership endeavored to consolidate relations with the Soviet Union in an international environment heavily influenced by the United States, the main international supporter of its Chinese Nationalist adversary, and American-associated states influential in Asian and world politics.[36]

Taken together, these circumstances and determinants led to a strong current in analyses of Chinese relations with the United States that emphasized Chinese imperatives of consolidation and development domestically and reactions internationally to perceived threats and occasional opportunities posed by circumstances involving the United States. In particular, as the Cold War spread from Europe and came to dominate international dynamics in

Asia for several decades beginning in the late 1940s, Chinese relations with the United States were seen as dominated in the 1950s and 1960s by Chinese efforts to deal with what emerged as a massive U.S.-led military, economic, and political containment of China. Chinese interactions with the United States in this period often were assessed in terms of Chinese reactions to perceived threats posed by the power and actions of the United States and associated powers.[37]

Heading the list of strengths that the Maoist leaders brought to bear as they began national leadership in China were the Chinese Communist Party's broad experience in political organization and related social and economic mobilization, and a strong revolutionary ideology. Mao Zedong and supporting leaders were committed to seeking revolutionary changes in China and in international affairs affecting China, and they had the determination and ability to move Chinese people along these paths. This set of determinants and circumstances led to another strong current in analyses of Chinese relations with the United States, one which emphasized the importance of the Chinese leadership's determination to challenge and confront the United States and its allies and associates in Asia as the Chinese Communist leadership sought to promote revolutionary change in Asian and world affairs. The analyses also showed a related tendency of the Chinese leadership to exploit episodes of confrontation with America as means to mobilize greater support within China for the often revolutionary changes sought there by the Maoist leadership.[38]

Assessments of the record of the Maoist period show a complicated mix of revolutionary imperatives and more conventional imperatives of security and nation-building driving Chinese decision-making. Adding to the mix was the emergence of the dominant role of Mao Zedong and his strong-man rule which came to determine Chinese decision-making regarding Chinese foreign relations in particular, notably relations with the United States and the Soviet Union. One consequence was the ability and the actual tendency of China to shift direction dramatically in foreign affairs. China's strong alignment with the Soviet Union in 1950 and break with Moscow ten years later exemplified the kinds of major shifts in China's foreign policy on issues important to the United States during this period.[39]

For their part, Chiang Kai-shek and the Chinese Nationalists appeared at the end of their struggle when they retreated to Taiwan after defeat on the Chinese mainland in 1949. Given the Truman administration's decisions to cut ties with the Nationalists and await opportunities to build relations with the triumphant Chinese Communists, it appeared to be only a matter of time before Communist forces would overwhelm the Nationalists on Taiwan. Those Nationalist leaders and officials less than fully committed to Chiang

Kai-shek and the Nationalist cause who had options other than joining Chiang on Taiwan tended to follow those alternative paths and settled in Hong Kong, the United States, or other safer locations. The two million Chinese who fled the mainland to Taiwan included leaders and officials who were loyal to Chiang and strongly anti-Communist, and large numbers of officials, soldiers, and dependents who had few other options.[40]

The outbreak of the Korean War and the subsequent U.S. policy of containment against expansion of Chinese Communist power and influence dramatically reversed the fortunes of Chiang and his associates on Taiwan. They sought to use the new circumstances to strengthen support from the United States and to consolidate their power in Taiwan. On this basis, they endeavored to go beyond U.S. efforts to contain Communist China by striving to lead efforts to roll back Communist rule on the mainland.[41]

U.S. Interests, Actions, and Perceptions

At the start of the Cold War, Asia seemed secondary in U.S. strategy. The United States demobilized rapidly after World War II. U.S. forces occupied Japan and U.S. naval and air forces patrolled the western Pacific, but overall U.S. military capabilities appeared unprepared for significant action in Asia. When the Korean War broke out unexpectedly, the United States abruptly reversed recent practice and began what became massive commitments of military power and related assistance to stop the spread of perceived communist expansion in Asia. Longstanding U.S. interest in sustaining a balance of power in East Asia favorable to the United States, as well as ongoing U.S. interests in fostering free economic access to the region and the spread of American values there, now were seen to require the United States to undertake the leading role in bearing the major costs, risks, and commitments associated with a system of containment that came to dominate U.S. policy in Asia in the 1950s and the 1960s and to determine the course of American policy toward China during this period.[42]

The American approach saw strategic concerns with shoring up the regional balance of influence against communist expansion in Asia dominate the U.S. foreign policy calculus toward China and other East Asian countries. Strong efforts by the U.S. government to mobilize domestic American support for the costs and risks associated with U.S. leadership of the containment effort overshadowed private calculations of American leaders and strategists that appeared to favor a more nuanced and flexible American approach that would have allowed for possible efforts to seek contacts and accommodation with Communist-ruled China. Eventually, U.S. elites and supporting groups began to chafe publicly in the 1960s at what they saw as a counterproductive

U.S. tendency to try isolating China as part of the Cold War containment strategy in Asia. Their efforts to encourage greater U.S. flexibility in dealing with the Chinese Communists failed in the face of strident Chinese opposition to the United States and a wide range of other adverse foreign influences at the start of China's Cultural Revolution in 1966 and the concurrent large increases in U.S. combat forces fighting Chinese-backed Communist forces in Vietnam.[43]

Encounters and Interaction in the 1950s and 1960s

Neither the government of Mao Zedong nor the Truman administration sought or foresaw U.S.-China war in early 1950. The Americans were surprised when North Korean forces, with the support of Soviet and Chinese leaders, launched an all-out military attack against South Korean forces in June 1950. The Chinese Communist leaders and their Korean and Soviet Communist allies apparently calculated that the better-armed North Koreans would attain victory quickly without provoking major or effective U.S. military response. Thus, it was their turn to be surprised when the United States quickly intervened militarily in the Korean War and also sent the U.S. Seventh Fleet to prevent Chinese Communist attack on Taiwan. U.S. forces and their South Korean allies halted the North Korean advance and carried out an amphibious landing at Inchon in September 1950 that effectively cut off North Korean armies in the South, leading to their destruction.[44]

The string of miscalculations continued. With UN sanction, U.S. and South Korea forces proceeded into North Korea. The Chinese Communists warned and prepared to resist them, but U.S. leaders thought the warnings were a bluff. By November hundreds of thousands of Chinese Communist forces were driving the U.S. and South Korean forces south in full retreat. Eventually, the Americans and their allies were able to sustain a line of combat roughly in the middle of the peninsula as the two armies faced off for over two more years of combat, casualties, and destruction.[45]

Chinese Communist leaders also launched domestic mass campaigns to root out pro-American influence and seize control of U.S. cultural, religious, and business organizations that remained in China. The United States began wide-ranging U.S. strategic effort to contain the expansion of Chinese power and Chinese-backed Communist expansion in Asia. A strict U.S. economic and political embargo against China; large U.S. force deployments, eventually numbering between one half and one million troops; massive foreign aid allocations to U.S. Asian allies and supporters; and a ring of U.S. defense alliances around China were used to block Chinese expansion and to drive a wedge between China and its Soviet ally. Meanwhile, led by often irresponsible congressional advocates, notably Senator Joseph McCarthy, congressional investigators in the early 1950s took aim at U.S. specialists on China and Asia, discrediting those with moderate and pragmatic views about the Chinese Communists and endeavoring to silence those in or out of government who were less than uniform in opposing the Chinese Communists and supporting Chiang Kai-shek and the Chinese Nationalists.[46]

The Dwight D. Eisenhower administration used threats and negotiations in reaching an armistice agreement that stopped the fighting in Korea in 1953. American efforts to strengthen military alliances and deployments to contain Chinese Communist–backed expansion continued unabated. They faced off against enhanced Chinese efforts in the wake of the Korean armistice to strengthen support for Communist insurgents working against American-backed forces in French Indochina and direct Chinese military probes and challenges against the United States and their Chinese Nationalist allies in the Taiwan Strait.[47]

Mao Zedong and his Communist Party–led administration continued their consolidation of control inside China, notably through mass campaigns led by Communist activists targeting landlords, leading urban political and economic elites, and others deemed abusive or uncooperative with Communist goals. They prepared for major nation-building efforts with the support of their Soviet and Warsaw Pact allies to establish an administrative structure, often along the lines of that of the Soviet Union, to govern Chinese civil administration, economic planning, military modernization, intelligence collection, and other endeavors. They sought efforts to tap into the surplus wealth being created in China's rural sector for investment in their planned expansion of China's industrial economy. After a brief period where peasants held land as a result of the mass campaign for land reform in rural China in the early 1950s, Chinese leaders saw the need to emulate the Soviet model and began to collectivize the land under government administration so as to better control the surplus rural wealth and to maximize its utility to the state's interests in promoting industrial development. The Soviet Union was providing over a hundred major projects in assistance to Chinese industrialization and modernization, but they had to be paid for it. Collectivization of the land and concurrently greater state control of the urban economy along Soviet lines was chosen as the appropriate way to deal with conditions in China while seeking economic modernization and development of the sinews of national and state power.[48]

These dramatic and massive shifts in domestic policy and direction occurred frequently in conjunction with crises and confrontations with the United States and its allies and associates around China's periphery in Asia. At one level, the Chinese determination to work against and confront the

U.S.-backed forces in Indochina and the Taiwan Strait reflected a deeply held determination to confound and wear down the American-fostered containment system. The Chinese Communist leadership held a strong revolutionary commitment to change the international order dominated by the United States and its allies and to support Communist-led forces struggling against this foreign imperialism.[49]

The U.S. effort also directly threatened China's national security and sovereignty, often in graphic and severe ways. The Eisenhower administration threatened China with nuclear attack in order to push it toward an armistice in Korea, and the U.S. government used the threat of nuclear attack at other times in the face of perceived Chinese provocations in the 1950s. Mao Zedong's China had no viable defense against U.S. nuclear weapons and put top priority on developing Chinese nuclear weapons to deal with such repeated U.S. intimidation. At the same time, the Chinese Communist leaders also were seen to continue to use the crisis atmosphere caused by confrontations with outside threats posed by the United States and its allies as a means to strengthen their domestic control and their mobilization of resources for advancement of nation-building and administrative competence.[50]

Defeat of U.S.-backed French forces in Indochina led to the 1954 Geneva Conference and accords that formalized French withdrawal from Indochina. After the conference, U.S. policy worked to support a non-Communist administration in South Vietnam, backing the regime when it resisted steps toward reunification set forth in the Geneva accords. The United States also deepened and broadened defense and other links with powers in Southeast Asia in order to check Chinese-backed Communist expansion in the region.[51]

President Eisenhower and Secretary of State John Foster Dulles were wary of Chiang Kai-shek and Chinese Nationalist maneuvers that might drag the United States into a war with the Chinese Communists over Taiwan. Chiang Kai-shek's Nationalists used the fortuitous turn of fate caused by the Korean War in order to consolidate their rule in Taiwan; and with American support they rapidly built Taiwan's military forces with the objective of eventually taking the battle to mainland China. The political atmosphere inside the United States was very supportive of Chiang and his harsh anti-Communist stance. The so-called China lobby supporting Chiang and his Nationalist administration included liberals as well as conservatives in such respected organizations as the Committee of One Million, which opposed Communist China taking China's seat in the United Nations. U.S. military and economic assistance to Chiang Kai-shek and the Nationalist forces on Taiwan expanded dramatically, and there was little public objection by the American government to Chiang's repressive authoritarian rule.[52]

Though Dulles and other leaders of the U.S. government were privately unsure of the wisdom of such close and formal U.S. commitment to Chiang's Nationalists, Washington eventually brought Taiwan into the web of formal military alliances that provided the foundation of the U.S. containment system against Chinese-backed communist expansion in Asia. The United States and Nationalist China signed a bilateral defense treaty in December 1954.[53]

The People's Republic of China (PRC) reacted with harsh rhetoric and military assaults against Nationalist Chinese–controlled islands off the coast of the Chinese mainland. The new and potentially very dangerous military crisis involving the United States and China so soon after the bloody conflict in Korea was not welcomed by Great Britain and other U.S. allies, or by some U.S. congressional leaders and other elites. The U.S. administration firmly backed the Chinese Nationalists and their Republic of China (ROC). U.S. forces helped Nationalist forces on some exposed islands to withdraw as the Taiwan Strait crisis of 1955 continued, raising fears of renewed U.S.-China war.[54]

Against this background, the Chinese Communist administration's stance against the United States moderated. The reasoning appeared related to a shift in Soviet policy toward the West following Stalin's death in 1953. The incoming Soviet leaders were more interested than the now-dead Soviet dictator in arranging advantageous modus vivendi with Western powers in Europe. While they continued to give some public support to their Chinese ally in its dispute with the Chinese Nationalists and the United States, they also signaled Soviet wariness about getting involved in Asian conflicts by playing down the applicability of the Sino-Soviet alliance to Asia, where Soviet commentary implied China was to bear the major responsibility for dealing with the United States and its allies and associates. The Chinese administration also began at this time trying to broaden productive economic and diplomatic ties with countries in nearby Asia and in Europe, and Chinese leaders found that their hard-line and confrontational behavior in the Taiwan Strait was counterproductive for this effort. Washington, for its part, had not sought to escalate military tensions with China, which complicated U.S. efforts to work with European and Asian allies in exploring Soviet moderation and building lasting alliance relationships to contain communist expansion in Asia.[55]

Thus, Beijing by early 1955 was faced with an increasingly counterproductive campaign over Taiwan, a potentially dangerous military confrontation with Washington, lukewarm support from its primary international ally, and increased alienation from world powers now being wooed by the Chinese administration. In this context, Chinese leaders understandably chose to shift to a more moderate stance when presented with the opportunity afforded by the American offer in mid-January 1955 of a cease-fire regarding the armed conflict in the Taiwan Strait. Beijing responded to the U.S. proposal with criticism but indirectly signaled interest in the offer by gradually reducing Chinese demands concerning Taiwan.[56]

Chinese Premier Zhou Enlai used the venue of the Afro-Asian Conference in Bandung, Indonesia, in 1955 to ease tensions and call for talks with the United States. Chinese leaders at this time attempted to engage in high-level dialogue with the United States. How serious the Chinese were in pursuing their avowed interest in such engagement with the United States was never shown as the Chinese overtures met with a nuanced but firm rebuff from the United States. Secretary of State Dulles was wary that direct talks with the PRC would undermine Chiang Kai-shek's Nationalist government on Taiwan. Though Dulles privately showed an interest in splitting China from alignment with the Soviet Union, the strategy called for maintaining a tougher U.S. stance against China than the comparatively accommodating USSR. On the other hand, Dulles faced congressional and Allied pressures to meet with the Chinese, so he agreed to low-level ambassadorial talks that began in Geneva in 1955.[57]

The two sides fairly expeditiously reached an agreement on repatriating detained personnel. The Chinese intended the agreement to lay the ground for higher-level talks with the United States. Americans officials from Dulles on down responded by using the wording in the agreement to make demands on the Chinese for release of detained U.S. personnel, notably captured U.S. spies, that they knew through private conversations with Chinese officials at the ambassadorial talks leading up to the agreements that China would not do. Washington soon charged Beijing with perfidy and disregard for agreements, souring the atmosphere in the talks. The U.S. side also pressed hard for a Chinese renunciation of force regarding Taiwan. Chinese negotiators came up with various formulas to bridge differences between the United States and China over this issue; at least one was positively received by the U.S. negotiators but was rejected by Washington. This issue came to stop progress in the talks, which were suspended for a time before resuming in Warsaw in 1958, when the two sides met periodically without much result. The talks did at least provide a useful line of U.S.-PRC communication during times of crisis, as both sides strove to avoid serious military conflict.[58]

Dulles's private strategy of vigorously pursuing a containment policy against China favored a tougher U.S. policy toward China than toward the Soviet Union. He endeavored thereby to force Beijing to rely on Moscow for economic and other needs the Soviet Union could not meet. In this and other ways, he hoped to drive a wedge between China and the USSR.[59]

In 1958, Mao Zedong's Communists used artillery barrages in an effort to challenge and halt the resupply of the Nationalist hold over the fortress island of Quemoy and other Nationalist-controlled islands located only a few miles off the coast of the Chinese mainland. The military attacks predictably created another major crisis and war scare, with the United States firmly supporting Chiang Kai-shek's forces and threatening nuclear attack. Chiang Kai-shek refused to consider withdrawal from the Quemoy fortre, s, where a large portion of his best troops were deployed as part of his broade. military preparations to attack mainland China and reverse Communist rule.

The absence of landing craft and other preparations for an invasion suggested that Mao was testing Nationalist and U.S. resolve regarding the offshore island and did not intend to invade Taiwan itself. The crisis atmosphere played into Mao's efforts at the time to use the charged atmosphere of the mass campaign to mobilize national resources for a massive "Great Leap Forward" in Chinese development. Later, foreign analysts argued persuasively that the domestic mobilization was a major Chinese objective in launching the military aggression on the offshore islands held by the Chinese Nationalists. Another line of analysis argued that the Chinese leader also used the confrontation with the United States to test Soviet resolve in supporting China in what was seen in China as a weakening Sino-Soviet alliance.[60]

The Chinese-Soviet alliance indeed began to unravel by the late 1950s, and 1960 saw a clear public break with the withdrawal of Soviet economic aid and advisers. U.S. policy makers had long sought such a split. Nonetheless, they were slow to capitalize on the situation as China remained more hostile than the Soviet Union to the United States and deepening U.S. involvement in Vietnam exacerbated U.S.-China frictions.

During the 1960 presidential election campaign, Senator John Kennedy criticized the "tired thinking" of the outgoing administration on issues regarding China; however, he said little about China once he assumed office in 1961. U.S. domestic opposition, Chinese nuclear weapons development, Chinese aggression against India, and Chinese expansion into Southeast Asia were among factors that seemed to block meaningful U.S. initiatives toward China. The administration took firm action in 1962 to thwart plans by Chiang Kai-shek to attack the Chinese mainland at a time of acute economic crisis in China caused by the collapse and abject failure of the Great Leap Forward campaign. The staggering damage to China from the three-year effort saw the premature deaths of thirty million people on account of starvation and nutrition deficits.[61]

Though publicly reserved about China policy, the Kennedy administration seemed to appeal to emerging American elite opinions seeking some moderation in the stern U.S. isolation and containment of China. However, scholarship has shown there was strong private antipathy on the part of Kennedy administration leaders to China's development of nuclear weapons and support for

communist-led insurgencies in Southeast Asia. The administration's backing of
Chiang Kai-shek in the United Nations also went beyond pledges under Eisenhower, with officials privately reassuring Chiang that the United States would
veto efforts to remove Nationalist China from the United Nations. Kennedy
was actively considering visiting Chiang in Taiwan.[62]

The administration of Lyndon Johnson, 1963–1969, saw U.S. Asian policy
dominated by escalating U.S. military commitment and related difficulties in
Vietnam. There was some movement within the U.S. government for a more
flexible approach to China, consistent with growing signs of congressional
and U.S. interest-group advocacy of a U.S. policy of containment without
isolation toward China. But they came to little as China entered the throes of
the violent and often xenophobic practices of the Cultural Revolution, and
the American forces in Vietnam faced hundreds of thousands of Chinese anti-
aircraft, railway, construction, and support troops sent to Vietnam. Johnson
was anxious to avoid prompting full-scale military involvement of China in
the Vietnam conflict. U.S. diplomats signaled these U.S. intentions in the
otherwise moribund U.S.-China ambassadorial talks in Warsaw, and Chinese
officials made clear that China would restrain its intervention accordingly.[63]

By early 1968, the bitter impasse in U.S.-China relations had lasted two
decades and seemed unlikely to change soon. The net result of the twists and
turns in Chinese domestic and foreign policy since the widespread starvation
and other disasters caused by the collapse of the Great Leap Forward were
years of violence and life-and-death political struggle among elites and other
groups mainly in Chinese cities during the Cultural Revolution that began
in 1966 and did not end until Mao's death in 1976. At first, the sharply deteriorating domestic situation in the early 1960s caused Mao to retreat from
regular involvement in administrative matters. His subordinates pursued
more moderate and pragmatic policies designed to revive agricultural and
industrial production on a sustainable basis without reliance on the highly
disruptive and wasteful mass campaigns and excessive collectivization of
recent years. The economy began to revive, but the progress was marred in
Mao's eyes by a reliance on the kinds of incentives prevalent in the "revision-
ist" practices of the Soviet Union and its allied states and the controlling
bureaucratic elites in those states seen as restoring the kind of unequal and
exploitative practices of capitalism.[64]

Mao found that two of the three main pillars of power and control in China,
the Communist Party and the Chinese government, continued to move in the
wrong direction. The third pillar of power and control, the Chinese military,
was under the leadership of Lin Biao following the purge of Defense Minister
Peng Dehuai, who dared to resist Mao's Great Leap policies during a leadership meeting in 1959. Lin positioned his leadership in support of Maoist

ideals of revolution, equality, and service to the people. Indoctrination and involvement in civil society and affairs often took precedence over professional military training. The distillation of Mao's wisdom from volumes of selected works was distributed throughout the Chinese military and the broader masses of China in the form of a plastic-covered "little red book," *Quotations from Chairman Mao Tse-Tung*, published with a preface by Lin Biao.[65]

Mao was not prepared to break with his party and government colleagues until 1966. By that time he had become sufficiently opposed to prevailing administrative practices and tendencies. Also, he had built up enough support outside normal administrative structures to challenge and reverse what were later portrayed as a drift toward revisionism and the restoration of capitalism. Relying on his personal charisma, organizational support from military leaders like Lin Biao, security forces controlled by radical leaders like Kang Sheng, and various political radicals and opportunists, Mao launched his unorthodox efforts that saw the creation of legions of millions of young Red Guards leading the attack against established authority in urban China. The result was confusion, some resistance from political and government leaders often unaware of Mao's commitment to the radical Red Guards and their allies, and ultimately mass purges and persecution of senior and lesser authorities amid widespread violence and destruction carried out by Red Guard groups. By 1968, numerous sections in cities in China had burned during clashes of rival Red Guard groups, and the party and government structure had collapsed. The military was called in to the cities to restore order. With Mao's support, they proceeded to transport the millions of Red Guards from the cities and to disperse them into various areas in the Chinese countryside, where they were compelled to stay and work for the indefinite future.[66]

The disaster and disruption seen in domestic affairs was duplicated in the shift toward radicalism in Chinese foreign relations. The Chinese public split with the Soviet Union deepened and broadened in the 1960s. Beijing not only opposed the Soviet Union on ideological grounds but also strongly attacked Moscow's willingness to cooperate with the United States in international affairs. Chinese leaders saw the newly independent Asian and African states providing an important arena for struggle with Moscow as well as the United States. Though weak economically and having little to spare following the deprivations of the Great Leap Forward, China provided economic and military aid to left-leaning governments and provided training, military assistance, and financial support to armed insurgents struggling against colonial powers or right-leaning third-world governments.[67]

Chinese Premier Zhou Enlai visited Africa in 1964 and said it was "ripe for revolution." China endeavored to compete with the Soviet Union in support of various anti-colonial insurgencies and to supply significant aid to African governments prepared to align closer to China than the Soviet Union or the West. In Asia, China strongly supported the Vietnamese communist forces directed by the North Vietnamese administration in Hanoi in the face of increased American military involvement in South Vietnam and other parts of Indochina. The Chinese administration also organized and/or strengthened support for communist-led insurgencies targeted against governments in Southeast Asia seen by China as pro-American or insufficiently accommodating to Chinese influence and interests. The left-leaning Sukarno government of Indonesia, the largest country in Southeast Asia, was a focus of Chinese support until the military coup in 1965 smashed communist and Chinese influence in the country through mass killings and arrests.[68]

Maoist China sacrificed conventional diplomacy in pursuing revolutionary fervor during the early years of the Cultural Revolution. The foreign minister and much of the senior foreign policy elite were purged. Ambassadors were recalled and forced to undergo extensive ideological retraining. Lower-level embassy officials often endeavored to show their loyalty to Mao and his revolutionary teaching by unauthorized demonstrations and proselytizing with often unreceptive and hostile foreign audiences. They and the staff of foreign policy organs in Beijing followed a radical line that alienated China from most foreign governments.

The nadir of Chinese diplomacy seemed evident in several developments in 1967. Huge Red Guard demonstrations were mobilized against the Soviet embassy in Beijing, which was kept under siege in January and February. Later in 1967, Red Guards invaded the Soviet Embassy's consular section and burned its files. When Moscow withdrew its diplomats' dependents in February 1967, some were beaten or forced to crawl under pictures of Mao Zedong on their way to planes to take them home. When Red Guard demonstrators in Hong Kong were arrested by British authorities for public disruption and disorder, a major crisis in Chinese-British relations ensued. A mob of thousands of Chinese surrounded British diplomatic offices in Beijing and set fires in the building. Escaping British diplomats came into the hands of the Chinese mob.[69]

The life-or-death struggles for power and attendant violent mass campaigns inside China, combined with militant Chinese policies in support of the Vietnamese and other communist insurgencies in Southeast Asia and a rigid Chinese stance on Taiwan, Korea, and other issues, continued to divide China and the United States. U.S. leaders saw little prospect for any significant movement in relations with the PRC as they grappled with consuming preoccupations associated with the failing U.S. effort against communist insurgents in Vietnam.[70]

Chiang Kai-shek endeavored to deepen the alliance relationship with the United States but found the Johnson administration reluctant to take actions that might embroil China more deeply in the Vietnam War. Despite China's radical and xenophobic posture, the newly independent third-world nations tended to be supportive of China being diplomatically recognized by them and by international bodies, notably the United Nations. Sentiment in the West also shifted somewhat in support of recognition of China, even if it came at the expense of past ties with Taiwan. France set the precedent by establishing ties with Beijing in 1964. The successful Chinese nuclear weapons test that year was followed by many more, underlining the rationale for formal relations with the Asian power.

As Chiang aged, he incrementally passed administrative authority to his son Chiang Ching-kuo, who focused less on plans for attacking the mainland and more on strengthening the economy and the Nationalist Party's support on Taiwan. The elder Chiang precluded compromise in the zero-sum competition with China for diplomatic recognition and representation in the United Nations. At one level, Taiwan seemed sure to lose this competition, but in 1968 with China in the midst of the Cultural Revolution and all its radical excesses, such losses seemed far off.[71]

4

Rapprochement and Normalization

Strategic Imperatives Opening U.S.-China Relations

THE ROOTS OF THE CONTEMPORARY, CLOSELY INTERTWINED Sino-American relationship began in what appeared to be very adverse circumstances. Maoist China had descended through phases of ideologically driven excess in foreign and domestic affairs, reaching a point of unprecedented international isolation, ideological rigidity, and wariness in foreign relations bordering on xenophobia. The United States had over five hundred thousand troops in Vietnam fighting a communist-led adversary supported by China with supplies, financing, and provision of many thousands of Chinese support troops. U.S. leaders were particularly fearful of an escalation of the prolonged and increasingly unpopular conflict that would somehow bring China more directly into a war that they were unsure how to win under existing conditions. The U.S. containment effort along China's periphery continued, as did U.S. political isolation and economic embargo against the Beijing regime. Nascent U.S. efforts to consider greater flexibility in relations with China ran up against Maoist hostility, disinterest, and contempt, and were overshadowed by the broad implications of the Vietnam quagmire.[1]

The dramatic turnabout leading to the opening in U.S.-China relations at the end of the 1960s and early 1970s has been subject to some different scholarly interpretations. One view sees a flagging of Mao's revolutionary drive and vigor, opening the way for the Chinese leader to consider and ultimately pursue pragmatic understanding with the United States.[2] Another sees a reconfiguring in the U.S. calculus of China's position in world politics and its implications for the United States. This view highlights the importance of an apparent trend whereby U.S. leaders privately came to see China in the late 1960s as less threatening than in the past; eventually they came to view the Maoist regime as a potential asset in American strategy focused increasingly on dealing with a rising and threatening Soviet Union.[3]

Despite these and other divergent views, assessments of this period and the opening in Sino-American relations find it hard not to give primacy to interpretations focused on the acute strategic necessities of both the United States and China amid circumstances of regional and international order featuring a rising and powerful Soviet Union challenging their core national interests. Only the threat of nuclear war with a domineering Soviet Union at a time of acute Chinese internal disruption and weakness appears sufficient to explain the remarkable turnabout in China's foreign policy calculus and approach to the United States at this time. Given China's size and the preoccupation Chinese rulers have long given to the tasks of managing the complicated internal affairs of this vast country, China historians and specialists of contemporary affairs often have given pride of place to Chinese domestic determinants in Chinese foreign policy. There was no better example during Maoist rule of how domestic Chinese policies and practices determined Chinese foreign policy than during the violent and disruptive early years of China's Cultural Revolution. Moving Chinese leaders out of their self-initiated isolation probably would have taken many years under more normal circumstances. But circumstances in the late 1960s were far from normal, giving rise to the real danger of the Soviet Union militarily invading China, destroying its nuclear and other strategic installations, and forcing China to conform to Soviet interests.[4]

For their part, U.S. leaders faced an unprecedented situation of Soviet military power seeming to reach parity with and in some critical areas surpassing that of the United States. The concurrent Vietnam quagmire drained American resources, and Moscow pumped up support for the Vietnamese communist resistance, seeking to further weaken the United States and strengthen the changing balance of power in Asian and world affairs. Finding a way to break this trend and deal more effectively with the Vietnam situation became critically important issues in American politics.[5]

It was fortuitous that strong strategic imperatives, which drove Chinese and U.S. leaders toward one another, developed at the same time. Otherwise, Maoist China in particular seemed positioned to continue resistance to the United States, while U.S. interest in greater flexibility toward China appeared likely to be overwhelmed by opposing U.S. interests and political inclinations.

There had been earlier occasions when one side or the other saw their interests served by a possible improvement in Sino-American relations. But it turned out that when one side showed some interest in improved contacts, the other rebuffed or ignored it. Thus, despite deeply rooted differences between the U.S. government and Chinese Communist leaders on ideological, economic, and international issues, United States–Chinese Communist interchange since the start of World War II witnessed a few instances where one side or the other saw their interests served by reaching out and seeking reconciliation and better ties with the other party. The Chinese Communists in particular tried a moderate and accommodating approach to the United States in greeting the American Military Observer Group to Yenan in 1944, and in the initial ambassadorial talks following Zhou Enlai's moderate overture at Bandung in 1955. The Americans tried more tentative overtures to Beijing in 1949 and showed interest in more flexibility toward China by the 1960s. Unfortunately, these initiatives and overtures failed, as there were never occasions when both sides sought improved relations at the same time, until internal and international weaknesses in 1968 and 1969 drove the United States and China closer together in a pragmatic search for means to deal with difficult circumstances.[6]

Encounters and Interaction, 1968–1989

Opening Contacts

Difficulties in the United States in 1968 were profound. It is hard to recall a one-year period since the start of the Cold War with so many shocking and adverse developments for American leaders and their constituents. The string of calamities and reversals began in January with the communist Tet Offensive throughout South Vietnamese cities. The assault often was carried out by Vietnamese thought to be supporting the American war effort. The U.S. and Allied forces counterattacked against the guerrillas in their own ranks and elsewhere in the supposedly pacified cities of South Vietnam, killing many thousands, but the uprising and mass killings shattered the Johnson administration's predictions of progress in the increasingly unpopular Vietnam War.[7]

U.S. commanders called for two hundred thousand more U.S. troops in addition to the more than half a million U.S. forces in the country. The vast majority of these American forces were draftees. They and their families and friends tended in growing numbers to question the purpose of the U.S. commitment to Vietnam and the massive costs in terms of American casualties and economic and military support. Anti-war demonstrations in the United States grew in size and frequency. Protest marches of two hundred thousand or more along the Mall in Washington, D.C., became more regular occurrences. Providing security for the White House compound adjoining the Mall became an increasing concern given the size of the demonstrations and the uncertainty over whether or not they would stay on the Mall or turn against the White House.

The rising anti-war sentiment in the United States changed the course of the 1968 presidential election campaign. President Johnson's mandate appeared to collapse when he did poorly in the New Hampshire primary in February. He ran against Senator Eugene McCarthy, an otherwise unexceptional opponent who emphasized an anti-war platform. Johnson pulled out of the race and redoubled peace efforts in talks with the Vietnamese communists in Paris.

Civil rights leader and anti-war proponent Martin Luther King Jr. traveled to Memphis in March in support of a strike by city trash handlers. King was killed by a rifleman while standing outside his motel. The assassination set off a rampage of urban looting and burning that afflicted several American cities. Washington, D.C., was closed for days as major parts of the city burned out of control. The fire service was prevented by snipers and mob violence. Order was restored only after the imposition of martial law by U.S. Army combat troops.

Amid this turmoil over the Vietnam War and race relations in the United States, the contentious Democratic primaries reached a conclusion in California in June, where Senator Robert Kennedy won. Kennedy was critical of the conduct of the war and drew vast crowds of African-Americans and others hopeful for government policies to heal fractured race relations in the United States. Like King three months earlier, Kennedy was assassinated, just after the California victory was secured.

With Kennedy dead, anti-war advocates gathered in Chicago in August to protest the likely selection of Johnson's vice president Hubert Humphrey as the Democratic standard-bearer. Chicago's Mayor Richard Daley and his police officers promised tough measures to deal with unauthorized demonstrations. They delivered on their promise: as American television audiences watched in shock, police officers clubbed and beat demonstrators, reporters, and others they deemed to be obstructing the smooth flow of the convention and nearby hotel receptions.

The Republicans at their convention in the summer nominated Richard Nixon. In a political comeback after retreating from public life in the early 1960s, Nixon said he had a plan to deal with the Vietnam morass. He did not speak very much about an opening to China. Nixon won the election and took office amid unprecedented tight security for fear of violence from anti-war protesters and others. Upon entering office, Nixon moved quickly to begin what would turn out to be the withdrawal of over six hundred thousand U.S. troops from around China's periphery in Asia. In his first year in office, he announced what later was called the Nixon Doctrine, a broad framework for Asia's future without massive U.S. troop deployments. One implication seemed to be the end of the U.S.-backed containment of China. Nixon also made several mainly symbolic gestures to the Chinese government while pursuing vigorous efforts in secret to develop communications with the Mao Zedong leadership.[8]

Meanwhile, in China, Mao succeeded in removing political rivals in the early years of the Cultural Revolution, but at tremendous cost. Many burnt urban areas testified to widespread violence and arson among competing groups. The party and government administration were severely disrupted. Experienced administrators were often purged, persecuted, or pushed aside by proponents of radical Maoist ideals or political opportunists. Expertise in economics, development, and other fields essential to nation-building came to be seen as a liability in the politically charged atmosphere of repeated mass campaigns. Political indoctrination and adherence to Mao Zedong Thought overshadowed education and training in practical tasks.[9]

Military forces called in to Chinese cities in order to restore order duly removed millions of disruptive Red Guards and began to lead the process of reconstituting a party and government infrastructure on the basis of military-led rule. Not surprisingly in this context, Defense Minister Lin Biao and his People's Liberation Army (PLA) associates rose to new prominence in the Chinese hierarchy. Military representation in various party and government bodies was high. Not all military leaders were as supportive of the radical policies and practices of the Cultural Revolution as Lin Biao and his associates in the high command. Some experienced civilian and military cadre had survived in office. But they appeared in the minority in a leadership featuring factional chieftains like the Gang of Four involving Mao's wife and three other extremist party Politburo members, and such luminaries as Mao's speechwriter and sometime confidant Chen Boda and security forces and intelligence operative Kang Sheng.[10]

Under these circumstances, China was not prepared for a national security shock. Chinese troops were engaged in domestic peacekeeping and governance. They also for many years followed Maoist dictates under the leadership of Defense Minister Lin Biao and eschewed professional military training in favor of ideological training and promoting popular welfare in China. Chinese military programs for developing nuclear weapons and ballistic missiles were excluded from the violence and disruption of the Cultural Revolution, but the PLA on the whole was poorly prepared to deal with conventional military challenges.[11]

In August 1968, the Soviet Union invaded Czechoslovakia and removed its leadership, putting in power a regime more compatible with Soviet interests.

The Soviet Union also made clear that it reserved the right to take similar actions in other deviant communist states. This view came to be known as the Brezhnev Doctrine, named after the Soviet party leader Leonid Brezhnev, who ruled from the mid-1960s until the early 1980s. Of course, Chinese leaders well knew that, from the Soviet perspective, there was no communist state more deviant than China. Moreover, since Brezhnev's takeover, the Soviet Union had backed political opposition to China with increasing military muscle, deploying ever-larger numbers of forces along the Manchurian border and, as a result of a new Soviet defense treaty with Mongolia, along the Sino-Mongolian border. The Soviet forces, mainly mechanized divisions designed to move rapidly in offensive operations, were configured in a pattern used by Soviet forces when they quickly overran Japanese forces in Manchuria and northern China in the last days of World War II.[12]

The Sino-Soviet dispute had emerged in the late 1950s as an ideological dispute with wide implications. Fairly quickly it became a major issue in bilateral relations, notably with the abrupt withdrawal of Soviet assistance from China in 1960. At that time, the dispute broadened to include stark differences on international issues and how to deal with the United States. Chinese accusations of Soviet weakness in the face of the firm U.S. stance against Soviet missiles in Cuba during the Cuban missile crisis of 1962 saw Soviet officials respond by accusing China of accommodating colonial "out-houses" held by Great Britain and Portugal in Hong Kong and Macau, respectively. Maoist China responded by reminding the world that imperialist Russia took by far the greatest tracts of Chinese territory by virtue of the so-called unequal treaties imposed on China by imperialist powers in the nineteenth and twentieth centuries. The Sino-Soviet debate now focused on competing claims to disputed border territories, against the background of new uncertainty over the legitimacy of the boundaries established by the unequal treaties. Sino-Soviet negotiations soon after Brezhnev took power following the ouster of Nikita Khrushchev in 1964 failed to resolve border uncertainties, prompting the new Soviet leader to make the force deployments and arrangements noted above in order to deal with the Chinese disputes from a position of strength. With the declared Soviet ambitions under terms of the Brezhnev Doctrine and Moscow's military preparations, the stage was set for the border dispute to evolve into the most serious national security threat ever faced by the People's Republic of China.[13]

The combination of perceived greater threat and internal weakness caused a crisis and debate in the Chinese leadership that lasted into the early 1970s. Chinese leadership decision-making in the Cultural Revolution was not at all transparent. Mao seemed to remain in overall command, but official Chinese media duly reflected competing views on how to deal with the new and apparently dangerous situation in relations with the Soviet Union.[14]

Some commentary, presumably encouraged by some Chinese leaders, favored reaching out to the United States as a means to offset the Soviet threat. In November 1968, the Chinese Foreign Ministry under Premier Zhou Enlai's direction called for renewed ambassadorial talks with the newly elected Nixon administration in a statement that was notable for the absence of the then-usual Chinese invective critical of the United States. The argument used in media commentary proposing a reaching-out to the United States was that the United States was in the process of being defeated in Indochina and was no longer the primary threat to China. It too faced challenge from the expanding USSR and China could take advantage of the differences between the competing superpowers in order to secure its position in the face of the newly emerging Soviet danger.[15]

Other commentary, presumably backed by other Chinese leaders, strongly opposed an opening to the United States. These commentaries were associated with Lin Biao and his lieutenants, along with the radically Maoist leadership faction, the Gang of Four. They argued in favor of continued strong Chinese opposition to both the United States and the Soviet Union. Though weakened by the defeat in Vietnam, the United States could not be trusted in dealings with China. In particular, any sign of Chinese weakness toward either superpower likely would prompt them both to work together in seeking to pressure China and gain at its expense.[16]

The latter leaders held the upper hand in Chinese leadership councils during much of 1969. Chinese media rebuked and ridiculed the new U.S. president as he took office. At the last moment Chinese leaders cancelled the slated ambassadorial talks in February. The Chinese authorities took the offensive in the face of Soviet military pressure along the border, ambushing a Soviet patrol on a disputed island in early March and publicizing the incident to the world. Far from being intimidated, Brezhnev's Soviet forces responded later in the month by annihilating a Chinese border guard unit, setting the stage for escalating rhetoric and military clashes throughout the spring and summer of 1969. The clashes were capped in August by an all-day battle along the western sector of the border that saw the Soviets inflict hundreds of casualties on the Chinese. Soviet officials followed with warnings to Americans, and other foreigners sure to relay the warnings to the Chinese, that the Soviet Union was in the process of consulting with foreign powers to assure they would stand aside as the Soviet Union prepared all-out attack on China, including the possible use of nuclear weapons.[17]

In the face of such threats and pressure, Chinese leaders were compelled to shift strategy. Zhou Enlai was brought forward to negotiate with Soviet leaders. It was clear that while negotiating with the USSR would temporarily ease tensions and the danger of war, China would not accept Soviet demands.

Beijing now viewed the USSR as China's number one strategic threat. Seeking international leverage, it took measures to improve strained Chinese relations with neighboring countries and with more distant powers. It was nonetheless evident that, while helpful, these improvements would not fundamentally alter China's strategic disadvantage in the face of Soviet intimidation and threat. Only one power, the United States, had that ability. Zhou and like-minded officials in the Chinese leadership were encouraged that the United States was weakened by the Vietnam War and that it was also beginning to withdraw sizeable numbers of troops from Asia and dismantle the U.S. military containment against China. On this basis, Beijing could pursue relations with Washington as a means to deal with the Soviet threat. However, Lin Biao and others continued to argue that both superpowers were enemies of China, and in the end they would cooperate together to isolate and control China.[18]

The debate seemed to get caught up with the broader struggle for power in this period of the Cultural Revolution. Mao Zedong came to side with the view associated with Zhou Enlai. Repeated initiatives by the Nixon administration to China ultimately succeeded in Sino-American ambassadorial talks being resumed in Warsaw in early 1970. China used the image of restored contacts with the United States in order to offset and undermine Soviet efforts to intimidate China. Chinese officials arranged for the meeting to be held in the secure area of their embassy in Warsaw. The usual venue, a palace provided by the Poles, was long suspected of being riddled with secret listening devices that would give the USSR and Warsaw Pact allies the full transcript of the U.S.-China discussions. The Chinese diplomats also made a point of being unusually positive to Western reporters during the photo opportunity as American officials were welcomed to the Chinese embassy at the start of the official talks. As Chinese officials presumably hoped, Soviet commentary on the secret talks and improved atmosphere in U.S.-China relations viewed the developments as complicating Soviet border negotiations with China and nuclear armament limitation talks with the United States. Soviet commentators even charged that Beijing, fearful of Soviet intentions, was seeking to come to terms with United States in order to play one nuclear power against the other.[19]

The Nixon administration's expansion of the Vietnam War by invading Cambodia in spring 1970 caused China to cancel the talks and slowed forward movement. Mao highlighted a mass demonstration in Beijing on May 20, 1970, where he welcomed the Cambodian leader Norodom Sihanouk, who had been deposed by the U.S.-led invading forces and their Cambodian allies. The Chinese chairman, in his last major public statement denouncing the United States, called on the people of the world to rise up against U.S. imperialism and their "running dogs." Outwardly, it appeared that Mao was siding with the Chinese advocates of a harder line against the United States. However, clandestine U.S.-China communication continued, as did the withdrawal of U.S. forces from Vietnam and other parts of Asia, so that by October 1970 Mao was prepared to tell visiting U.S. journalist Edgar Snow that Nixon could visit China.[20]

The shift in Mao's stance was accompanied by other moves that appeared to undermine the leadership standing of Lin Biao and his radical allies in the Chinese leadership. A key radical leader, Chen Boda, dropped from public view in late 1970 in what later was shown to be intensified factional maneuvering leading up to the alleged coup plans by Lin and his allies.[21]

What role differences over the opening to the United States played in the life-or-death struggle in the Chinese leadership remains hidden by pervasive secrecy in Chinese leadership decision-making. Emblematic of the significance of the opening to the United States in Chinese politics at the time was the unusual greeting of U.S. National Security Advisor Henry Kissinger upon his arrival in Beijing on his secret mission in July 1971 to open U.S. China relations. The first Chinese official to greet Kissinger on arrival was not a protocol officer from the foreign ministry or some other appropriate official; it was Marshall Ye Jianying. Ye was one of the most senior Chinese military leaders. He survived the Cultural Revolution, advised Mao to use connections with the United States in the face of the Soviet threat, later played a key role in the arrest of the Gang of Four following Mao's death in 1976, and became president of China. His approach was close to that of Zhou Enlai and at odds with that of Lin Biao.[22]

The announcement of Kissinger's successful secret trip appeared to represent a serious defeat for Lin Biao and his allies in their debate with opponents on how to deal with the Soviet Union and the United States. The setback came amid rising pressures and adverse developments affecting the military leader. The stakes apparently were very high. Two months later, Lin, his wife, son, and close aides were dead as a result of an air crash in Mongolia as they were allegedly trying to escape China following a failed coup attempt against Mao and his opponents. The military high command in the PLA that had risen to power under Lin's tenure as defense minister were arrested, removed from power, and not seen again until they eventually were brought out for public trial along with Gang of Four and other discredited radical leaders in the years after Mao's death.[23]

Though nothing like the intense factional struggles of Maoist China, U.S. leadership and popular opposition to an opening to China were feared by President Nixon and his top aides. In particular, it was clear to the American leaders that they would have to sacrifice U.S. official relations with Taiwan in order to meet the conditions Chinese leaders set for establishing relations with the United States. How the Chiang Kai-shek administration in Taiwan would react to this new adverse turn of fate was uncertain. The so-called China lobby, both supportive of Chiang and the Chinese Nationalists and strongly anti-communist, had become a feature of American domestic politics for over twenty years. Chiang and the lobby had particular influence among conservatives in the president's Republican Party. Nixon had close and personal ties with the lobby.[24]

President Nixon, National Security Advisor Kissinger, and the small group of top aides involved in the opening to China dealt with potential domestic opposition through secrecy and what arguably could be seen as deception. Their motives focused on the advantages for the United States in a new relationship with China in regard to handling the difficult process of reaching an acceptable peace agreement to end the U.S. involvement in the Vietnam War and in dealing with the Soviet Union in arms limitation and other negotiations from a position of greater strength. A new order in Asian and world affairs featuring positive American-Chinese relations seemed much less costly and more compatible for U.S. interests than the previous U.S. confrontation with and containment of China. President Nixon and his administration also seemed acutely aware that the political opportunity of an American opening to China could fall into the hands of a Democratic Party opponent, and they were determined to preclude such an outcome.[25]

For a time, it was difficult for scholars to construct the full picture of the Nixon administration approach to China because much of the record initially remained secret and public pronouncements, memoirs, and other documents from administration leaders sometimes seemed very much at odds with what was actually the administration's policy and practice. It was clear that U.S. leaders now centered their strategies and approaches in East Asia on improving relations with China, and that U.S. relations with Taiwan would decline, though the scope and extent of the decline was left ambiguous. Relations with Japan and other East Asian allies and friends also appeared secondary and were sometimes viewed as declining assets or liabilities. Also clear was evidence that the United States sought, through the new relationship with China, a means to secure U.S. interests following the failure of U.S. military intervention in Vietnam and the rising danger posed by expanding power of the Soviet Union in the Asian region as well as elsewhere. And the ambitions of the Nixon administration to use the dramatic opening to China to garner personal prestige at home and abroad and strong domestic political support in the run-up to the 1972 U.S. presidential race seemed evident.[26]

The American people, their representatives in Congress, the media, and others with an interest were notably left in the dark for many years regarding the full extent of the U.S. compromises on Taiwan carried out in the early contacts between Kissinger and Nixon and Chinese leaders. The Nationalist Chinese administration was in a similar situation. The record reconstructed by recent scholarship shows that Kissinger met Chinese conditions involving a full break in U.S. official relations with Taiwan and other interaction with Taiwan during his initial meetings with Zhou Enlai in 1971, and that Nixon backed these steps in his initial meetings with Chinese leaders the following year. These compromises were kept from public view and also kept from many U.S. officials responsible for the conduct of U.S. policy toward China and Taiwan, amid statements and actions by the administration indicating continued support for Taiwan and ambiguity about what the future course of U.S. policy might be.[27]

On the basis of the compromises by Kissinger and Nixon, recent scholarship judges that the Chinese leadership could reasonably have concluded Taiwan would soon be theirs, as the United States would remove itself from involvement in the issue. Unfortunately, Nixon and his associates had only begun to build support in the United States and internationally for this dramatic change in policy. It was unclear whether majorities in the Congress, the media, public opinion, and the major political parties would accept it. Nixon and his aides avoided building this support as they focused on developing relations with China in secret on a foundation of compromises and accommodations poorly understood in the United States and abroad. They made a strong case that such secrecy was needed in order to avoid complications in the process of normalization. That argument would be followed by later U.S. administrations with mixed success and some serious negative consequences for long-term U.S.-China relations. Notably, Chinese expectations that Taiwan would soon be theirs and that the United States would remove itself from involvement in Taiwan were sorely and repeatedly tested by U.S. actions demonstrating continued support for Taiwan, backed by American leaders often unaware of or opposed to the Nixon-Kissinger secret compromises on Taiwan.[28]

The July 1971 announcement of Nixon's trip to China came as a surprise to most Americans, who supported the initiative; Americans watched with interest the president's February 1972 visit to China. Supporting Kissinger's secret pledges in the July 1971 meetings in Beijing, Nixon privately indicated to Chinese leaders he would break U.S. ties with Taiwan and establish diplomatic relations with China in his second term. In the Shanghai Communiqué signed at the end of President Nixon's historic visit to China, both sides registered opposition to "hegemony"—a code word for Soviet expansion—laid out differences on a variety of Asian and other issues, and set forth the U.S. intention to pull back militarily from Taiwan and to support a "peaceful settlement of the Taiwan question by the Chinese themselves." Subsequently, both sides agreed to establish U.S.-Chinese Liaison Offices staffed with senior diplomats in Beijing and Washington in 1973, despite the fact that the United States still maintained official relations with the Chinese Nationalist government in Taipei.[29]

Normalization of Relations

Progress toward establishing formal U.S.-China relations, the so-called normalization of relations, was delayed in the mid-1970s on account of circumstances mainly involving the United States. A politically motivated break-in at the Watergate office complex in Washington, D.C., and cover-up of the crime involved President Nixon in criminal activity. As congressional investigation led toward impeachment, Nixon resigned in August 1974. His promise to normalize relations with China in his second term ended with his resignation. President Gerald Ford privately reaffirmed Nixon's pledge to shift diplomatic recognition from Taiwan to China, but then he backtracked in the face of U.S. domestic opposition and international circumstances.[30]

Chinese leaders for their part were preoccupied with Mao's declining health and subsequent death in September 1976, and the most important leadership succession struggle in the history of the People's Republic of China. The leadership turmoil in China at this time saw Zhou Enlai die in January. His purported successor, recently rehabilitated veteran leader Deng Xiaoping, gave the eulogy at the memorial service for Zhou and then disappeared from public view, purged from the leadership for a second time. The radical Gang of Four seemed to exert more influence for a time, but the demonstration of support for Zhou and his relatively moderate policies, in the form of thousands of Beijing people placing flowers and wreaths in his memory at the monument for revolutionary martyrs in the capital in April, appeared to indicate that the days of radicalism were numbered. The death of senior military leader Zhu De in July preceded Mao's by two months, setting the stage for the struggle for succession.[31]

That China had far to go in creating a foreign policy that dealt with the United States and other countries in the world in conventional and normal ways was underlined by the tragedy of an earthquake in July that demolished the industrial city of Tangshan, 105 miles southeast of Beijing, and severely damaged nearby areas including the capital and the major port and industrial city of Tianjin. It later was disclosed that hundreds of thousands of Chinese died in the quake and that the needs for relief were enormous. Nevertheless, in a remarkable and extremely damaging demonstration of Maoist "self-reliance," the radical leadership in Beijing at the time refused to acknowledge these needs or to allow foreign countries and groups to assist in efforts to save lives and reduce misery.[32]

A coalition of senior leaders managed to stop the Gang of Four from gaining power after Mao's death. The coalition included veteran cadre who had survived the Cultural Revolution and administrators who had risen to prominence during the turmoil but also endeavored to avoid the harm caused by excessively radical policies. The four radical leaders were arrested. After a few years, they were put on public trial in 1980 once the Communist Party leadership had sufficiently reunited and come to overall judgment about what was correct and incorrect behavior during the Cultural Revolution. Reaching such judgment was particularly time-consuming and difficult since Chairman Mao Zedong, still seen as the revered leader of China, was personally responsible for support of the radicals and so much of the turmoil they and others carried out during the Cultural Revolution.[33]

Following the arrest of the Gang of Four, leadership changes in China slowly evolved toward a reversal of the disruptive policies of the past and restoration to power of senior cadre committed to pragmatic reform in the interest of Chinese development and sustaining Communist rule in China. Deng Xiaoping was once again brought back to power. By the time of the third plenary session of the Eleventh Central Committee in December 1978, Deng was able to consolidate a leading position within the administration and to launch the economic and policy reforms that provided the foundation for China's recent approach to the United States and international affairs. Deng and his colleagues constantly were compelled to maneuver amid competing interests and preferences within the Chinese leadership and the broader polity in order to come up with changes they felt would advance China's wealth and shore up the legitimacy of the Chinese Communist Party, which had been severely damaged by the excesses and poor performance of the past.[34]

Not only were Chinese leaders preoccupied internally, but their priorities internationally in the latter 1970s were less focused on consummating normalization with the United States and more focused on dealing with Soviet intimidation and threat. The United States was weakened internally by Nixon's resignation, and the Ford government was hobbled by the president's pardon of Nixon. Ford was in a poor position to continue strong support for the struggling South Vietnamese government and the neighboring Cambodian government aligned with the United States. Strong Soviet assistance to Vietnamese communist forces bolstered their efforts to take control of the south. The Cambodian regime collapsed, and Chinese-backed Khmer Rouge insurgents entered Phnom Penh in March 1975. The new regime immediately began carrying out their radical and brutal policies that would see the evacuation of the capital and the massive repression and deaths of over one million Cambodians. North Vietnamese forces launched an all-out assault in South Vietnam. The Saigon regime disintegrated; the Americans and what Vietnamese associates they could bring with them fled in ignominious defeat; and the communist forces barged through the gates of the presidential palace and occupied Saigon in late April.[35]

Chinese officials showed considerable alarm at the turn of events around China's periphery. Stronger efforts by the Soviet Union to use military power and relations with allies around China, like Vietnam and India, to contain and pressure the PRC mimicked the U.S.-led containment effort against China earlier in the Cold War. Under these circumstances, Chinese leaders focused on shoring up U.S. resolve and the resolve of other governments and forces seen as important in what China depicted as a united front against expanding Soviet power and influence in Asian and world affairs. The Chinese leaders appeared prepared to wait for the United States to meet Chinese conditions on breaking all U.S. official ties with Taiwan, including the U.S.-Taiwan defense treaty, before moving ahead with full normalization of PRC relations with the United States.[36]

Desiring to complete the normalization of U.S.-China relations begun by President Nixon, President Jimmy Carter felt compelled to wait until after his success in spring 1978 in gaining Senate passage of a controversial treaty transferring control of the Panama Canal to Panama. A visit by Secretary of State Cyrus Vance to China in 1977 showed that Chinese leaders were not prepared for significant compromise on Taiwan. President Carter was aware that a complete ending of U.S. official relations with Taiwan would alienate many in the U.S. Senate, and he needed the support of these senators for the two-thirds Senate vote of ratification on the Panama Canal treaty. Once the Senate approved the Panama treaty in spring 1978, Carter moved forward expeditiously with normalization with China.[37]

National Security Adviser Zbigniew Brzezinski was in the lead in seeking rapid progress in normalizing U.S.-China relations in 1978 and in subsequent steps to advance U.S.-China relations as a means to counter Soviet power and expansion. Soviet and Soviet-backed forces had made gains and were making inroads that seemed at odds with U.S. interests in different parts of Africa, the Middle East, Central America, and Southwest and Southeast Asia. Chinese officials were in the lead among international advocates in warning the United States to avoid the dangers of "appeasement" and to stand firm and work with China against the expanding Soviet power. Carter followed Brzezinski's advice over that of Secretary of State Cyrus Vance, who gave a higher priority to working constructively with the USSR, notably in order to reach U.S.-Soviet arms control agreements.[38]

The process of U.S. administration decision-making followed the practices of the Nixon period. Like their Nixon-administration counterparts, the Carter administration leaders were concerned with the reactions of U.S. supporters of Taiwan and others opposed to American normalization with China. To outmaneuver anticipated opposition and complications, Carter, Brzezinski, and their senior aides worked hard to preserve the secrecy of the negotiations with China. Though the broad direction of U.S. policy was understood to be moving toward normalization with China, the process of the talks with Beijing and the content of U.S. concessions were held back. The Carter administration agreement to normalize diplomatic relations with China would follow through in a public way on many of the secret agreements the U.S. leaders had already made with China over Taiwan. Though some in the Carter administration were concerned with preserving important U.S. ties with Taiwan after normalization, Brzezinski showed little interest, and Carter seemed contemptuous of congressional backers of Taiwan. Key Carter officials didn't expect Taiwan to survive the change in relations.[39]

The United States–China Communiqué announced in December 1978 established official U.S. relations with the People's Republic of China under conditions whereby the United States recognized the PRC as the government of China, acknowledged that Taiwan was part of China, ended official U.S. relations with the Republic of China government on Taiwan, and terminated the U.S. defense treaty with the ROC on Taiwan. Official U.S. statements underscored U.S. interest that Taiwan's future be settled peacefully and that the United States would continue sales of defensive arms to Taipei.[40]

U.S. and especially Chinese leaders used the signs of improved U.S.-China relations in the communiqué and during Chinese leader Deng Xiaoping's widely publicized visit to the United States in January 1979 to highlight Sino-American cooperation against "hegemony," notably a Soviet-backed Vietnamese military assault against Cambodia beginning in late December 1978. Returning from the United States, Deng launched a large-scale Chinese military offensive into Vietnam's northern region. Chinese forces withdrew after a few weeks but maintained strong artillery attacks and other military pressure against Vietnamese border positions until the Vietnamese eventually agreed to withdraw from Cambodia ten years later. Carter administration officials voiced some reservations about Deng's confrontational tactics against Soviet and Vietnamese expansionism, but Sino-American cooperation against the USSR and its allies increased.[41]

In pursuing normalization of relations with China, President Carter and National Security Adviser Brzezinski followed the pattern of secret diplomacy used successfully by President Nixon and National Security Adviser Kissinger in early interaction with China. Their approach allowed for very little consultation with Congress, key U.S. allies, or the Taiwan government regarding the conditions and timing of the 1978 normalization agreement. In contrast to general U.S. congressional, media, and popular support for the surprise Nixon opening to China, President Carter and his aides clearly were less successful in winning U.S. domestic support for their initiatives. Many in Congress were satisfied with the stasis that developed in U.S.-PRC-ROC relations in the mid-1970s and unconvinced that the United States had strategic or other need to pay the price of breaking a U.S. defense treaty and other official ties with a loyal government in Taiwan for the sake of formalizing already existing relations with the PRC. Bipartisan majorities in Congress resisted the president's initiatives and passed laws, notably the Taiwan Relations Act (TRA), that tied the hands of the administration on Taiwan and other issues.[42]

The Taiwan Relations Act was passed by Congress in March 1979 and signed by President Carter on April 10, 1979. The initial draft of the legislation was proposed by the Carter administration to govern U.S. relations with Taiwan once official U.S. ties were ended in 1979. Congress rewrote the legislation, adding or strengthening provisions on U.S. arms sales, economic relations, human rights, congressional oversight, and opposition to threats and use of force. Treating Taiwan as a separate entity that would continue to receive U.S. military and other support, the law appeared to contradict the U.S. stance in the U.S.-PRC communiqué of 1978 establishing official U.S.-PRC relations. Subsequently, Chinese and Taiwan officials and their supporters in the United States competed to incline U.S. policy toward the commitments in the U.S.-PRC communiqué or the commitments in the TRA. U.S. policy usually supported both, though it sometimes seemed more supportive of one set of commitments than the other.[43]

Running against President Carter in 1980, California Governor Ronald Reagan criticized Carter's handling of Taiwan. Asserting for a time that he would restore official relations with Taipei, Reagan later backed away from this stance but still claimed he would base his policy on the Taiwan Relations Act. The Chinese government put heavy pressure on the Reagan administration, threatening serious deterioration in relations over various issues but especially continuing U.S. arms sales to Taiwan.[44]

Viewing close China-U.S. relations as a key element in U.S. strategy against the Soviet Union, Secretary of State Alexander Haig led those in the Reagan administration who favored maintaining close China-U.S. relations and opposed U.S. arms sales to Taiwan that might provoke China. For a year and a half, Haig and his supporters were successful in leading U.S. efforts to accommodate PRC concerns over Taiwan, especially regarding U.S. arms sales to the ROC, in the interest of fostering closer U.S.-China cooperation against the Soviet Union. The United States ultimately signed with China the August 17, 1982, communiqué. In the communiqué, the United States agreed gradually to diminish arms sales, and China agreed it would seek peaceful reunification of Taiwan with the mainland. Subsequent developments showed that the vague agreement was subject to varying interpretations. President Reagan registered private reservations about the agreement, and his administration also took steps to reassure Taiwan's leader of continued U.S. support.[45]

Looking back at the first decade of opening and developing U.S.-China contacts leading to the normalization of relations, prevailing assessments show a strong tendency on the part of U.S. leaders to focus on relations with China as the key element in a new U.S. approach to East Asian and world affairs. The war in Vietnam, the growing challenge of an expanding Soviet Union, the seeming decline in U.S. power and influence in East Asian and world affairs, and major U.S. internal disruptions and weaknesses seemed to support emphasis on a new U.S. approach to China with important benefits for U.S. foreign policy and other interests. U.S. leadership attention focused on doing what was needed to advance the new China relationship and gave secondary attention to longstanding U.S. allies and other close relationships in East Asia or manipulated them in ways that would accord with the China-first emphasis in U.S. policy. Emblematic of this trend, Nixon's surprise announcement in July 1971 that he would visit China was so shocking and disturbing to the longstanding and more conservative China policy of the government of Prime Minister Eisaku Sato of Japan that it brought down the Japanese government. Available scholarship shows that Nixon deliberately withheld information of the American shift so he could "stick it to Japan" and show U.S. frustration with Japan's trade and economic policies working against U.S. interests.[46]

The U.S. emphasis on China came with significant costs for the United States and U.S. interests, though scholarship tends to depict the benefits of the U.S. approach as justifying the costs.[47] Notably, U.S. leaders came to overestimate the power, influence, and utility of China in assisting U.S. efforts to withdraw from Vietnam and to shore up international opposition to Soviet expansion. By so doing, they gave advantage to China in negotiations over contentious U.S.-China issues regarding Taiwan and other disputes. Seeking sometimes-unattainable advantages from improved relations with China, U.S. leaders sacrificed relations with an ally, Taiwan, and treated relations with Japan and other U.S. Asian allies and associates in ways that subordinated those relations to U.S. interests in improving relations with China. They also sacrificed attention to those U.S. values and interests in Asian and world affairs that were inconsistent with a pragmatic pursuit of better ties with China.

The elitist approach of U.S. leaders followed a pattern of secret diplomacy and deal-making that undermined the U.S. administration's credibility with the Congress and significant segments of the U.S. media and public opinion. It also undermined the constitutionally mandated shared powers the executive and legislative branches hold in the conduct of U.S. foreign policy. This experience established an atmosphere of suspicion and cynicism in American domestic politics over China policy and set the stage for often bitter and debilitating fights in U.S. domestic politics over China policy in ensuing years that on balance are seen not to serve the overall national interests of the United States.[48]

The Pan-Asian Approach of George Shultz and Chinese Accommodation

Amid continued strong Chinese pressure tactics on a wide range of U.S.-China disputes, U.S. policy shifted with Haig's resignation in 1982 and the appointment of George Shultz as secretary of state. Reagan administration officers who were at odds with Haig's emphasis on the need for a solicitous U.S. approach to China came to the fore. They were led by Paul Wolfowitz, who was chosen by Shultz as assistant secretary of state for East Asian affairs; Richard Armitage, the senior Defense Department officer managing relations with China and East Asia; and the senior National Security Council staff aide on Asian affairs and later assistant secretary of state for East Asian affairs, Gaston Sigur. While officers who had backed Haig's pro-China slant were transferred from authority over China policy, the new U.S. leadership contingent with responsibility for East Asian affairs shifted U.S. policy toward a less solicitous and accommodating stance toward China, while giving much higher priority to U.S. relations with Japan, as well as other U.S. allies and friends in East Asia. There was less emphasis on China's strategic importance to the United States in American competition with the Soviet Union, and there was less concern among U.S. policy makers about China possibly downgrading relations over Taiwan and other disputes.[49]

The scholarship on the U.S. opening to China beginning in the Nixon administration reviewed above focuses on powerful strategic and domestic imperatives that drove the United States and China to cooperate together in a pragmatic search for advantage for their respective national and leadership interests. It underlines the primacy of China in American foreign policy in Asia while relations with Japan and other East Asian allies and friends remained secondary and were sometimes viewed as declining assets or liabilities.[50]

Some scholars discern an important shift in U.S. strategy toward China and in East Asia more broadly beginning in 1982.[51] The reevaluation of U.S. policy toward China under Secretary of State George Shultz is seen to bring to power officials who opposed the high priority on China in U.S. strategy toward East Asia and the world, and who gave much greater importance to U.S. relations with Japan and other U.S. allies in securing U.S. interests amid prevailing conditions. The reevaluation on the whole is depicted as working to the advantage of the United States. It notably is seen to have added dimensions related to a changing balance of forces affecting Chinese security and other interests in Asian and world affairs, which prompted heretofore demanding Chinese leaders to reduce pressures on the United States for concessions on Taiwan and other disputed issues. The changes in Chinese policy helped to open the way for several years of comparatively smooth U.S.-China relations after a period of considerable discord in the late 1970s and early 1980s.

Other scholars explain the improvement in U.S.-China relations at this time through analyses focused on the dynamics of U.S.-China relations.[52] They discern U.S. compromises and accommodations in negotiations and relations with China that assuaged Chinese demands and met Chinese interests over Taiwan and other issues. They tend to avoid analysis of how any shift in emphasis in U.S. policy away from a focus on China and toward a greater emphasis on Japan and the East Asian region might have altered Chinese calculations and the overall dynamic in U.S. interaction with China.

The analysis in the assessment detailed below supports the former view. It shows that the Chinese leaders grudgingly adjusted to the new U.S. stance, viewing their interests best served by less pressure and more positive initiatives to the Reagan administration, seen especially in their warm welcome for the U.S. president on his visit to China in 1984. Cooperative Chinese relations with the United States were critically important to the Chinese leadership in maintaining Chinese security in the face of continuing pressure from the Soviet Union and in sustaining the flow of aid, investment, and trade essential to the economic development and modernization underway in China—the linchpin of the Chinese Communist leadership's plans for sustaining their rule in China. Meanwhile, the Reagan leadership learned not to confront important Chinese interests over issues like Taiwan in overt and egregious ways, seeking to continue U.S. military and other support for Taiwan in ways less likely to provoke strong Chinese reaction. Thus, the accommodations that characterized U.S.-China relations in Reagan's second term in office were mutual, but they involved significant Chinese adjustments and changes influenced by the new posture toward China undertaken by Secretary of State Shultz and his colleagues.

In this author's assessment, the scholarship that portrays the improvement in U.S.-China relations at this time largely based on the dynamics in U.S.-China relations seems too narrowly focused. In this scholarship, the United States is seen to make compromises in ways that accommodate Chinese interests and thus allow for smoother U.S.-China relations. By limiting the focus to the dynamics of U.S.-China ties, this scholarship seems to miss the importance of the shift in U.S. emphasis during the tenure of George Shultz. Overall, that shift seems to have significantly enhanced U.S. power and leverage over China in negotiations over Taiwan and other disputes and compelled China to make concessions on its part in order to insure a positive relationship with the United States advantageous to Chinese interests. This changed dynamic, with the United States in a more commanding position vis-à-vis China, also was much more acceptable to congressional members, media, and others in U.S. politics who had been alienated by the secrecy and perceived excessive U.S. deference to China in the previous decade. It made executive-congressional relations over China policy much smoother than in the previous six years.

China's Shifting Strategic Calculus and the Importance of the United States

The significance of the shifts in American policy toward China and Asia undertaken during the tenure of Secretary Shultz and under the direction of such influential U.S. officials as Wolfowitz, Armitage, and Sigur are shown below to be important for China's broader international calculations influencing its approach toward the United States. Chinese foreign policy at this time was strongly influenced by Chinese assessments of the relative power and influence of the Soviet Union and the United States and the effects these had on key Chinese interests of security and development. Throughout much of the 1970s, China had been more vocal than the United States in warning of the dangers of expansion by the Soviet Union, seen as the greatest threat to China's security and integrity. Chinese officials and commentary depicted Soviet efforts to contain China in Asia through its military buildup and advanced nuclear ballistic missile deployments along the Sino-Soviet border, its deployments of mobile mechanized divisions in Mongolia, its stepped-up naval activity in the western Pacific along the China coast, its military presence in Vietnam, including active use of formerly U.S. naval and air base facilities, and its ever-closer military relationship with India and growing involvement with and eventual invasion of Afghanistan. These Soviet actions were seen as part of a wider expansion of Soviet power and influence that China judged needed to be countered by a united international front including China and led by the United States.[53]

For much of the 1970s, particularly after the resignation of President Nixon, Chinese officials and commentary saw the United States vacillate between a tough line toward the USSR and an approach seeking détente and accommodation with Moscow. Concern over U.S. resolve toward Moscow saw China criticize Secretary of State Henry Kissinger for being too soft toward Moscow during the Ford administration, favoring instead the harder line advocated by Defense Secretary James Schlesinger. Carter administration officials like UN envoy Andrew Young, who took a moderate view toward Soviet-backed Cuban troop deployments and other Soviet expansion in Africa, were roundly criticized in Chinese media. More cautious official commentary registered reservations about Secretary of State Cyrus Vance's approach in seeking arms limitation talks with Moscow, while Chinese officials and commentary registered approval of National Security adviser Brzezinski's tough anti-Soviet stance.[54]

Over time, and especially after the Soviet invasion of Afghanistan in late 1979, Chinese leaders began to recalculate the balance of forces affecting their interests and their respective approaches to the Soviet Union and the United States. The previous perceived danger that the United States would "appease" the Soviet Union and thereby allow Moscow to direct its pressure against China now appeared remote. Carter's last year in office and Reagan's initial stance toward the USSR saw a large increase in U.S. defense spending and military preparations. Closely allied with the United States, European powers and Japan also were building forces and taking firm positions against the USSR. Meanwhile, increased complications and weaknesses affecting the power of the Soviet Union included problems of leadership succession, economic sustainability, and tensions in Poland and elsewhere in the Warsaw Pact. Faced with such adverse circumstances prior to his death in 1982, Brezhnev reached out with positive initiatives toward China, attempting to improve relations.[55]

Against this background, Chinese officials saw an ability to exert a freer hand in foreign affairs and to position China in a stance less aligned with the United States. The priority to stay close to the United States in order to encourage resolute U.S. positions against Soviet expansion was no longer as important as in the recent past. Also, there were new opportunities to negotiate with Soviet leaders calling for talks. Beijing moved by 1981 to a posture more independent of the United States and less hostile toward the USSR. China's new "independent foreign policy" also featured a revival of Chinese relations with the developing third world and in the international communist movement, which had been neglected in favor of emphasis on the anti-Soviet front in the 1970s.[56]

However, the shift in Chinese policy away from the United States and somewhat closer to the Soviet Union did not work very well. Chinese leaders continued to speak of their new independent foreign policy approach, but they seemed to change their international calculations based on perceptions of shifts in the international balance of power affecting China. By 1983, Chinese leaders showed increasing concern about the stability of the nation's surroundings in Asia at a time of unrelenting buildup of Soviet military and political pressure along China's periphery, and of serious and possibly prolonged decline in relations with the United States. They decided that the foreign policy tactics of the previous two years, designed to distance China from the policies of the United States and to moderate and improve Chinese relations with the Soviet Union, were less likely to safeguard the important Chinese security and development concerns affected by the stability of the Asian environment.[57]

The Chinese leaders appeared to recognize in particular that Beijing would have to stop its pullback from the United States for fear of jeopardizing this link so important for maintaining its security and development interests in the face of persistent Soviet pressure in Asia. Thus, in 1983, Beijing began to retreat from some of the tactical changes made the previous two years under the rubric of an independent approach to foreign affairs. The result was a substantial reduction in Chinese pressure on the United States over Taiwan and other issues; increased Chinese interest and flexibility in dealing with the Reagan administration and other Western countries across a broad range of economic, political, and security issues; and heightened Sino-Soviet antipathy. Beijing still attempted to nurture whenever possible the increased influence it had garnered by means of its independent posture in the developing third world and the international communist movement, but it increasingly sided with the West against the USSR in order to secure basic strategic and economic interests.[58]

A key element in China's decision to change tactics toward the United States was an altered view of the likely course of Sino-American-Soviet relations over the next several years. When China began its more independent approach to foreign affairs and its concurrent harder line toward the United States in 1981–1982, it had hoped to elicit a more forthcoming U.S. attitude toward issues sensitive to Chinese interests, notably Taiwan. Beijing probably judged that there were possibly serious risks of alienating the United States, which had provided an implicit but vital counterweight serving Chinese security interests against the USSR for over a decade and was assisting more recent Chinese economic development concerns. But the Chinese seemed to have assessed that their room to maneuver had been increased because:

- The United States had reasserted a balance in East-West relations likely to lead to a continued major check on possible Soviet expansion. Chinese worries about U.S. "appeasement" of the USSR seemed a thing of the past.
- The Soviet ability to pressure China had appeared to be at least temporarily blocked by U.S. power, the determination of various U.S. allies to thwart Soviet expansion, and Soviet domestic and international problems. China added to Soviet difficulties by cooperating with the United States in clandestine operations supporting fighters resisting the Soviet occupation of Afghanistan
- At least some important U.S. leaders, notably Secretary of State Alexander Haig and his subordinates in the State Department, continued

to consider preserving and developing good U.S. relations with China as a critically important element in U.S. efforts to confront and contain Soviet expansion [59]

By mid-1983, China saw these calculations upset. In particular, the United States under Secretary of State George Shultz adopted a new posture that was seen to publicly downgrade China's strategic importance. The adjustment in the U.S. position occurred after the resignation of Haig, perhaps the strongest advocate in the Reagan administration of sustaining good relations with China as an important strategic means to counter the USSR. Secretary Shultz and such subordinates as Paul Wolfowitz were less identified with this approach. Shultz held a series of meetings with government and nongovernmental Asian specialists in Washington in early 1983 to review U.S. Asian policy in general and policy toward China in particular. The results of the reassessment—implicitly but clearly downgrading China's importance to the United States—were reflected in speeches by Shultz and Wolfowitz later in the year.[60]

U.S. planners now appeared to judge that efforts to improve relations with China were less important than in the recent past because:

- China seemed less likely to cooperate further with the United States (for example, through military sales or security cooperation against the Soviet Union at a time when the PRC had publicly distanced itself from the United States and had reopened talks on normalization with the USSR).
- At the same time, China's continued preoccupation with pragmatic economic modernization and internal development made it appear unlikely that the PRC would revert to a highly disruptive position in East Asia that would adversely affect U.S. interests in the stability of the region.
- China's demands on Taiwan and a wide variety of other bilateral disputes, and the accompanying threats to downgrade U.S.-China relations if its demands were not met, seemed open-ended and excessive.
- U.S. ability to deal militarily and politically with the USSR from a position of greater strength had improved, particularly as a result of the large-scale Reagan administration military budget increases and perceived serious internal and international difficulties of the USSR.
- U.S. allies, for the first time in years, were working more closely with Washington in dealing with the Soviet military threat. This was notably true in Asia, where Prime Minister Yasuhiro Nakasone took positions and initiatives underlining common Japanese-U.S. concerns against the Soviet danger, setting the foundation for the close "Ron-Yasu" relationship between the U.S. and Japanese leaders.

- Japan and U.S. allies and friends in Southeast Asia—unlike China—
  appeared to be more important to the United States in protecting against
  what was seen as the primary U.S. strategic concern in the region—
  safeguarding air and sea access to East Asia, the Indian Ocean, and the
  Persian Gulf from Soviet attack. China appeared less important in dealing with this perceived Soviet danger.[61]

Western press reports quoting authoritative sources in Washington alerted
China to the implications of this shift in the U.S. approach for PRC interests.
In effect, the shift seemed to mean that Chinese ability to exploit U.S. interest
in strategic relations with China against the Soviet Union were reduced, as
were U.S. interest in avoiding disruptions caused by China and other negative consequences flowing from a downgrading of China's relations with the
United States. Chinese ability to use these facets in order to compel the United
States to meet Chinese demands on Taiwan and other questions seemed less
than in the recent past. Underlining these trends for China was the continued
unwillingness of the United States throughout this period to accommodate
high-level PRC pressure over Taiwan, the asylum case of Chinese tennis
player Hu Na, the Chinese representation issue in the Asian Development
Bank, and other questions. The Reagan administration publicly averred that
U.S. policy would remain constant whether or not Beijing decided to retaliate,
or threatened to downgrade relations by withdrawing its ambassador from
Washington, or some other action.[62]

Moreover, Chinese commentary and discussions with Chinese officials
suggested that Beijing perceived its leverage in the United States to have
diminished at this time. Chinese media duly noted the strong revival in the
U.S. economy in 1983 and the positive political implications this had for
President Reagan's reelection campaign. China also had to be aware, through
contacts with leading Democrats, notably House of Representatives Speaker
Tip O'Neill, who visited China at this time, that Beijing could expect little
change in U.S. policy toward Taiwan under a Democratic administration.
As 1983 wore on, the Chinese saw what for them was an alarming rise in the
influence of U.S. advocates of self-determination for Taiwan among liberal
Democrats. In particular, Senator Claiborne Pell took the lead in gaining passage of a controversial resolution in the Senate Foreign Relations Committee
that endorsed, among other things, the principle of self-determination for
Taiwan—anathema to Beijing.[63]

Meanwhile, although Sino-Soviet trade, cultural, and technical contacts
were increasing, Beijing saw few signs of Soviet willingness to compromise on
basic political and security issues during vice-ministerial talks on normalizing
Sino-Soviet relations that began in October 1982. And the Soviet military

buildup in Asia—including the deployment of highly accurate SS-20 intermediate-range ballistic missiles—continued.[64]

In short, if Beijing continued its demands and harder line against the
United States of the previous two years, pressed the United States on various
issues, and risked downgrading relations, it faced the prospect of a period
of prolonged decline in Sino-American relations—possibly lasting until the
end of Reagan's second presidential term. This decline brought the risk of
cutting off the implicit but vitally important Chinese strategic understanding with the United States in the face of a prolonged danger to China posed
by the USSR.

The Chinese also recognized that a substantial decline in Chinese relations
with the United States would have undercut their already limited leverage with
Moscow; it probably would have reduced Soviet interest in accommodating
China in order to preclude closer U.S.-China security ties or collaboration
against the USSR. It also would have run the risk of upsetting China's ability
to gain greater access not only to U.S. markets and financial and technical
expertise but also to those of other important capitalist countries. Now that
the Chinese economy was successfully emerging from some retrenchments
and adjustments undertaken in 1981–1982, the Western economic con-
nection seemed more important to PRC planners. Yet many U.S. allies and
friends, especially Japan, were more reluctant to undertake heavy economic
involvement in China at a time of uncertain U.S.-China political relations.
The United States also exerted strong influence in international financial institutions that were expected to be the source of several billions of dollars of
much-needed aid for China in the 1980s.

China also had to calculate as well that a serious decline in U.S.-China relations would likely result in a concurrent increase in U.S.-Taiwan relations. As
a result, Beijing's chances of using Taiwan's isolation from the United States
to prompt Taipei to move toward reunification in accord with PRC interests
would be set back seriously.

In Chinese domestic politics, any backing away from a firm line toward
the United States on Taiwan and other sensitive issues almost certainly represented a difficult compromise for those leaders who had push this approach
in 1981–1982. Nonetheless, Deng Xiaoping appeared to have the political
standing to carry out the adjustment and moderation without serious negative implications.

Moderation toward the United States

Appearing anxious to moderate past demands and improve relations with
the United States, the Chinese responded positively to the latest in a series

of Reagan administration efforts to ease technology transfer restrictions—
announced by Commerce Secretary Malcolm Baldridge during a trip to China
in May 1983. The Chinese followed up by agreeing to schedule the long-de-
layed visit by Secretary of Defense Caspar Weinberger in September, and to
exchange visits by Premier Zhao Ziyang, a Chinese senior leader, and President Reagan at the turn of the year. Not to appear too anxious to improve
relations with China, Reagan administration officials were successful in getting Premier Zhao Ziyang to visit Washington for a summit in January 1984,
before the U.S. president would agree to go to China later that year.

Beijing media attempted to portray these moves as Chinese responses
to U.S. concessions and as consistent with China's avowed "independent"
approach in foreign affairs and its firm stance on U.S.-China differences
over Taiwan and other issues. But as time went on, it became clear just how
much Beijing was prepared to moderate past public demands and threats of
retaliation over Taiwan and other issues for the sake of consolidating Sino-
American political, economic, and security ties.[65]

- In 1981, Beijing had publicly disavowed any interest in military purchases
  from the United States until the United States satisfied China's position
  on the sale of arms to Taiwan. It continued to note that it was dissatisfied
  with U.S. arms transfers to Taiwan after the August 1982 communiqué,
  which continued at a pace of over $700 million a year; but it now was
  willing to negotiate with the United States over Chinese purchases of U.S.
  military equipment.
- Beijing muffled previous demands that the United States alter its position
  regarding Taiwan's continued membership in the Asian Development
  Bank.
- China reduced criticism of official and unofficial U.S. contacts with
  Taiwan counterparts. It notably avoided criticism of U.S. officials being
  present at Taipei-sponsored functions in Washington. Beijing was even
  willing to turn a blind eye to the almost thirty members of Congress who
  traveled to Taiwan in various delegations in January 1984—coincident
  with Zhao Ziyang's trip to Washington. It even welcomed some of the
  members who traveled on to the mainland after visiting Taiwan.
- Beijing allowed Northwest Airlines to open service to China in 1984, even
  though the airline still served Taiwan. This was in marked contrast with
  the authoritative and negative Chinese position adopted in 1983 in response to Pan American Airline's decision to reenter the Taiwan market
  while also serving the mainland.
- China reduced complaints about the slowness of U.S. transfers of technology to China and about the continued inability of the administration

to successfully push through legislative changes that would have allowed the Chinese to receive American assistance.[66]

China's greatest compromise was to give a warm welcome to President Reagan, despite his continued avowed determination to maintain close U.S. ties with "old friends" on Taiwan. Visits by Speaker O'Neill and others made clear to China the importance of the China visit in serving to assist the U.S. president's reelection bid in the fall. Chinese leaders also understood that the president was unlikely to accommodate China interests over Taiwan and some other sensitive issues during the visit. Indeed, Chinese reportage made clear that there was no change in the president's position on the Taiwan issue during the visit. Thus it appears that the best the Chinese hoped for was to try to consolidate U.S.-PRC relations in order to secure broader strategic and economic interests, while possibly expecting that such a closer relationship over time would reduce the president's firm position on Taiwan and other bilateral disputes.

The Reagan administration, meanwhile, attempted to add impetus to the relationship by accommodating Chinese concerns through the avoidance of strong rhetorical support for Taiwan that in the past had so inflamed U.S.-PRC tensions, and by moving ahead on military and technology transfers to the PRC. Nevertheless, when the U.S.-China nuclear cooperation agreement, which had been initialed during the president's visit, became stalled because of opposition from nonproliferation advocates in the United States who were concerned about reports of China's support for Pakistan's nuclear weapons program, China went along with administration explanations of their inability to reverse the adverse situation with only minor complaint.[67]

In short, by mid-1984 it appeared that, at a minimum, Beijing was determined to further strengthen military and economic ties with the United States and to soft-pedal bilateral differences that had been stressed earlier in the decade. On the question of Taiwan, Beijing retreated to a position that asked for U.S. adherence to the joint communiqué and accelerated reductions of U.S. arms sales to Taiwan, but was not prepared at this time to make a significant issue of what they saw as U.S. noncompliance unless seriously provoked. This meant giving lower priority to Chinese complaints about President Reagan's interpretations of the communiqué at odds with China's position and lower priority to Chinese complaints over the U.S. president's continued strong determination to support U.S. interests in helping the defense of Taiwan. The new Chinese position also meant downplaying Chinese criticism of methods used by the United States to calculate the value of arms sales to Taiwan at high levels, thereby allowing over a half billion dollars of U.S. sales to the island's armed forces for years to come. It also meant that China chose not to contest vigorously the ultimately successful maneuvers used by Taiwan and U.S. defense manufacturers that allowed the United States to support, through commercial transfers of equipment, technology, and expertise, the development of a new group of jet fighters, the Indigenous fighter aircraft, for the Taiwan air force.[68]

Continued Sino-Soviet Differences

China's incentive to accommodate the United States was reinforced by Beijing's somber view of Sino-Soviet relations. China appeared disappointed with its inability to elicit substantial Soviet concessions—or even a slowing in the pace of Soviet military expansion in Asia—during the brief administration of Yuri Andropov (d. 1984). Beijing saw the succeeding government of Kanstantin Chernenko (d. 1985) as even more rigid and uncompromising. In response, China hardened its line and highlighted public complaints against Soviet pressure and intimidation—an approach that had the added benefit of broadening common ground between China and the West, especially the strongly anti-Soviet Reagan administration.[69]

The Sino-Soviet vice-ministerial talks on normalizing relations were revived in October 1982 following their cancellation as a result of the Soviet invasion of Afghanistan in late 1979. These talks were unable to bridge a major gap between the positions of the two sides on basic security and political issues. Beijing stuck to its preconditions for improved Sino-Soviet relations involving withdrawal of Soviet forces from along the Sino-Soviet border and from Mongolia (later China added specific reference to Soviet SS-20 missiles targeted against China); an end to Soviet support for Vietnam's military occupation of Cambodia; and withdrawal of Soviet forces from Afghanistan.[70]

In part to get around this roadblock, a second forum of vice-foreign-ministerial discussions began in September 1983. The discussions covered each side's views of recent developments in the Middle East, Central America, the Indian Ocean, Afghanistan, and Indochina; concerns over arms control, including the deployment of SS-20 missiles in Asia; and other questions. No agreement was noted.

Progress in both sets of talks came only in secondary areas of trade, technology transfers, and educational and cultural exchanges. Both sides attempted to give added impetus to progress in these areas coincident with the exchange of high-level Sino-American visits in early 1984. In particular, Moscow proposed and Beijing accepted a visit to China by Soviet First Deputy Prime Minister Ivan Arkhipov. The visit was timed to occur just after President Reagan's departure from China in early May 1984. It was postponed on account of rising Sino-Soviet frictions.

Cherneko's leadership went out of its way to publicize strong support for Mongolia and Vietnam against China and underlined Soviet unwillingness to make compromises with China at the expense of third countries. Beijing also saw Moscow as resorting to stronger military means in both Europe and Asia in order to assert Soviet power and determination against China and others. In February and March, the Soviet Union deployed two of its three aircraft carriers to the western Pacific; one passed near China in late February, on its way to Vladivostok. And in March, the USSR used an aircraft carrier task force to support its first joint amphibious exercise with Vietnam, which was conducted fairly close to China and near the Vietnamese port city of Haiphong. This followed the reported stationing of several Soviet medium-range bombers at Cam Ranh Bay, Vietnam, in late 1983—the first time Soviet forces were reported to be stationed outside areas contiguous with the USSR.

Meanwhile, the Chinese escalated their military pressure against the Vietnamese—taking their strongest action precisely at the time of President Reagan's visit to China in late April and early May 1984. Beijing at the same time escalated charges regarding the Soviet threat to Chinese security, especially via Vietnam, and attempted to establish publicly an identity of interests with both Japanese Prime Minister Nakasone, during a visit to China in March, and President Reagan in April–May, on the basis of opposition to Soviet expansion in Asia. The result was the most serious downturn in Sino-Soviet relations since the Soviet invasion of Afghanistan in late 1979.

The Success of the U.S. Pan-Asian Approach to China

In sum, the record of developments in China's approach toward and relations with the United States and the Soviet Union in 1983 and 1984 show that the pan-Asian approach adopted by Secretary of State George Shultz and the senior officials responsible for Asian affairs during this period of the Reagan administration worked effectively in support of American interests in policy toward China in several important ways. It notably played into an array of concerns and uncertainties in Chinese foreign policy calculations and interests, causing the Chinese leaders to shift to a more accommodating posture toward the United States that played down issues that in the recent past Chinese officials had said threatened to force China to take steps to downgrade U.S.-China relations. U.S. officials made sure their Chinese counterparts understood that the United States was no longer as anxious, as evident in the first decade of Sino-American rapprochement and normalization, to seek China's favor in improving Sino-American relations as a source of leverage against Moscow. The United States was increasingly confident in its strategic position vis-à-vis the Soviet Union, and had begun a process to roll back the gains the Soviets had made in the previous decade in various parts of the developing world. It was China that appeared to face greater difficulties posed by Soviet military buildup and expansion. China needed the U.S. relationship as a counterweight to this Soviet posture, and it increasingly needed a good relationship with the United States to allow for smooth and advantageous Chinese economic interchange with the developed countries of the West and Japan and the international financial institutions they controlled.

Under the circumstances, the Chinese leaders grudgingly adjusted to the new U.S. stance, viewing their interests best served by less pressure and more positive initiatives to the Reagan administration, seen notably in their warm welcome for the U.S. president on his visit to China in 1984. As noted above, some scholarship portrays the improvement in U.S.-China relations at this time largely from dynamics in U.S.-China relations. In general, the United States is seen to make compromises in ways that accommodate Chinese interests and thus allow for smoother U.S.-China relations. By limiting the focus to the dynamics of U.S.-China ties, this scholarship seems to miss the importance of the shift in U.S. emphasis during the tenure of George Shultz. Overall, that shift seems to have significantly enhanced U.S. power and leverage over China in negotiations over Taiwan and other disputes and compelled China to make concessions on its part in order to insure a positive relationship with the United States advantageous to Chinese interests. This changed dynamic, with the United States in a more commanding position vis-à-vis China, was much more acceptable to congressional members, media, and others in U.S. politics who had been alienated by the secrecy and perceived excessive U.S. deference to China in the previous decade. It set the stage for relatively smooth U.S. domestic politics over China policy for the remainder of the Reagan administration.

5

Tiananmen, Taiwan, and Post–Cold War Realities, 1989–2000

Collapse of U.S. Policy Consensus and Emerging Domestic Debate on China

UNEXPECTED MASS DEMONSTRATIONS CENTERED in Beijing's Tiananmen Square and other Chinese cities in spring 1989 represented the most serious challenge to China's post-Mao leadership. Deng Xiaoping was decisive in resolving Chinese leadership differences in favor of hard-liners supporting a violent crackdown on the demonstrators and a broader suppression of political dissent that began with the bloody attack on Tiananmen Square on June 4, 1989. Reform-minded leaders were purged and punished.[1]

Anticipating shock over and disapproval of the Tiananmen crackdown from the United States and the West, Deng nonetheless argued that the negative reaction would have few prolonged adverse consequences for China. The Chinese leader failed to anticipate the breadth and depth of U.S. disapproval that would profoundly influence U.S. policy into the twenty-first century. American public opinion of China's administration dropped sharply. It never recovered the positive views of the Chinese administration that prevailed in the years prior to Tiananmen and reflected a wary and negative view of China on the part of a majority of Americans even twenty years later. The U.S. media switched coverage and opinion of China, portraying the policies and practices of the Chinese administration in a much more critical light than in the years leading up to Tiananmen. Twenty years later, American and Chinese specialists continued to see U.S. and Western media remaining focused on the negative in reporting and commentary dealing with the Chinese administration. U.S. leaders were shocked by the brutal display of power by China's authoritarian leaders. Expectations of rapid Chinese political reform dropped; they were replaced by outward hostility at first, followed by often-grudging pragmatism about the need for greater U.S. engagement with the Chinese administration as it rose in prominence in Asian and world affairs. The U.S. engagement was tempered by a private wariness and suspicion of the longer-term intentions of the Chinese administration that remained a prominent feature of U.S. expectations of China well into the next century.[2]

The negative impact of the Tiananmen crackdown on the American approach to China was compounded by the unforeseen and dramatic collapse of communist regimes in the Soviet bloc and other areas, leading to the demise of the Soviet Union in 1991. These developments undermined the perceived need for the United States to cooperate pragmatically with China despite its brutal dictatorship on account of a U.S. strategic need for international support against the Soviet Union. The Soviet collapse also destroyed the strategic focus of American foreign policy during the Cold War. The ability of the U.S. president to use Cold War imperatives to override pluralistic U.S. domestic interests seeking to influence American foreign policy declined. A variety of existing and emerging American interest groups focused on China's authoritarian regime in strongly negative ways, endeavoring to push U.S. policy toward a harder line against China. Meanwhile, Taiwan's authoritarian government was moving steadily at this time to promote democratic policies and practices, marking a sharp contrast to the harsh political regime in mainland China and greatly enhancing Taiwan's popularity and support in the United States.[3]

Taken together, these circumstances generally placed the initiative in U.S.-China relations with U.S. leaders and broader forces in the United States. Chinese leaders at first focused on maintaining internal stability as they maneuvered to sustain workable economic relations with the United States and other developed countries while rebuffing major U.S. and other Western-led initiatives that infringed on Chinese internal political control or territorial and sovereignty issues involving Taiwan, Tibet, and Hong Kong. Leadership debate about how open China should be to promoting economic reform at home and how welcoming China should be to economic interchange with the West as it consolidated authoritarian rule at home appeared to be resolved following Deng Xiaoping's tour of southern China in 1992. Deng urged continued rigorous economic reform and opening to the benefits of foreign trade, investments, and technology transfer. As the Chinese government presided over strong economic growth beginning in 1993, and the U.S. and other international attention that came with it, Chinese leaders reflected more confidence as they dealt with U.S. pressures for change. However, the Chinese leaders generally eschewed direct confrontation that would endanger the critically important economic relations with the United States unless China was provoked by U.S., Taiwanese, or other actions.[4]

U.S. policy in the decade after Tiananmen worked explicitly against the central interest of the Chinese leadership to sustain the rule of the Communist Party in China. Even when the U.S. government leaders emphasized a pragmatic policy of engagement with China's leaders, they often used rationales that the engagement would lead to the demise of the authoritarian Communist Party rule in China. U.S. policy also increased support for Taiwan, for the interests of the Dalai Lama in Tibet, and for forces in Hong Kong seen as critical of Chinese administration goals and threatening to the overall territorial integrity and sovereignty of China. The United States also was in the lead in criticizing a range of Chinese foreign policies; it was seen to be strengthening strategic and other pressures on China through reinforcing U.S. military relations with Japan and other allies and improving American military as well as political and economic relations with other nations around China's periphery. In response, Chinese leaders and broader public opinion saw U.S. policy and intentions in a negative way.[5]

Over time, years of pragmatic Sino-American engagement policies and generally positive treatment of the United States in state-controlled Chinese media in the first decade of the twenty-first century resulted in an improvement in Chinese public opinion about the United States. Privately, Chinese leaders were reported to remain deeply wary and suspicious of the policies and intentions of the United States. Strong public Chinese antipathy toward the United States and U.S. policy and practice toward China also showed from time to time, over sensitive issues or during times of crisis in U.S.-China relations.[6]

Although American leaders held the initiative in relations with China during the years after the Tiananmen incident, they had a hard time creating and implementing an effective and integrated policy. Coherent U.S. policy toward China proved elusive in the midst of contentious American domestic debate over China policy during the 1990s. That debate was not stilled until the September 11, 2001, terrorist attack on America muffled continued U.S. concerns over China amid an overwhelming American concern to deal with the immediate, serious, and broad consequences of the global war on terrorism.[7]

In the aftermath of Tiananmen, President George H. W. Bush tried to keep China policy under his control and to move U.S. relations with China in directions he deemed constructive. Yet he and his administration were repeatedly criticized by Congress, the media, and organized groups with differing interests in policy toward the PRC but with an agreed emphasis on a harder

U.S. approach to China. In this atmosphere, Bush's more pragmatic approach to China became a distinct liability for the president, notably during his failed reelection campaign in 1992.[8]

President Clinton entered office on an election platform critical of the "butchers of Beijing." His administration developed a clear stance linking Chinese behavior regarding human rights issues with U.S. trade benefits to China. Majorities in Congress and many nongovernmental groups and the media favored this position. However, the policy came under increasing pressure from other groups and their allies in the Congress and the administration who were strongly concerned with U.S. business interests in relations with China's rising market. The opposition prompted President Clinton to end the policy of linkage in May 1994.[9]

The president's decision did not end the battle for influence over China policy on the part of competing U.S. interest groups and their supporters in the Congress and the administration. Pro-Taiwan interests mobilized in early 1995 to change U.S. policy in order to allow the Taiwan president to travel to the United States in a private capacity. After senior U.S. officials assured China that no visa would be granted, President Clinton decided to allow the visit. His reversal triggered a major crisis and military face-off between the United States and China over Taiwan in 1995–1996. There were periodic live-fire Chinese military exercises in the Taiwan Strait, including tests of short-range Chinese ballistic missiles, over a period of nine months beginning in mid-1995 and culminating in large exercises coincident with Taiwan's first direct election of its president in March 1996. The U.S. government did little in public reaction to the exercises at first, but by 1996 senior U.S. leaders privately, and eventually publicly, strongly warned Chinese leaders against them. In the end, the United States sent two aircraft carrier battle groups to the Taiwan area to face off against the perceived Chinese military provocations during the Taiwan presidential elections.[10]

Seeking to restore calm and avoid repetition of dangerous crises with China, the Clinton administration accommodated Chinese interests as they shifted to a strong emphasis on pragmatic engagement with China, highlighted by U.S.-China summits in Washington and Beijing in 1997 and 1998, respectively. Through often-difficult negotiations, the United States and China were able to reach agreement in late 1999 leading to China's entry into the World Trade Organization (WTO). Related to this accord, the Clinton administration secured congressional passage of a law granting China the trading status of Permanent Normal Trade Relations (PNTR) in 2000. The law removed the previous annual legal requirement for the president to publicly notify Congress of his intention to seek most favored nation (MFN) status for American trade with China, and for the president's notification to be subject to possible legislation of disapproval by Congress. That legal requirement provided the focus of annual and often raucous congressional debates over the pros and cons of harsher U.S. measures against China in the years after the Tiananmen crackdown.[11]

Clinton's policy shift toward engagement with China met strong opposition in Congress and the media and among nongovernment groups pressing for a harder American China policy. In China, the U.S. bombing of the Chinese embassy in Belgrade in May 1999 saw the Chinese administration react by directing mass demonstrations that destroyed or severely damaged U.S. diplomatic properties in Beijing and other cities. Beijing leaders also openly debated their continued emphasis on engagement with the United States, eventually coming to the conclusion that shifting to a more confrontational Chinese approach against U.S. "hegemonism" was not in the overall interests of the Chinese administration.[12]

Post–Cold War Imperatives and American Debate over China Policy

Understanding the changes in U.S. policy toward China in the 1990s requires going beyond the Tiananmen crackdown and other immediate issues in U.S.-China relations to assess the implications of the post–Cold War debate in U.S. foreign policy. Because security issues and opposition to Soviet expansion no longer drove U.S. foreign policy, economic interests, democratization abroad, and human rights were among concerns that gained greater prominence in American foreign policy. Various U.S. advocacy groups and institutions interested in these and other foreign policy concerns also showed greater influence in policy-making, including policy-making regarding China. Historically, such fluidity and competition among priorities had more often than not been the norm in American foreign policy-making. As noted in chapter 2 and chapter 3, Woodrow Wilson and Franklin Roosevelt both set forth comprehensive concepts of a well-integrated U.S. foreign policy, but neither framework lasted long. The requirements of the Cold War were much more effective in establishing rigor and order in U.S. foreign policy priorities. The influence of these requirements in driving U.S. interest in rapprochement and normalization with China was described in chapter 4. By the 1990s, that era was over.

In its place was a changed array of forces influencing American foreign policy in general and policy toward China in particular. There was a shift away from the elitism of the past and toward much greater pluralism. This increased the opportunity for inputs by nongovernmental groups, including lobby groups with interests in foreign policy, notably policy toward China.[13]

The elitist model of American foreign policy-making that prevailed through much of the Cold War included the following characteristics:

- Domination of the process by the executive branch, particularly by the White House, the State Department, and the Pentagon.
- Presidential consultation with a bipartisan leadership in Congress and mobilization through them of broad congressional support for the administration's foreign policy.
- Parallel consultations with a relatively small group of elites outside government, some of whom were specialists on the particular issue under consideration and others of whom had a more general interest in foreign policy as a whole.
- Mobilization of public support through the major newspapers and television programs, other media outlets, and civic organizations.[14]

This process transformed in much more pluralistic directions and took on quite different characteristics following the 1980s:

- A much greater range of agencies within the executive branch became involved in foreign policy, with the rise of economic agencies (Commerce, Treasury, and U.S. Trade Representative) of particular importance.
- A reallocation of power within the government, moving away from dominance by the executive branch and giving more power to Congress.
- Much greater participation of nongovernmental organizations including lobbying groups, which attempted to shape foreign policy to conform with their interests.
- Much less consensus within Congress and within the broader American public over the direction of U.S. foreign policy.

Among divergent American views about foreign policy in the post–Cold War period were three discernable schools of thought.[15] The first school stressed the relative decline in U.S. power and its implications for U.S. ability to protect its interests abroad. It called for the United States to work harder to preserve important interests while adjusting to limited resources and reduced influence. This school of thought—reflected in the commentary of such leaders as George H. W. Bush, Henry Kissinger, and others—argued that these circumstances required the United States to work closely with traditional allies and associates. In Asia, it saw that it was inconsistent with U.S. goals not to preserve longstanding good relations with Japan and other allies and friends whose security policies and political-cultural orientations complemented U.S. interests. It urged caution in policy toward other regional powers—Russia, China, and India. All three countries were preoccupied with internal development issues and did not appear to want regional instability. All sought closer economic and political relations with the West and with other advancing economies. Washington would be well advised, according to this view, to work closely with these governments wherever there were common interests. In considering U.S. assets available to influence regional trends, proponents of this view called on the United States to go slow in reducing its regional military presence.[16]

A second school of thought argued for major cutbacks in U.S. international activity, including military involvement, and a renewed focus on solving domestic American problems. Variations of this view were seen in the writings of William Hyland, Patrick Buchanan, and other well-known commentators of the time, and in the political statements of the independent candidate in the 1992 presidential election, Ross Perot. Often called an "America First" or "Neoisolationist" school, it contended that the United States had become overextended in world affairs and was being taken advantage of in the current world security-economic system. It called for sweeping cuts in spending for international activities, favoring U.S. pullback from foreign bases and major cuts in foreign assistance and foreign technical-information programs. Some in this school favored trade measures that were seen as protectionist by U.S. trading partners.[17]

A third school of thought argued for policy that would promote more vigorously U.S. interests in international political, military, and economic affairs and would use U.S. influence to pressure countries that do not conform to the U.S.-backed norms on an appropriate world order. Supporters of this stance wanted the United States to maintain military forces with worldwide capabilities, to lead strongly in world affairs, and to minimize compromise and accommodation in promoting American interests and values.

Those who supported this view perceived a global power vacuum, caused mainly by the collapses of the Soviet empire, which allowed the United States to exert greater influence.[18] In the immediate post–Cold War years, some advocates of this third view were most vocal in pressing for a strong U.S. policy in support of democracy and human rights. They opposed economic or trading policies of other countries seen as inequitable or predatory. They pressed for a strong policy against proliferation of weapons of mass destruction. Members of this school also argued variously for sanctions against countries that practiced coercive birth control, seriously polluted the environment, harbored terrorists, or promoted the drug trade. Proponents of this view came from both the left and the right in the American political spectrum. In Congress, they included conservative Republican Newt Gingrich and liberal Democrat Nancy Pelosi, both of whom would serve as speaker of the U.S. House of Representatives.

As far as U.S. policy toward China was concerned, during the 1990s, advocates of the third group—proponents of active U.S. leadership and international intervention—were forceful in calling for policies opposing Chinese human rights violations, weapons proliferation, and protective trade practices. They pressed Beijing to meet U.S.-supported international norms and called for retaliatory economic and other sanctions. By contrast, the more cautious and accommodating first group believed that the advocates of strong assertion of U.S. values and norms were unrealistic about U.S. power and were unwilling to make needed compromises with the Chinese government in order to protect and support U.S. interests and regional stability and avoid strategic enmity.[19]

As the decade wore on, it was unclear what approach to China would prevail in U.S. policy. Some in the George H. W. Bush and Clinton administrations advocated a moderate, less confrontational policy of "engagement" with China, for fear that doing otherwise could promote divisions in and a possible breakup of China with potentially adverse consequences for U.S. interests in Asian stability and prosperity. Impressed by subsequent growth in Chinese economic and national strength later in the decade, many U.S. officials, business interests, and others sought opportunities in closer economic and other relations with China. They also promoted engagement in order to guide China's power into channels of international activity compatible with American interests.

A tougher approach was supported by U.S. officials and advocates outside the U.S. government who stressed that China's leaders were biding their time, conforming to many international norms in order to avoid difficulties as China built national strength. Once the Chinese administration succeeded with economic and related military modernization and development, Beijing was expected to become even less inclined to sacrifice nationalistic and territorial ambitions for the sake of cooperation in engagement policies by the United States and the West. Given this reasoning, U.S. leaders were urged to be firm with China, to rely on military power as a counterweight to rising Chinese power, to remain firm in dealing with economic and security disputes with China, and to work closely with U.S. allies and friends along China's periphery in dealing with actual or potential Chinese assertiveness. Senator John McCain was identified with this view.[20]

An even tougher U.S. approach to China at this time was advocated by some leaders in the Congress along with commentators and interest group leaders who believed that China's political system needed to change before the United States could establish a constructive relationship with Beijing. China's Communist leaders were perceived as inherently incapable of participating in truly cooperative relationships with the United States. U.S. policy should aim to change China from within while maintaining vigilance against disruptive Chinese foreign policy. Prominent congressional leaders such as Senator Jesse Helms, Representative Frank Wolf, and Representative Christopher Smith were associated with these views.[21]

Nongovernment advocacy groups interested in influencing China policy found fertile ground in the often-acute debate in the 1990s over the proper American approach to China and the broader debate over the appropriate course of U.S. foreign policy after the Cold War. The groups endeavored to muster recruits, gain financial support, and build coalitions by focusing on issues related to China policy. Their concerns focused on issues like human rights, trade disputes, weapons proliferation, and other topics. Competing coalitions of interest groups fought bitterly, especially during major crises such as the decisions of the Bush and Clinton administrations to grant MFN tariff treatment to China.[22]

In general, the organized American interest groups active in China policy following the end of the Cold War can be divided among those dealing with economic interests, specific values or causes, ethnic issues, and issues important to foreign governments and foreign economic interests. Within the economic realm, the National Association of Manufacturers, the Chamber of Commerce, and the Business Roundtable endeavored to promote such business concerns as foreign trade and investment beneficial to American companies. The Emergency Committee for American Trade worked successfully to ensure that the United States would continue nondiscriminatory trading relations with China.[23]

Often at odds with these pro-business groups were groups representing organized labor. They favored more trade restrictions; they often viewed Chinese exports to the United States as a threat to U.S. jobs; and they also weighed in on a variety of social justice issues including human rights and labor rights and the use of prison labor to produce Chinese exports.[24]

A number of public interest or citizen groups have common concerns of a non-economic or non-occupational nature. Many of these organizations focus on a single issue or a small group of issues. Examples include groups concerned with independence or greater autonomy for Tibet (e.g., the International Campaign for Tibet); freedom for political prisoners in China (e.g., Amnesty International and Human Rights Watch); religious freedom and freedom from coercive birth control and abortions (e.g., The Family Research Council, very active in the 1990s); as well as those concerned with curbing Chinese practices that endanger the regional and international environment or that promote instability and possible conflict through the proliferation of weapons of mass destruction and related technology (e.g., the Wisconsin Project, prominent in the 1990s in focusing on egregious Chinese failings in the area of weapons proliferation.)[25]

Ethnic groups have long been a key factor in American foreign policy. Although Chinese-Americans represent about 1 percent of the U.S. population, they have not become a unified ethnic bloc influencing U.S. foreign policy. However, there were instances when segments of this group have been active in the politics of U.S. foreign policy-making. Expatriate Chinese students heavily lobbied Congress and the administration during the years immediately following the 1989 Tiananmen crackdown. Their influence waned as the students became divided over their goals regarding U.S. policy toward China. A much more cohesive ethnic group has been the over half-million Americans who trace their family background to Taiwan. Taiwanese-Americans have formed a variety of organizations that have actively encouraged U.S. foreign policy to respect Taiwan's separate status and autonomy from the mainland. Many of these groups are strong advocates of independence for the island.[26]

Foreign governments, foreign businesses, and other elites also work actively to influence U.S. foreign policy. Government, business, and other leaders of Taiwan have been active for many years in pressing their points of view on the U.S. government. With the break in official Taiwan relations with the U.S. administration in 1979, they have focused more effort to lobby the Congress. Reports have linked the Taiwan administration and other groups supportive of Taiwan with sometimes-large campaign contributions to U.S. political candidates. Taiwan government and nongovernment entities also have been prominent in promoting academic, think-tank, media, local government, and other research and exchanges that enhance goodwill and positive feelings between Taiwan and the United States.[27]

The mainland Chinese administration, business leaders, and other elites were much less active on these fronts, though their efforts to influence U.S. foreign policy continue to grow. Media and congressional reports in the 1990s focused on charges that the Chinese government clandestinely was funneling campaign contributions to U.S. candidates. Chinese government and business leaders found they were more attractive to and influential with U.S. officials and elites as a result of the rapid growth of the Chinese economy. Against this background, the Chinese administration was successful in promoting regular exchanges with the Congress. The Chinese administration also worked closely with like-minded U.S. business leaders and officials in sustaining vibrant economic interchange with the United States.[28]

Relations during the Bush and Clinton Administrations

Developments in U.S.-China relations after the Tiananmen crackdown in 1989 and though the 1990s witness repeated cycles of crisis heavily influenced by the newly active domestic debate in the United States over American policy toward China. The first major turning point came during the George H. W. Bush administration with U.S. reaction to Tiananmen and the concurrent ending of the Cold War and emergence of Taiwan democratization. The second turning point came with President Clinton's advocacy in 1993 and then his withdrawal in 1994 of linkage between Chinese human rights practices and the granting of nondiscriminatory U.S. trade status to China. A third and more serious crisis resulted from Clinton's decision in 1995 to allow the Taiwan president to visit the United States; Chinese military demonstrations in the Taiwan area ultimately prompted the deployment of two U.S. aircraft carrier battle groups to the area in 1996. In 1999 contentious negotiations over China's entry into the WTO, Chinese mass demonstrations following the U.S. bombing of the Chinese embassy in Belgrade, and a crescendo of congressional opposition to and criticism of the president and his China policy represented a fourth period of crisis since 1989.[29]

What would turn out to be a twisted course of U.S. policy in this decade at first saw President George H. W. Bush strive to preserve cooperative ties amid widespread American outrage and pressure for retribution and sanctions against the Chinese leaders. President Bush had served as the head of the U.S. Liaison Office in China in the mid-1970s. He took the lead in his own administration (1989–1993) in dealing with severe problems in U.S.-China relations caused by the Tiananmen crackdown and the decline in U.S. strategic interest in China as a result of the collapse of the Soviet bloc. He resorted to secret diplomacy to maintain constructive communication with senior Chinese leaders; while senior administration officials said all high-level official contact with China would be cut off as a result of the Tiananmen crackdown, President Bush sent his national security advisor and the deputy secretary of state on secret missions to Beijing in July and December 1989. When the missions became known in December 1989, the congressional and media reaction was bitterly critical of the administration's perceived duplicity.[30]

Bush eventually became frustrated with the Chinese leadership's intransigence and took a tough stance on trade and other issues, though he made special efforts to ensure that the United States continued most favored nation tariff status for China despite opposition by a majority of the U.S. Congress, much of the American media, and many U.S. interest groups newly focused on China. Reflecting more positive U.S. views of Taiwan, the Bush administration upgraded U.S. interchange with ROC by sending a cabinet-level official to Taipei in 1992, the first such visit since official relations were ended in 1979. He also seemed to abandon the limits on U.S. arms sales set in accord with the August 1982 U.S. communiqué with China by agreeing in 1992 to a sale of 150 advanced F-16 jet fighters to Taiwan, worth over $5 billion. The president's motives for the sale were heavily influenced by a need to appear to be protecting U.S. manufacturing jobs at the F-16 plant in Texas, a key state in the Bush reelection plan.[31]

Presidential candidate Bill Clinton used sharp attacks against Chinese government behavior, notably the Tiananmen crackdown, and President Bush's moderate approach to China to win support in the 1992 election. The presidential candidate's attacks, though probably reflecting sincere anger and concern over Chinese behavior, also reflected a tendency in the U.S. China debate in the 1990s to use China issues, particularly criticism of China and U.S. policy toward China, for partisan reasons. The president-elect, and U.S. politicians in following years, found that criticizing China and U.S. policy toward China provided a convenient means to pursue political ends. For candidate Clinton and his aides, using China issues to discredit the record of the Republican candidate, George H. W. Bush, proved an effective way to take votes from the incumbent. Once he won the election and was in office, President Clinton showed little interest in China policy, leaving the responsibility to subordinates.[32]

In particular, Assistant Secretary of State for East Asia Affairs Winston Lord in 1993 played the lead administration role in working with congressional leaders, notably Senate Majority Leader George Mitchell and a House of Representatives leader on China and human rights issues, Representative Nancy Pelosi, and others to establish the human rights conditions the Clinton administration would require before renewing MFN tariff status for China. The terms he worked out were widely welcomed in the United States at the time. However, the Chinese government leaders were determined not to give in on several of the U.S. demands, and they appeared to calculate that U.S. business interests in a burgeoning Chinese economy would be sufficient to prevent the United States from taking the drastic step of cutting MFN tariff treatment for China and risking the likely retaliation of the PRC against U.S. trade interests. U.S. business pressures pushed Clinton to intervene in May 1994 to reverse existing policy and allow for unimpeded U.S. renewal of MFN status for China.[33]

Pro-Taiwan interests in the United States, backed by U.S. public relations firms in the pay of entities and organizations in Taiwan, took the opportunity of congressional elections in 1995 giving control of the Congress to pro-Taiwan Republican leaders to push for greater U.S. support for Taiwan, notably a visit by ROC President Lee Teng-hui to his alma mater, Cornell University. Under heavy domestic political pressure, President Clinton intervened again and allowed Taiwan's president to visit the United States despite the strenuous opposition of China.[34]

The resulting military confrontation with China in the Taiwan Strait involving two U.S. aircraft carrier battle groups saw the Clinton administration eventually move to a much more coherent engagement policy toward China that received consistent and high-level attention from the president and his key aides, and was marked by two U.S.-China summit meetings in 1997 and 1998. By the end of the Clinton administration, progress included U.S.-China agreement on China's entry into the World Trade Organization (WTO) and U.S. agreement to provide permanent normal trade status for China. However, the new approach failed to still the vigorous U.S. domestic debate against forward movement in U.S. relations with China on an array of strategic, economic, and political issues.[35]

As in the case of Clinton's attacks on George H. W. Bush, many of the attacks on Clinton's engagement policy with China after 1996 were not so much focused on China and China issues for their own sake as on partisan or other concerns. Most notably, as congressional Republican leaders sought to impeach President Clinton and tarnish the reputation of his administration, they endeavored to dredge up a wide range of charges regarding illegal Chinese fund-raising, Chinese espionage, and Chinese deviations from international norms regarding human rights, nuclear weapons and ballistic missile proliferation, and other questions in order to discredit President Clinton's moderate engagement policy toward China, and in so doing cast serious doubt on the moral integrity and competence of the president and his aides.[36]

The Clinton policy of engagement with China also came under attack from organized labor interests within the Democratic Party, some of which used the attacks on the administration's China policy as a means to get the administration to pay more attention to broader labor interests within the party. In a roughly similar fashion, social conservatives in the Republican Party used sharp attacks against continuation of U.S. most favored nation tariff status for China (a stance often supported by congressional Republican leaders) despite Chinese coercive birth control policies; they did this in part as a means to embarrass and pressure the Republican leaders to pay more positive attention to the various agenda issues of the social conservatives.

During the 1990s, congressional criticism of China and moderation in U.S. policy toward China was easy to do and generally had benefits for those making the criticism. The criticism generated positive coverage from U.S. media strongly critical of China, and it generated positive support and perhaps some fund-raising and electioneering support for the congressional critics by the many interest groups in the United States that focused criticism on Chinese policies and practices at this time. The Chinese government, anxious to keep the economic relationship with the United States on an even keel, was disinclined to punish such congressional critics or take substantive action against them. More likely were Chinese invitations to the critical congressional members for all-expenses-paid trips to China in order to persuade them to change their views by seeing actual conditions in China. Finally, President Clinton, like President George H. W. Bush, often was not in a position to risk other legislative goals by punishing congressional members critical of his China policy.

As President Clinton and his White House staff took more control over China policy after the face-off with Chinese forces in the Taiwan Strait in 1996, they emphasized—like George H. W. Bush—a moderate policy of engagement, seeking change in offensive Chinese government practices through a gradual process involving closer Chinese integration with the world economic and political order. The U.S.-China relationship improved but also encountered significant setbacks and resistance. The high points included the U.S.-China summits in 1997 and 1998, the Sino-American agreement on China's entry into the WTO in November 1999, and passage of U.S. legislation in 2000 granting China permanent normal trade relations status. Low points included strong congressional opposition to the president's stance against Taiwan independence in 1998; the May 1999 bombing of the Chinese Embassy in Belgrade and Chinese demonstrators trashing U.S. diplomatic properties in China; strident congressional criticism in the so-called Cox Committee report of May 1999 charging administration officials with gross malfeasance in guarding U.S. secrets and weaponry from Chinese spies; and partisan congressional investigations of Clinton administration political fund-raising that highlighted some illegal contributions from sources connected to the Chinese regime and the alleged impact they had on the administration's more moderate approach to the PRC.[37]

Chinese leaders had long sought the summit meetings with the United States. Coming in the wake of Chinese meetings with other world leaders in the aftermath of the international isolation of China caused by the Tiananmen crackdown, the summit meetings with the U.S. president were a clear signal to audiences at home and abroad that the Communist administration of China had growing international status and that its position as the legitimate government of China now was recognized by all major world powers.[38]

The benefits for the United States in the summit meetings were more in question, though the Clinton administration justified these steps as part of its efforts to use engagement in seeking change in offensive Chinese government practices through a gradual process involving closer Chinese integration with the world economic and political order. U.S. and other critics failed to accept this rationale and honed their criticism on what they viewed as unjustified U.S. concessions to Chinese leaders. Heading the list were perceived concessions in the U.S. president articulating limits on American support for Taiwan in the so-called "Three No's." Speaking in Shanghai in June 1998 during his visit to China, President Clinton affirmed that the United States did not support

Taiwan independence; two Chinas; or one Taiwan, one China; and that the United States did not believe Taiwan should be a member of an organization where statehood is required. The Clinton administration claimed the Three No's were a reaffirmation of longstanding U.S. policy, but the president's action was roundly criticized in the Congress and U.S. media as a new gesture made to accommodate Beijing and undermine Taipei.[39]

Progress in U.S. negotiations leading to eventual agreement on China's entry into the WTO was not without serious difficulties and negative consequences. The United States took the lead among the WTO's contracting parties in protracted negotiations (1986–1999) to reach agreements with China on a variety of trade-related issues before Chinese accession could move forward. Chinese Premier Zhu Rongji visited Washington in April 1999, hoping to reach agreement with the United States on China's entry into the World Trade Organization. An agreement was reached and disclosed by the Americans, only to be turned down by President Clinton. The setback embarrassed Zhu and raised serious questions in the Chinese leadership about the intentions of President Clinton and his administration. Recovering from the setback, Zhu was able to complete the U.S.-China negotiations in November 1999, paving the way for China's entry into the WTO in 2001. U.S. legislation passed granting China permanent normal trade relations (PNTR) in 2000. This ended the need for annual presidential requests and congressional reviews regarding China keeping normal trade relations tariff status, previously known as most favored nation tariff status.[40]

Making such progress in U.S.-China relations was difficult because of incidents and developments affecting U.S.-China relations and vitriolic U.S. debate over the Clinton administration's China policy. Heading the list was the U.S. bombing of the Chinese embassy in Belgrade, the most important incident in U.S.-China relations after the Tiananmen crackdown. The reaction in China included mobs stoning the U.S. embassy in Beijing and burning U.S. diplomatic property in Chengtu. Both governments restored calm and dealt with some of the consequences of the bombing, but China and the United States never came to an agreement on what happened and whether the United States explained its actions appropriately.[41]

Taiwan President Lee Teng-hui added to Taiwan Strait tension that worried American policy makers when he asserted in July 1999 that Taiwan was a state separate from China and that China and Taiwan had "special state-to-state relations." Chinese leaders saw this as a step toward Taiwan independence and reacted with strong rhetoric, some military actions, and by cutting off cross-strait communication links.[42]

Complementing difficulties abroad were the many challenges at home to the Clinton administration's moderate policy of engagement toward China.

The U.S. media ran repeated stories in the second term of the Clinton administration linking the president, Vice President Gore, and other administration leaders with illegal political fund-raising involving Asian donors, some of whom were said to be connected with the Chinese government. Congressional Republican Committee chairmen, Senator Fred Thompson and Representative Dan Burton, held hearings, conducted investigations, and produced information and reports regarding various unsubstantiated allegations of illegal contributions from Chinese backers in return for the Clinton administration turning a blind eye to Chinese illegal trading practices and Chinese espionage activities in the United States.[43]

More damaging to the administration and its engagement policy toward China was the report of the so-called Cox Committee. Formally known as the Select Committee on U.S. National Security and Military/Commercial Concerns with the People's Republic of China, and named for its Chairman, Republican Congressman Christopher Cox, the committee released in May 1999 an eight-hundred-page unclassified version of a larger classified report. It depicted longstanding and widespread Chinese espionage efforts against U.S. nuclear weapons facilities allowing China to build American advanced nuclear warheads for use on Chinese missiles that were made more accurate and reliable with the assistance of U.S. companies. It portrayed the Clinton administration as grossly negligent in protecting such vital U.S. national security secrets. The report added substantially to congressional, media, and other concerns that the United States faced a rising security threat posed by China's rapidly expanding economic and military power.[44]

China Policy Debate in Perspective: Strengths, Weakness, and Importance

Looking back at Tiananmen from the perspective of the end of the Clinton administration in 2000, it was fair to assert that the domestic American debate over China policy had emerged powerfully in the 1990s and would continue to have a primary influence in the American approach to China for the foreseeable future. The incoming George W. Bush administration in January 2001 adopted a tougher policy toward China more consistent with the widespread criticism of the Clinton administration's more moderate engagement policy. Bush's approach calmed the critics for the time being. A more lasting and significant impact on the China policy critics came with the September 11, 2001, terrorist attack on America. Though not comparable to the strategic danger posed by Soviet expansion during the height of the Cold War, the new challenge of terrorism became the focus of U.S. government, media, and interest group attention. Those in the United States endeavoring to use criticism of China and their attacks on moderation in U.S. policy toward China had a much harder time getting the attention of officials, donors, and the general public. The China debate as a force that pushed U.S. policy toward a significantly harder line against China basically was overwhelmed by perceived American requirements to focus on other issues related to the complicated U.S. war on terrorism. As the danger of terrorism to the United States appeared to subside and the popularity of the Bush administration also declined, the domestic U.S. debate over China began to revive again in the middle of the decade. But it remained a secondary force influencing American China policy. It was more a drag on forward movement and improvement in U.S. relations with China than it was a significant determinant of a more negative and critical American policy toward China.[45]

Closer examination shows that the rapid and unforeseen decline in the salience of the American domestic debate about China policy during the first year of the George W. Bush administration reflects some important weaknesses of the critics and their arguments in favor of a tougher stance toward China. In fact, a comparison of the U.S. China policy debate in the 1990s against the U.S. debate over China policy debate in the late 1970s and early 1980s appears to illustrate weaknesses in the resolve and approach of the critics in the later period. The resolve and commitment of critics seen in episodes in the late 1970s and early 1980s related to the passage of the Taiwan Relations Act and resistance to perceived excesses in U.S. accommodation of China at the expense of U.S. relations with Taiwan, Japan, and other interests appear stronger than the resolve and commitment on the part of many of the various individuals and groups seeking a tougher U.S. approach to China after the Cold War. The comparison of the two periods of criticism of prevailing U.S. policy leads to a conclusion that even though the number of critics and their support in the 1990s was larger and broader than those of critics of U.S. policy in the late 1970s and early 1980s, the commitment of the leaders and followers was comparatively thin and expedient in the post–Cold War period.[46]

Comparing the U.S. Debates on China—Late 1970s/Early 1980s versus Post–Cold War

The domestic debate and the related domestic interests have sometimes been an important determinant pushing forward the direction of U.S. policy toward China, including Taiwan and related issues. More often, they have been an obstacle slowing the momentum of U.S. policy. From Nixon through Carter and into early Reagan, the domestic factors generally were a brake slowing the policies led by the administration to move the United States away from ties with Taiwan and closer to the PRC. For several years following the end of the Cold War, they generally were a driver pushing U.S. policy against China and toward closer ties with Taiwan, though they reverted to the status of brake during the second term of the Clinton administration.[47]

As noted in chapter 4, the debate in the Nixon-Reagan period (1972–1983) involved important tangible costs and benefits for the United States. The U.S. strategic posture vis-à-vis the Soviet Union and the future of Taiwan headed the list of the serious issues at stake for the United States. Reflecting deep uncertainty about U.S. power and purpose in world affairs, U.S. policy was prepared to make major sacrifices in order to pursue respective paths in the debate, and indeed U.S. policy ultimately sacrificed official relations with Taiwan and took the unprecedented step of ending a defense treaty with a loyal ally for the sake of the benefits to be derived from official relations with the PRC, notably in regard to assisting the United States in dealing with expanding Soviet power.[48]

The major protagonists in the U.S. domestic debate over policy toward the PRC and Taiwan at this time argued their case mainly because they were sincerely concerned about the serious implications and consequences of the direction of U.S. policy in this triangular relationship. Partisan interests and the influence of interest groups or constituent groups also played a role, but less so than in the U.S. China policy debate of the 1990s. The fact that a Democratic-controlled Congress took the lead in the Taiwan Relations Act and in other legislative actions in modifying the perceived oversights and excesses of the Democratic Carter administration in tilting in favor of Beijing and against Taiwan in the late 1970s and 1980 showed that partisan interests played a secondary or relatively unimportant role in the U.S. domestic debate. Significantly, this pattern persisted even after the Democratic-controlled Congress rewrote and passed the Taiwan Relations Act in April 1979. Democratic senators and representatives remained active in resisting the Carter administration's continuing perceived "tilt" toward the PRC and away from Taiwan. Among notable critics and skeptics of the U.S. policy at this time were such Democrats as Adlai Stevenson, John Glenn, Richard Stone, and George McGovern.[49]

The congressional opposition of the day did reflect an important element of institutional rivalry between the executive branch and the Congress that colored the U.S. domestic debate during this period. Congress appeared determined to protect its perceived prerogatives in U.S. foreign policy, while U.S. administration officials were equally determined to protect the prerogatives of the executive branch in foreign affairs.[50]

Although the U.S. domestic debate became more prominent and important in influencing the course of U.S. policy toward China and Taiwan and related issues after the Tiananmen incident and the end of the Cold War in the late 1980s and the early 1990s, major features of the debate were markedly different from the debate in the 1970s and early 1980s. The differences underlined that the resolve and commitment of the critics generally was weaker in the 1990s than in the 1970s.[51]

- U.S. policy makers in the executive branch and the Congress were confident of U.S. power and influence in the world, especially now that the Soviet empire had collapsed—a marked contrast from the U.S. strategic uncertainty that underlined the U.S. policy debate in the 1970s and early 1980s.
- In the 1970s, U.S. officials faced and made major sacrifices in pursuit of U.S. policy toward the PRC and Taiwan. The protagonists in the U.S. China policy debate after the Cold War had little inclination to sacrifice tangible U.S. interests for the sake of their preferred stance in the U.S.-PRC-Taiwan triangle or other China policy-related questions. Thus, those in Congress, the media, and elsewhere in U.S. domestic politics who were vocal in seeking an upgrading in U.S. treatment for Taiwan President Lee Teng-hui, demanding he be granted a visa to visit Cornell University in 1995, largely fell silent when Beijing reacted to the visit with forceful actions in the Taiwan Strait that posed a serious danger of U.S.-China military confrontation. The majority of congressional members opposing the annual waiver granting continued MFN tariff treatment to Chinese imports had no intention of seeking a serious cutoff of U.S.-China trade. They often explained that they were merely endeavoring to send a signal to the administration and to China over their dissatisfaction with U.S. and Chinese policies.
- Many were active in the U.S. domestic debate for partisan or other ulterior motives—a marked contrast from the 1970s, when the foreign policy issues themselves seemed to be the prime drivers in the U.S. domestic debate. Bill Clinton used the China issue to attack the record of the Bush administration, only to reverse course after a time in office, returning to the engagement policy of the previous president. The strident rhetoric coming from Republican congressional leaders critical of the Clinton administration's engagement policy in its second term seemed to have similarly partisan motives. Labor-oriented Democrats used the China issue to discredit the pro-business leanings of the leaders of the Clinton administration, while social conservatives in the Republican Party focused in on China's forced abortions and suppression of religious freedom to embarrass their party leaders and prompt them to devote more attention to the social conservatives' political agenda in U.S. domestic politics.[52]

- Reflecting the less serious commitment by critics in the 1990s was the fact that the U.S. China debate notably subsided whenever the United States faced a serious foreign policy challenge. Thus, the vocal congressional debate over China policy stopped abruptly following the Iraqi invasion of Kuwait in 1990, and the Congress remained quiet about China throughout the U.S. "Desert Shield" and "Desert Storm" operations. Once the war was over and the need for Chinese acquiescence in the United Nations over the U.S.-led war against Iraq ended in 1991, the China debate resumed immediately, with many Democrats in Congress and elsewhere seeking to use the China issue for partisan purposes in order to tear down President Bush's then-strong standing in U.S. opinion polls regarding his handling of foreign affairs. As noted earlier in this chapter, the September 11, 2001, attack on America dampened the U.S. China debate, which was then focused notably on the threat to U.S. interests posed by a rising China. After several months, media organs like the *Washington Times* and some in Congress resumed lower-keyed efforts to focus on the China threat, while pro-Taiwan groups tried to use the rebalancing of Bush administration policy directions more favorable to China by arguing for concurrent favorable U.S. treatment for Taiwan.[53] These moves were small and of little consequence; they seemed to underline the weakness of U.S. critics of China or advocates of policies opposed by China in a U.S. foreign policy environment focused on dealing with terrorism-related issues.[54]

Chinese Priorities and Calculations: Managing Crisis-Prone Relations

Whatever their strengths and weaknesses, the shifts in U.S. policy prompted by the U.S. debate over China policy after the Cold War posed major and repeated challenges for Chinese leaders. Once it became clear to Chinese leaders that the strategic basis of Sino-American relations had been destroyed by the end of the Cold War and the collapse of the Soviet Union and that it would take a long time for political relations to return to more moderate engagement after the trauma of the Tiananmen incident, Chinese leaders worked throughout the 1990s to reestablish "normalized" relations with the United States on terms as advantageous as possible to China. With the U.S.-China summits of 1997 and 1998, relations arguably were normalized, but they remained far from stable. Chinese leaders continued to give high priority to managing differences with the United States while benefiting from advantageous economic and other ties with the U.S. superpower.[55]

Throughout the post–Cold War period, Chinese officials reflected vary-ing degrees of suspicion regarding U.S. intentions and remained well aware of fundamental ideological, strategic, and other differences with the United States.[56] In general, Chinese officials settled on a bifurcated view of the United States. This view held that U.S. leaders would extend the hand of "engage-ment" to the Chinese government when their interests would be served, but that U.S. leaders were determined to "contain" aspects of China's rising power and block aspects of China's assertion of influence in world affairs that were seen as contrary to U.S. interests. The Chinese emphasis on cooperat-ing with the "soft" U.S. "hand of engagement" or reacting to the "hard" U.S. "hand of containment" varied. The general trend from 1996 to 2001, and after adjustments in U.S.-China relations in 2001, was to give more emphasis to the positive and less emphasis to the negative on the part of both the Chinese and U.S. administrations.[57]

Presidents George H. W. Bush and Bill Clinton were clear about U.S. differ-ences with China in several key areas. Despite Chinese disapproval, the United States was determined to expend such a vast array of resources on defense that it would remain the world's dominant power, and also the dominant military power along China's periphery in East Asia, for the foreseeable future. The United States would continue to provide support, including sophisticated arms, to Taiwan; and the United States endeavored to use growing govern-ment, commercial, and other nongovernmental contacts with China, as well as other means, to foster an environment that promoted political pluralism and change in the authoritarian Chinese communist system.

For its part, Beijing strove for a post–Cold War world order of greater multipolarity; China would be one of the poles and would have greater op-portunity for advantageous maneuvering than in a superpower-dominated order. China strove for a gradual decline in U.S. power and influence in East Asia and globally, and Beijing called for cutbacks in U.S. military sales and other support to Taiwan in order to help create advantageous conditions for the reunification of the island with mainland China. Finally, CCP leaders were determined to maintain the primacy of their rule in the face of economic, social, and political challenges at home and abroad, including challenges sup-ported by the United States.

A critical problem for Chinese leaders in dealing with the United States in the 1990s involved mixing their strategies and goals with those of the United States in ways advantageous to China. In general, the Chinese approach focused on trying to work constructively with U.S. power, concentrating on areas of common ground, building interdependent economic relations, and minimizing differences wherever possible. This was difficult to achieve, especially when U.S. policy concentrated on the stark differences between the

United States and China over human rights, Taiwan, weapons proliferation, and trade issues. In some instances, Chinese officials chose to confront the United States with threats of retaliation if the United States pursued pressure tactics against China. For the most part, however, Chinese leaders bided their time, endeavoring to avoid complications that would ensue from protracted confrontation with the United States. At bottom, they believed that China's growing economy and overall international importance would steadily win over foreign powers to a cooperative stance and encourage politically important groups in the United States, especially business groups, to press for an accommodating U.S. approach to China.

Following this general line of approach in the 1990s, Beijing managed to end the diplomatic isolation that stemmed from the Tiananmen crackdown, weakened the Clinton administration advocates of conditioning most favored nation tariff treatment of Chinese imports to the United States, and prompted the president to end this policy in 1994. With the Sino-American summits of 1997 and 1998, Beijing clearly established the Chinese leaders as legitimate and respected actors in world affairs.[58]

Chinese officials duly noted during the 1990s and later that they had few illusions about beneficent U.S. policy toward China. But they repeatedly affirmed to Western specialists and others that they—whether they personally liked it or not—also saw Chinese interests best served by trying to get along with the United States. They cited the following reasons:[59]

- The United States remained the world's sole superpower. As such, it posed the only potential strategic threat to China's national security for the foreseeable future. A confrontation with such a power would severely test China's strength and undermine Chinese economic and political programs.
- As the world's leading economic power, the United States had markets, technology, and investment important for Chinese modernization. It also played an important role in international financial institutions heavily involved in China; Western financial actors and investors viewed the status of U.S. relations with China as an important barometer determining the scope and depth of their involvement in China.
- Internationally, establishing cooperative relations with the United States facilitated smooth Chinese relations with Western and other powers that were close to Washington. Antagonistic U.S.-China relations would mean that China would have to work much harder, and presumably offer more in the way of economic and other concessions, to win over such powers.
- The United States continued to play a key strategic role in highly sensitive areas around China's periphery, notably Korea, Japan, the South China

Sea, and especially Taiwan. It controlled sea lanes vital to Chinese trade. Cooperative U.S.-China relations allowed Beijing to continue to focus on domestic priorities with reasonable assurance that its vital interests in these sensitive areas would not be fundamentally jeopardized by antagonistic actions by the United States. Indeed, good U.S.-China relations tended to increase Chinese influence in these areas.

On balance, the record of Chinese relations with the United States in the 1990s showed considerable achievement for China. Beijing reestablished extensive high-level contacts with the U.S. administration and saw the end of most Tiananmen-related sanctions against China. By 1998, the Clinton administration appeared sincerely committed to pursuing a policy of generally accommodating engagement with China. Administration officials in the United States endeavored to work closely with the Chinese administration to reduce differences over U.S. world primacy, the U.S. strategic posture in East Asia, U.S. support for Taiwan, and U.S. support for political pluralism in China. Chinese officials took satisfaction in the fact that the improvement in relations resulted much more from shifts toward accommodation of China's rising power and influence by the U.S. administration than from adjustments by the Chinese government in dealing with issues sensitive to the United States.

While assessments among Chinese officials differed regarding the status and outlook of U.S.-China relations, the prevailing view in 1999 was one of caution. There remained plenty of evidence that U.S. policy continued to have elements of containment along with the seemingly accommodating engagement. Political forces in the United States, many interest groups, and the media still lined up against Chinese interests on a range of human rights concerns, strategic issues, Taiwan, and economic questions. Many Chinese officials remained suspicious of the ultimate motives of some members of the Clinton administration as well. As a result, Beijing was privately wary as it continued to seek advantages by building cooperative relations.[60]

The Challenges of Shifting U.S. Policies

The Clinton administration decision in 1993 to condition MFN status for China on China's progress in human rights issues posed a major problem for the Chinese leadership. It was met indirectly by the rapid growth of the Chinese economy, which attracted strong U.S. business interest, and the interest in turn of many visitors from Congress and the administration concerned with the growth of the U.S. economy and economic opportunity abroad. By early 1994, Chinese officials were well aware that proponents for continuing the human rights conditions on MFN treatment for China had become isolated in the administration and centered in the State Department. The private reservations among senior officials in U.S. departments concerned with business, notably the Treasury Department and the Commerce Department, about these conditions on China's MFN status had become clear through their earlier visits to China and through other interactions. Moreover, U.S. business groups had moved into high gear in warning that conditions on MFN treatment could jeopardize U.S. access to the burgeoning Chinese market.[61]

Sino-American disagreements over human rights conditions in China and MFN status rose sharply during Secretary of State Warren Christopher's March 11–14, 1994, visit to Beijing.[62] Before and during Secretary Christopher's visit, Chinese leaders appeared defiant in the face of U.S. human rights requirements. Most notably, Chinese security forces detained prominent dissidents immediately prior to the secretary's visit and also detained some Western journalists covering interaction between Chinese dissidents and Chinese security forces. In public interchange during the secretary's visit, Chinese leaders strongly warned against U.S. use of trade or other pressure to prompt changes in China's human rights policy.

This tough approach reflected a determination to rebuff overt U.S. pressure seen as targeted against the core Chinese leadership concern of sustaining Communist Party rule in China. It also reflected the fact that the secretary's trip coincided with the annual convening of the National People's Congress. That meeting was the focal point of dissident activism in Beijing, and Chinese leaders were determined to take a hard line toward those both at home and abroad who pressed for political change.

Perhaps of most importance, Chinese leaders calculated that the time was right to press the United States to alter its human rights policy, especially the linkage with MFN renewal. They saw the Clinton administration leaders divided on the issue. They saw members of the U.S. Congress as much more supportive than in the recent past of maintaining MFN treatment for China. Congress was perhaps influenced, too, by the fact that while the United States had been debating the issue, countries that were political allies to the United States but economic competitors, like Japan, Germany, and France, had been sending high-level officials to China—underlining their willingness to help fill the vacuum should U.S.-China economic relations falter with the withdrawal of MFN tariff treatment.[63]

Reflecting a calculus of costs and benefits, Chinese leaders adopted a tough stance during the Christopher visit. Those in the U.S. government favoring linkage of MFN treatment and human rights conditions were further isolated, and U.S. leaders were forced to change their policy or lose the considerable economic opportunities in the Chinese market. In the end, Chinese leaders were generally pleased with President Clinton's May 26, 1994, decision to "delink" MFN treatment to China from U.S. consideration of Chinese human rights practices.

Subsequently, Chinese officials and commentators in official Chinese media were anxious for the United States and China to take advantage of the improved atmosphere in bilateral relations to push for more far-reaching and comprehensive progress in the U.S.-China relationship.[64] Whatever hopes Chinese leaders held about advancing relations with the United States were dashed by President Clinton's reversal of past policy, permitting Taiwan President Lee Teng-hui to make an ostensibly private visit to Cornell University in June 1995.

Beijing's tough military and polemical responses and the Clinton administration's eventual dispatch of carrier battle groups to Taiwan highlighted mixed lessons for China.[65]

On the positive side, Chinese officials claimed several achievements resulting from the PRC's forceful reaction to Lee Teng-hui's visit to the United States:

- It intimidated Taiwan, at least temporarily, preventing it from taking further assertive actions to lobby in the U.S. Congress or elsewhere for greater international recognition. Pro-independence advocates in Taiwan also had to reassess previous claims that the PRC was bluffing in its warnings against Taiwan independence.
- It prompted second thoughts by some pro-Taiwan advocates in the Congress and elsewhere in the United States as to the wisdom of pursuing their agenda at this time. International officials seeking to follow the U.S. lead in granting greater recognition to Taiwan had to reevaluate their positions as well.
- It resulted in heightened sensitivity by the Clinton administration regarding China. This led to official reassurances to the PRC that U.S. policy toward Taiwan would not deviate from past practice; it also led to an invitation for the Chinese president to visit the United States, a summit meeting long sought by Chinese leaders; and it led to tightly controlled management of significant developments in U.S. policy toward China by the president and his senior advisers, who now sought to pursue an active engagement policy with China and to avoid significant deterioration of relations.

At the same time, Beijing appeared to have overplayed its hand in pressing the United States for pledges against Taiwan official visits to the United States and in pressing Taiwan's people to abandon Lee Teng-hui in favor of a leader more committed to reunification with the mainland. Beijing also appeared to recognize that it was not productive to continue strident accusations in official Chinese media during 1995–1996 that the United States was attempting to contain China, or to shun dialogue with the United States.

Given China's perceived need to sustain a working relationship with the United States for the foreseeable future, Beijing officials tried, for example through President Jiang's meeting with President Clinton in 1995, to find and develop common ground while playing down differences. Whereas Beijing had appeared prepared in mid-1995 to freeze contacts with the Clinton administration, awaiting the results of the 1996 U.S. elections, Beijing now appeared to have judged that endeavoring to work constructively with the current U.S. government was in China's best interests. Also, Jiang Zemin told U.S. reporters in October 1995 that lobbying Congress would be an important priority in the year ahead, and Chinese specialists also said that the PRC would put more effort into winning greater understanding and support from other U.S. sectors, notably the media and business.[66] For its part, the Clinton administration continued strong efforts to avoid serious difficulties with China; to emphasize a policy of engagement with the PRC; and to seek high-level contacts, summit meetings, and tangible agreement with China on sensitive issues.

The events of the next two years in U.S.-China relations were highlighted by the summit meetings of Presidents Jiang and Clinton in Washington in 1997 and Beijing in 1998. Despite the continued debate in the United States over the Clinton administration's new commitment to a policy of engagement with China, Chinese officials and specialists claimed to be confident that China's rising power and influence in world affairs, and its willingness to cooperate with the United States on issues of importance to both countries, made it unlikely that the U.S. opponents of the engagement policy would have a serious, lasting impact on U.S.-China relations.[67]

The events of 1997 and 1998 seemed to bear out the Chinese view. The U.S.-China summit meetings capped the Beijing leaders' decade-long effort to restore their international legitimacy after the Tiananmen incident. The results redounded to the benefit of the presiding Chinese leaders, especially President Jiang Zemin. Jiang was anxious to carve out a role as a responsible and respected international leader as part of his broader effort to solidify his political base of support at home. Basically satisfied with the results of the smooth summit meetings with the U.S. president, Beijing saw little need to take the initiative in dealing with continuing U.S.-China differences like human rights, trade, and weapons proliferation. It was the U.S. side that felt political pressure to achieve results in these areas.

Responding to repeated U.S. initiatives to reach agreements at the summit meetings and elsewhere on these kinds of questions, Chinese officials took the opportunity to make demands of their own, especially regarding U.S. policy toward Taiwan. At the same time, Beijing was willing marginally to improve human rights practices, and it curbed nuclear and cruise missile exchanges with Iran, for the sake of achieving a smoother and more cooperative U.S.-China relationship.

In sum, despite strong and often partisan debate in the United States over policy toward China, Chinese officials were well pleased with the progress they had made in normalizing relations with the United States from the low points after the Tiananmen crackdown of 1989 and the confrontation over Taiwan in 1995–1996. The progress had been made largely by changes in U.S. policy toward China, and with few concessions by Beijing in key areas of importance to China. The summits of 1997 and 1998 represented the capstone of the normalization effort, in effect strongly legitimating the PRC leaders at home and abroad—a key Chinese goal after the Tiananmen incident. Once this was accomplished, Chinese leaders could turn to their daunting domestic agenda with more assurance that the key element of U.S.-China relations was now on more stable ground.

At the same time, Chinese leaders had few illusions about U.S. policy. They saw plenty of opportunities for continued difficulties. American behavior continued to be seen as fitting into the pattern of engagement and containment—the "two hands" of U.S. policy seen by Chinese officials and specialists. The main trend in 1997 and 1998 was toward greater engagement, and China endeavored to encourage that. But there remained many forces in Congress, in the media, and among U.S. interest groups that were prepared to challenge any forward movement in U.S.-China relations. And the fact remained that although it was clearly in China's interest to cooperate with the United States under existing circumstances, the two countries continued to have fundamentally contradictory interests over the international balance of influence, the U.S. strategic role in East Asia, U.S. support for Taiwan, and U.S. support for political change in China.[68]

Events in 1999, highlighted by the U.S. bombing of the Chinese embassy in Belgrade, posed new challenges for Chinese leadership efforts to sustain workable economic and other ties with the United States while defending key Chinese interests of sovereignty and nationalism. Chinese mob violence against U.S. diplomatic properties was accompanied by a virulent leadership debate over how to deal with the United States that was not resolved for months. In the end, Chinese leaders decided their interests were best served by working with the U.S. administration to restore calm and to continue U.S.-China engagement that was beneficial to China.

Amid the contentious U.S. presidential campaign of 2000, where policy toward China figured as an issue of some importance, senior Chinese officials told senior Clinton administration officials that China was intent on approaching the United States constructively, regardless of which candidate won the election. Such comment was seen by these U.S. officials as supporting a coherent and consistent Chinese strategy toward the United States. This strategy appeared similar to that seen in 1997 and 1998 in that it accepted U.S. leadership in world affairs and in Asian affairs and sought Chinese development in a peaceful international environment where the United States maintained primacy.[69]

However, the limitations, fragility, and apparent contradictions of this Chinese moderate approach toward the United States also were starkly evident. Whatever this strategy entailed, it did not show Chinese willingness to curb harsh commentary and the use of military force in challenging U.S. power and influence in Asian and world affairs. Thus, Chinese officials and commentary in 2000 and until mid-2001 continued to be full of invective against the United States, opposing alleged U.S. power politics, hegemonism, and Cold War thinking. China repeatedly criticized the United States over a variety of key foreign policy issues, such as U.S. plans for national missile defense in the United States and theater missile defense abroad, NATO expansion, enhanced U.S. alliance relations with Japan, and U.S. policy and practices in dealing with Iraq, Iran, Cuba, and other countries.[70] Chinese aircraft and ships monitoring U.S. surveillance aircraft and ships in international waters near China carried out dangerous maneuvers in apparent efforts to harass and deter the Americans from carrying out their objectives.

6

U.S.-China Policy Priorities and Implications for Relations in the Twenty-First Century

G EORGE W. BUSH BECAME PRESIDENT IN 2001 with a policy toward China tougher than the policy of his predecessor. Seeking to sustain economic relations with China, the new president was wary of China's strategic intentions and took steps to deter China from using military force against Taiwan. Relations deteriorated when on April 1, 2001, a Chinese jet fighter crashed with a U.S. reconnaissance plane, an EP-3, in international waters off the China coast.

Many specialists predicted continued deterioration of relations, but both governments worked to resolve issues and establish a businesslike relationship that emphasized positive aspects of the relationship and played down differences. The terrorist attack on America in September 2001 diverted U.S. attention away from China as a potential strategic threat. Preoccupied with leadership transition and other issues in China, Chinese leaders worked hard to moderate previous harsh rhetoric and other tactics in order to consolidate relations with the United States.

Some specialists tended to emphasize as the cause for the turnabout in relations greater Chinese leadership confidence and maturity, which they argued prompted the Chinese government to deal more moderately and with restraint regarding some of the seeming challenges posed by the new U.S. administration and its policies regarding Taiwan, weapons proliferation, ballistic missile defense, and the overall greater U.S. assertiveness and national security power in Asian and world affairs.[1]

Another group of specialists was less convinced that U.S.-China relations were destined to converge substantially over Asian and world affairs. These specialists emphasized the importance of what they saw as the Bush administration moving fairly rapidly from an initial toughness toward China to a stance of accommodation and compromise. The shift toward a moderate U.S. stance prompted Chinese leaders in turn to pursue greater moderation in their overall approach to Asian and world affairs.[2]

A third view involved specialists, including this writer, who gave more weight to the Bush administration's firm and seemingly effective policies toward China, which were seen to have curbed assertive and potentially disruptive Chinese tendencies and served to make it in China's interests to avoid confrontation, seek better U.S. ties, and avoid challenge to U.S. interests in Asian and world affairs. This view held that it was more China than the United States that took the lead in seeking better ties in 2001, and that greater U.S.-China cooperation in Asia-Pacific affairs depended not so much on Chinese confidence and maturity as on effective U.S. use of power and influence to keep assertive and disruptive Chinese tendencies in check and to prevail upon China to limit emphasis on differences with the United States.[3]

This writer's perspective on why the third view best explains the surprising improvement in U.S.-China relations at this time is explained in chapter 7. Whatever one's view of the causes of the improvement, the fact of the matter is that the course of U.S.-China relations was smoother than at any time since the normalization of those relations. U.S. preoccupation with the wars in Afghanistan and Iraq and the broader war on global terrorism meant that U.S. strategic attention to China as a threat remained a secondary consideration for American policy makers. Chinese leaders for their part continued to deal with an incomplete leadership transition and the broad problem of trying to sustain a one-party authoritarian political regime amid a vibrant economy and rapid social change. In this context, the two powers, despite a wide range of continuing differences ranging from Taiwan and Tibet to trade issues and human rights, managed to see their interests best served by generally emphasizing the positive. In particular, they found new common ground in dealing with the crisis caused by North Korea's nuclear weapons program beginning in 2002, and the Chinese appreciated Bush administration pressure on Taiwan's leader Chen Shui-bian in order to avoid steps toward independence for Taiwan that could lead to conflict in the Taiwan Strait.

Domestic criticism of U.S. policy toward China began to revive in 2005 as the war on terrorism wore on and the conflict in Iraq reflected major setbacks for the Bush administration. Economic and trade issues dominated the China policy debate. At the same time, congressional, media, and interest groups revived criticism of China on a variety of other issues involving notably human rights, international energy competition, and foreign relations with perceived rogue regimes.

Democrats led by longstanding critics of China won majority control of both houses of the Congress in the November 2006 elections. Democratic Party candidates for the 2008 presidential election generally were critical of the Bush administration's free-trade policies, which saw the U.S. annual trade deficit with China of over $250 billion and coincided with the loss of good-paying manufacturing jobs in the United States. They also tended to take a tougher line than the U.S. administration on human rights, Tibet, and other issues in U.S.-China relations. In the face of American criticism of China and of U.S. government moderation toward China, the Bush administration, some in Congress, and some U.S. interest groups emphasized pursuit of constructive engagement and senior-level dialogues as means to encourage China to behave according to U.S.-accepted norms as a "responsible stakeholder" in the prevailing international order and thereby show that the positives in U.S.-China relations outweighed the negatives.[4]

Priorities and Issues in U.S. Policy toward China

A close examination of the debates over issues in U.S.-China relations in the post–Cold War period generally appears to support the view that the U.S. debate over policy toward China at this time had more to do with developments in the United States, especially changed U.S. perceptions of Chinese government policies and behavior, than with changes in those Chinese policies and behavior. From one perspective, the Chinese authorities generally have been following broadly similar policies in the post-Mao (d. 1976) period designed to build national wealth and power, maintain territorial integrity and achieve unification with Taiwan, enhance the leadership of the authoritarian Communist Party, and improve the economic livelihood and social opportunities for the Chinese people. Their challenge to U.S.-supported norms regarding such subjects as human rights, weapons proliferation, environmental protection, the use of force to settle territorial disputes, and other sensitive issues have continued to wax and wane over the years. They often pose serious problems for the United States and U.S. interests, but on balance they are less serious today than they were in the Mao period or even during much of the rule of Deng Xiaoping.[5]

However, the shock of the 1989 Tiananmen incident and the end of the Cold War fundamentally changed the way the United States dealt with China. A pattern prevailing into the twenty-first century saw the U.S. administration generally continue to seek closer ties, including frequent high-level leadership meetings and various senior official dialogues, in order to develop areas of common ground while managing differences. The U.S. administration and the Chinese administration typically highlighted the many positive results from U.S.-China cooperation and dialogue. In recent years these have included cooperation in facilitating mutually advantageous trade and investment relations, cooperation in managing such regional crises and threats as the Asian economic crisis of 1997–1998, the crises in 1994 and again beginning in 2002 over North Korea's nuclear weapons program, the 1998 crisis prompted by nuclear weapons tests by India and Pakistan, and the global war on terrorism beginning in 2001. Under the rubric of engagement or cooperation, the U.S. administration officials and their Chinese counterparts presided over an ever-increasing economic interdependence between the United States and China, supplemented by growing cultural and political contacts and developing military contacts.

In contrast, a variety of U.S. groups were in the lead among U.S. critics who applied pressure in the Congress, the media, and in other public discourse to encourage a firmer U.S. policy designed to press the Chinese government to conform more to U.S.-backed norms. As discussed in chapter 5, some of these groups and advocates had varied motives that related less to China and its government's behavior and more to partisan or other ulterior benefits these groups and advocates derived from taking a tough stand against Chinese practices. The influence of the critics was evident in the varying intensity and scope of congressional debate and criticism of administration China policy in the post–Cold War period.

Meanwhile, each U.S. administration had differences within its own ranks on how to deal with China, and the administrations varied in their commitment to developing constructive ties and common ground with China.[6] The George W. Bush administration initially emphasized the competitive as well as the cooperative aspects of U.S.-China relations. It gave more emphasis to U.S. relations with Japan and other regional allies rather than to U.S. relations with China as means for dealing with Asian affairs. It focused U.S. military planning more on the implications of China's arms buildup, especially opposite Taiwan, and took strong positions on Taiwan, Tibet, human rights, and missile defense issues at odds with Chinese interests. The impasse over the EP-3 collision, the detention of the crew, and negotiations to return the plane resulted in a halt in military and many other official contacts. The clouded relationship then began to improve, witnessing closer cooperation between the U.S. and Chinese administrations.[7]

Reflecting a prevailing pattern in recent years, the George W. Bush administration, as with previous U.S. governments, came to emphasize a policy of closer interaction and generally positive engagement with China. In the post–Cold War period, administration officials tended to judge that China believed good relations with the United States were important, and that

Chinese leaders made some shifts in their policies in directions favored by the United States. Thus, China phased out its nuclear cooperation with Iran, joined the World Trade Organization, and assisted the United States in the Six Party talks dealing with North Korea's nuclear weapons program.

The 107th Congress (2001–2003) coincided with the start of the George W. Bush administration and showed a decline in the scope and intensity of domestic American debate over China policy for several reasons. First, the early actions of the Bush government supported firmer policies toward China that were backed by many in Congress regarding Taiwan, Tibet, human rights, and security concerns. These actions helped to calm the strong congressional debate over China policy that prevailed in the previous Congress. Second, partisan attacks on the U.S. administration's engagement policy toward China also diminished as the Bush White House and the Congress both were controlled by a Republican Party leadership intent on showing unity and party discipline on sensitive issues including China policy.[8] Third, U.S. preoccupation with the war on terrorism, including the U.S.-led military attacks on Afghanistan and Iraq, made it more difficult for U.S. interest groups and other activists to gain the public and private attention in Congress and elsewhere that they seemed to need in order to pressure for changes in U.S. policies toward China.

Congress and China Policy

To help to grasp the scope and depth of the U.S. domestic debate over China policy during the first decade of the twenty-first century, it is instructive to review the issues that were raised in debates, notably in the U.S. Congress. Because of its receptivity to U.S. domestic political movements and constituent pressures, Congress has remained a focal point for those Americans and U.S. groups pressing for change in U.S. policy toward China. The record of the post–Cold War debate in Congress over China policy is long and wide ranging. It deals with clusters of sensitive issues involving human rights and democratic political values, security issues, economic questions, and sovereignty issues, especially regarding Taiwan and Tibet. Highlights of the issues considered in congressional debate and actions at the outset of the twenty-first century are noted below. They provide evidence of the broad range of American interests that were trying to influence policy toward China and the directions they wanted China policy to follow. In general terms, the pattern shows these groups often opposed improvements or other forward movement in U.S.-China relations until the Chinese government changed its policies and practices more in accord with U.S.-supported norms. The groups sometimes favored sanctions or other pressures to force the Chinese government to change, although U.S. business interests and others with a strong economic stake in China often were effective in sustaining constructive trade relations.

After the intense U.S. domestic debates over China policy in the 1990s, the overall impact of the groups and the actions of Congress served in the first decade of the twenty-first century more as a drag on forward movement in U.S.-China relations than an impetus for tougher U.S. policy toward China. There was little support for serious retrogression in key areas of U.S.-China relations. And, as in the case of the 1990s, there was almost no support for a U.S. policy that would lead to military confrontation or strategic containment of China.[9]

A high point of revived congressional pressure on the administration's China policy came with the inauguration of the Democratic Party–controlled 110th Congress in 2007; Democratic leadership continued with stronger majorities in control of the 111th Congress beginning in 2009. While some forecast major challenges to existing U.S. China policy from domestic U.S. critics in the Congress and those working through the Congress, the outcome was more in line with predictions of a much more mixed outlook with pressures for a tougher U.S. China policy offset by important countervailing factors.[10]

Congress dealt with each of the policy priorities and issues noted below in a variety of ways, through press releases and statements reacting to U.S. media stories highlighting negative Chinese practices, legislation, hearings, so-called dear colleague letters, formal letters to the administration, speeches in and out of Congress, and other means.[11]

Human Rights Issues

China's human rights abuses have remained among the most visible and constant points of contention in U.S.-China relations in the post–Cold War period. China's human rights record presents a mixed picture, with both setbacks and minor improvements providing plenty of ammunition for U.S. policy debate in the Congress and elsewhere. Among the more positive developments in China's human rights record, the Chinese government signed two key human rights agreements: the UN Covenant on Economic, Social, and Cultural Rights (October 27, 1997) and the International Covenant on Civil and Political Rights (March 12, 1998). The government also was allowing local, competitive elections in rural areas in China and implemented legislation to make political and judicial processes more transparent and to hold law enforcement officials more accountable for their actions.

Crackdowns against dissidents and the Falun Gong group. In 1999, American news accounts began to give wide coverage to reports that the Chinese government was arresting prominent activists and giving out harsh jail sentences for what most Americans considered to be routine and benign civil acts. On July 22, 1999, the government outlawed Falun Gong, a spiritual movement in China said to combine Buddhist and Taoist meditation practices with a series of exercises. The government arrested Falun Gong leaders, imposed harsh prison sentences, closed Falun Gong facilities, and confiscated Falun Gong literature. At that time, the Chinese government also cracked down on democracy activists trying to register a new independent political party, the Chinese Democracy Party. Promoters of the new party were convicted on subversion charges and given long prison sentences.[12]

Chinese officials also harshly suppressed dissents among ethnic minorities, particularly in Tibet and in the Xinjiang-Uighur Autonomous Region, in China's far west. In April 1999, Amnesty International issued a report accusing the Chinese government of gross violations of human rights in Xinjiang, including widespread use of torture to extract confessions, lengthy prison sentences, and numerous executions. Harsh Chinese suppression continued as the global war on terrorism saw the Chinese administration brand dissidents in Xinjiang as terrorists with some links to Al Qaeda and other international terrorist organizations. Although U.S. administration officials warned after September 11, 2001, that the global anti-terror campaign should not be used to persecute Uighurs or other minorities with political grievances against Beijing, some believe that the U.S. government made a concession to the PRC on August 26, 2002, when it announced that it was placing one small group, the East Turkestan Islamic Movement, on the U.S. list of terrorist groups.[13]

A significant episode of anti-China activism and rhetoric in Congress accompanied public protests in the United States and harsh American and other Western media criticism of China's crackdown of dissent and violence in Tibet in 2008. Congressional leaders called for a boycott of the summer 2008 Olympic Games, but President Bush announced firmly that he would attend the games.

Chinese prisons/prison labor. Prisons in China were widely criticized for their conditions, treatment of prisoners, and requirements that prisoners perform productive work. From the standpoint of U.S. policy, one issue was the extent to which products made by Chinese prisoners were exported to the U.S. market, a violation of U.S. law. Meanwhile, periodic reports of Chinese security forces taking organs from executed prisoners and selling them on the black market prompted repeated congressional hearings, queries, and condemnations.[14]

Family planning/coercive abortion. Controversies in U.S. population planning assistance continued in recent years concerning China's population programs. Abortion, and the degree to which coercive abortions and sterilizations occur in China's family planning programs, remained a prominent issue in these debates.[15]

Religious freedom. U.S. government reports including the Department of State's Annual Reports on International Religious Freedom and the report issued on May 1, 2000, by the U.S. Commission on International Religious Freedom criticized Chinese government policies on religious practices. They provided a focal point for congressional hearings and statements. Although some foreign commentators noted recent moderation and even encouragement by Chinese officials regarding freer religious practices, the strong U.S. criticism of China's record on religious freedom continued.[16]

Internet and media restrictions. The growth of Internet, cell phone, and text messaging led to new Chinese regulations begun in 2005 that prompted some congressional hearings and other actions. A key issue was the extent to which U.S. Internet firms collaborated with Chinese authorities in helping the latter control Internet use in China.[17]

Issues in U.S.-China Security Relations

Once one of the stronger foundations of the relationship, U.S.-China security and military relations never fully recovered after they were suspended following the 1989 Tiananmen Square crackdown. The EP-3 incident resulted in a temporary halt regarding most military contacts.

China's military expansion. Some officials in the George W. Bush administration, backed by officials in Congress, the media, and others, focused on China's military buildup regarding a Taiwan contingency concerning U.S. military intervention and involvement. They pressed for stronger U.S. measures to deal with this situation, which in turn reinforced U.S.-China military competition and complicated bilateral military relations. [18]

WMD proliferation. The Bush administration, backed by many in the Congress, also took a tougher position against China's proliferation of weapons of mass destruction (WMD).[19] One key security issue for the United States was China's record of weapons sales, technology transfers, and nuclear energy assistance, particularly to Iran and Pakistan.

Espionage. Beginning in the late 1990s, U.S. media sources reported about ongoing investigations of cases of alleged Chinese espionage against the United States dating back to the 1980s. The most serious case involved China's alleged acquisition of significant information about the W-88, an advanced miniaturized U.S. nuclear warhead, as a result of alleged security breaches at the Los Alamos nuclear science laboratory between 1984 and 1988. Another serious instance, first reported in late April 1999 by the *New York Times*, involved allegations that a Taiwan-born Chinese-American scientist, Wen Ho Lee, had downloaded critical nuclear weapons codes, called legacy codes, from a classified computer system at Los Alamos to an unclassified computer system accessible by anyone with the proper password. Alleged Chinese espionage featured prominently in the 1999 Cox Commission report. This congressional commission was sharply critical of the U.S. administration's counterespionage activities against China.[20]

Subsequently, U.S. media focused attention on a complicated case involving an alleged Chinese double agent whose sexual relationship with senior FBI counterintelligence officers seemed to undermine the integrity of U.S. government efforts to curb Chinese espionage. Suspicions of Chinese espionage were voiced in Congress when the State Department decided to purchase computers for use in classified communications from a Chinese company. The controversy caused the department to halt the purchase.[21] Developments later in the decade featured arrests and convictions of individuals illegally funneling advanced U.S. technologies to China at the behest of Chinese administration clandestine agents.

Economic Issues

Trade deficit. Issues involving trade with China factored heavily into U.S. policy debates. The U.S. trade deficit with China surged from a $17.8 billion deficit in 1989 to around $100 billion in 2000. It more than doubled in the five following years and was $256 billion in 2008.[22]

Intellectual property rights. China's lack of protection for intellectual property rights (IPR) was long an issue in U.S.-China relations and became more important in the 109th and 110th Congresses. According to calculations from U.S. industry sources in 2006, IPR piracy cost U.S. firms $2.5 billion in lost sales a year and the IPR piracy rate in China for U.S. products remained estimated at 90 percent. Backed by Congress, U.S. administration officials repeatedly pressed Chinese officials to better implement IPR regulations.[23]

Currency valuation. In recent years until 2005, the PRC pegged its currency, the renminbi (RMB) to the U.S. dollar at a rate of about 8.3 RMB to the dollar—a valuation that many critics in Congress and elsewhere in the United States concluded kept the PRC's currency undervalued, making PRC exports artificially cheap and making it harder for U.S. producers to compete. On July 1, 2005, the PRC changed this valuation method. The resulting slow appreciation in the RMB from this action was not sufficient to assuage U.S. congressional concerns.[24]

Chinese purchase of U.S. government securities. A related concern was Chinese purchases of U.S. Treasury bills and other U.S. government securities as a means of recycling China's massive trade surplus with the United States while maintaining a relatively low value of the Chinese currency relative to the U.S. dollar. The Chinese investments seemed very important to the stability of the U.S. economy. Some congressional and other U.S. critics warned of U.S. overdependence on this type of investment by China.[25]

Bid for Unocal. The bid of a Chinese state-controlled oil company to acquire the U.S. oil firm Unocal in 2005 set off an uproar in the Congress and U.S. media. The congressional debate over the alleged dangers of the transaction to U.S. energy security was so intense that the Chinese firm withdrew the bid after two months.[26]

China's International Rise

A set of issues emerged in the 109th and 110th Congresses focused on the critical implications of China's economic growth and increasing international engagement and influence for U.S. economic, security, and political interests in various parts of the world. To feed its growing needs for resources, capital, and technology, Chinese officials, businesses, and others successfully sought trade agreements, oil and gas contracts, scientific and technological cooperation, and multilateral security, political, and economic arrangements with countries around its periphery and throughout the world. China's growing international economic engagement was backed by China's growing military power and went hand in hand with expanding Chinese political influence. China notably used unconditional economic exchanges and assistance to woo governments and leaders seen as rogues or outliers by the United States and other developed countries. Chinese practices undercut Western pressures on these officials and governments. China's increased influence also extended to many key allies and associates of the United States and to regions like Latin America where the United States exerted predominant influence.[27]

Sovereignty Issues: Taiwan, Tibet

Taiwan. Taiwan remained the most sensitive and complex issue in U.S.-China relations. Beijing was engaged in a military buildup focused on a Taiwan contingency involving the United States.

In 2001, the George W. Bush administration offered the largest package of U.S. arms to Taiwan in ten years and allowed Taiwan President Chen Shuibian to tour more freely and to meet with congressional representatives during stopovers in the United States. President Bush publicly pledged to come to Taiwan's aid with U.S. military power if Taiwan were attacked by mainland China. The steps were welcomed in Congress, but they deepened Beijing's judgment that the United States would remain at odds with China over the Taiwan issue for the foreseeable future.[28]

As the Taiwan administration of President Chen Shui-bian advanced, beginning in 2003, pro-independence proposals seen as destabilizing by the Bush administration, the U.S. president and his aides took steps to curb those potentially destabilizing actions. In general, these steps elicited only minor objections from the normally pro-Taiwan Congress.[29] The calming of cross-strait tensions as a result of Taiwan President Ma Ying-jeou's policies of reassurance toward China beginning in 2008 was welcomed in the Congress.

Tibet. The Dalai Lama long had some strong supporters in the U.S. Congress and among other U.S. opinion leaders, and these continued to put pressure on the White House to protect Tibetan culture and accord Tibet greater status in U.S. law despite Beijing's strong objections.[30] The Tibet issue flared again in U.S.-China relations in 2007. Congress awarded the Congressional Gold Medal to the Dalai Lama in a public ceremony. President Bush met the Dalai Lama during his visit to Washington and took part in the congressional award ceremony. China protested strongly.[31] Congressional leaders spoke out firmly against the Chinese crackdown on dissent and violence in Tibet in 2008.

China and the 110th Congress

The strong victory of the Democratic Party in the November 7, 2006, congressional elections underlined a broad desire of the American electorate for change in the policies and priorities of the George W. Bush administration. In the House of Representatives, the Democratic Party moved from a deficit position of thirty seats against the Republican majority to an advantage of thirty seats over the Republicans, and in the Senate it erased the Republican Party's ten-seat advantage, gaining a one-seat majority.

The implications of the Democratic victory seemed serious for U.S. policy in the Asia-Pacific and particularly for U.S. policy toward China, the focus of greatest controversy in the U.S. Congress regarding Asia-Pacific countries. The Democratic majority of the 110th Congress, led by opinionated and often confrontational leaders Representative Nancy Pelosi and Senator Harry Reid, pressed for change in a partisan atmosphere charged by preparations for the U.S. presidential election of 2008. The Democratic majority was forecast to pursue strong trade and economic measures that, if successful, would seriously disrupt U.S. economic relations with China and the free trade emphasis of the Bush administration. Mainstream commentator Thomas Friedman predicted a civil war in American politics over the massive U.S. trade deficit and related economic issues with China. Democrats pushing more activist approaches regarding human rights and environmental initiatives added to anticipated serious complications in U.S. relations with China.[32]

In contrast to such dire warnings, however, factors of power, priorities, politics, and personalities diluted the push for substantial change in U.S. policy in Asia, and toward China in particular. These factors resulted in a more balanced assessment of what the Democratic-led Congress could actually accomplish in changing U.S. policies and practices in Asia, especially regarding China. On the one hand, there were frequent episodes of congressional proposals, postures, and maneuvers regarding U.S. policies and practices regarding China. On the other hand, the impact of these congressional actions seemed not to change the course of U.S. relations with China in major ways. Overall the experience showed that the equilibrium that emerged in relations between the U.S. and Chinese administrations would not be substantially challenged by the continuing U.S. domestic debate over priorities in policy toward China.[33]

Power. The U.S. Constitution gave the executive the leading role in foreign affairs. In the face of a determined president like George W. Bush, the Democratic-led Congress appeared to have only a few levers to force change in areas that impact on U.S. relations with Asia, and especially China. Congress played a direct role in any decision to extend the president's so-called Trade Promotion Authority, which allowed expedited congressional consideration of free trade agreements (FTAs), including one that was negotiated with South Korea. The authority ended in mid-2007. Without it, congressional approval and Bush administration consideration of additional FTAs in Asia or elsewhere were less likely. The relevance of this issue for China was indirect at best.

Congress also controlled government spending—the "power of the purse." This could be used to block, redirect, or tailor administration requests for U.S. government spending and U.S. foreign assistance. The relevance of this issue to China was low, especially as official U.S. aid was not allowed to go to China.

Congressional opposition could hold up and possibly halt administration personnel appointments or policy initiatives needing congressional approval. In its last years, the Bush administration did not appear to anticipate major or controversial personnel changes regarding China and broader Asia policy or substantial policy initiatives requiring congressional action. Congressional oversight involving hearings, investigations, and reports was more active with the Democrats in control, but it usually exerted only limited power to steer the course of U.S. policy.

Priorities. Democratic leaders in the House and Senate voiced varied priorities. They tended to focus initially on such domestic issues as raising the minimum wage, controlling government spending deficits, strengthening job security for U.S. workers, preserving Social Security, and providing limited tax relief for middle-class taxpayers. Finding ways to change the adverse course of the U.S.-led war in Iraq dominated the foreign policy agenda.

Against this background, most issues affecting Asia, including China, received lower priority. Attention focused on finding ways to deal more effectively with the massive U.S. trade deficits and perceived unfair trade and economic policies regarding countries in Asia, notably China. Some Democratic leaders and members favored strong emphasis on human rights, labor conditions, and environmental concerns in governing U.S. policy to China and other concerned Asian countries, but others did not.

Politics. The bruising fight among House Democrats leading to the selection of Representative Steny Hoyer as house majority leader over the wishes of Speaker designate Nancy Pelosi was a reminder that the Democrats would not follow their leaders in lockstep as Republicans did under Speaker Newt Gingrich following the Republican landslide victory of 1994. Even if Speaker Pelosi wanted to push House Democrats to follow her past leanings to be tough in relations with China and on other Asian issues regarding human rights and trade, the makeup of the Democratic caucus and likely committee leadership strongly suggested less-than-uniform support. Conservative Democratic members increased as a result of the 2006 election and were reluctant to press too hard on human rights, environment, and other issues when important U.S. business and security interests were at stake. Many Democratic members supported free trade and resisted what they saw as protectionist measures of Democratic colleagues against China, Japan, and other Asian trading partners. They were backed by polling data of the Chicago Council on Global Affairs, which showed that Americans were fairly comfortable with the economic rise of China.[34]

Personalities. Given loose Democratic leadership control, individual members in key committee assignments mattered in the Democratic-led Congress and its approach to China issues. Because they differed among themselves on key issues, they were likely to have difficulty coming up with united positions in pressing for meaningful change in Bush administration policies regarding Asia and China in particular.[35]

The public positions of House leader Pelosi and Senate leader Reid were tough on trade and related economic and human rights issues regarding China. Representative Sander Levin and some other members of the House Ways and Means Committee and other economic policy committees also favored a tougher U.S. stance on trade issues, especially with China, and regarding trade issues with Japan that affected key U.S. industries, notably autos. However, they were offset by committee moderates headed by the Ways and Means Committee's leading Democrat, Charles Rangel. In the Senate, the leading Democrat on the Finance Committee, Max Baucus, also held moderate views supported by others on the committee that eschewed protectionism.

Leading Democrats in the House Committee on International Relations had records of vocal opposition to human rights violations, notably by China's authoritarian administration. These meshed well with the views of Representative Pelosi but were at odds with the large number of Democratic members who joined various working groups designed to foster pragmatic exchanges with and more informed and effective U.S. policy toward China. On balance, these groups moderated the congressional tendency to engage in "China-bashing" seen during annual congressional debates in the 1990s on China's trading status with the United States.

In sum, prevailing circumstances showed why U.S. policy toward China would not change substantially as a result of the Democratic victory in 2006. China's massive trade and foreign exchange surpluses and perceived unfair currency and trading practices generated legislation and other actions to apply pressure on the Bush administration to toughen the U.S. approach to China, but they appeared to fall short of forcing significant protectionist measures against China. Despite congressional pressure, the Bush administration's Treasury Department consistently refused to have China labeled a currency manipulator in its periodic reports to Congress. An increase in congressional rhetoric and posturing against Chinese human rights violations and other practices offending U.S. norms was balanced by growing congressional interest in working pragmatically with China in study groups and exchanges. Any congressional interest in pressing the Bush administration to increase support for Taiwan despite China's objections seemed offset by the turbulent political situation in Taiwan in the last years of the administration of President Chen Shui-bian and the fracturing of the Taiwan lobby in Washington as a result of partisan and divisive politics in Taiwan.

Chinese Policy Priorities

Those endeavoring to understand the priorities that determine the foreign policy of the People's Republic of China (PRC) after the Cold War and into the twenty-first century have a wealth of books, articles, and other assessments and analyses by scholars and specialists in Chinese foreign policy. These works document ever-expanding Chinese interaction with the outside world through economic exchanges in an era of globalization, and broadening Chinese involvement with international organizations dealing with security, economic, political, cultural, and other matters. They demonstrate a continuing trend toward greater transparency in Chinese foreign policy decision-making and policy formation since the beginning of the era of Chinese reforms following the death of Mao Zedong in 1976. As a result, there is considerable agreement backed by convincing evidence in these writings about the course and goals of contemporary Chinese foreign policy and how they affect the United States.[36]

In the post-Mao period, Chinese Communist Party (CCP) leaders have focused on economic reform and development as the basis of their continued survival as the rulers of China. Support for economic liberalization and openness has waxed and waned, but the overall trend has emphasized greater market orientation and foreign economic interchange as critical in promoting economic advancement, and by extension, supporting the continued CCP monopoly of political power. For a time, the leaders were less clear in their attitudes toward political liberalization and change, with some in the 1980s calling for substantial reform of the authoritarian communist system. Since the crackdown at Tiananmen in 1989, there has been a general consensus among the party elite to control dissent and other political challenges, allowing for only slow, gradual, and often halting political change that can be closely monitored by the authorities.[37]

In foreign affairs, post-Mao leaders retreated from the sometimes-strident calls to change the international system and worked pragmatically to establish relationships with important countries, especially the United States and Japan but also China's neighbors in Southeast Asia and elsewhere, who would assist China's development and enhance Beijing's overall goal of developing national wealth and power. The collapse of Soviet communism at the end of the Cold War posed a major ideological challenge to Chinese leaders and reduced Western interest in China as a counterweight to the USSR. But the advance of China's economy soon attracted Western leaders once again, while the demise of the USSR gave China a freer hand to pursue its interests, less encumbered by the long-term Soviet strategic threat.[38]

Against this backdrop, Chinese leaders by 1997 were anxious to minimize problems with the United States and other countries in order to avoid complications in their efforts to appear successful in completing three major tasks for the year, involving: the July 1997 transition of Hong Kong to Chinese rule; the reconfiguration of Chinese leadership and policy at the Fifteenth CCP Congress in September 1997; and the Sino-American summit of October 1997.[39]

Generally pleased with the results of these three endeavors, Chinese leaders headed by President and party chief Jiang Zemin began implementing policy priorities for 1998. At the top of the list was an ambitious multi-year effort, begun in earnest after the National People's Congress (NPC) meeting in March 1998, to transform tens of thousands of China's money-losing state-owned enterprises (SOEs) into more efficient businesses by reforming them (for example, selling them to private concerns, forming large conglomerates, or other actions). Beijing also embarked on major programs to promote economic and administrative efficiency and protect China's potentially vulnerable financial systems from any negative fallout from the 1997–1998 Asian economic crisis and subsequent uncertainties.

As a result of the September 1997 party congress and the March 1998 NPC meeting, a new party-government team was in place. Making collective leadership work is an ongoing challenge for China's top leaders. President Jiang Zemin gained in stature and influence, but his power still did not compare to that exerted by Mao Zedong and Deng Xiaoping. When it came time for Jiang and his senior colleagues to retire, there was a distinct possibility of a renewed struggle for power and influential positions by up-and-coming leaders. In the event, the leadership transition was handled cautiously, with Jiang slow to hand over the control of military power to the new generation of party leaders headed by Hu Jintao. Once he had assumed the leadership of the Chinese party, government, and military by 2004, Hu moved carefully in consolidating his leadership position. He seemed well aware that if a major economic, political, or foreign policy crisis were to emerge, leadership conflict over what to do, how to do it, and who should do it could be intense. Hu and his associates dealt with such major issues as the crisis caused by the outbreak of SARS in China in 2002–2003 and the North Korean nuclear crisis beginning in 2003 with generally effective policies that endeavored to support the leadership's interest in preserving Communist rule in China. The results of the Seventeenth Congress of the Chinese Communist Party in October 2007 appeared to underline a continuing cautious approach to political change and international and domestic circumstances that was designed to reinforce Communist Party rule in China.[40]

There was little sign of disagreement among senior leaders over the broad recent policy emphasis on economic reform, though sectors affected by reform often resist strenuously. The ambitious plans for economic reform, especially reform of the SOEs, were needed if China's economy was to become sufficiently efficient to sustain the growth rates seen as needed to justify continued communist rule and to develop China's wealth and power. China joining the World Trade Organization (WTO) in 2001 strengthened the need for greater economic efficiency and reform.

The reforms also exacerbate social and economic uncertainties, which reinforce the administration's determination to maintain a firm grip on political power and levers of social control. The repression of political dissidents and related activities begun in 1998 continued into the next decade and appeared likely to last for the duration of the economic reform efforts.

The results of the Seventeenth Party Congress in October 2007 strongly underscored the emphasis of the Hu Jintao administration gave to dealing more attentively than the Jiang Zemin leadership with the many negative consequences of China's rapid economic growth and social change. These negative consequences included glaring inequities between urban and rural sectors and coastal and interior areas; pervasive corruption by self-serving government and party officials; environmental degradation; misuse of scarce land, water, and energy resources; and the lack of adequate education, health care, and social welfare for hundreds of millions of Chinese citizens. The Hu Jintao leadership emphasized using scientific methods to promote sustainable development conducive to fostering a harmonious Chinese order under the leadership of the CCP administration.[41]

Against this background, foreign affairs generally remained an area of less urgent policy priority. Broad international trends, notably improved relations with the United States, support the efforts by the Chinese authorities to pursue policies intended to minimize disruptions and to assist their domestic reform endeavors. The administration remains wary of the real or potential challenges posed by a possible economic crisis, by Taiwan, by efforts by Japan and the United States to increase their international influence in ways seen as contrary to Beijing's interests, by India's great power aspirations and nuclear capability, by North Korea's nuclear weapons development, and other concerns. The PRC has voiced special concern over the implications for China's interests of U.S. plans and reported plans to develop and deploy theater ballistic missile defense systems in East Asia and a national missile defense for the United States. Chinese officials also voiced concern over the downturn in U.S.-China relations at the outset of the George W. Bush administration, but appeared determined to cooperate with the U.S.-led anti-terrorism campaign begun in September 2001.

In recent years, Chinese leaders are seen to be focused on promoting China's economic development while maintaining political and social stability in China. These efforts undergird a fundamental determination of the CCP administration to be an exception to the pattern of collapsing communist regimes at the end of the Cold War and to reinvigorate and sustain its one-party rule in China. Foreign policy is made to serve these objectives by sustaining an international environment that supports economic growth and stability in China. This is done partly through active and generally moderate Chinese diplomacy designed to reassure neighboring countries and other concerned powers, notably the United States, the dominant world power in Chinese foreign policy calculations. Chinese efforts try to demonstrate that rising Chinese economic, military, and political power and influence should not be viewed as a threat, but should be seen as an opportunity for greater world development and harmony. In the process, Chinese diplomacy gives ever-greater emphasis to engagement and conformity with the norms of regional and other multilateral organizations as a means to reassure those concerned over possible negative implications of China's increased power and influence.[42]

Chinese foreign policy places great emphasis on seeking international economic exchange beneficial to Chinese development. A large influx of foreign direct investment (FDI), foreign aid, foreign technology, and foreign expertise has been critically important in China's economic growth in the post-Mao period. In recent years, China has become the center of a variety of intra-Asian and other international manufacturing and trading networks that have seen China emerge as the world's third- or second-largest trading nation and the largest consumer of a variety of key world commodities and raw materials. In stark contrast to the "self-reliant" Chinese development policies of the Maoist period, which severely restricted foreign investment and curbed Chinese economic dependence on the outside world, China today depends fundamentally on a healthy world economy in which Chinese entrepreneurs compete for advantage and promote economic development as an essential foundation for continued rule of the CCP administration.

At the same time, the world economy depends increasingly on China. Now a member of the World Trade Organization (WTO) and other major international economic organizations, the Chinese government exerts ever-greater influence in international economic matters as a key manufacturing center for world markets and an increasingly prominent trading nation with a positive balance of trade and the largest foreign exchange reserves in the world.

Chinese nationalism and Chinese security priorities also are important determinants in contemporary Chinese foreign policy. The CCP administration has placed greater emphasis on promoting nationalism among Chinese people as communism has weakened as a source of ideological unity and legitimacy on account of the collapse of the Soviet Union and other communist regimes and the Chinese government's shift toward free-market economic practices. Nationalism supports the CCP administration's high priority to prevent Taiwan independence and restore this and other territory taken from China by foreign powers when China was weak and vulnerable during the nineteenth and twentieth centuries. Chinese leaders are forthright in building advanced military power and voicing determination to take coercive measures to achieve nationalistic goals, especially regarding Taiwan, even in the face of opposition by the power of the United States and its allies and associates. More broadly, Chinese leaders seek to build what they call "comprehensive national power"—particularly economic, military, and political power—as China seeks an as yet not clearly defined leading role as a great power in Asian and world affairs.

Meanwhile, Chinese administration and popular attention focused with great national pride on China's hosting of the August 2008 Olympic Games. The Chinese administration seemed determined to avoid actions at home or abroad that might complicate their successful Olympic Games. The administration used the occasion to showcase China's many positive accomplishments to wide audiences abroad and to reinforce the legitimacy and power of the Communist administration in the eyes of the Chinese people and international audiences.

Debate over China's Priorities

Despite considerable agreement among specialists about the course of and many of the goals in Chinese foreign policy after the Cold War, there also is considerable debate over the durability of China's recent approach. Some specialists judge that China's leaders are following a firm strategy that will last well into the twenty-first century. Others argue that China's approach is subject to change, particularly as major uncertainties and variables could push Chinese foreign policy in directions different from the recent course.[43]

Chinese government officials and some Chinese and foreign scholars and specialists emphasize that the mix of Chinese government priorities and prevailing conditions in the post–Cold War period provide the basis of a Chinese strategy of peace and development that will last for decades.[44] The State Council of the People's Republic of China issued a White Paper from its Information Office in December 2005 that provided an outline of this view of China's strategy in foreign affairs. Entitled *China's Peaceful Development Road*, the document stressed that to achieve peaceful development has been the "unremitting pursuit" of the Chinese people and administration for almost thirty years and that China's approach will remain along these lines and compatible with Chinese and international circumstances for decades to come. Key features of the Chinese approach were said to include striving to sustain a peaceful international environment helpful to Chinese development and the promotion of world development and peace; achieving Chinese development beneficial to China and its economic partners through growing economic interchange conforming to economic globalization; and doing China's part to build a harmonious world with sustained peace and common prosperity featuring more democratic international decision-making than that prevailing in the past. While acknowledging problems and conflicts in contemporary world affairs, the overall optimistic assessment said that "there are more opportunities than challenges" in the world today and that the rise of China was one of the most salient international opportunities, as "China's development will never pose a threat to anyone."[45]

Among more detailed assessments of China's overall foreign policy strategy by prominent Chinese officials and specialists was an article published in

2006 by two prominent specialists of the Chinese government organization the Academy of Social Sciences.[46] This study said there were four important concepts underpinning China's strategy in world affairs. They are (1) A drive for great power in world affairs; (2) A need for a stable international environment supportive of China's economic development; (3) A restraint on the part of Chinese leaders in world politics in order to avoid onerous obligations and commitments that would hamper China's growth and development. This restraint was strong during the leadership of Deng Xiaoping in the 1990s; and, (4) A recognition by post-Deng Xiaoping (d. 1997) leaders that China's success at home and abroad depends on ever-closer interaction with world affairs requiring China to take up more international responsibilities than in the past.

In practice, according to the two Chinese specialists, the Chinese strategy involves several important initiatives:

- Seeking comprehensive cooperation and partnerships with all states around China's periphery and important governments elsewhere in the world.
- Emphasizing and demonstrating Chinese self-restraint in order to add to a benign image of China as not a threat but an opportunity for the world.
- Willingness to put aside past repeated and vocal complaints against U.S. dominance and "hegemony" in world politics so long as the United States does not challenge Chinese interests regarding Taiwan, Communist Party rule in China, and related issues.
- A Chinese approach to economic development that opens the Chinese economy ever more widely to international influence so that as China rises in economic importance, the benefits of its rise are spread widely throughout the world, and China's new position is less likely to be seen as a threat to the international economy or to the economies of countries that interact with China.
- Ever-greater Chinese involvement with regional and other multilateral bodies. This effort is designed to enhance China's international profile on the one hand while on the other hand it channels Chinese power into these institutions, thereby reducing the suspicions of neighbors and significant world powers, notably the United States.

Among foreign assessments, a cogent analysis by the prestigious Institute for International and Strategic Studies entitled *China's Grand Strategy: A Kinder, Gentler Turn* was published in late 2004 and focused on the growing concerns in the United States and among some of China's neighbors in Asia over the rise of Chinese economic, military, and political power and influence as a key driver in contemporary Chinese strategy in world politics.[47] The strengthening of negative perceptions of China's rise by the United States and other powers would inevitably lead to the rise of new balancing coalitions against China, it averred, upsetting China's still-incomplete efforts to develop and accumulate comprehensive national power sufficient to secure Chinese internal and international interests. Thus, an important objective in China's strategy in world affairs is to assure the continued smooth growth of Chinese wealth and power while simultaneously preventing the emergence of balancing coalitions that might arise in response to such growth.

To do this, China has settled on an approach affirming Beijing's permanently peaceful intentions; emphasizing good neighbor relations designed to wean states, especially neighboring ones, away from potentially balancing behavior or coalitions; using China's economic strength as leverage to increase dependence on the part of potential rivals; and accommodating and appeasing the reigning hegemony, the United States—at least until the point where Beijing can cope with American power independently—while exploiting Asian and international dissatisfaction with the United States in order to enhance China's own efforts to create buffers and guard against U.S. pressure and dominance. China's broader international goals include giving notice of its arrival as a great power, forging friendly relations with more distant governments for the purposes of developing new allies and access to needed commodities, and preempting these countries from aiding the United States in any future effort to pressure China.

In contrast to the above assessments of a coherent strategy in Chinese foreign relations based on clear priorities of Chinese leaders are the findings of foreign specialists, including this writer, who emphasize complications and uncertainties in Chinese foreign policy that make it far from sure that the prevailing moderate Chinese approach will continue without interruption. In the area of Chinese national security, Thomas Christensen argued at the start of this decade that while the priorities of the Chinese leadership seemed clear, "many of the means to reach the regime's domestic and international security goals are so fraught with complexity, and sometimes contradiction, that a single, integrated grand plan is almost certainly lacking, even in the innermost circles of the Chinese leadership compound."[48]

U.S. government assessments repeatedly underlined uncertainty about China's strategy and longer-term objectives and what they meant for the United States. Speaking in Japan in March 2005 during her first trip to Asia as the secretary of state in the second term of the George W. Bush administration, Condoleezza Rice affirmed the basic judgment in U.S. government circles that while China's growth in economic, military, and political power and influence was a reality, it was unclear whether the Chinese government had determined to use this power in ways that benefited or undermined U.S. goals of regional and international stability and cooperation. She described China's rising power as "a new factor" in world affairs that "has the potential for good or for bad," and she asserted it was the role of the United States and its partners to "try and push and prod and persuade China toward the more positive course."[49]

Bush administration discourse on China came to emphasize the positive during the president's second term. Deputy Secretary of State Robert Zoellick did so in November 2005 in a speech calling on China to behave as a "responsible stakeholder" in sustaining an international order beneficial to China and others. Secretary of Defense Robert Gates said in 2007 that he did not view China as an adversary. At the same time, however, the United States took military preparations and other steps widely seen in China and abroad as contingency plans or hedges in the event of aggressive Chinese military or other actions.[50]

Uncertainties Influencing China's Policy in World Affairs

This writer and others who argue for caution in defining and assessing Chinese strategy in contemporary world affairs are supported by a variety of recent scholarship and evidence highlighting major uncertainties governing Chinese foreign policy and behavior.[51] For one thing, there is plenty of evidence that the course of Chinese policy leading to the current emphasis on peace and development has not been smooth. Even in the brief period since the end of the Cold War, there have been many twists and turns, along with various international crises and policy debates in China on the best course to take in prevailing circumstances. Chinese leaders decided to pursue a much more assertive stance against outside powers than that espoused by the current peace and development line when they launched China's tough stance and provocative military actions in the Taiwan Strait in 1995–1996. Chinese leaders openly debated whether or not to adopt a more uncompromising position against U.S. "hegemonism" following the U.S. bombing of the Chinese embassy in Belgrade in 1999. The Chinese government for several days allowed illegal violence against Japanese diplomatic and business installations during an upsurge of anti-Japanese sentiment in China in April 2005.

For another, foreign specialists cannot come up with a clear view as to whether the prevailing Chinese approach to world affairs reflects Chinese confidence, strength, and determination to continue the current course or reflects vulnerability and uncertainty in the face of circumstances at home and abroad that could prompt change in China's international approach. The result is a mixed and often confusing situation pointing out Chinese leaders' confidence in some areas and uncertainty in others, with the level of confidence or uncertainty in some key policy areas prone to change over time with changing circumstances. For example, those who track Chinese officials' asserted confidence or uncertainty over the key issue of Taiwan have documented several cycles of optimism and pessimism by Chinese officials in recent years brought on by changing policies of the Taiwan administration.[52] In an authoritative compendium on recent Chinese policies in Asia, foreign experts came to markedly different conclusions on whether or not China's leaders were confident in dealing with foreign affairs.[53]

U.S.-China Relations Add to Uncertainty in Chinese Foreign Policy

Relations with the United States are widely acknowledged as the most important bilateral relationship and a key determinant in Chinese foreign policy. Whether China's approach to international affairs continues along the self-proclaimed strategic direction of peace and development or whether it veers toward assertiveness and confrontation or in some other direction is widely seen in China and abroad to depend heavily on the state of play in China's relations with the United States.

Lack of clarity in predictions of the future course of U.S.-China relations underlines ambivalence about the future direction of Chinese foreign policy. Professor Aaron Friedberg, a prominent international affairs specialist and former deputy director of the U.S. vice president's national security staff, wrote an assessment in late 2005 dealing with underlying uncertainties in U.S.-China relations.[54] He questioned whether U.S.-China relations over the next decades would be marked by convergence toward deepening cooperation and peace or whether there would be deterioration leading to growing competition and possibly war. Assessing the enormous consequences of either path for China, the United States, and the international order, Friedberg warned that, despite these consequences and the many studies of U.S.-China ties, the bottom line is profound uncertainty, with few willing to predict the outlook without major caveats and conditions.

In sum, the priorities of China's leaders have emerged gradually in the post–Cold War period. They appear to focus on preserving stability at home and abroad, and advancing economic exchanges and development that help to legitimate continued rule by the Communist Party of China. Also important are broader Chinese interests to exert greater influence in Asian and world affairs, to promote nationalistic goals, notably regarding Taiwan, and to develop China's military as well as economic and political power. These priorities sometimes come into conflict with one another. When this happens, Chinese policy tends to shift direction. Shifts also have occurred during important international crises and presumably could occur as a result of future crises.

In many respects, the Chinese priorities seem compatible with U.S. interests in promoting stability, peace, and development in Asian and world affairs. Chinese policies and practices are conforming ever more to U.S.-backed international norms. Nevertheless, the longer-term implications of the rise of Chinese power remain very mixed for the United States. Persisting wariness also characterizes the American response to the increasingly salient roles China plays in international economics and world political affairs. The concurrent growth of Chinese military power focused on contingencies involving the United States over Taiwan and Asian issues is seen as a more direct threat to the United States.

7

An Emerging U.S.-China Equilibrium in the Twenty-First Century

U.S.-CHINA RELATIONS DURING THE FIRST DECADE of the twenty-first century evolved toward a positive equilibrium that appears likely to continue into the near future. Based on consideration of the respective policy priorities of the United States and China detailed in chapter 6 and on developments affecting U.S.-China relations in recent years, it appears that both the U.S. and Chinese administrations have become preoccupied with other issues, and they seem reluctant to exacerbate tensions with one another. Growing economic interdependence and cooperation over key issues in Asian and world affairs reinforce each government's tendency to emphasize the positive and pursue constructive relations with one another. The emerging positive stasis in U.S.-China relations provides a basis for greater cooperation over economic, security, and other interests and issues.

However, differences in these interests and issues also have remained strong; they represent major obstacles to further cooperation between the two countries. Policy makers in both countries continue to harbor suspicions about each other's intentions. They remain on alert for changing circumstances regarding Taiwan, Japan, North Korea, international economic trends, U.S. and Chinese domestic politics, and other developments that could seriously complicate the bilateral relationship.

A pattern of dualism in U.S.-China relations has arisen as part of the positive equilibrium in this decade. The pattern involves constructive and cooperative engagement on the one hand and contingency planning or hedging on the other. It reflects the mix noted above of converging and competing interests and prevailing leadership suspicions and cooperation.

Chinese and U.S. contingency planning and hedging against one another sometimes involves actions like the respective Chinese and U.S. military buildups that are separate from and develop in tandem with the respective engagement policies the two leaderships pursue with each other. At the same time, dualism shows as each government has used engagement to build positive and cooperative ties while at the same time seeking to use these ties to build interdependencies and webs of relationships that have the effect of constraining the other power from taking actions that oppose its interests. While the analogy is not precise, the policies of engagement pursued by the United States and China toward one another have featured respective "Gulliver strategies" that are designed to tie down aggressive, assertive, or other negative policy tendencies of the other power through webs of interdependence in bilateral and multilateral relationships.

The recent positive stasis in U.S.-China relations is based on an increasing convergence of these respective engagement policies and Gulliver strategies. But the fact remains that these Gulliver strategies reflect underlying suspicions and conflicting interests that feature prominently in the calculations of both the U.S. and Chinese administrations as they pursue their relations with one another.[1]

Beginning in the last half of the 1990s, Chinese leaders reviewed and reassessed their previous, more confrontational approach to U.S. pressures against China and longstanding Chinese opposition to U.S. dominance and so-called "hegemony" in Asian and world affairs. These U.S. pressures and dominance previously had been seen as antithetical to Chinese interests and as requiring strong opposition and resistance by China.

There was debate among foreign and Chinese specialists regarding the significance of this reassessment. According to some foreign specialists who interviewed numerous Chinese officials and foreign policy specialists, the Chinese leaders by the latter 1990s settled on a strategy that played down differences with and resistance to the United States, in favor of an approach of ever-greater cooperation with the American government. This approach was said to remain sensitive to U.S. intrusions on core Chinese interests involving Taiwan, but it deemphasized past Chinese concerns regarding U.S. policies and behavior designed to solidify U.S. leadership in Asian and world affairs.[2]

Against this background, some U.S. and Chinese specialists judged that the new Chinese approach of pragmatic adjustment met and would continue to meet U.S. approval and result in ever-increasing convergence and cooperation in U.S.-China relations. They maintained that the Chinese adjustment was based on greater maturity and confidence among Chinese leaders as they dealt with the United States and world affairs. Chinese maturity and confidence were seen as based on the Chinese leaders' success in promoting decades of remarkable economic growth along with military modernization and social change in China. Indeed, the maturity and confidence was understood to lie behind much of the "new thinking" said to be influencing greater Chinese involvement in regional and other multilateral organizations, and to offset traditional Chinese views of having been victimized by outside powers and needing to be on guard to prevent future exploitation or oppression.[3]

An opposing school of thought among U.S. and Chinese specialists, which includes this writer, judges that the circumstances surrounding Chinese foreign policy and Chinese policy toward the United States have remained far too uncertain to posit a truly lasting Chinese strategy of cooperation and convergence with the United States. There have been remarkable twists and turns in Sino-American relations, even following the reported Chinese leadership decision in the latter 1990s, to pursue a moderate policy toward the United States. The stability of what is seen as an inherently fragile relationship was challenged this decade by antipathy in the United States over Chinese policies and practices in economic, security, and other areas, and by the policies and practices of Taiwan, North Korea, Japan, and other international actors.[4]

This writer and other specialists in this group remain unconvinced that Chinese leaders are confident and mature in their recent moderate approach to the United States. Rather, Chinese leaders are seen as often vulnerable and uncertain as they react and respond to policies and practices, particularly those of the powerful and sometimes unpredictable U.S. government but also including the leaders of Taiwan, Japan, Russia, North Korea, and India. They adjust to changing circumstances, weighing in each instance the costs and benefits of maintaining or changing policies, and thereby seek to sustain important Chinese leadership priorities and advance the development of what they call China's comprehensive national power.[5]

In recent years, Chinese leaders are seen by this group of analysts as hedging their bets as they endeavor to persuade the United States and other important world powers of China's avowed determination to pursue the road of peace and development. Thus, the new thinking seen in greater Chinese international activism and positivism regarding multilateral organizations and world politics appears to be only one part of recent Chinese foreign policy. Such positive and cooperative new thinking seems balanced by a concurrent large-scale buildup in Chinese military forces backed by assertions in Chinese white papers on national security, other official commentary, and assertive diplomatic and military actions that make clear that Chinese leaders are quite prepared to protect their interests in strong and assertive ways under circumstances seen to warrant such actions. In the meantime, the new Chinese diplomatic and international activism and positivism not only foster a positive and beneficent image for China; they are seen by these analysts as serving an important practical objective of fostering norms and practices in regional and international organizations and circumstances that create a buffer against perceived U.S. efforts to "contain" China and to impede China's rising power. Roughly consistent with the image of the "Gulliver strategy" noted earlier, they foster webs of interdependent relationships that tie down and hamper unilateral or other actions by the U.S. superpower that could intrude on important Chinese interests in Asian and world affairs.[6]

Evolving U.S. Policy—Bush's Initial Approach to China and China's Reaction

George W. Bush had a reputation of toughness toward China but no clearly articulated policy. The new U.S. administration's approach to the Chinese administration was based in large measure on a fundamental uncertainty—China was rising and becoming more prominent in Asia and world affairs, but U.S. leaders were unsure if this process would see China emerge as a friend or foe of the United States.[7] The administration dealt with this ambiguous China situation within a broader U.S. international strategy that endeavored to maximize U.S. national power and influence in key situations, including relations with China. This involved strengthening:

- U.S. military and economic power;
- U.S. relations with key allies—in Asia, Japan, South Korea, and Australia—received high priority; and
- U.S. relations with other power centers—the Bush administration was successful in moving quickly, before September 11, 2001, to build closer relations with the two major flanking powers in East Asia, Russia and India.[8]

In 2001, the new U.S. president and his leadership team displayed a notably less solicitous approach to China than displayed by the outgoing Clinton administration. The Clinton administration during its second term adopted an engagement policy toward China that received the top priority among U.S. relations with Asia. The administration was anxious to avoid serious downturns in U.S.-China relations over Taiwan and other issues; it also repeatedly sought negotiations with Beijing to develop "deliverables"—agreements and other tangible signs of forward movement in U.S.-China relations. President Clinton, senior U.S. officials, and U.S. specialists repeatedly made clear that key objectives of growing U.S. engagement with China were to enmesh China in webs of interdependent relationships with the United States, international organizations, world business, and others that would constrain and ultimately change Chinese policies and practices at home and abroad that were seen as offensive to or opposed to U.S. interests.[9]

PRC bargainers used a prevailing atmosphere of strong, public Chinese criticism of U.S. policies and warnings of Chinese actions against Taiwan in order to press for U.S. concessions in areas of importance to them, notably regarding U.S. relations with Taiwan. Chinese criticism of U.S. policy had a broad scope involving Taiwan and a wide range of issues in U.S. foreign and security policy including missile defense, NATO expansion, U.S.-Japan security cooperation, U.S. human rights policy, U.S. efforts in the United Nations to sanction Iraq, and U.S. policy toward Cuba, Iran, the Middle East, and other areas in the developing world. As noted in chapter 5, Clinton administration concessions fueled the white-hot U.S. domestic debate over the proper direction of U.S. China policy.[10]

By contrast, the Bush administration lowered China's priority for U.S. decision makers, placing the PRC well behind Japan and other Asian allies and even Russia and India for foreign policy attention.[11] This kind of downgrading of China's importance in U.S. policy had last been carried out in the Reagan administration under the supervision of Secretary of State George Shultz. It appeared to be no accident that the key architects of the policy shift in 2001, notably Deputy Secretary of State Richard Armitage, were among key decision makers in the similar U.S. shift in U.S. China policy that began in 1983. Armitage and his key aides in the State Department and close associates in the National Security Council Staff were in the lead in moving U.S. policy from the strong emphasis on compromising with China and doing what was necessary in order to preserve good relations with China in the latter years of the Clinton administration.

Following the crash between a Chinese jet fighter and a U.S. reconnaissance plane over the South China Sea during the so-called EP-3 incident of April 2001, the Bush administration did not resort to high-level envoys or other special arrangements used by the Clinton administration to resolve difficult U.S.-China issues. It insisted on working through normal State Department and Defense Department channels that did not raise China's stature in U.S. foreign policy. In an unusual step showing that the administration was speaking firmly with one voice during the incident, U.S. officials were instructed to avoid all but the most essential contacts with Chinese officials in Washington and elsewhere.[12]

Bush administration interest in seeking negotiations with China in order to create "deliverables" and other agreements remained low. Its reaction to the EP-3 episode, markedly increased U.S. support for Taiwan, and a new U.S. focus on China as a potential threat showed Beijing leaders that the Bush government, while seeking to broaden areas of cooperation where possible, was prepared to see U.S.-China relations worsen if necessary.

Chinese leaders by mid-2001 seemed to recognize that if U.S.-China relations were to avoid further deterioration, it was up to China to take steps to improve ties. In a period of overall ascendant U.S. influence and leverage in Asian and world affairs, Beijing saw its interests best served by a stance that muted differences and sought common ground. Chinese officials thus significantly adjusted their approach to the United States. They became more solicitous and less acrimonious in interaction with U.S. officials. Chinese officials and media toned down public Chinese rhetoric against the United States. They gave some tentative signs of public PRC support for the U.S. military presence in East Asia. The U.S. side also signaled an interest to calm the concerns of friends and allies in Asia over the state of U.S.-China relations and to pursue areas of common ground in trade and other areas with the PRC.[13]

The anti-terrorism campaign after September 11, 2001, saw an upswing in U.S.-China cooperation, though China was somewhat tentative and reserved in supporting the U.S. war against Afghanistan. President Bush's visits to Shanghai in October 2001 and Beijing in February 2002 underlined differences as well as common ground. The U.S. president repeatedly affirmed his strong support for Taiwan and his firm position regarding human rights issues in China. His aides made clear China's lower priority in the administration's view of U.S. interests as the Bush administration continued to focus higher priority on relations with Japan and other allies in Asia and the Pacific. The Bush administration imposed sanctions on China over issues involving China's reported proliferation of weapons of mass destruction more times in its first year than were imposed during the eight years of the Clinton administration. The U.S. Defense Department's Quadrennial Defense Review unmistakably saw China as a potential threat in Asia. U.S. ballistic missile defense programs, opposed by China, went forward; rising U.S. influence and prolonged military deployments were at odds with Chinese interest to secure China's western flank.[14] The U.S. Defense Department's annual reports on the Chinese military pulled few punches in focusing on China's military threat to Taiwan and to U.S. forces that might come to Taiwan's aid in the event of a conflict with the PRC. The Bush administration's September 2002 National Security Strategy Report called for better relations with China but clearly warned against any power seeking to challenge U.S. interests with military force.[15]

It was notable that China's increased restraint and moderation toward the United States came even in the face of these new departures in U.S. policy and behavior under the Bush administration, particularly presidential pledges along with military and political support for Taiwan, strong missile defense programs, and strong support for alliance-strengthening with Japan and expanded military cooperation with India. In the recent past, such U.S. actions would have prompted severe Chinese public attacks and possibly military countermeasures.

U.S. leaders showed an increased willingness to meet Chinese leaders' symbolic needs for summitry, and the U.S. president pleased his Chinese counterpart by repeatedly endorsing a "constructive, cooperative, and candid" relationship with China. Amid continued Chinese moderation and concessions in 2002, and reflecting greater U.S. interest in consolidating relations and avoiding tensions with China at a time of growing U.S. preoccupation with the war on terrorism, Iraq, and North Korea, the Bush administration broadened cooperation with China and gave U.S. relations with China a higher priority as the year wore on. An October 2002 meeting between President Bush and President Jiang Zemin at the U.S. president's ranch in Crawford, Texas, highlighted this trend. Concessions and gestures, mainly from the Chinese side dealing with proliferation, Iraq, release of dissidents, U.S. agricultural imports, Tibet, and Taiwan, facilitated the positive Crawford summit.[16] Meanwhile, senior U.S. leaders began to refer to China, and Jiang Zemin, as a "friend."[17] They adhered to public positions on Taiwan that were acceptable to Beijing. They sanctioned an anti-PRC terrorist group active in China's Xinjiang region. The U.S. Defense Department was slow to resume high-level contacts with China, reflecting continued wariness in the face of China's ongoing military buildup focused on dealing with Taiwan and U.S. forces that may seek to protect Taiwan, but formal relations at various senior levels were resumed by late 2002.[18]

U.S. Moderation and Chinese Response

Looking back, it appears that patterns of Bush administration policy and behavior toward China began to change significantly in 2003. U.S. officials sometimes continued to speak in terms of "shaping" Chinese policies and behavior through tough deterrence along with moderate engagement. However, the thrust of U.S. policy and behavior increasingly focused on positive engagement. China also received increasingly high priority in U.S. policy in Asia and the world.

The determinants of the U.S. approach appeared to center on the Bush administration's growing preoccupations with the war in Iraq, the mixed record in other areas in the war on terror and many complications in the Middle East, and broad international and growing domestic disapproval of Bush administration policies. The North Korean nuclear program emerged as a major problem in 2003, and the U.S. government came to rely heavily on China to help to manage the issue in ways that avoided major negative fallout for the interests of the U.S. government. Though Asian policy did not figure prominently in the 2004 presidential campaign, Senator John Kerry, the Democratic candidate, used a televised presidential debate to challenge President Bush's handling of North Korea's nuclear weapons development. President Bush countered by emphasizing his reliance on China in order to manage the issue in accord with U.S. interests.[19]

The Bush administration's determination to avoid trouble with China at a time of major foreign policy troubles elsewhere saw the president and senior U.S. leaders strongly pressure Taiwan's government to stop initiating policies seen as provocative by China and possible causes of confrontation and war in U.S.-China relations.[20] The strong rhetorical emphasis on democracy promotion in the Bush administration's second term notably avoided serious pressures against China's authoritarian system.

The U.S. government's emphasis on positive engagement with China did not hide the many continuing U.S.-China differences or U.S. efforts to plan for contingencies in case rising China turned aggressive or otherwise disrupted U.S. interests. The United States endeavored to use growing interdependence, engagement, and dialogues with China to foster webs of relationships that would tie down or constrain possible Chinese policies and actions deemed negative to U.S. interests.[21]

On the whole, the Chinese administration of President Hu Jintao welcomed and supported the new directions in U.S. China policy. The Chinese leaders endeavored to build on the positives and play down the negatives in relations with the United States. This approach fit well with the Chinese leadership's broader priorities of strengthening national development and Communist Party legitimacy that were said to require China to use carefully the "strategic opportunity" of prevailing international circumstances seen as generally advantageous to Chinese interests. As in the case of U.S. policy toward China, Chinese engagement with the United States did not hide Chinese contingency plans against suspected U.S. containment and the Chinese use of engagement and interdependence as a type of Gulliver strategy to constrain and tie down possible U.S. policies and actions deemed negative to Chinese interests.[22]

Debate over the Challenge of China's Rise in Asia

China expanded military power along with economic and diplomatic relations in Asian and world affairs at a time of U.S. preoccupation with the war in Iraq and other foreign policy problems. Debate over the implications of China's rise for U.S.-China relations was important in Bush administration deliberations for several years, and it remained strong among congressional, media, and nongovernment specialists and interest groups.

Within the Bush administration, there emerged three viewpoints or schools of thought, though U.S. officials frequently were eclectic, holding views of the implications of China's rise from various perspectives.[23]

On one side were U.S. officials who judged that China's rise in Asia was designed by the Chinese leadership to dominate Asia and in the process to undermine U.S. leadership in the region.[24] Recently China promoted regional efforts that excluded or opposed the United States and efforts to undermine U.S. allies and friends, notably Japan and Taiwan. China also endeavored to widen gaps between the United States and some of its allies (for example, Australia) over policy toward China, thereby weakening U.S. influence. China also continued a robust military buildup targeted against U.S. forces in Asia.

A more moderate view of China's rise in Asia came from U.S. officials who judged that China's focus in the region was not on isolating and weakening the United States in Asia but on improving China's position mainly in order to sustain regional stability, promote China's development, reassure neighbors and prevent balancing against China, and isolate Taiwan. Nevertheless, the Chinese policies and behavior, even though not targeted against the United States, contrasted with perceived inattentive and maladroit U.S. policies and practices. The result was that China's rise was having an indirect but substantial negative impact on U.S. leadership in Asia.

A third school of thought became more prominent in recent years. It is identified with former U.S. Special Trade Representative and Deputy Secretary of State Robert Zoellick, who by 2005 publicly articulated a strong argument for greater U.S. cooperation with China over Asian and other issues as China rose in regional and international prominence.[25] This viewpoint held that the United States has much to gain from working directly and cooperatively with China in order to encourage the PRC to use its rising influence in "responsible" ways in accord with broad American interests in Asian and world affairs. This viewpoint seemed to take account of the fact that the Bush administration was already working closely with China in the Six-Party Talks to deal with North Korea's nuclear weapons development, and that U.S. and Chinese collaboration or consultations continued on such sensitive topics as the war on terror, Afghanistan, Pakistan, Iran, Sudan, Myanmar/ Burma, and even Taiwan, as well as bilateral economic, security, and other issues. Thus, this school of thought put less emphasis than the other two on competition with China and more emphasis on cooperation with China in order to preserve and enhance U.S. leadership and interests in Asia as China rises.

Bush administration policy came to embrace the third point of view. Senior U.S. leaders reviewed in greater depth the implications of China's rise and the strengths and weaknesses of the United States in Asia. The review showed that U.S. standing as Asia's leading power was basically sound. U.S. military deployments and cooperation throughout the Asia-Pacific region were robust. The U.S. economic importance in the region was growing, not declining. Overall, it was clear that no other power or coalition of powers was even remotely able or willing to undertake the costs, risks, and commitments of the United States in sustaining regional stability and development essential for the central interests of the vast majority of regional governments.[26]

China's rise—while increasingly important—thus came to be seen as posing less substantial and significant challenge for U.S. interests than many of the published commentaries and specialists' assessments might have led one to believe. Against this background, the Bush administration increasingly emphasized positive engagement and dialogues with China, encouraging China to act responsibly and building ever-growing webs of relationships and interdependence. This pattern fit well with Chinese priorities regarding national development in a period of advantageous international conditions while building interdependencies and relationships that constrain possible negative U.S. policies or behaviors.

Bush's Legacy: Positive Equilibrium in U.S.-China Relations

The positive stasis in U.S.-China relations that emerged at this time met the near-term priorities of the U.S. and Chinese governments. Converging U.S. and Chinese engagement policies tried to broaden common ground while they dealt with differences through engagement policies that included respective Gulliver strategies designed to constrain each other's possible disruptive or negative moves.

Neither the Chinese leadership nor the U.S. administration sought trouble with the other. Both were preoccupied with other issues. Heading the list of preoccupations for both governments was dealing with the massive negative consequences of the international economic crisis and deep recession begun in 2008. Other preoccupations of the outgoing Bush administration included Iraq, Afghanistan, Pakistan, Iran, broader Middle East issues, North Korea, and other foreign policy problems which came on top of serious adverse economic developments.

The global economic decline added to Chinese leaders' preoccupations in dealing with the results of the October 2007 Seventeenth Chinese Communist Party Congress and the Eleventh National People's Congress in March 2008. Those meetings and subsequent developments showed a collective leadership with Hu Jintao first among equals but not dominant that continued to debate appropriate ways to meet a wide variety of pressing economic, social, political, and other issues at home and abroad. The leaders sought with only mixed results lines of policy and action that avoided major cost and risk to China's ruling party leadership while endeavoring to promote Chinese development and the stability of one-party rule. There remained uncertainty about the major leadership transition expected at the Eighteenth Congress in 2012—a serious matter in an authoritarian political system like China's.[27]

The U.S. and Chinese administrations worked hard to use multiple formal dialogues, high-level meetings and communications, and official rhetoric emphasizing the positive in the relationship in order to offset and manage negative implications from the many differences and issues that continued to complicate U.S.-China relations. Neither leadership emphasized the major differences over key policy issues regarding economic, military, and political questions.

Both administrations registered close collaboration over North Korea's nuclear weapons program. They worked in parallel to manage the fallout from Taiwan President Chen Shui-bian's repeated efforts to strengthen Taiwan's sovereignty and standing as a country separate from China. Chen's moves provoked China and were opposed by the United States. The U.S. and Chinese governments supported Taiwan's new president, Ma Ying-jeou, who pursued an overall easing of Taiwan-China-U.S. tensions over cross-strait issues. Meanwhile, much more limited collaboration between China and the United States influenced such international hot spots as Sudan, Iran, and Myanmar/Burma, with leaders on both sides speaking more about Sino-American cooperation than Sino-American differences over these sensitive international questions.[28]

Unfortunately for those hoping for significantly greater cooperation between the United States and China, dramatic increases in cooperation seemed absent because of major conflicting interests and disputes over a wide range of issues. Cautious U.S. and Chinese leaders seeking to avoid trouble with one another had a hard time overcoming these obstacles. Some disputes may be hard to control, resulting in surprising upsurges in U.S.-China tensions.

As noted in chapter 1, China's many disagreements with the United States can be grouped into four general categories of disputes, which have complicated U.S.-China relations for years. China's moderation toward the United States since 2001 reduced the salience of some of these issues, but they remained important and were reflected in Chinese policies and actions. The risk-adverse Hu Jintao leadership appeared to have little incentive to accommodate the United States on these sensitive questions.

The four categories in priority order are: (1) opposition to U.S. support for Taiwan and involvement with other sensitive sovereignty issues, notably

Tibet; (2) opposition to U.S. efforts to change China's political system; (3) opposition to the United States playing the dominant role along China's periphery in Asia; and (4) opposition to many aspects of U.S. leadership in world affairs. Some specific issues in the latter two categories include U.S. policy in Iraq, Iran, and the broader Middle East; aspects of the U.S.-backed security presence in the Asia-Pacific; U.S. and allied ballistic missile defenses; U.S. pressure on such governments as Burma, North Korea, Sudan, Zimbabwe, Cuba, and Venezuela; U.S. pressure tactics in the United Nations and other international forums, and the U.S. position on global climate change.[29]

As noted in chapter 1, U.S. differences with China continue to involve clusters of often-contentious economic, security, political, sovereignty, foreign policy, and other issues. Economic issues center on inequities in the U.S. economic relationship with China that include a massive trade deficit, Chinese currency policies and practices, U.S. dependence on Chinese financing of U.S. government budget deficits, and Chinese enforcement of intellectual property rights. Security issues focus on the buildup of Chinese military forces and the threat they pose to U.S. interests in Taiwan and the broader Asia-Pacific. Political issues include China's controversial record on human rights, democracy, religious freedom, and family planning practices. Sovereignty questions involve disputes over the status of Taiwan, Tibet, Xinjiang, and Hong Kong. Foreign policy disputes focus on China's support for such "rogue" states as Sudan, Myanmar/Burma, Iran, Cuba, Zimbabwe, and Venezuela; and Chinese trade, investment, and aid to resource-rich and poorly governed states in Africa that undermines Western sanctions designed to pressure these governments to reform.[30]

Given the many issues they faced, the outgoing Bush administration was disinclined to take dramatic steps forward in relations with China. Such steps probably would have required compromises unacceptable to important U.S. constituencies and partners abroad. It was more advantageous to follow and reinforce the recent equilibrium along generally positive lines in U.S. policy and relations toward China.

Against this background, the outlook for U.S. relations with China at the end of the Bush administration seemed focused on sustaining the positive equilibrium developed during the Bush years. The most serious force for significant negative change seemed to be U.S. domestic debate over China. In its last years, the Bush administration was preoccupied with many issues and appeared tired and reactive. It had a harder time in its waning days in controlling the consequences of a broad range of U.S. interest groups and commentators that were sharply critical of various Chinese administration policies and practices. Such groups and critics also became more active and prominent as they endeavored to influence the policy agenda of the new U.S. administration as it came to power. They sought to push forward their various proposals before the incoming government set its policy agenda.

The U.S. election in November 2008 underlined a call for change.[31] The Democrats increased their majorities in both the House of Representatives and the Senate. The Democratic-controlled Congress at least in theory could muster the votes needed to halt filibusters and override presidential vetoes. Reminiscent of the efforts of Speaker Newt Gingrich and his Contract with America in 1995, such a Congress might be capable of setting the agenda of U.S. policy, including key issues in China policy.

After the elections, there were two key areas where this projected trend appeared to foreshadow possibly serious problems for U.S. relations with China.

Trade and Economic Relations

Organized labor and other key groups affiliated with the Democratic Party have been arguing for years that the U.S. economic relationship with China hurts American workers; they cite the massive U.S. trade deficit with China to underscore this point. Their arguments gain much greater political traction during a U.S. recession when overall unemployment rises.[32]

Organized labor and related groups also were important politically in the close race for the Democratic Party's presidential nomination. Neither of the leading Democratic contenders, Barack Obama and Hillary Clinton, could have afforded to alienate these political forces; they tended to appeal for their support with pledges to pursue tougher policies than the free-trade policies of the Bush administration. They sometimes sharply criticized China's economic policies as unfair to American workers. Meanwhile, many congressional incumbents and aspirants focused on adverse economic conditions and saw the very unbalanced trade relationship with China as a salient target in their campaign rhetoric.[33]

Charges of unfair Chinese economic practices leading to the massive U.S. trade deficit with China were supported by attacks on Chinese currency policies, intellectual property rights violations, and industrial and national security espionage. There was a danger of sharp American backlash as Chinese firms now move to use some of China's massive foreign exchange reserves to invest in U.S. companies and as they begin to enter sensitive U.S. markets such as autos.

Most economists see punitive U.S. laws and restrictions on trade and investment with China as counterproductive for U.S. national interests.[34] Nevertheless, the likelihood of such protectionist actions increased with the Democratic gains in the Congress and a Democratic president.

Climate Change

The Bush administration was the main target of burgeoning criticism in the United States and the world because of its record on environmental protection and climate change. All the U.S. presidential candidates and the vast majority of congressional contenders promised to shift U.S. policy dramatically. Such a shift after January 2009 could mean that China would become the new target of U.S. and perhaps international criticism regarding this set of sensitive issues.[35] China's recent diplomatic activism and arguments in international forums dealing with environmental protection and climate change may not assuage broad American concern regarding China's massively wasteful use of energy in the production of goods and services.[36] China has become the top greenhouse gas producer. If the United States faces up to its responsibilities on environmental protection and climate change, American officials and public opinion may expect no less of China. The United States seems to be prepared to help with the transfer of expertise and technology provided China can safeguard intellectual property rights and pay a fair price. Overall, American demands probably would mean greater costs for China either in implementing meaningful efforts to curb greenhouse gases or in bearing the consequences of being seen as an international outlier on this important issue.

Other Issues

Taiwan. Both China and the United States acknowledge that Taiwan poses the most sensitive issue in the relationship. During his eight years in office, Taiwan President Chen Shui-bian repeatedly pushed pro-independence initiatives that were opposed by Chinese and U.S. leaders. His replacement by President Ma Ying-jeou, who seeks to reach out to Beijing, helped to calm the waters in the strait and thereby reduce U.S.-China discord over Taiwan. However, it was easy to exaggerate how easily and how much progress will be achieved. In particular, Ma's national security plan advocated acquisition of over sixty advanced F-16 aircraft from the United States. President George H. W. Bush sold 150 F-16s to Taiwan in 1992.

The Bush government was under congressional pressure to go forward with the sale but was reluctant to do so. At the end of its term, it went forward with a large arms sales package that did not include several weapons systems desired by Taiwan, notably F-16 aircraft. China reacted strongly to the Bush administration action. It remains opposed to all U.S. arms sales to Taiwan, and how it would react to such a significant transfer is uncertain. The pressures for the sale may build and become an issue of controversy in the new U.S. government and in its relations with China.[37]

North Korea. North Korea had only begun to climb to the top rungs of U.S. policy concerns when the Bush administration left office. Few anticipated the scope and intensity of North Korean provocations and defiance in 2009, which prompted an Obama administration policy review and the seeking of actions from China that Beijing in the past had been very reluctant to do.

Episodes of U.S. hostility to China. Prevailing attitudes toward China in the United States seemed to make episodes of contention likely in the period ahead. Observers were correct in noting that the United States and China were so interdependent economically and had so many areas of growing cooperation internationally that a significant break between the two countries was unlikely. However, this situation did not preclude episodes of friction and contention generated from the United States that can pose substantial problems for China. Spikes of U.S. antagonism toward China occurred even in periods of otherwise good U.S. relations with China. When a Chinese oil company sought in 2005 to purchase the U.S. oil company Unocal, the outpouring of anti-China comment from the U.S. media and the Congress overwhelmed the sale. In 2007, toxic Chinese pet food, toys, health products, and other consumer goods produced a storm of media controversy, congressional hearings, and other investigations.[38] The outpouring of media coverage on the March 2008 uprisings in Tibet underlined the continuing tendency of the U.S. media to focus on reporting about aspects of China that the American public and their officials find objectionable. Annual Gallup polls of American opinion toward various countries show that a majority of Americans polled have an unfavorable view of China.[39] As noted earlier, interest groups, including many with an agenda very critical of China's policies and practices, are active in the initial year of the new U.S. government.

The Obama Administration and U.S.-China Relations

President Barack Obama came to power facing daunting domestic and foreign crises. The United States led world economies into steep decline in 2008 and continued falling in 2009. Active efforts by U.S. and other governments to deal with the causes and effects of the global financial crisis showed little sign of substantially reversing economic fortunes. A prolonged recession seemed likely.[40]

Economic calamity overshadowed the new U.S. government's preoccupation in the broader Middle East–Southwest Asian region. Anticipated withdrawals of U.S. combat forces from Iraq were balanced by significant increases in U.S. forces battling the Taliban in Afghanistan.[41] A weak Pakistan featured an ungoverned border region with Afghanistan that harbored al Qaeda and

Taliban militants working to overthrow the U.S.-backed administration in Kabul. Pakistani terrorists also threatened India. Developments in the Middle East stalled prospects for advancing peace amid deep regional and global concerns over Iran's apparently active pursuit of nuclear weapons.[42]

In the rest of the Asia-Pacific region, the global economic crisis put a premium on close U.S. collaboration with major international economies, notably Asian economies like China and Japan, in promoting domestic stimulus plans, rescuing failing economies, and avoiding egregious protectionism. How cooperative China and other Asian and world economic leaders would be in working with the United States to deal with the crisis remained open to question. On balance, it appeared from an American perspective in 2009 that no major stakeholder in the international economy, including China and the United States, had much to gain from pushing controversial policies that would further undermine international confidence in the existing economic system and thwart meaningful efforts at economic recovery.

To the surprise of many, North Korea climbed to the top of the Obama government's policy agenda through a string of provocative actions culminating in North Korea's withdrawal from the Six-Party Talks and its second nuclear weapons test in May. The Obama government had seemed poised to use the Six-Party Talks and bilateral discussion with North Korea in seeking progress in getting North Korea to fulfill its obligations under agreements signed in recent years. The escalating North Korean provocations and strident defiance of UN Security Council resolutions and international condemnation compelled a U.S. policy review. Obama government leaders from the president on down also consulted closely with concerned powers, notably key allies Japan and South Korea and China, in assuring a firm response from the UN Security Council in June that imposed sanctions in addition to those imposed after North Korea's first nuclear test and called for interdiction of suspected weapons shipments to and from North Korea. The United States also planned its own unilateral sanctions in order to pressure Pyongyang to halt the provocations and return to the negotiations. Available evidence in 2009 showed considerable skepticism that negative and positive incentives from the United States and other concerned powers would lead to lasting improvement in North Korea's behavior. Few were optimistic that the crisis atmosphere would subside soon.[43]

Meanwhile, longstanding U.S. concern with the security situation in the Taiwan Straits declined as the newly installed government of President Ma Ying-jeou reversed the pro-independence agenda of his predecessor in favor of reassuring China and building closer cross-strait exchanges. The Obama administration indicated little change from Bush administration efforts to support the more forthcoming Taiwan approach and avoid U.S. actions that would be unwelcome in Taipei and Beijing as they sought to ease tensions and facilitate communication.[44]

The Obama administration and the strong Democratic majorities in both houses of the Congress also gave high priority to promoting international efforts on the environment and climate change. Such efforts appeared ineffective without the participation of Asia's rising economies, particularly China, the world's largest emitter of greenhouse gases. An American approach of prolonged consultation and dialogue with China to come up with mutually acceptable approaches to these issues seemed likely.[45]

The Obama government seemed intent on building on the strengths in the U.S. leadership position in relations with Asia, including China, as it sought to remedy some of the perceived shortcomings in Bush administration policies. In general, Obama administration leaders saw the United States in a generally strong position in Asia as it dealt with China and regional issues.

Media and specialist commentary, as well as popular and elite sentiment in Asia, tended to emphasize the shortcomings of U.S. policy and leadership in Asia throughout much of the twenty-first century. Heading the list were widespread complaints regarding the Bush administration's hard-line policy toward North Korea, its military invasion and occupation of Iraq, and assertive and seemingly unilateral U.S. approaches on wide-ranging issues including terrorism, climate change, the United Nations, and Asian regional organizations. The United States appeared alienated and isolated, and increasingly bogged down with the consequences of its invasion of Iraq and perceived excessively strong emphasis on the so-called war against terrorism.[46]

By contrast, Asia's rising powers and particularly China seemed to be advancing rapidly. China used effective diplomacy and rapidly increasing trade and investment relationships backed by China's double-digit economic growth in order to broaden influence throughout the region. China also carried out steady and significant increases in military preparations.[47]

This basic equation of Chinese strengths and U.S. weaknesses became standard fare in mainstream Asian and Western media. It was the focus of findings of many books and reports of government departments, international study groups, and think tanks authored often by well-respected officials and specialists. The common prediction was that Asia was adjusting to an emerging China-centered order, and U.S. influence was in decline.[48]

Over time, developments showed the reality in the region was more complex. Japan clearly was not in China's orbit; India's interest in accommodation with China was very mixed and overshadowed by a remarkable upswing in strategic cooperation with the United States; Russian and Chinese interest in close alignment waxed and waned and appeared to remain secondary to their respective relationships with the West; and South Korea, arguably the area of greatest advance in Chinese influence at a time of major tensions in the U.S.-ROK relationship earlier in the decade, changed markedly beginning in 2004 and evolved to a situation of often wary and suspicious South Korean relations with China seen today.

Former U.S. officials pushed back against prevailing assessments of U.S. decline with a variety of tracts underlining the U.S. administration's carefully considered judgment that China's rise actually was not having a substantial negative effect on U.S. leadership in Asia, which remained healthy and strong.[49] As noted above, Bush administration officials increasingly rallied around this public position, first articulated by Robert Zoellick, saying further that the United States should encourage China to behave as a so-called responsible stakeholder in the international system. This line of approach was continued during the Obama administration.[50]

The basic determinants of U.S. strength and influence in Asia seen in the recent more balanced assessments of China's rise and U.S. influence in Asia involve the following factors:[51]

Security. In most of Asia, governments are strong, viable, and make the decisions that determine direction in foreign affairs. Popular, elite, and media opinion may influence government officials in policy toward the United States and other countries, but in the end the officials make decisions on the basis of their own calculus. In general, the officials see their governments' legitimacy and success resting on nation-building and economic development, which require a stable and secure international environment. Unfortunately, Asia is not particularly stable, and most governments privately are wary of and tend not to trust each other. As a result, they look to the United States to provide the security they need to pursue goals of development and nation-building in an appropriate environment. They recognize that the U.S. security role is very expensive and involves great risk, including large-scale casualties if necessary, for the sake of preserving Asian security. They also recognize that neither rising China nor any other Asian power or coalition of powers is able or willing to undertake even a fraction of these risks, costs, and responsibilities.

Economic. The nation-building priority of most Asian governments depends importantly on export-oriented growth. Chinese officials recognize this, and officials in other Asian countries recognize the rising importance of China in their trade; but they all also recognize that half of China's trade is done by foreign-invested enterprises in China, and half is processing trade—both features that make Chinese and Asian trade heavily dependent on exports to developed countries, notably the United States. In recent years, the United States has run a massive and growing trade deficit with China and a total trade deficit with Asia valued at over $350 billion at a time of an overall U.S. trade deficit of over $700 billion. Asian government officials recognize that China, which runs a large overall trade surplus, and other trading partners of Asia are unwilling and unable to bear even a fraction of the cost of such large trade deficits that nonetheless are very important for Asian governments. Obviously, the 2008–2009 global economic crisis is having an enormous impact on trade and investment. Some Asian officials are talking about relying more on domestic consumption, but tangible progress seems slow as they appear to be focusing on an eventual revival of world trade that would restore previous levels of export-oriented growth involving continued heavy reliance on the U.S. market.[52]

Government engagement and Asian contingency planning. The Obama administration inherited a U.S. position in Asia buttressed by generally effective Bush administration interaction with Asia's powers—China, Japan, and India. The U.S. Pacific Command and other U.S. military commands and organizations have been at the edge of wide-ranging and growing U.S. efforts to build and strengthen webs of military relationships throughout the region. Part of the reason for the success of these efforts has to do with active contingency planning by many Asian governments. As power relations change in the region, notably on account of China's rise, Asian governments generally seek to work positively and pragmatically with rising China on the one hand; but on the other hand they seek the reassurance of close security, intelligence, and other ties with the United States in case rising China shifts from its current generally benign approach to one of greater assertiveness or dominance.[53]

Nongovernment engagement and immigration. Unlike China and other powers in Asia, active American nongovernment interaction with Asia has developed for two centuries and continues today, putting the United States in a unique position where the American nongovernment sector has such a strong and usually positive impact on the influence the United States exerts in the region. Meanwhile, over forty years of generally color-blind U.S. immigration policy since the ending of discriminatory U.S. restrictions on Asian immigration in 1965 has resulted in the influx of millions of Asian migrants who call America home and who interact with their countries of origin in ways that undergird and reflect well on the U.S. position in Asia.

In sum, the findings of these assessments of U.S. strengths show that the United States is deeply integrated in Asia at the government and nongovernment level. U.S. security commitments and trade practices meet fundamental security and economic needs of Asian government leaders, and those leaders know it. The leaders also know that no other power or coalition of powers is able or willing to meet even a small fraction of those needs. Asian contingency planning seems to work to the advantage of the United States, while rising China has no easy way to overcome pervasive Asian wariness of Chinese longer-term intentions. On balance, the assessments show that the Obama administration can work to fix various problems in U.S. policy in Asia with confidence that U.S. leadership in the region remains broadly appreciated by Asian governments and unchallenged by regional powers or other forces. The new administration's initial interactions with Asia appeared to reflect this generally positive view.

In the case of China, the new U.S. government seemed prepared to build on what was deemed as an overall positive legacy from the Bush administration.[54] The pattern of dualism in U.S.-China relations continues as a central feature of the outwardly positive equilibrium in the post–Cold War period. Constructive and cooperative engagement on the one hand and contingency planning or hedging on the other remain important features of the equilibrium. They reflect the continued mix of converging and competing interests and prevailing leadership suspicions and cooperation.[55]

The exchange of visits by top-level officials followed the pattern in the latter years of the Bush administration in calling for deepening dialogue and development of "positive and constructive" relations. A positive atmosphere prevailed in meetings between Presidents Obama and Hu at international gatherings in 2009 and the summit meeting during the U.S. president's visit to China in November 2009. Nonetheless, the differences between the two countries are readily apparent on the U.S. side, where they are repeatedly highlighted by U.S. media and U.S. interest groups concerned about various features of Chinese governance and practice, and where the majority of Americans give an unfavorable rating to the Chinese government. They are less apparent in the more controlled media environment of China, though Chinese officials and government commentaries make clear strong opposition to U.S. efforts to support Taiwan and to foster political change in China as well as to key aspects of U.S. alliances and U.S. security presence and arrangements around China's periphery and U.S. positions on salient international issues ranging from the military use of space to fostering democratic change.[56]

The positive features of the relationship tend to outweigh the negatives because:

- Both governments gain from cooperative engagement—the gains include beneficial economic ties, as well as cooperation over North Korea, the war on terrorism, Pakistan, and even Taiwan. It also includes smaller progress on Iran and even less on Sudan and Myanmar/Burma.
- Both governments recognize that, because of ever-closer U.S.-China interdependence, focusing on negative aspects in U.S.-China relations would be counterproductive to their interests.

- Both governments recognize that, because of other major policy preoccupations they both have, focusing on negative aspects in U.S.-China relations would be counterproductive to their interests.

At bottom, it seems fair to conclude that the recent U.S. relationship with China rests upon a common commitment to avoid conflict, cooperate in areas of common interest, and prevent disputes from shaking the overall relationship.[57] Against this background, the Obama government seems most likely to advance relations with China in small ways. It probably will show sufficient resolve to avoid conflict with China over trade, currency, environmental, security, Taiwan, Tibet, human rights, and other issues that appear counterproductive for what seem to be more important U.S. interests in preserving a collaborative relationship with China and avoiding frictions with such an important economy at a time when international economic cooperation seems of utmost importance.[58]

Those in the United States who seek to give greater prominence to differences with China seem overwhelmed for now, particularly by the salience of the global economic crisis and the perceived U.S. need to be seen to cooperate with China in restoring international economic confidence. Events in China or U.S.-China relations could bring their issues to the fore, as they did in the 2008 Chinese crackdown on dissent and violence in Tibet.

8

Security Issues in
Contemporary U.S.-China Relations

IN THE COURSE OF U.S. NORMALIZATION WITH CHINA since the late 1960s, security issues moved from being the main source of converging interests between the United States and China to the main source of divergence and mutual distrust between the two countries. Throughout the entire period, security issues have never been uniformly positive or negative for the relationship; their implications usually have been mixed. However, the broad pattern shows important convergence of Sino-American security interests against the Soviet Union in the period from the late 1960s through the early 1980s. U.S.-China security ties were cut drastically after the 1989 Tiananmen crackdown. Since then the United States and China restored businesslike security ties and developed common ground on a variety of international security questions. These positive elements were offset by differences on a range of security issues. The differences arose against a background of changing Asian and international power relations caused in part by China's rising power and prominence in international affairs, and particularly by China's strong military modernization focused on Asian issues of key concern to the United States. China's growing military role in Asia was supported by expanding Chinese nuclear and unconventional attack capabilities and espionage directed at the United States.

Convergence against the Soviet Threat

As discussed in chapter 4, the United States and China aligned together after decades of intense Cold War conflict and confrontation because of common security interests in the face of an expanding threat posed by the Soviet Union. Maoist China was racked by factional leadership disputes and committed to radical domestic and foreign policies and practices, but the Chinese leadership saw the need and wisdom of working closely with the United States in the face of the pressure China was receiving from the USSR. The Nixon administration and later U.S. governments were prepared to put aside or play down a long list of American differences with China over foreign policy, economics, and values in order to give pride of place in American foreign policy to developing the new opening to China for the benefit of U.S. interests in Asian and world affairs challenged in particular by expanding Soviet power.[1]

Both governments judged they had a lot at stake in how they worked together and in parallel to deal with security dangers posed by the Soviet Union. China was particularly vocal in complaining repeatedly in the 1970s and early 1980s that the United States was not firm enough in dealing with Soviet expansion or that the United States was too interested in bilateral agreements with Moscow that would benefit the United States but have adverse consequences for China. It took years for Chinese leaders to overcome a previous assumption that the United States would be more likely to cooperate with the Soviet Union against Chinese interests than to cooperate with China against the USSR. American leaders were concerned during this period with the possibility of a Sino-Soviet rapprochement and the negative impact this would have on U.S. foreign policy and security. They worked hard to keep China on the U.S. side in an international arena seen heavily influenced by trilateral U.S.-Soviet-Chinese relations.[2]

The Shanghai Communiqué of 1972 and other official statements of both China and the United States during the 1970s and early 1980s made clear the large number of security as well as economic, political, and other issues that continued to divide the two countries. Despite secret U.S. concessions to China over Taiwan at the start of the Sino-American normalization process, the slow pace of U.S. withdrawal from official relations with Taiwan and the continued U.S. commitments to the island government were at the center of a set of key differences between the United States and China that were of fundamental importance to China. The United States was disappointed with China's position regarding the U.S. war in Vietnam. Chinese leaders seemed from the American perspective to straddle the fence in opening closer relations with the United States while continuing support for the Vietnamese Communists fighting Americans in Indochina.[3]

The two powers were at odds over the Korean Peninsula, where they were on opposite sides, China supporting Kim Il-song's North Korea and the United States sustaining a strong alliance with and large military presence in South Korea. The close U.S. alliance with Japan and China's avowed fear of revived Japanese "militarism" were important sources of differences between the United States and China, though China and Japan quickly normalized their relations in 1972, and China seemed more concerned in this period in shoring up Japanese resolve to join with the United States and China in struggling against the danger posed by the expanding Soviet Union. Elsewhere in international politics, where China's influence was comparatively small as Beijing was slowly rebuilding its international relationships tattered by the binge of self-righteous radicalism during the Cultural Revolution, Chinese leaders followed a path that focused opposition against the Soviet Union but also demonstrated strong differences with the United States. Chinese officials publicly opposed the two superpowers, the Soviet Union and the United States. The Chinese priority was on building a strong international united front against expanding Soviet "hegemonism," but they continued to register strong differences with U.S. policies in the Middle East, Africa, Latin America, and other parts of the developing world, as well as U.S. positions in international organizations and American views on international economic and political issues.[4]

Balancing American security interests with China and the Soviet Union was a repeated challenge for U.S. policy makers. The prevailing U.S. tendency to "play the China card," to lean closer to China in seeking U.S. advantage against the Soviet Union, remained controversial in American politics and government decision-making. Secretary of State Cyrus Vance and critics in and out of government saw U.S. interests better served by seeking negotiations and improved relations with the USSR through arms control and other agreements. China's actual utility in assisting the United States in dealing with the expanding Soviet power also seemed limited. What exactly China would do in assisting the United States in a security confrontation with the Soviet Union was subject to debate.[5] In addition, China's sometimes-strident positions and provocative actions against the USSR or its allies raised the danger of military conflict that alarmed some U.S. officials. For example, China's military invasion of Soviet-backed Vietnam in 1979 prompted numerous statements of disagreement from prominent Americans.[6]

How U.S. support for China in the face of the common danger posed by the Soviet Union would impact other important U.S. security issues remained controversial. The United States was reluctant to build close military ties with China; U.S. arms sales to the Chinese government were not an option until the early 1980s. Not only were such sales and the closer U.S. alignment with China seen as limiting U.S. options in relations with the Soviet Union, but U.S. arms sales to China also had implications for longstanding U.S. allies and associates in Asia who remained wary of Chinese intentions and expanding military capabilities. Nonetheless, the Carter administration and the early

Reagan administration continued efforts to solidify U.S. security and other relations with China on an anti-Soviet basis. The full extent of American security cooperation with China against the Soviet Union did not become clear until years later. It involved extensive Sino-American clandestine operations directed against Soviet forces occupying Afghanistan following the Soviet invasion of December 1979, and agreements allowing U.S. intelligence agents to monitor Soviet ballistic missile tests from sites in China.[7]

Tiananmen and Post–Cold War Divergence

U.S. sanctions against China in reaction to the Tiananmen crackdown focused heavily on the U.S.-China military relationship. The George H. W. Bush administration suspended military-to-military contacts and arms sales to China. U.S. legislation in February 1990 enacted into law sanctions imposed on U.S. arms sales and other military cooperation. In April, China cancelled what had been the most significant U.S. arms transfer to China, the so-called "Peace Pearl" program to upgrade avionics of Chinese fighter planes.[8]

The Clinton administration began to revive military-to-military meetings with China. However, relations were marred by the Sino-American military face-off in the Taiwan Strait as a result of China's provocative military exercises there in 1995–1996; the trashing of U.S. diplomatic properties in China following the U.S. bombing of the Chinese embassy in Belgrade in 1999; and, during the first months of the George W. Bush administration, the crash of the EP-3 U.S. surveillance aircraft with a Chinese fighter jet in 2001.[9]

During this period, Congress stuck to a harder line toward China than that of the administration. It passed into law strict limits on the types of military exchanges the United States could carry out with China and required reports on the purpose and scope of such exchanges. It also required classified and unclassified annual reports on the purpose and scope of China's military buildup and its implications for American interests.[10]

The U.S. reaction to the Tiananmen crackdown and the shifts in U.S. policy toward China and Taiwan as a result of the decline and demise of the Soviet Union and the emergence of newly democratic Taiwan raised fundamental security questions in China regarding the United States. Though U.S. administrations continued with varying vigor to pursue engagement with China, U.S. leaders repeatedly made clear their interest in promoting change in China's authoritarian political system. The top priority of the Chinese Communist Party leadership was to preserve their rule in China, and the Chinese military and broader security apparatus focused on this task accordingly. As a result, Chinese security and other leaders came to view the U.S. government and related nongovernment organizations and groups, notably the U.S. media, which encouraged and fostered democratic change in China, as a fundamental threat to this key Chinese national security goal.[11]

The shift in American support for Taiwan also was seen in China as fundamentally at odds with Chinese national security objectives regarding preservation of Chinese sovereign claims and security. The fact that the Clinton administration, seen by Chinese officials as sometimes irresolute on security issues, sent two aircraft carrier battle groups to face off against Chinese forces in the Taiwan area at the height of the Taiwan Strait crisis in 1996 had important lessons for Chinese national security planners. From that time forward, Chinese security planners seemed to have little doubt that a key aspect of Chinese military preparations to counter Taiwan's moves toward independence must involve building the military capability to impede or deter U.S. military intervention in a possible conflict between China and Taiwan. Meanwhile, the U.S. threat to Chinese national security and sovereignty also took other concrete forms for China as American leaders became more prominent in support for the Dalai Lama and his calls for greater Tibetan autonomy, and as they supported legislation and administrative actions pressing for democratic change and greater autonomy for Hong Kong as it passed from British to Chinese rule in 1997.[12]

Recent Developments: Some Convergence, Continued Wariness

Sino-American tensions over security issues involving Taiwan, Tibet, and continued one-party authoritarian rule in China have continued into the first decade of the twenty-first century. American complaints at this time, reviewed in chapter 6, included disputes over Chinese military assertiveness around its periphery, China's still-unsatisfactory record regarding proliferation of WMD; China's development of anti-satellite, cyber attack, and other military capabilities sensitive to the United States; Chinese espionage targeting U.S. defense systems and national security interests; and perceived secrecy and deception regarding the purpose and scope of China's continued strong drive toward military modernization. A broader challenge affecting these issues has been posed by China's rise to great power status in this decade. The rise of Chinese military power has particularly important implications for American interests and raises fundamental uncertainties that reinforce wariness and distrust in contemporary U.S.-China relations.

From the perspective of American defense planners and strategists, the Chinese military buildup of the past two decades has focused in considerable part on building a capability to impede and deny U.S. forces access to the

Taiwan area in the event of a China-Taiwan military conflict or confrontation. The scope of this "anti-access" effort seems to be broadening as Chinese military capabilities grow to include the South China Sea and East China Sea, where Chinese security forces periodically challenge and confront patrolling U.S. naval vessels and military aircraft. Related challenges appear in Chinese efforts to counter U.S. dominance in space and to use cyber attacks and other unconventional means to erode U.S. military capabilities.[13]

As noted in earlier chapters, the United States has a fundamental interest in sustaining naval and other access to East Asia. And since the Japanese attack on Pearl Harbor, it has undertaken the obligations of leadership in sustaining a favorable balance of power in the region in order to protect that access and other American interests. The conflicts of the Cold War allowed for an equilibrium to emerge in East Asia and the western Pacific where—in general terms and with some notable exceptions—the United States sustained dominance along the maritime rim of East Asia and the western Pacific, while continental Asia came to be dominated by China. Ten years ago, this stasis was labeled the "Geography of Peace" by international relations specialist Robert Ross.[14]

Today, the situation is changing. China has long chafed under superpower pressure along its periphery. Its military modernization gives top priority to upgrading power projection by air and naval forces along China's maritime borders. While the United States seemed satisfied with the stasis Ross discussed at the end of the 1990s, American concern with Chinese anti-access efforts grows in tandem with the increasing Chinese military capabilities to carry out the broadening scope of their anti-access goals.[15]

Key security issues involving Taiwan, Chinese one-party rule, sovereignty, and resistance to superpower presence along China's periphery provide the foundation for Chinese security differences with the United States and help to explain the suspicion and wariness that characterizes contemporary Sino-American relations. Of course, as explained in chapter 7, prevailing discourse between the U.S. and Chinese governments emphasizes the positive for a variety of mainly pragmatic reasons important to the respective interests of the two governments. Security differences are dealt with discreetly, notably in dialogues dealing with U.S.-China military contacts and security issues in Asian and world affairs.[16]

The two administrations also have developed considerable common ground on important security issues. China used to be seen by the United States as an outlier regarding issues of proliferation of weapons of mass destruction (WMD) and related delivery systems. Into the 1990s, China passed nuclear weapons technology and missile systems to Pakistan and engaged in suspicious nuclear technology cooperation and missile development and sales with Iran and other nations deemed hostile to the United States. Under pressure from the United States and reflecting recalibration of Chinese foreign policy and national security priorities, China moved to a position much more consistent with American interests on WMD proliferation.[17] Most notably, the United States and China have deepened cooperation and common ground in dealing with North Korea's nuclear weapons and ballistic missile programs and the danger they pose for stability on the Korean peninsula and elsewhere.[18] China also has worked cooperatively and in parallel with the United States in dealing with international terrorism following the terrorist attack on America in September 2001, in managing tensions between nuclear-armed Pakistan and India in South Asia, and in managing crises precipitated by pro-independence initiatives by Taiwan president Chen Shui-bian (2000–2008). China has endeavored to moderate and then support Western-backed efforts in the UN Security Council to curb Iran's suspected nuclear weapons development program. It also has been among the most active participants in sending security forces abroad as UN peacekeepers.[19]

Chinese growing accommodation of and cooperation with the United States over North Korea, WMD proliferation, Iran, and other sensitive issues seem related to the apparent decision of Chinese leaders in the current decade to deal carefully with complications that could arise with the United States as China rises in Asian and world affairs. Chinese leaders came to recognize that China's rising power and prominence could lead to strongly adverse reactions from the United States and other powers, especially in nearby Asia. They acknowledged that China's vocal opposition to various U.S. foreign policies in Asian and world affairs and repeated public opposition to U.S. hegemonism during the 1990s, when combined with rising Chinese power and various Chinese actions U.S. interests challenging U.S. security interests, could lead to balancing behavior by the United States that could severely complicate Chinese modernization efforts.[20]

Chinese Efforts at Reassurance—Strengths and Limitations

China's foreign policy approach shifted in the twenty-first century in order to take account of concerns over the possible negative reactions of the United States and other powers to China's rising international prominence and influence. More emphasis was given to reassuring China's neighbors, and new emphasis was given to reassuring the United States; all were told that China's rise would not affect their interests in adverse ways. Opposition to "hegemonism" (a code word for the United States used prominently by Chinese officials and media throughout the 1990s) had been one of the two main stated goals in major Chinese foreign policy pronouncements for decades. It was dropped from major Chinese foreign policy statements or received only passing reference. In its place emerged a policy of reassurance with a strong focus on the United States. The process of this evolution and change in Chinese foreign policy took several years and culminated in a major foreign policy document, "China's Peaceful Development Road," released by the Chinese government in December 2005. A few years later, China's foreign policy goal was recast by party leader Hu Jintao, who stressed China's seeking to promote a "harmonious world" as the Chinese administration strove to achieve greater harmony inside China. The net effect of the new emphasis on "harmony" reinforced Chinese efforts to reassure American and other foreign leaders concerned with the implications of China's rise.[21]

Beginning in 2003, Chinese leaders entered a new stage in China's efforts to define China's approach toward its neighboring countries and what China's approach meant for the United States and U.S. interests in Asia and the world. Premier Wen Jiabao addressed the topic of China's peaceful rise in a speech in New York on December 9, 2003. The exact purpose and scope of the new emphasis on China's "peaceful rise" remained less than clear. There seemed to be debate among Chinese leaders in 2004 and 2005 over whether Chinese officials should use the term "rise" to define China's approach to Asia and the world. Some Chinese officials and specialists voiced concern that this could be interpreted as a challenge to the United States and other powers, and should be avoided. They favored a more neutral term such as China's "peaceful development." The issue seemed to be settled with the Peaceful Development Road white paper released in December 2005.[22]

According to senior Party strategists and other officials, Chinese motives rested on a leadership review of the negative experiences of China's past confrontations with the United States, Asian neighbors, and other powers, and the negative experiences of earlier rising powers, such as Germany and Japan in the twentieth century. They concluded that China could not reach its goals of economic modernization and development through confrontation and conflict. As a result, they incorporated and advanced the moderate features of China's recent approach to Asia and the world into their broader definition of China's peaceful foreign policy approach.[23]

A central feature of the new Chinese approach was a very clear and carefully balanced recognition of the power and influence of the United States. In the 1990s, the Chinese leadership often worked against and confronted U.S. power and influence in world affairs. China resisted the U.S. superpower-led world order, seeking a multi-polar world of several powers where China would enjoy more influence and room for maneuver. By contrast, in this decade, Chinese leaders reevaluated this approach and adopted a more pragmatic attitude to the continued unipolar world led by the United States.[24]

Greater pragmatism and a strong desire to offset views in the United States that saw rising China as a competitor and a threat prompted Chinese leaders and officials to narrow sharply their view of areas of difference with the United States. They avowed that most differences with the United States now centered on the Taiwan issue and U.S. continued support for Taiwan. The wide range of other Chinese complaints about U.S. "hegemonism" in the post–Cold War period was said to be reduced. This seemed to conform to actual Chinese practice, though at times there were strong rhetorical attacks in the Chinese media against U.S. policies and practices not related to Taiwan.[25]

In this improved atmosphere, Chinese leaders sought to build closer ties with America. They wished to integrate China more closely in the Asian and world system, which they saw as likely to continue to be dominated by U.S. power for many years to come. They pursued closer partnership with the U.S. leaders and wanted to avoid taking steps that would cause the U.S. leaders to see China as a danger or threat that would warrant a concerted U.S. resistance to Chinese development and ambitions. At the same time, they were not abandoning their past differences with U.S. hegemonism. They still disapproved of perceived U.S. domination and unilateralism seen in U.S. practices in Iraq, U.S. missile defense programs, U.S. strengthening alliance relations with Japan, NATO expansion, and other areas that were staples in the repertoire of Chinese criticism of U.S. practices in the 1990s. But Chinese officials were not prepared to raise such issues as significant problems in U.S.-China relations, unless they impinged directly on core Chinese interests. As a result, most important Chinese criticism of U.S. policy focused on issues related to disputes over Taiwan.[26]

According to Chinese officials and specialists, Chinese leaders pursued the peaceful approach because they needed the appropriate environment to deal with massive internal difficulties and to avoid creating foreign opposition as China developed greater economic and other power and influence. Chinese leaders were said to judge that China faced a period of "strategic opportunity" to pursue its important and complicated nation-building tasks without major distractions, and they wanted to assure that complications and distractions did not emerge in China's relations with the United States. The duration of this strategic opportunity was said to include the first two decades of the twenty-first century.[27]

Whether or not the new emphasis on reassurance to the United States would work effectively was uncertain, according to Chinese officials and specialists. Domestically, it was uncertain whether nationalistic Chinese public opinion would uniformly accept the newly moderate approach to the United States. The viability of the new approach also was seen to depend on forces outside China that were capable of taking actions that would seriously disrupt Chinese foreign relations. The list of potential disrupters included leaders in North Korea, Taiwan, Japan, India, and Russia.[28]

Because of its perceived power and influence, the United States loomed large in Chinese calculation of possible problems for China's peaceful foreign policy approach. In general, the success or failure of the Chinese initiative depended on the reaction of the United States. If U.S. policy turned from the recent trend of pragmatically seeking convergence with China and resumed an approach of viewing China as a strategic competitor, Chinese leaders were thought likely to reevaluate their foreign policy and adopt a more confrontational posture in return. This was seen as especially likely if U.S. hardening affected Chinese interest in Taiwan.[29]

Chinese officials and specialists were well aware that there remained broad segments of U.S. opinion and interest groups disposed to be negative and suspicious of China and its policies.[30] Many American groups had participated actively in the vocal debates over U.S. China policy in the 1990s and saw a wide range of continuing differences between China and the United States over political, economic, security, and other issues. In the view of these Americans, the U.S.-China relations remained the most complicated and contentious U.S. bilateral relationship after the Cold War. The major shift in U.S. strategic attention to the war on terrorism and the conflicts in Iraq and Southwest Asia had distracted attention away from China, but had not ended suspicion and wariness by many Americans.

These Americans were not inclined to accept without careful verification Chinese assurances of peaceful intent. The new Chinese emphasis on reassurance and peaceful approach did not necessarily assuage American critics of China. For example, U.S. security planners and related specialists in intelligence and other departments in the U.S. government and supporting nongovernment agencies devoted extensive and continuing attention to potential or real threats from China. This came particularly in response to the Chinese military buildup after the Taiwan Strait crisis of 1995–1996, and the accompanying stream of rhetoric and articles by Chinese strategists and other commentators pointing to China's willingness and ability to resort to various means of asymmetrical warfare in order to defeat U.S. forces should they intervene in a Taiwan contingency. As a result, the willingness of these U.S. government and nongovernment specialists to take at face value Chinese assertions of peaceful intent were balanced by their continued awareness that Chinese military forces continued to add sophisticated capabilities to PLA forces targeted at Taiwan and at U.S. forces that would intervene in a Taiwan contingency. Without explicitly addressing China's military doctrine, force structure, and increased military capabilities, China's new peaceful approach to the United States and others was not very meaningful to these Americans. They judged it difficult for the United States to be a true partner of a country that continued to develop and expand military capabilities targeted at Americans.[31]

Chinese National Security Strategy and Military Modernization

An important reason for American wariness of Chinese intentions was the apparent disconnect between China's national development policy and China's national security policy. Chinese officials were the first to highlight that China in recent years has crafted a relatively clear national development policy. That Chinese approach was laid out authoritatively in the December 2005 "China's Peaceful Development Road." The approach is consistent with the thrust of Chinese leadership pronouncements since 2003, emphasizing Chinese leaders' determination to avoid trouble abroad and to seek international cooperation and a harmonious world order as China develops and rises peacefully in importance in Asian and world affairs in the twenty-first century.[32]

Unfortunately, the December 2005 document makes no reference to military conflict, the role of the rapidly modernizing PLA, and other key national security questions. When asked about this, one senior Chinese Foreign Ministry official said in May 2006 that China's national security policy is less clearly developed than China's national development policy.[33] In fact, however, the broad outlines of Chinese national security policy are fairly clearly laid out in official Chinese documents and briefings.[34] Chinese national security documents and briefings, and the remarkable recent advances in China's military modernization in the post–Cold War period, are in the lead among Chinese statements and behaviors that have called into question just how peaceful and cooperative China's approach to Asia and the world actually will be and what the implications for U.S. interests in Asian and world affairs might be.[35]

Paul Godwin and other specialists on the Chinese military pointed out apparent contrasts and contradictions in recent Chinese official pronouncements and actions dealing with trends in international security. As noted above, authoritative Chinese foreign policy pronouncements emphasized China's view of an emerging harmonious world order in which China was rising peacefully in national strength and international influence. China often was seen as occupying its most influential position in world affairs in the modern era. In contrast, white papers on national security,[36] recent public presentations by authoritative Chinese military representatives, and the continuation of an impressive buildup and modernization of the Chinese military forces in recent years revealed Chinese leadership's strong concern about China's security in the prevailing regional and international order. This concern continued despite over fifteen years of double-digit percentage increases in China's defense budgets and despite the view of many foreign specialists that China was becoming Asia's undisputed leading military power and an increasingly serious concern to American security planners as they sought to preserve stability and U.S. leadership in Asia.[37]

Chinese military modernization programs have been underway for twenty-five years. They have reached the point where they strongly suggest that the objective of the Chinese leadership is to build Asia's most powerful defense force.[38] China's military growth complicated China's relations with the United States and some Asian neighbors, notably Taiwan and Japan. Leaders from the United States and some Asian countries were not persuaded by Chinese leadership pledges to pursue the road of peace and development. They saw Chinese national security policies and programs as real or potential threats to their security interests.[39]

Chinese national security pronouncements duly acknowledged that with the end of the Cold War, the danger of global war—a staple in Chinese warning statements in the 1970s and 1980s—ended. However, recent Chinese national security statements rarely highlighted the fact that Chinese defense policy was being formulated in an environment less threatening to China than at any time in the last two hundred years. Typically, in the December 2004 white paper on national defense, the international system was represented as stable, but "factors of uncertainty, instability, and insecurity" were viewed as increasing.[40]

PLA pronouncements and Western scholarship made clear that the United States remained at the center of the national security concerns of Chinese leaders.[41] Authoritative PLA briefings in 2008 presented growing U.S. military power as the most serious complication for China's international interests, China's main security concern in the Asian region, and the key military force behind Chinese security concerns over Taiwan, Japan, and other neighbors.[42]

Chinese statements and the PLA buildup opposite Taiwan underlined that Taiwan was the most likely area of U.S.-China military conflict. The United States and its close ally Japan were portrayed as the principal sources of potential regional instability in Asia. Japan was explicitly criticized for various increased military activities and for its alleged interference in Taiwan.[43]

PLA and other Chinese officials registered strong determination to protect Chinese territory and territorial claims, including areas having strategic resources such as oil and gas. As Chinese-Japanese and other territorial conflicts involving energy resources in the East and South China Seas grew in scope and intensity, they intruded ever more directly on these PLA priorities. Chinese concerns increased over U.S. and allied forces controlling sea lines of communication, which were essential for increasing oil flows to China. The Chinese administration appeared uncertain as to how serious was the strategic danger posed by the vulnerability of China's energy flows from the Middle East and Africa through the Strait of Malacca and other chokepoints in Southeast Asia, and what should be done about it. Chinese national security officials openly debated these issues.[44] The Chinese administration pursued solutions, such as overland oil and gas pipelines that would bypass the Strait of Malacca and the steady buildup of Chinese naval capabilities, including the development of Chinese aircraft carriers, that would provide more military capability to protect Chinese trade, energy flows, and other maritime communications.[45]

U.S. Influence on China's Defense Modernization

A factor that adds substantially to the uncertainty in U.S.-China security relations and to the mutual wariness that characterizes U.S.-China relations on these issues involves the actions of the United States and how they are perceived by Chinese leaders. Given recent history, the concern Chinese leaders have had over the strategic intentions of the United States regarding China and Chinese interests concerning Taiwan, Japan, Asia, and world affairs is not unwarranted. The George W. Bush administration worked more closely with Taiwan's government in efforts to support Taiwan's defense against China than any U.S. administration since the break in official U.S. relations with Taiwan in 1979. It also worked more closely in defense collaboration with Japan, which focused on Taiwan and other possible contingencies regarding China, than at any time since the normalization of U.S. and Japanese relations with China in the 1970s. Policy statements such as the National Security Strategy of the United States of 2002 and the Quadrennial Defense Report of 2006 made clear that the United States military was able and willing to take steps to sustain Asian stability in the face of possible adverse consequences of China's rising military strength. Bush administration leaders emphasized U.S. uncertainty over China's longer-term strategic intentions; they affirmed they were not fully persuaded by Chinese pronouncements on peace and development and remained unsure whether China will be a friend or a foe of the United States. They built up U.S. forces in Asia and collaborated with Japan, Australia, and other allies and partners including India, in part to ensure that U.S. interests and Asian stability will be sustained in the face of possible disruptive or negative actions by Chinese military forces.[46]

In this context, it appeared reasonable for Chinese leaders to carry out the acquisition, development, and advancement of military capabilities specifically designed to defeat U.S. forces, especially if they were to intrude in a confrontation regarding China's avowed top priority, restoring Taiwan to Chinese sovereignty. And as the Chinese leaders devoted ever-higher priority to this military buildup, the United States advancement of its military deployments and defense cooperation with Taiwan, Japan, and others also seemed logical in order to deter Chinese attack and preserve stability. Of course, the result was an escalating arms race and defense preparations that seemed very much at odds with the harmonious international environment Chinese leaders sought to nurture and sustain. In effect, the respective Chinese and U.S. defense buildups and preparations regarding Taiwan demonstrated that Chinese leaders were not prepared to pursue uniformly "the road to peace and development" set forth in the document "China's Peaceful Development Road." The emphasis on peace and development and a harmonious international environment clearly were goals of Chinese foreign policy, but Chinese leaders at the same time were hedging their bets, notably with an impressive array of military acquisitions that provided capabilities they judged necessary.[47]

Recent Trends and Prospects in Military Modernization

Overall, Chinese defense acquisition and advancement showed broad ambitions for Chinese military power. While they appeared focused recently on dealing with U.S. forces in the event of a Taiwan contingency, these forces can be used by Chinese leaders as deemed appropriate in a variety of circumstances.

Salient Chinese defense acquisitions and modernization efforts include: [48]

- Research and development in space systems to provide wide area intelligence, surveillance, and reconnaissance, and the development of anti-satellite systems to counter the surveillance and related efforts of potential adversaries; development of cyber attack and means of defense;
- Cruise missile acquisitions and programs that improve the range, speed, and accuracy of Chinese land-, air-, and sea-launched weapons;
- Ballistic missile programs that improve the range, survivability (through mobile systems in particular), reliability, accuracy, and response times of tactical, regional, and intercontinental-range weapons to augment or replace current systems; development of ballistic missiles with warheads capable of targeting naval surface combatants;

- Construction and acquisition of advanced conventional-powered submarines with subsurface-launched cruise missiles and guided torpedoes, and nuclear-powered attack and ballistic missile submarines to augment or replace older vessels in service;
- Development and acquisition of more capable naval surface ships armed with advanced anti-ship, antisubmarine, and air-defense weapons;
- Air force advances, including hundreds of modern multi-role fighters, advanced air-to-air missiles, airborne early warning and control system aircraft, aerial refueling capabilities, and unmanned aerial vehicles;
- Air-defense systems involving modern surface-to-air missiles and air-defense fighters;
- Improved power projection for ground forces, including more sea- and airlift capabilities, special operations forces, and amphibious warfare capabilities;
- Research and development of defense information systems and improved command, control, communications, and computer systems; and
- Increase in the tempo and complexity of exercises in order to make the PLA capable in joint interservice operations involving power projections, including amphibious operations.

The Chinese advances mean that no single Asian power can match China's military power on continental Asia. With the possible exception of Japan, no Asian country will be capable of challenging China's naval and air power in maritime East Asia. Should Beijing choose to deploy naval and air forces to patrol the sea lines of communications in the Indian Ocean, only India conceivably would be capable of countering China's power.

Looking to the future, it is possible to bound the scope of China's military buildup. Available evidence shows that it is focused on nearby Asia. A major possible exception is the long-range nuclear weapons systems that target outside Asia, notably the United States. China has used these to deter the United States and other potential adversaries by demonstrating a retaliatory, second-strike capability against them. Other challenges with implications beyond nearby Asia involve cyber attack and anti-satellite weapons.[49]

The objectives of the Chinese military buildup seem focused first on Taiwan, preventing its move toward independence and assuring that China's sovereignty will be protected and restored. More generally, Chinese forces can be deployed to defeat possible threats or attacks on China, especially China's economically important eastern coastline. Apart from conflict over Taiwan, Chinese forces are designed to deal with a range of so-called local war possibilities. These could involve territorial disputes with Japan, Southeast Asian countries, or India, or instability requiring military intervention in Korea.

Meanwhile, the Chinese military plays a direct role in Chinese foreign policy, which seeks to spread Chinese international influence, reassure neighboring countries and others of Chinese intentions, and nurture an international environment that will allow China to rise in power and influence without major disruption. This role likely will involve continued active diplomacy by Chinese military officials; increasing numbers of military exercises with Asian and other countries; some Chinese arms sales to and training of foreign military forces; and more active participation by Chinese national security officials in regional and other multilateral security organizations and agreements.[50]

The Chinese military is on course to continue a transformation from its past strategic outlook, that of a large continental power requiring large land forces for defense against threats to borders. The end of the threat from the Soviet Union and the improvement of China's relations with India, Vietnam, and others have eased this concern. China is likely to move further away from a continental orientation requiring large land forces to a combined continental/maritime orientation requiring smaller, more mobile, and more sophisticated forces capable of protecting China's inland and coastal periphery. Unlike the doctrine of protracted land war against an invading enemy prevalent until the latter years of the Cold War, Chinese doctrine probably will continue its more recent emphasis on the need to demonstrate an ability to strike first in order to deter potential adversaries and to carry out first strikes in order to gain the initiative in the battlefield and secure Chinese objectives.

To fulfill these objectives, Chinese forces will need, and will further develop, the ability to strike or respond rapidly; to take and maintain the initiative in the battlefield; to prevent escalation; and to resolve the conflict quickly and on favorable terms. Chinese military options will include preemptive strikes and the use of conventional and nuclear forces to deter and coerce adversaries. Chinese forces will expand power-projection capabilities, giving Chinese forces a solid ability to deny critical land and sea access (for example, Taiwan Strait) to adversaries, and providing options for force projection further from Chinese borders.[51]

To achieve these objectives, Chinese conventional ground forces will evolve, consistent with recent emphasis, toward smaller, more flexible, highly trained, and well-equipped rapid reaction forces with more versatile and well-developed assault, airborne, and amphibious power-projection capabilities. Special operations forces will play an important role in these efforts. Navy forces will build on recent advances with more advanced surface combatants and submarines having better air defense, antisubmarine warfare, and anti-ship capabilities. Their improved weaponry of cruise missiles and torpedoes, an improved naval air force, and greater replenishment-at-sea capabilities will broaden the scope of their activities and pose greater challenges to potential adversaries. Air forces will grow with more versatile and modern fighters, longer-range interceptor/strike aircraft, improved early warning and air defense, and longer-range transport, lift, and midair refueling capabilities.

These forces will be used increasingly in an integrated way consistent with an emphasis on joint operations that involves more sophisticated command, control, communications, computers, intelligence, and strategic reconnaissance (C4ISR), early warning, and battlefield management systems. Improved airborne and satellite-based systems will improve detection, tracking, targeting, and strike capabilities, and enhanced operational coordination of the various forces.

Chinese strategic planners are sure to build on the advantages Chinese strategic missile systems provide. Estimates vary, but it appears likely that Chinese plans call for more than 1,500 short-, medium-, and intermediate-range solid-fueled, mobile ballistic missiles (with a range under four thousand miles), and short-range cruise missiles, with increased accuracy, and some with both nuclear and conventional capabilities. China is also modernizing a small number of longer-range nuclear missiles capable of hitting the continental United States, and seems likely to develop a viable submarine-launched nuclear missile that would broaden Chinese nuclear options. Chinese nuclear missiles will have smaller and more powerful warheads with potential multiple independently targeted reentry vehicles or multiple reentry vehicle capabilities. The emphasis on modern surveillance, early warning, and battle management systems with advanced C4ISR assets seen in Chinese planning regarding conventional forces also applies to nuclear forces.

These advances will build on China's existing military abilities. They pose a long list of serious concerns for the United States, as well as Taiwan, Japan, and some other Chinese neighbors, and an overall strategic reality of increasing Chinese military power that influences the strategic outlook of most Chinese neighbors. Those abilities include:

- The ability to conduct intensive, short-duration air and naval attacks on Taiwan, as well as prolonged air, naval, and possibly ground attacks. China's ability to prevail against Taiwan is seen as increasing steadily, especially given lax defense preparedness and political division in Taiwan. Massive U.S. military intervention is viewed as capable of defeating a Chinese invasion, but Chinese area denial capabilities could substantially impede and slow the U.S. intervention.
- Power-projection abilities to dislodge smaller regional powers from nearby disputed land and maritime territories and the ability to conduct air and sea denial operations for two hundred miles along China's coasts.

- Strong abilities to protect Chinese territory from invasion, to conduct ground-based power projection along land borders against smaller regional powers, and to strike civilian and military targets with a large and growing inventory of ballistic missiles and medium-range bombers armed with cruise missiles.
- Limited ability to project force against the territory of militarily capable neighboring states, notably Russia, India, and Japan.
- Continued ability to deter nuclear and other attacks from the United States and Russia by means of modernized and survivable Chinese nuclear missile forces capable of striking at these powers.

As China's military capabilities continue to grow more rapidly than those of any of its neighbors, and as China solidifies its position as Asia's leading military power, the situation clearly poses serious implications for, and some complications in, China's foreign policy. As we have discussed, Chinese officials have worked hard and with some success to persuade skeptical neighbors and the United States that China's rising power and influence will be peaceful and of benefit to all. However, many neighboring officials and those in the United States, sometimes publicly but more often privately, remain concerned.

The history of the use of force in Chinese foreign policy provides little assurance to Americans or others that China's current peaceful emphasis will be sustained. The Chinese government has resorted to the use of force in international affairs more than most governments in the modern period. The reasons have varied and include Chinese determination to: deter perceived superpower aggression; defend Chinese territory and territorial claims; recover lost territory; and enhance China's regional and global stature. Studies of Chinese leaders' strategic thinking have led to the conclusion that modern Chinese leaders, like those in the past, have been more inclined than not to see the use of military force as an effective instrument of statecraft.[52]

Though facing superpower adversaries with much greater military might, Mao Zedong frequently initiated the use of military force to keep the more powerful adversary off balance and to keep the initiative in Chinese hands. Deng Xiaoping was much more focused than Mao on conventional Chinese nation-building and sought to foster a peaceful environment around China's periphery in order to pursue Chinese economic modernization. However, Deng also undertook in 1979 strong Chinese military action against Soviet-backed Vietnam, and he continued for several years to confront Soviet power throughout China's periphery despite China's military weakness relative to the Soviet superpower. In the post–Cold War period, Chinese officials judged that the Taiwan president's visit to the United States in 1995 so challenged Chinese interests that it warranted nine months of military tensions in the

Taiwan Straits. These tensions included live-fire military exercises, ballistic missile tests near Taiwan ports, and a private warning from a senior Chinese military leader of China's determination to use nuclear weapons to deter U.S. intervention in a Taiwan confrontation.[53]

China's growing stake in the international status quo and its dependence on smooth international economic interchange are seen to argue against Chinese leaders' resorting to military force to achieve international objectives. At the same time, the rapid development of Chinese military capabilities to project power and the change in Chinese doctrine to emphasize striking first to achieve Chinese objectives are seen to increase the likelihood of Chinese use of force to achieve the ambitions and objectives of the Chinese administration. Against this background, it is not surprising that an active debate continues in the United States and elsewhere about Chinese national security intentions and whether they will override the Chinese administration's public emphasis on promoting peace and development in Chinese foreign affairs. Prudence argues for increased U.S. defense preparations in the face of China's rise. As those American efforts continue, they reinforce longstanding Chinese suspicions that the positive hand of U.S. engagement is accompanied by the negative hand of U.S. containment. Deeply rooted Chinese suspicions of U.S. intentions and policies are reinforced.

In the recent period of pragmatic accommodation between the U.S. and Chinese governments, Chinese and American security officials have tended to register their reservations and concerns in dialogues or less prominent briefings and statements. As far as Chinese concerns and differences with the United States on security issues are concerned, fairly typical were briefings by a delegation from the Academy of Military Sciences (AMS) visiting Washington, D.C., in October 2008. The Chinese delegates took aim at a long list of U.S. security activities that concerned China and were seen by the AMS delegates to underline a U.S. security posture "hostile" to China. The delegates wanted the United States to disavow and abandon these alleged aspects of its security posture. They included:

- U.S. statements and actions seen by China to show that the United States viewed China as a potential adversary, that it sought to change China's authoritarian political system, and that it endeavored to complicate and hold back China's rising international role;
- Perceived U.S. support for Taiwan independence, U.S. refusal to support Taiwan's reunification with China, and U.S. use of Taiwan as a "card," a source of leverage, in negotiations with China;
- U.S. support for forces in Tibet and Xinjiang that undermine Chinese sovereignty;

- U.S. force deployments and defense arrangements in Asia that surround China with adverse strategic pressures;
- Strengthened U.S.-Japan alliance that is directed at countering rising China;
- U.S. nuclear weapons strategy which sees China as an enemy;
- U.S. and Japanese ballistic missile defense efforts that are targeted against China's growing ballistic missile capabilities; and
- U.S.-backed Western arms embargo against China.

Uncertainty over Asian Security and Regional Dynamics

One other factor strengthening Chinese and U.S. wariness and distrust over security and other issues despite China's recent emphasis on reassuring the United States and others about Chinese moderation and peaceful intentions involves the complicated and uncertain strategic environment in Asia. The post–Cold War order in Asia is not clear or set. It is subject to an array of variables that could push the security situation and power dynamics in the region in very different directions. What this means is that the current balance in Chinese priorities, giving public emphasis to moderation and reassurance, while sustaining a strong defense buildup in a de facto arms race with the United States, could change as the overall situation in Asia changes. It also means that U.S. policy and practice could change in order to take account of changing regional dynamics, perhaps leading to greater tension in Sino-American relations. Obviously, future developments in Asia could result in greater convergence between the United States and China. Unfortunately, the recent security dynamics between China and the United States and the mutual military buildups of Chinese and U.S. forces underline recent factors that make both sides wary of being put at a disadvantage as a result of the uncertain and shifting balances in Asia.[54]

The post–Cold War strategic environment in Asia remains uncertain because it is influenced by a variety of factors with uncertain trajectories. In general there appear to be five main determinants or sets of determinants that affect the recent policy environment in the Asia-Pacific region in ways relevant to China, the United States, and their policies and concerns with each other over security and other issues:

1. Reactions to changes in major regional power relationships, including China's rising power; India's rising power; Japan's on-again, off-again international assertiveness following a prolonged period of economic

stagnation and political weakness; and Indonesia's slow comeback from weakness and leadership drift;

2. Regional concern about sustaining economic growth amid growing challenges of economic globalization and related freer flow of information;

3. Growing regional interest in and convergence around sub-regional and regional multilateral groups and organizations that address important economic and security concerns of Asia-Pacific countries;

4. Regional reactions to broad security changes brought about by the global war on terror begun in 2001 and by changes on the Korean Peninsula prompted mainly by North Korea's provocative pursuit of nuclear weapons, ballistic missiles, and other weapons; and

5. Regional concern over U.S. security, economic, and political policies and objectives, ranging from apprehension over perceived excessive U.S. activism, unilateralism, and pressures on the one hand to worries over possible U.S. pullbacks and withdrawal from Asia-Pacific affairs on the other.[55]

With the exception of the global war on terror, these determinants are not new, though all have become stronger in recent years. They have led to more fluid security and power relationships in the Asia-Pacific region than at any time since the Cold War. Taken together, the determinants provide impetus for greater activism by Asian-Pacific governments to foster their interests using an often-wide array of means amid an increasingly challenging and fluid environment. Their effect on U.S.-China relations has been to prompt greater activism by both powers and to sustain mutual wariness and uncertainty amid changing regional power dynamics.[56]

9

Economic and Environmental Issues in Contemporary U.S.-China Relations

T HE RAPID GROWTH OF THE CHINESE ECONOMY and close integration of Chinese development into the global economy have been the most salient accomplishments of the reforms pursued by Chinese leaders since the death of Mao. China's economic modernization has had a staggering impact on the lives of Chinese people. It is the foundation of the legitimacy of the ruling Chinese Communist Party, the source of China's growing military power, and the main reason for China's international prominence in the early twenty-first century. The implications of Chinese economic development also have had negative features at home and abroad, notably regarding trade disputes and environmental protection.[1]

As the world's leading economy, source of foreign investment and technology, and importer of Chinese products, the United States has had an important influence on and in turn has been influenced in important ways by China's economic advance and integration into existing international economic structures and interactions. On the whole, the burgeoning Sino-American economic relationship has had a positive effect on relations between the two countries. In the post–Cold War period, it has replaced the strategic cooperation between the United States and China against the Soviet Union that had provided the key foundation of U.S.-China cooperation in the 1970s and 1980s. The two world economies have become increasingly interdependent. They have become so salient for each country's development that by the first decade of the twenty-first century, hints of serious economic dispute or confrontation between the great economic powers had profound impacts on world markets detrimental to the well-being of each country.[2]

The rapid growth of China's economy and U.S.-China economic relations have largely conformed with and been driven by forces of international economic globalization. The overall process has had profound effects, both positive and negative, on broad swaths of opinion, economic, and other interest groups, and political leaders in both societies. On the whole, China's rapid growth and rise to great power status as a leading world economy have shown the process in recent years as highly beneficial to China's interests. The Chinese administration has generally eschewed major initiatives that have the potential to disrupt existing economic relationships seen as largely beneficial for Chinese interests.[3]

Complaints and initiatives to change existing economic relations have come in recent years largely from the U.S. side of the Sino-American relationship. They were particularly salient in the wake of the Tiananmen crackdown when the U.S. administration and the Congress considered whether to place conditions on U.S. provision of most favored nation trading status for China. Those efforts ended in U.S. agreement with China on China's entry into the WTO and the passage of U.S. legislation granting China permanent normal trade status in 2000.[4]

More recent U.S. initiatives and complaints reflect a wide range of U.S. interests and constituencies concerned with perceived unfair or disadvantageous aspects of the massive U.S.-China economic relationship. They are supported by varying numbers of congressional members and generally less vocal officials in the U.S. government. The U.S. administration has followed a pattern of dealing with such economic and trade disputes through a variety of bilateral discussions and dialogues with Chinese counterparts. The Chinese administration favors this approach in dealing with these and other issues. It reacts negatively to American public pressure or U.S. policy initiatives on trade and related economic issues which it tends to see as protectionist or otherwise adverse to Chinese interests. Chinese officials also were openly critical of U.S. financial management and other policies that negatively affected China's economy in the 2008–2009 global financial crisis and recession.[5]

Periodic U.S. complaints and initiatives on economic and trade issues often cause public U.S. disagreements with China as the United States presses for change and China resists U.S. demands on various economic questions. The overall impact of the disputes and complaints has done little to change the direction of closer integration of the U.S. and Chinese economies, but they have challenged and served as a drag on efforts by the U.S. and Chinese governments to advance positive aspects of the relationship.[6]

China's Economic Importance

Since the beginning of economic reforms following the death of Mao Zedong in 1976, China has become one of the world's fastest-growing economies. From 1979 to 2007, the average annual growth rate of China's gross domestic product (GDP) was over 9.8 percent. The Chinese economy in 2007 was nearly fourteen times larger than it was in 1979, and per capita GDP was more than ten times larger.[7]

Economists generally attribute much of China's rapid economic growth to two main factors: large-scale capital investment (financed by large domestic savings and foreign investment); and rapid productivity growth. The two factors appear to have worked together during the reform period. Economic reforms led to higher efficiency in the economy, which boosted output and increased resources for additional investment in the economy.[8]

In foreign affairs, the growing importance of the Chinese economy was manifested most notably by the growth in economic interchange between China and countries throughout the world, notably the United States. Most important in this regard was the growth of trade and foreign investment in China. International trade played a key role in increasing Chinese influence around the world and in enabling China to import the technology, resources, food, and consumer goods needed to support economic growth, to finance China's military buildup and other aspects of its national power, and to maintain the legitimacy of the Communist Party government. Greater Chinese access to foreign markets also enabled China to attract foreign investment. Foreign-affiliated companies played a key role in generating economic growth and employment and in the manufacture of world-class products. China's joining the WTO in 2001 added to reasons for strong foreign investment in China, which in turn boosted the size of Chinese foreign trade. Chinese exports and imports in 2004 were both more than twice as large as those just three years earlier, in 2001.[9]

Over half of Chinese foreign trade in recent years has been so-called processing trade, where a commodity crosses China's border, perhaps several times, before the final product is produced and the value of each cross-border transfer is duly registered in Chinese import and export figures. In effect, such processing trade results in a good deal of double-counting in Chinese import and export figures, which tends to exaggerate the actual size and importance of Chinese foreign trade. This consideration aside, the fact remains that the internationally recognized figures for Chinese exports surpassed those of the United States in 2007.[10]

Though China sometimes ran trade surpluses and sometimes ran trade deficits in the reform period since the late 1970s, for over a decade China has run trade surpluses. The surplus was $262 billion in 2007 and about $300 billion in 2008. The U.S. global trade deficit in 2007 was $791 billion. Merchandise trade surpluses and large-scale foreign investment saw China accumulate the world's largest foreign exchange reserves. The value of the reserves reached $1.9 billion in late 2008.[11]

In assessing China's major trading partners, it is important to keep in mind differences of Chinese trade data with those of some of its major trading partners. This is due to the fact that a large share of China's trade (both exports and imports) passes through Hong Kong, which reverted back to Chinese rule in July 1997 but is treated as a separate customs area by most countries, including China and the United States. China treats a large share of its exports through Hong Kong as Chinese exports to Hong Kong for statistical purposes, while many countries including the United States that import Chinese products through Hong Kong generally attribute their origin to China for statistical purposes.

As a result, trade data from the United States showed that the importance of the U.S. market to China's export sector was much higher than was reflected in Chinese trade data. Based on U.S. data on Chinese exports to the United States, and Chinese data on total Chinese exports, it was estimated that Chinese exports to the United States as a share of total Chinese exports grew from 15 percent in 1986 to 33 percent in 2004.[12]

Reflecting the importance of foreign investment in the Chinese economy and trading relationships, a growing level of Chinese exports was from foreign-funded enterprises in China. According to Chinese data in recent years, about half of its trade was conducted by such enterprises. A large share of these enterprises was owned by investors from Hong Kong and Taiwan, as well as growing numbers of investors from South Korea, Japan, the United States, and Southeast Asia. Some of the foreign entrepreneurs shifted their labor-intensive, export-oriented firms to China to take advantage of low-cost labor and other cost benefits. A significant share of the products made by such firms was exported to the United States. Chinese data indicated that the share of China's exports produced by foreign-invested enterprises in China rose from 2 percent in 1986, to 41 percent in 1996, to 57 percent in 2004 and 58.5 percent in 2005.[13]

China's abundance of cheap labor made it internationally competitive in many low-cost, labor-intensive manufactures. As a result, manufactured products constituted an increasingly large share of China's trade. Meanwhile, a large share of China's imports, such as raw materials, components, parts, and production machinery, was used to manufacture products for export. For example, China imported cotton and textile-production machinery to produce textile and apparel items. A substantial amount of China's imports comprised parts and components that were assembled in Chinese factories and then exported. Major products in these efforts included consumer electronics and computers.[14]

Viewed in comparison to the United States, the world's top economy, the recent growth of Chinese trade was impressive.[15] In 1995, U.S. total trade was $1.39 trillion or five times that of China's $281 billion. In 2007, U.S. total trade of $3.116 trillion was 1.4 times that of China's $2.175 trillion. China became a major trading nation and a competitive rival to the United States in certain industries. Given the rise of international supply chains, China's economy also complemented that of the United States in certain areas. U.S. companies joined many other foreign firms in relying on China to manufacture products designed, advertised, and distributed by the home (American-based) part of the multinational corporation; or they manufactured in the United States using Chinese components; or they produced components in the United States for assembly in China.

In 2007 China ranked second only to the European Union (extra EU-trade only) in total merchandise exports, and third after the United States and the EU in imports. Japan and Canada held fourth and fifth places in both exports and imports respectively. Projections showed that China's total trade could surpass that of the United States in 2011, and that China's trade could be double that of the United States ten years after that.[16] As this trend developed, Chinese trading partners might rely more on China than on the United States both as a market for exports and source of imports. However, such a possible shift was offset by the fact—well illustrated in the 2008–2009 international economic crisis—that Chinese trade and the trade of Asian and other countries linked with production chains focused on China—depended very heavily on exports to the United States and the European Union.[17]

The scope of Chinese trade grew commensurate with its rapidly increasing size. China surpassed the United States as an exporter in several regions of the world; the United States far surpassed China as an importer in some of these areas, and it also was ahead of China in overall world trade. Specifically, China surpassed the United States in overall trade with Northeast Asia, Southeast Asia, and Australia/Oceania. China was catching up to the level of U.S. trade with South Asia and the Middle East. U.S. trade with Europe, Latin America, and Africa remained well ahead of China's growing trade with these areas.[18]

China's rising trade prominence in international markets went hand in hand with the rise in China's importance as a destination for and source of foreign direct investment. As much of Chinese trade was done by foreign-invested enterprises in China, China was in the lead among developing countries in receiving foreign investment. Annual utilized FDI in China reached over $70 billion in 2007, and the cumulative amount of FDI in

China at that time was ten times that amount. FDI in China in 2008 was valued at $90 billion.[19]

At the same time, Chinese companies beginning at the start of the decade were urged by the Chinese administration to increase the more limited Chinese investment abroad. It remained difficult to measure the extent and importance of these investments and their significance for data on foreign investment into China. In recent years, over half of Chinese overseas investment was shown in Chinese data to go to Hong Kong, the Cayman Islands, and the British Virgin Islands. The accounting rules in these locales were such that they were seen to provide tax havens and to allow Chinese firms to seek advantage by investing there, and from those locations to send investment back into China.[20]

By the end of 2006, Chinese government figures showed over five thousand domestic Chinese investment entities had established nearly ten thousand overseas direct invested enterprises in 172 countries or territories around the world. The accumulated FDI stock reached $90 billion, of which non-finance FDI was $75 billion and $15 billion was in finance-related FDI. FDI from China accounted for about 0.8 percent of global FDI stocks and 2.7 percent of global FDI outflows (thirteenth in the world).[21] By way of comparison, in 2006 the cumulative stock of FDI was over $2.8 trillion for the United States.[22]

The pace and scope of Chinese investment increased in more recent years, with Chinese officials advising in late 2008 that China's "direct investment overseas" was expected to reach $45 billion in 2008 and others claiming that such broadly defined investment would reach over $60 billion in 2010. How much of these flows would go to tax havens, how much would involve finance and non-finance investment, and other uncertainties remained to be determined, though the rise of China's importance as an international investor was clearly growing.[23]

China's foreign aid was difficult to assess, given a lack of official and reliable data. The China Statistical Yearbook 2003–2006 released an annual aid figure of $970 million, but specialists judged this did not include loans, a main form of Chinese aid. A former U.S. government foreign aid official, Georgetown University Professor Carol Lancaster, judged in 2007 that China's annual aid ranged in value between $1.5 and $2 billion.[24] Studies that inventoried various reports of loans and state-sponsored investment and other official Chinese financing came up with much larger figures, though aid specialists judged that much of these efforts would not qualify as aid and that it was difficult to determine when and whether reported aid and loan pledges were actually ever made and disbursed. Chinese financing at times involved interest-free or concessional loans, but it also involved trade and investment agreements, including arrangements whereby Chinese loans were to be repaid by commodities (for example, oil) produced as a result of the development financed with China's help.[25]

China also was important as a recipient of considerable foreign assistance. Because of the difficulties in assessing the costs and scope of Chinese assistance efforts and the varied and complicated channels of foreign assistance to China, there remained considerable uncertainty as to whether or not China had reached a point where it was no longer a net recipient of foreign assistance. China was a leading recipient of international assistance in the 1980s and the 1990s.[26]

Impact of global economic crisis, 2008–2009. Although Chinese financial institutions were not believed to have heavily invested in U.S. sub-prime securities, the global economic crisis that began in the U.S. financial sector in 2008 had a major impact on China's economy. China's leading trading partners, the United States, the European Union, and Japan, were pushed into a deep recession exacerbated by a major crisis in world credit markets that markedly slowed lending needed for growth. Chinese trade and foreign investment coming to China declined; the overall rate of growth of the Chinese economy also declined. The Chinese government implemented a two-year, $586 billion stimulus package, mainly dedicated to infrastructure projects. Interest rates were cut repeatedly as were real estate taxes. The government increased export tax rebates for textile, garments, toys and other export products hard hit by the decline in foreign demand for Chinese products. It endeavored to revise tax policies and provide financial support to domestic firms.[27]

China's international role in the crisis developed cautiously. Some Chinese and Asian commentators at first asserted that China and its neighbors could confidently ride out the economic crisis in U.S. and Western financial markets. They appeared in retreat by the end of 2008 as the impact of the financial turmoil and recession in America and Europe began to have a major effect on China and the region's trade, manufacturing, currency values, and broader economic stability.[28]

Like its Asian neighbors, the Chinese administration also was cautious in taking the lead in international financial arrangements and commitments that could involve significant risks for the Chinese economy in what increasingly appeared to be a period of prolonged adverse international economic conditions.[29] On the whole, Chinese leaders stuck to the position that China's top priority in the crisis was to sustain growth at home. Despite China's continued large cumulative trade and current account surpluses, the Chinese administration took steps to keep the value of its currency low relative to the U.S. dollar and some other currencies and to stimulate export growth through tax changes and other measures. These recent steps helped Chinese export manufacturers, but they seemed to work to the disadvantage of China's international trade competitors in Asia and elsewhere. Meanwhile, despite sometimes-prominent Chinese criticisms of the existing international economic order in the World Bank, the IMF, and the WTO that was said to have disadvantaged developing countries and supported the primacy of the U.S. dollar, Chinese government investors, for the time being at least, continued to see their interests best served by heavy investment of their foreign exchange reserves in U.S. Treasury securities.[30]

U.S. Trade Deficit with China

The U.S. trade deficit with China has continued to grow in recent years, though it leveled off in 2008 and declined somewhat in 2009. According to U.S. data, the deficit was $232 billion in 2006, $256 billion in 2007, and $266 billion in 2008. The deficit with China was the largest with any country or group of countries in an overall U.S. trade deficit valued at $800 billion in 2008. The overall U.S. trade deficit and the trade deficit with China were expected to decline as a result of the economic recession in the United States in 2009.[31]

The decline may reduce but almost certainly will not end longstanding complaints voiced by many in Congress, the media, and interest groups in the United States who focus on the massive trade deficit as a key indicator that China's economic and trade policies are unfair and disadvantageous for the United States. Chinese officials publicly and privately resent U.S. attempts to "politicize" the trade deficit, which Chinese trade figures show as much less than shown by U.S. trade figures. They tend to see the American complaints as "protectionist" efforts by special interests in the United States which have been disadvantaged by international economic trends associated with economic globalization. They tend to find little fault in Chinese policies or practices, and view American criticisms of China as unjustified.[32]

U.S. exports to China grew markedly in recent years but from a relatively low base compared with massive U.S. imports from China. The U.S. merchandise sold was wide ranging, including leading goods categories of waste and scrap, semiconductors and other electronic components, aircraft and parts, and agricultural products. Chinese merchandise sold to the United States tended to move from low-value consumer products of past years to more advanced technology products, like computers, in recent years. An important dimension of the recent increase in U.S. imports of Chinese manufactured goods is the movement in production facilities from other Asian countries to China. Various manufactured products that used to be made in Japan, Taiwan, Hong Kong, South Korea, and Southeast Asian nations and then exported to the United States are now being made in China (in many cases by foreign firms in China using components and materials imported from foreign countries) and exported to the United States.[33]

The diversity of Chinese products sold to the United States includes agricultural exports. The United States long viewed China as a major market for U.S. agricultural goods, and U.S. farmers sold $12 billion in products to China in 2008. In recent years, China has become the third largest supplier of agricultural products to the United States, valued at $4.7 billion in 2008.[34]

Growing Investment Ties

China's investments in U.S. assets can be broken down into two categories: holdings of U.S. securities (for example, U.S. Treasury securities, U.S. government agency securities, corporate securities, and stocks) and foreign direct investment. According to U.S. government data, China's total holdings of U.S. securities at the end of 2008 were estimated at $1.2 billion. China ranked a close second to Japan, which had holdings valued at $1.25 billion. China's holdings of U.S. securities were growing fast and were expected to surpass Japan's in 2009. The largest type of U.S. securities held by China is U.S. Treasury securities, which were valued at $727 billion in December 2008. China at that time had overtaken Japan and was the largest holder of U.S. Treasury securities. Meanwhile, U.S. holdings of Chinese securities are comparatively small. The U.S. government estimated the value of such holdings (mainly equities such as stocks) at $97.2 billion in 2007. This represented a small percentage (1.3 percent) of total U.S. holdings of foreign securities.[35]

Regarding bilateral FDI, China's FDI in the United States is quite small, valued at $1.1 billion (cumulative at the end of 2007), according to U.S. government data. U.S. FDI in China in 2007 was valued at $28.3 billion. China was still relatively low, twenty-first, among the destinations for U.S. FDI. However, for certain U.S. companies, investment and sales in China loomed very large. China has the world's largest mobile phone network and six hundred million mobile phone users; it is the largest market for commercial aircraft outside the United States; it has the largest number of Internet users in the world; and recently China became the world's largest market for new cars. U.S. firms invest substantially in China as they endeavor to expand to meet the needs of these Chinese markets.[36]

Implications of Chinese Holdings of U.S. Securities

On one hand, U.S. government leaders and other Americans encourage Chinese investment in such U.S. securities as a means for the United States to meet its investment needs and to fund the large U.S. federal budget deficit. On the other hand, U.S. policy makers raise concerns that the Chinese investment could give China increased leverage over the United States on major economic or other issues. For example, some Chinese officials have been reported to suggest that China could dump (or threaten to dump) a large share of its holdings in order to prevent the United States from imposing trade sanctions against China over its currency policies. Other Chinese officials were reported to have stated that China should diversify its investments of its foreign exchange reserves away from dollar-denominated assets to those that offer higher rates of return. The global economic crisis of 2008–2009 heightened U.S. concerns that China might reduce its U.S. assets holdings.[37]

If China attempted to reduce its holdings of U.S. securities, they would be sold to other investors (foreign and domestic), who would presumably require higher interest rates than those prevailing in order to be enticed to buy them. In 2007, one analyst estimated that a Chinese move away from long-term U.S. securities could raise interest rates by as much as fifty basis points. Higher interest rates would cause a decline in investment spending and other interest-sensitive spending. A reduction in Chinese holdings of U.S. Treasury securities would cause the overall foreign demands for U.S. assets to fall, and this would cause the U.S. dollar to depreciate. If the value of the dollar depreciated, the trade deficit would decline, as the price of U.S. exports fell abroad and the price of imports rose in the United States. (The extent that the dollar declined and U.S. interest rates rose would depend on how willing other foreigners were to supplant China's reduction in capital inflows. A greater willingness would lead to less dollar depreciation and less of an increase in interest rates, and vice versa.) The magnitude of these effects would depend on how many U.S. securities China sold; modest reductions would have negligible effects on the economy given the vastness of U.S. financial markets.[38]

Since China recently has held over $1 trillion of U.S. government assets, any reduction of its U.S. holdings could potentially be large. If there were a large reduction of its holdings, the effect on the U.S. economy still would depend on whether the reduction was gradual or sudden. Here, it should be noted that economists point out that a slow decline in the U.S. trade deficit and dollar could even have an expansionary effect on the U.S. economy, if the decrease in the trade deficit had a more stimulative effect on aggregate demand in the short run than the decrease in investment and other interest-sensitive spending resulting from higher interest rates. For example, the dollar declined by about 40 percent in real terms and the trade deficit declined continually in the late 1980s, from 2.8 percent of GDP in 1986 to nearly zero during the early 1990s. Yet economic growth was strong throughout the late 1980s.[39]

A potentially serious short-term problem would arise if China decided to suddenly reduce Chinese-held liquid U.S. financial assets significantly. The effect could be compounded if this action triggered a more general financial reaction (or panic), in which most foreigners responded by reducing their holdings in U.S. assets. The initial effect could be a sudden and large depreciation in the value of the dollar, as the supply of dollars on the foreign exchange market increased, and a sudden and large increase in U.S. interest rates, as an important funding source for investment and the budget deficit was withdrawn from the financial markets. Dollar depreciation would reduce the trade deficit, but the large increases in interest rates could swamp the trade effects and cause or worsen a U.S. recession. Large increases in interest rates reduce the market value of debt securities, cause prices on the stock market to fall, undermine efficient financial intermediation, and jeopardize the solvency of various debtors and creditors.[40]

The U.S. Treasury secretary and the chairman of the Federal Reserve responded to congressional queries in the latter part of the Bush administration regarding the implications of a Chinese sell-off of U.S. government securities. They maintained that such actions were not critically important for U.S. economic well-being because foreign holdings of U.S. Treasury securities represented only a small part of total U.S. credit market debt. For example, it was noted that in 2007 China's total holdings of U.S. Treasury securities were equal to the value of U.S. Treasury Securities sold in one day.

Meanwhile, it was widely assumed in the United States and China that the likelihood that China would suddenly reduce its holdings of U.S. securities was low because doing so did not appear to be in China's economic interests. First, a sell-off of China's U.S. holdings could diminish the value of these securities in international markets, which would lead to large losses on the sale, and would in turn decrease the value of China's remaining dollar-denominated assets. This would also occur if the value of the dollar were greatly diminished in international currency markets due to China's sell-off. Second, such a move would diminish U.S. demand for Chinese imports, either through a rise in the value of the Chinese yuan against the U.S. dollar or a reduction in U.S. economic growth. The United States purchased about 30 percent of China's total merchandise exports in 2007. Decline in U.S. purchase of Chinese exports would negatively impact China's economy, which heavily depends on exports for economic growth. Meanwhile, any major action by the Chinese government that destabilized the U.S. economy could provoke protectionist sentiment and action in the United States against China.[41]

For their part, Chinese officials have expressed concern over the safety of their large holdings of U.S. debt. They seem recently worried that growing U.S. debt will spark inflation in the United States and a sharp deterioration of the U.S. dollar, which would diminish the value of China's dollar assets. Chinese officials sometimes voice frustration over the implications of China's heavy investment in U.S. government securities. They also complain about the salience of the U.S. dollar in international trade and economic exchange, calling for other means than the U.S. dollar for conducting international economic transactions. Nevertheless, for the time being at least, Chinese purchases of U.S. government securities continue, and steps to support a move away from the U.S. dollar in international transactions remain small and tentative.[42]

Recent U.S.-China Trade Issues

Apart from U.S.-China disagreements caused by the prevailing U.S. trade deficit and the implications of China's holding of U.S. securities, tensions have risen in U.S.-China relations on a variety of trade issues. On the U.S. side, they include concerns over unsafe Chinese food and consumer products; China's currency policies and practices, which many in the United States blame for the size of the U.S. trade deficit with China and the loss of U.S. manufacturing jobs; China's mixed record regarding implementing its obligations in the WTO, including its failure to provide adequate protection of U.S. intellectual property rights (IPR); and Chinese industrial policies used to promote and protect domestic industries. Chinese officials view the U.S. complaints as myopic and unfair. They sometimes voice suspicions that the United States uses them and other practices and policies in order to hold back Chinese economic development and hobble China's rise to world prominence and influence. Chinese officials regularly call on the United States to end restrictions on high technology U.S. exports to China, to follow other developed countries in recognizing China's market economy status under WTO rules, and to eschew protectionism and politicizing of trade issues in U.S.-China relations.[43]

Concerns about Product Safety

Throughout 2007 and 2008, Americans and a large array of other international consumers showed increasing concern over what they found to be a wide variety of unsafe food and consumer products coming from China. U.S. policy makers were called on to press China to improve enforcement of health and safety standards of its exports as well as to strengthen the ability of U.S.

regulatory agencies to ensure the health and safety of imports from China, as well as other countries.[44]

The long list of U.S. complaints that emerged in this period involved toxic, tainted, or faulty seafood, pet food, medicine, toys, and tires, among others. Nonfeasance and malfeasance on the part of Chinese producers and regulators, along with less-than-rigorous oversight by U.S. regulators and concerned businesses, were at the root of the problems caused by these products.[45]

Amid frequent and highly critical U.S. and other international media exposés of unsafe products coming from China, U.S. government institutions took remedial steps. The Food and Drug Administration (FDA) in March 2007 issued warnings and announced voluntary recalls on over 150 brands of pet foods from China. In May 2007, the FDA issued warnings on certain toothpaste products found to originate in China that contained poisonous chemicals. In June 2007, the administration announced import controls on several kinds of farm-raised fish, shrimp, and eels from China. On September 12, 2008, the FDA issued a health information advisory on infant formula in response to reports of contaminated milk-based infant formula manufactured and sold in China.[46]

2007 also was a particularly busy period for the U.S. Consumer Product Safety Commission, which found that over four-fifths of its numerous recall notices involved Chinese products. Over this period more than seventeen million Chinese manufactured toys were recalled because of excessive lead levels. Other reasons for recalls of toys from China involved chemicals toxic if ingested, finger entrapment, and burn hazards. In reaction, Chinese suppliers and U.S. companies purchasing Chinese products improved quality standards so that recalls in 2008 were down sharply.[47]

Perceived lax oversight by U.S. companies purchasing Chinese products for sale in the United States and perceived lax oversight by the FDA, CPSC, and other U.S. bodies prompted the passage in the United States of the Consumer Product Safety Improvement Act of 2008. But malfeasance by Chinese companies and officials and a poor regulatory system in China was widely seen in the United States and increasingly in China as a critical problem in China's trade with the United States and other countries. Among perceived weaknesses in the Chinese regulatory system were weak consumer protection laws and poorly enforced regulations; lack of inspections and ineffective penalties for code violators; understaffed and underfunded regulatory agencies; restrictions on media coverage; proliferation of fake goods and unlicensed producers; and widespread government corruption.[48]

The Chinese government initially reacted defensively in the face of U.S. and other international complaints in 2007, criticizing the American charges as exaggerated and self-serving. However, the Chinese administration soon recognized that the credibility of Chinese products on the international market was at stake. In response, it took numerous steps to strengthen food and drug safety supervision, increase inspections, and crack down on corruption. Numerous agreements were signed with CPSC and other U.S. bodies to improve assurances regarding the quality of Chinese products sold in the United States. Critical shortcomings in the Chinese efforts remained. Notably, foreign media and other reports said that Chinese media were not able to expose evidence of the wide scope of the contaminated milk in China for months in 2008, until the completion of the August 2008 summer Olympic Games in Beijing. The foreign media indicated that Chinese authorities judged that a successful Chinese image from the games was more important than the health threat posed by the tainted milk.[49]

China's Currency Policy

Criticism in the United States over China's currency policy emerged in recent years against the background of the massive and growing U.S. trade deficit with China and complaints from U.S. manufacturing firms and workers over competitive challenges posed by Chinese imports that benefit from the Chinese currency's value relative to the U.S. dollar. Unlike most advanced economies, China does not maintain a market-based floating exchange rate. Between 1994 and 2005, China pegged its currency, the renminbi (RMB) or yuan, to the U.S. dollar at about 8.28 yuan to the dollar. In July 2005, China appreciated the RMB to the dollar by 2.1 percent and moved to what it called a "managed float," based on a basket of major foreign currencies, including the U.S. dollar. In order to maintain a target rate of exchange with the dollar and other currencies, the Chinese government has maintained restrictions and controls over capital transactions and has made large-scale purchases of U.S. dollars and dollar assets. According to the Bank of China, from July 21, 2005 to March 31, 2009, the dollar-yuan exchange rate went from 8.11 to 6.84, an appreciation of 18.6 percent.[50]

Many U.S. policy makers, business leaders, union representatives, and academic specialists have charged that China's currency policy has made the RMB significantly undervalued relative to the U.S. dollar. Estimates of undervalue range from 15–40 percent. The American critics maintain that China's currency policy makes Chinese exports to the United States cheaper and U.S. exports to China more expensive than they would be if exchange rates were determined by market forces. They complain that this policy has particularly hurt several U.S. manufacturing sectors (such as textiles and apparel, furniture, plastics, machine tools, and steel), which are forced to compete against low-cost imports from

China. The Chinese currency policy is seen by the American critics to add to the size and growth of the U.S. trade deficit with China. Responsive to these complaints, representatives in Congress have introduced numerous bills in recent years designed to pressure China to either significantly appreciate its currency or let it float freely in international markets.[51]

What has received secondary attention in the often-heated U.S. debate over China's currency policy is that the low value of the yuan relative to the dollar has some benefits for the U.S. economy. Imported Chinese goods are cheaper than they would be if the yuan were market-determined. This lowers prices for U.S. consumers and dampens inflationary pressures. It also lowers prices for U.S. firms that use imported Chinese inputs in their production, making such firms more competitive. When the United States runs a trade deficit with China, this requires a capital inflow from China to the United States, such as Chinese purchases of U.S. Treasury securities. This, in turn, lowers U.S. interest rates and increases U.S. investment spending.[52]

Chinese officials have argued that China's currency policy is not meant to favor exports over imports, but instead to foster domestic economic stability. They have expressed concern that abandoning its currency policy could cause an economic crisis in China and would especially hurt its export industries at a time of painful economic reforms and challenging international competition. Chinese officials view economic stability as critical to sustaining political stability; they fear an appreciated currency could reduce jobs and lower wages in several sectors and thus cause worker unrest.[53]

Section 3004 of the 1988 U.S. Omnibus Trade and Competitiveness Act requires the Secretary of the Treasury to issue a report every six months on international economic policy, including exchange rate policy, and to determine if any country is manipulating its currency in order to prevent an effective balance of payments adjustment or to gain an unfair competitive advantage in international trade. After China changed its currency policy in July 2005, the Bush administration continued to press China to further reform its currency and its financial sector. But the U.S. government declined to cite China for currency manipulation. The Obama administration has adhered to this position, though members of Congress and others are pressing the new U.S. government to cite China as a currency manipulator in order to pressure it to appreciate and reform its currency policy and practice.[54]

Further complicating the issue of China's currency policy is China's large holdings of U.S. debt such as Treasury securities, discussed above. Some Americans and others warn that threatening China over its currency policy could induce the Chinese government to slow its purchases of U.S. securities, or even sell off current holdings of U.S. Treasury securities, which could contribute to higher U.S. interest rates. On the other hand, other Americans are concerned that China's large holdings provide Beijing with what they see as unacceptable leverage over the United States; and some see China's currency policy and resulting large purchases of U.S. government securities as a contributing factor in the ongoing global economic crisis and recession.[55]

WTO Implementation Issues

An important benchmark in Chinese leaders' embrace of economic globalization and interdependence was the decision to join the WTO under terms requiring major concessions from China to its international trading partners. On September 13, 2001, China concluded a WTO bilateral trade agreement with Mexico, the last of the original thirty-seven WTO members to have requested such an accord. On September 17, 2001, the WTO Working Party handling China's WTO application announced that it had resolved all outstanding issues regarding China's WTO accession. China's WTO membership was formally approved at the WTO Ministerial Conference in Doha, Qatar, on November 10, 2001. On November 11, 2001, China notified the WTO that it had formally ratified the WTO agreements, which enabled China to enter the WTO on December 11, 2001.[56]

Under the WTO accession agreement, China set forth various concessions and actions to accommodate the interests of its major trading partners. It agreed to:

- Reduce the average tariff for industrial goods to 8.9 percent and for agricultural goods to 15 percent; most tariff cuts were to come by 2004;
- Limit subsidies for agricultural production to 8.5 percent of the value of farm output and end export subsidies for agricultural exports;
- By 2004, grant full trade and distribution rights to foreign enterprises (with some exceptions);
- Provide nondiscriminatory treatment to all WTO members; foreign firms in China were to be treated no less favorably than Chinese firms for trade purposes; price controls would not be used to provide protection to Chinese firms;
- Implement the WTO's standards on intellectual property rights seen in the organization's Trade-Related Aspects of Intellectual Property Rights (TRIPS) Agreement;
- Accept a twelve-year safeguard mechanism, available to other WTO members in cases where a surge in Chinese exports cause or threaten to cause market disruption to domestic producers;

- Fully open the Chinese banking system to foreign financial institutions by 2006; joint ventures in insurance and telecommunications would be permitted with various degrees of foreign ownership allowed.[57]

The subsequent record of implementation of the Chinese agreement with the WTO was a source of considerable criticism from the United States and some others among China's major trading partners. These criticisms, in turn, prompted Chinese government complaints. As a result of burgeoning Chinese exports, notably involving textiles and apparel, the United States, the European Union, and others imposed restrictions on Chinese imports of these products that met with vocal complaints from the Chinese government. Surges in Chinese exports involving agricultural products were a frequent source of complaint from some of China's Asian trading partners, who tried to restrict the imports in ways that antagonized the Chinese authorities.[58]

The U.S. government took the lead among WTO members in reaching the agreements leading to China's joining the organization. It viewed the U.S. market as by far China's largest export market and had a growing concern over the unprecedented U.S. trade deficit with China. As a result, it maintained a leading role in measuring Chinese compliance with WTO commitments, and its complaints met with dissatisfaction and criticism from the Chinese government.[59]

The U.S. Special Trade Representative (USTR) issued annual reports assessing China's WTO compliance, as did prominent U.S. nongovernmental organizations such as the U.S.-China Business Council. These reports tended to give China mixed evaluations. On the one hand, China was seen making significant progress in meeting such commitments as formal tariff reductions; but the reports raised a host of concerns involving quotas, standards, lack of transparency, and protection of intellectual property rights, all of which were seen to impact negatively on U.S. trade interests. The U.S. complaints focused on what U.S. analysts viewed as unfair restrictions on U.S. soybean and other agricultural exports to China; confusing and discriminatory Chinese regulations of service enterprises that impeded U.S. firms from succeeding in the Chinese market; unfair competition from Chinese state-owned enterprises (SOEs), which received subsidies through advantageous loans from government-controlled Chinese banks; and health and safety requirements and technical standards that U.S. analysts saw as designed to protect unfairly Chinese producers. The USTR reports gave special emphasis to U.S. complaints over Chinese treatment of U.S. intellectual property rights (IPR).[60]

The USTR's December 2008 report on China's compliance with WTO obligations stated that although China agreed to make SOEs operate according to free-market principles when it joined the WTO, SOEs were still being subsidized, especially through the banking system. In addition, China was attempting to promote the development of several industries such as autos, steel, telecommunications, petroleum, and high-technology products, deemed by the government as important to China's future economic development. Beijing implemented policies to promote and protect them in ways inconsistent with China's WTO obligations.[61]

When China joined the WTO, it agreed to provide a full description of all its subsidy programs, but as of 2009 it had failed to do so. In addition, China agreed to make its state-owned enterprises operate according to market principles, yet such firms continue to receive direction and subsidies. Some major issues of continued concern to the United States include the following:[62]

- In December 2006, the Chinese government designated several large industries (military equipment, power generation and distribution, oil, telecommunications, coal, civil aviation, and shipping) as critical to the nation's economic security and stated it must retain "absolute control" and limit foreign participation.
- U.S. officials have expressed disappointment that China has failed to develop a science-based trading protocol for importing beef from the United States, which would enable the United States to resume beef trade with China.
- In July 2005, the Chinese government issued new guidelines on steel production, which reportedly included provisions for the preferential use of domestically produced steel-manufacturing equipment and domestic technologies and other measures adverse to foreign investors and imports. The guidelines and other actions were criticized by the U.S. steel industry and some U.S. officials. U.S. pressures led the USTR to begin a Steel Dialogue with China, which first met in March 2006, in order to discuss issues of concern to the U.S. steel industry.
- The Chinese government took repeated actions in recent years that discouraged the importation of auto parts, and required use of domestic technology and minimum levels of domestic content in autos made or sold in China.

The United States has initiated several WTO dispute resolution cases against China involving perceived infractions involving the above-noted pattern of Chinese discrimination against foreign goods while protecting domestic Chinese producers, as well as infractions involving intellectual property rights. China has initiated action against the United States regarding the use of anti-dumping and countervailing measures against Chinese products.

Intellectual Property Rights (IPR)

The United States, along with Japan and other developed countries, for many years pressed Chinese authorities to improve China's IPR protection regime. In 1991, the United States threatened to impose $1.5 billion in trade sanctions against China if it failed to strengthen its IPR laws. Although China later implemented a number of new IPR laws, it often failed to enforce them, which led the United States to once again threaten China with trade sanctions. The two sides reached a trade agreement in 1995, which pledged China to take immediate steps to stem IPR piracy by cracking down on large-scale producers and distributors of pirated materials and prohibiting the export of pirated products; to establish mechanisms to ensure long-term enforcement of IPR laws; and to provide greater market access to U.S. IPR-related products.[63]

Under the terms of China's WTO accession, China agreed to immediately bring its IPR laws into compliance with the WTO agreement on Trade-Related Aspects of Intellectual Property Rights (TRIPS). The USTR stated on a number of occasions that China made great strides in improving its IPR protection regime, noting that it passed several new IPR-related laws, closed or fined several assembly operations for illegal production lines, seized millions of illegal audiovisual products, curtailed exports of pirated products, expanded training of judges and law enforcement officials on IPR protections, and expanded legitimate licensing of film and music production in China.[64]

However, the USTR indicated that much work needed to be done to improve China's IPR protection regime. Business groups in the United States continued to complain about significant IPR problems in China, especially in terms of illegal reproduction of software, retail piracy, and trademark counterfeiting. According to the U.S. Congressional Research Service, it was estimated that counterfeits accounted for 15 to 20 percent of all products made in China and accounted for 8 percent of China's GDP. China's enforcement agencies and judicial system often lacked the resources or the will needed to enforce vigorously IPR laws; convicted IPR offenders generally faced minor penalties. In addition, while market access for U.S. and other foreign IPR-related products improved, high tariffs, quotas, and other barriers continued to hamper U.S. exports; such trade barriers were believed by U.S. analysts to be partly responsible for illegal IPR-related smuggling and counterfeiting in China. Industry analysts estimated that IPR piracy in China cost U.S. firms $2.6 billion in lost sales in 2003, compared to estimated losses of $1.9 billion in 2002. The piracy rate for IPR-related products in China (such as motion pictures, software, and sound recordings) was estimated at around 90 percent by U.S. analysts. In addition, China accounted for a significant share of imported counterfeit products seized by U.S. Customs and Border Protection officers ($62.5 million, or 66 percent of total goods seized, in FY-2003).

Under an April 21, 2004, U.S.-China trade agreement, China pledged to "significantly reduce" IPR infringement levels by increasing efforts to halt production, imports, and sales of counterfeit goods and lowering the threshold for criminal prosecution of IPR violations. On October 6, 2004, the U.S. State Department announced it would allocate $210,000 to IPR enforcement training to Chinese government officials (for example, judges, police, legislators, etc.). Nevertheless, according to the International Intellectual Property Rights Alliance, IPR piracy in China cost U.S. firms $3.5 billion in lost sales in 2007.[65]

Following a long list of U.S. government measures to prompt the Chinese government and Chinese businesses to respect U.S. intellectual property rights and to adhere to obligations undertaken in bilateral agreements and multilateral commitments, the USTR in 2008 stated in a report that its top IPR protection and enforcement priorities involved China and Russia. Among other charges, the USTR meshed its complaint with the ongoing controversy over the safety of products imported from China by stating that Chinese counterfeit products, such as pharmaceuticals, electronics, batteries, auto parts, industrial equipment, and toys "pose a direct threat to the health and safety of consumers in the United States, China, and elsewhere."[66]

U.S. firms contend that IPR piracy in China has worsened in recent years, despite Chinese government agreements to strengthen IPR enforcement and stamp out major piracy concerns. American and other foreign businesses charge that poor IPR protection is one of the most significant obstacles for doing business in China. Following its indictment of Chinese practices in 2007, the International Intellectual Property Rights Alliance estimated that piracy of business software and records and music in China cost U.S. firms $3.5 billion in 2008, the same as in 2007, making China the highest-value offender of any of the forty-eight countries and territories surveyed. Of the $221 million worth of pirated goods seized by the U.S. Customs and Border Protection officers in 2008, four-fifths came from China. The Motion Picture Association of America mixed its continued condemnation of pirated movies in China with charges of blatant Chinese discrimination against foreign films. It charged that in China nine out of ten movie DVDs are fake and part of the reason is that the Chinese government only allows twenty foreign films into the Chinese market each year. American music producers estimated that the piracy rate for their products also was 90 percent.[67]

Chinese government information supports the view of rampant IPR violations in China. The government information backs estimates that counterfeits constitute between 15 and 20 percent of all products made in China and are equivalent to about 8 percent of China's annual gross domestic product. Among notable areas of violation, the government estimates that five hundred million pirated books are produced in China each year. The reasons for continued widespread violations vary with the central authorities not as resolute as American companies would like to see in establishing enforcement mechanisms and disciplining local officials who allow and even encourage widespread IPR abuse; Chinese-owned companies also have not yet reached a stage where they are a major force in pressing the government to protect their own brands and IPR-related products.[68]

Reflecting strong American frustration with China's record of IPR violations, the USTR filed two cases in the WTO in April 2007 regarding Chinese IPR violations. The cases represented the most comprehensive and complex cases the United States had filed against a WTO member. Most WTO cases involve specific restrictions on specific products; however, the two USTR cases challenged a broad range of China's IPR policies; they could potentially lead the WTO to authorize the United States to impose a significant level of sanctions against China.[69]

U.S. Measures against Trade with China

Among measures that the United States can and has taken against perceived Chinese unfair trade practices is the application of U.S. countervailing laws to China. As noted above, there are widespread American complaints that Chinese policy and practice provides significant subsidies to many domestic Chinese industries such as preferential bank loans and grants, debt forgiveness, and tax breaks and rebates. In addition, China's currency policy is widely seen to constitute a form of government export subsidy. Against this background, American critics say that countervailing U.S. laws, which seek to address the negative impact foreign government subsidies on exported products may have on U.S. producers in the United States, should be applied to non-market economies such as China.[70]

Until recently, the Commerce Department maintained that U.S. countervailing laws could not be applied to a non-market economy because of the assumption that most production and prices in such an economy are determined by the government, and thus it would be impractical to determine the level of government subsidy that might be conveyed to various exported products. However, in November 2006, the Commerce Department decided to pursue a countervailing case against certain imported Chinese coated free sheet paper products. In March 2007, the Commerce Department issued a preliminary ruling to impose countervailing duties ranging from 11 percent to 20 percent against the products in question. The U.S. government department contended that, while China was still a non-market economy, for the purposes of U.S. trade laws, economic reforms in China have made several sectors of the economy relatively market based, and therefore it is possible to identify the level of government subsidies given to the Chinese paper firms in question.[71]

As of 2009, thirteen countervailing cases were brought against a number of other Chinese products. American industry advocates and supporting members of Congress have called on the U.S. administration to expand the use of countervailing measures against Chinese products. Some congressional members have proposed codifying the use of countervailing laws against non-market economies, and others have sought to make China's undervalued currency a factor in determining the need of countervailing duties.[72]

Another set of American trade measures against perceived Chinese unfair trade practices is the application of safeguard provisions related to the Chinese agreement to enter the WTO. When China entered the WTO, it agreed to allow the United States to continue to treat it as a non-market economy for twelve years for the purpose of safeguards. This provision enables the United States to impose restrictions such as quotas and/or increased tariffs on imported Chinese products that have increased in such quantities that they have caused or threatened to cause market disruption to U.S. domestic producers. The Bush administration on six different occasions chose not to extend relief to various industries under China-specific safeguards. Controversy over the influx of Chinese textiles and apparel into the United States posed a particular problem following the elimination of U.S. textile and apparel quotas on Chinese goods in January 2005. According to the U.S. Department of Commerce, China was the largest supplier of textiles and apparel to the United States in 2008 with imports valued at $32.7 billion representing 35 percent of U.S. imports of these goods; from 2002 to 2008, U.S. textile and apparel imports from China rose by 274 percent. The sharp rise in textile and apparel imports from China, and U.S. industry contention that these imports were disrupting U.S. markets, prompted the Bush administration to seek an agreement with China to limit such Chinese exports to the United States. In November 2005, China agreed to restrict various textile and apparel exports to the United States according to specified quota levels from January 2006 through the end of 2008. The Obama government took a different and seemingly tougher approach in September 2009 when it imposed tariffs on Chinese tires entering the U.S. market.[73]

Environmental and Climate Change Issues

The George W. Bush administration was notorious among environmental activists concerned with global warming and climate change. Under the leadership of President Bush, the U.S. government took the lion's share of domestic and international criticism for policies and practice seen as at odds with growing international efforts supported by various developed and developing nations to curb environmental pollution, greenhouse gas emissions, and global climate change. Emblematic of Bush administration policies and of the reasons for international and domestic criticism of Bush administration policies was the U.S. government's refusal to support the Kyoto Protocol on climate change.[74]

China's rapid economic development has been accompanied by massive air and water pollution and greenhouse gas emissions. During recent years, China has emerged as the number one emitter of greenhouse gases. China's poor record in reversing environmental degradation associated with its rapid economic development and in curbing the rapid growth of greenhouse gas emissions from Chinese power plants, factories, and other sources was widely acknowledged, even by Chinese leaders. But Chinese policies and practices failed to generate much friction between the Chinese government and a U.S. administration under constant international and domestic attack for its alleged passive or even hostile approach to key aspects of international efforts to curb global warming, climate change and related environmental degradation.[75]

This situation began to change dramatically with the approach of the U.S. presidential and congressional elections of November 2008. All the U.S. presidential candidates and the vast majority of congressional contenders promised to shift U.S. policy regarding environmental degradation and climate change. In fact, the shift began in earnest in 2009, setting the stage for Americans and others concerned with environmental pollution and climate change to view Chinese policies and practices in a new, more attentive and more critical light.[76]

The incoming Obama government chose to build on mechanisms inherited from the outgoing Bush administration and engaged in bilateral dialogues with Chinese counterparts seeking forward movement on environmental and climate change issues. Others in the Congress, the U.S. media, and the wide range of American activists associated with global warming and environmental issues tended to be more vocal and critical regarding China's environmental record. As the United States moved to take action on environmental protection and climate change, American officials, especially in Congress, and public opinion were often explicit in expecting no less of China.[77]

Against the backdrop of almost twenty years of prominent policies and efforts by senior Chinese leaders to curb environmental damage and limit adverse consequences of economic development such as greenhouse gas emissions and climate change, the Chinese administration in recent years has undertaken a new series of steps in order to curb environmental damage and also to check possible damage to China's international standing as a responsible actor in world affairs. In 2009, it was unclear how well these steps would work in actually curbing environmental damage associated with Chinese development, in offsetting international attention to China's negative record in areas of pollution and climate change, and in avoiding serious disputes with a U.S. government markedly more sensitive than the previous U.S. government to issues of environmental degradation and to China's important role in those matters.[78]

The Obama government seemed to seek to avoid major friction with China as it sought common ground on important issues like global economic revival, North Korea's nuclear weapons development, and terrorist threats and instability in Southwest Asia. Nevertheless, there remained the distinct possibility that China's recent diplomatic activism and arguments in international forums dealing with environmental protection and climate change would not assuage broad American concern regarding China's growing negative impact on the environment, notably the massively wasteful use of energy in the production of goods and services and the associated burgeoning greenhouse gases coming from China.[79]

In China, the vast majority of greenhouse gas emissions come from power generation and other support for industrial production. In this decade, that production has focused more on heavy industry and high energy-consuming products. The situation is worsened because Chinese industrial production is very energy inefficient. The ratio of China's emissions to the value of production is twice the global average. Russia's is slightly lower than China's, and India's is substantially lower. The United States has a ratio less than one half of China's; Japan has a ratio one quarter that of China.[80]

Chinese leaders for almost two decades have shown sensitivity to environmental practices in China and the consequences on the Chinese and world environment of China's rapid growth. They have worked hard, on the one hand, to avoid being considered an international laggard on environmental practices, while, on the other, avoiding environmental obstacles to the rapid development of China's economy. On the positive side, Chinese leaders since the early 1990s have taken serious steps to deal with worsening environmental conditions in China. Premier Li Peng, a political hard-liner who played a key role in the Tiananmen crackdown of 1989, was particularly instrumental in putting ecology on the political map in China. Laws were passed on air, water, solid waste, and noise pollution. Enforcement mechanisms were bolstered and funds for cleanup, inspection, education, and enforcement increased repeatedly in the 1990s.[81]

In January 1999, a top environmental official announced that China would boost spending on "green" projects to 1.5 percent of GDP between 1997 and 2000. Altogether, in 1996 to 2000, plans called for investing almost $60 billion in environmental programs. State-owned banks and the State Environmental Protection Agency (SEPA) in 1997 announced that no loans would be issued to seriously polluting firms; in 1996, some sixty thousand enterprises—mostly rural factories with no environmental safeguards—were shut down. In January 1997, Beijing set up a national center to disseminate environmentally sound technology; and on March 1, 1997, the government announced the adoption of five new sets of international environmental protection standards.

Despite good intentions at the top, Beijing had serious problems, especially compliance and follow-through with funding and implementation of promised programs. In the late 1990s, China had only about twenty thousand enforcement officials nationwide to inspect industrial firms throughout the country; enforcement authority remained weak and fragmented; and penalties were anemic. Local officials tended to judge proposed projects by the number of jobs they created and the revenue they generated rather than by the environmental damage or good they did.[82]

With close to 10 percent annual growth and massive foreign investment focused on manufacturing, China faced enormous environmental problems at the start of the twenty-first century. Demand for electric power grew rapidly and was met predominantly by coal-fired plants. Autos clogged roads in major cities. Air pollution went from bad to worse. Efforts to develop hydropower using dams on China's rivers were controversial as the projects would displace large numbers of people and have major environmental impacts on people in China and other countries downstream from the new dams. Serious depletion of water resources in northern China was exacerbated by water pollution, pervasive throughout China.[83]

The Hu Jintao leadership has given more emphasis than its predecessors to the need for sustainable development in China. However, the results thus far have been similar to the mixed record of the recent past. Official Chinese media and Chinese officials noted significant improvement in water pollution levels in some Chinese rivers during the Tenth Five-Year Plan (2001–2005), but not in others. Recent efforts to curb air pollution included 182 projects to reduce sulfur dioxide emissions, and closures of over six thousand heavily polluting enterprises. Air pollution levels were said to have improved in some cities, but sulfur dioxide remained a major problem.[84]

In the latter part of the decade, Chinese officials sometimes were cautious in predicting improvements, especially with the projected rapid rise of automobile use in China, along with the pollution and land, water, and natural resource use associated with China's rapid economic growth. At a meeting in Beijing in January 2006, Chinese officials responsible for environmental protection agreed that an investment of 1.5 percent of GDP was required to effectively curb pollution and an investment of 3 percent of GDP was needed to substantially improve the environment, but it remained unclear where the money for the environmental goals would come from.[85]

The nation still lacks a powerful national body that is able to coordinate, monitor, and enforce environmental legislation: The State Environmental Protection Agency (SEPA) is understaffed, has few resources, and must compete with other bureaucracies for attention. The devolution of decision-making authority to local levels has placed environmental stewardship in the hands of officials who frequently are more concerned with economic growth than the environment. Meanwhile, the deficiency of capital and the lack of will to promote the massive spending necessary to reverse several decades of environmental damage indicated that environmental restoration was remote in the near future.[86]

The international consequences of China's environmental problems are varied and usually negative. Dust storms from eroding land in northern China pollute the atmosphere in Korea and Japan, leading to popular and sometimes official complaints and concerns. Air pollution from China affects locales to the east as far away as the Pacific coast of the United States. Chinese dams on the Mekong River negatively impact the livelihood of people in Cambodia and Vietnam, complicating official relations. Extensive international publicity regarding China's poor environmental record makes international opinion less patient with Chinese government explanations that China, as a developing country, should not be held to strict environmental standards. As a result, China's image in world affairs declines.[87]

China avoided the negative international spotlight when the United States refused to agree to the Kyoto Protocol to reduce polluting and other emissions. The U.S. position became the focal point of international criticism, with little attention devoted to China's refusal to agree to any binding steps to curb greenhouse gas emissions and other Chinese pollution. In January 2006, China joined with the United States and others in the inaugural ministerial meeting of the Asia-Pacific Partnership on Clean Development and Climate. The meeting elicited broad statements and promises by representatives from China, the United States, Japan, and others that were viewed by some as a positive step forward. Others saw these statements as a diversion from these states' unwillingness to be bound by the international standards set forth in the Kyoto Protocol.[88]

In response to growing domestic and international pressures for stronger Chinese actions to curb environmental damage, the Chinese administration adopted a number of measures in 2007 and 2008. China established senior-level working groups to deal with international concerns that China conform more to growing world efforts to curb the negative effects of climate change. Chinese diplomats and senior officials were in the forefront in bilateral and multilateral meetings in calling attention to China's concerns over climate change. They emphasized that China and other developing countries should not see their growth thwarted by environmental restrictions and that developed countries should bear the initial responsibility for concrete actions to deal with the growing issue. At home, Chinese officials took new measures to curb investment in energy intensive industries and to improve the poor standard of energy efficiency in Chinese manufacturing.[89]

Unfortunately, as in the past, Chinese targets in these areas often were not met. A core of the Chinese plan to address climate change, announced in 2007, was a goal to lower energy intensity of production by 20 percent. The country fell short of its annual milestones, set in energy policies in both 2007 and 2008. In July 2008 Premier Wen Jiabao and the State Council warned that meeting China's energy intensity and emission reduction goals "remained an arduous task." Related goals include more than doubling renewable energy use by 2020, expansion of nuclear power, closure of inefficient industrial facilities, tightened efficiency standards for buildings and appliances, and forest coverage expanded to 20 percent of China. According to official Chinese media, Minister of the National Development and Reform Commission Zhang Ping reported on December 24, 2008, that China "had failed to realize the goals of energy savings, emission control and economic restructuring in the past two years." By way of example, he said, "the government had set a goal to reduce energy consumption per unit of gross domestic product by 20 percent from 2006 to 2010. But it could cut only 1.79 percent and 3.66 percent in 2006 and 2007." Looking out, Zhang warned that "the worsening global financial crisis" posed "a serious challenge to us in achieving our goals."[90]

10

Taiwan Issues in
Contemporary U.S.-China Relations

THE INTERESTS, POLICIES, AND PRACTICES OF THE UNITED STATES and China usually have been at odds over Taiwan. While giving ground on U.S. relations with Taiwan in seeking to foster beneficial U.S. relations with China, the
United States nonetheless has tended to side with Taiwan, which remained in
strong competition with China until 2008. The history of the normalization
of U.S.-China relations shows repeated efforts by both countries to move
forward in developing U.S.-China relations while dealing with differences
over Taiwan. Seemingly successful understandings and agreements have been
compromised and reversed; both sides have periodically resorted to military,
diplomatic, and economic pressures to support their goals; the result has been
mutual wariness and suspicion.[1]

A new situation fostering détente and cooperation in cross-strait relations
and in U.S. relations with China over Taiwan emerged with the election of
Taiwan President Ma Ying-jeou in March 2008. The new Taiwan administration followed moderate policies and sought to reassure China, marking a
sharp contrast with the intense Taiwan-China competition that prevailed up
to that time. The result was significant easing of cross-strait tensions affecting
U.S.-China relations. Nonetheless, in late 2009 it was too early to tell whether
the recent developments signaled a fundamental shift in longstanding and
often competing and conflicting U.S. and Chinese interests and policies regarding Taiwan.

As explained in chapter 4, the process of normalization of U.S.-China relations saw Henry Kissinger and Richard Nixon privately pledge to meet firm
Chinese demands about ending U.S. official relations with Taiwan in return

for the perceived strategic and other benefits the United States would gain from the breakthrough in official relations with China. To avoid controversy in American domestic politics and in U.S. interaction with Taiwan and other concerned powers, these commitments remained hidden from the American public, the Congress, most officials in the Nixon government, Taiwan, and other foreign governments. The U.S.-China normalization process stalled on account of Nixon's forced resignation over the Watergate scandal. Unaware of the Kissinger-Nixon secret commitments, American public opinion and mainstream views in Congress supported continuing U.S. ties with Taiwan while moving ahead with China.

The Carter administration endeavored to complete the normalization of diplomatic relations and eventually met most Chinese demands on ending U.S. official ties with Taiwan. China seemed basically satisfied, though Carter's insistence on continuing some U.S. arms sales to Taiwan after breaking official relations remained an outstanding dispute. The backlash in the United States severely complicated the Carter understanding with China. Bipartisan congressional leaders rewrote the administration's proposed bill governing future unofficial relations with Taiwan and passed the Taiwan Relations Act, which underlined continued strong U.S. interest in protecting Taiwan from Chinese pressure and sustaining close economic, arms sales, and other ties with Taiwan.

Ronald Reagan highlighted his record of support for Taiwan in defeating Carter in the 1980 presidential election. Strong Chinese pressure against the seeming reversal of U.S. policy resulted in a compromise over U.S. arms sales to Taiwan in a Sino-American communiqué of 1982. Whatever Chinese expectations continued about the United States withdrawing from Taiwan diminished further with concurrent U.S. efforts to support Taiwan in international organizations, to transfer to Taiwan the technology and expertise to produce its own jet fighters, and to increase high-level U.S. officials' meetings with Taiwan counterparts. American officials from Reagan on down saw U.S. interests well served by preserving a balance in American relations with Taiwan and China where Taiwan would be sufficiently supported by the United States through military and other means that it would not feel compelled to come to terms with China on reunification or other issues seen as adverse to Taiwan's interests. Reagan's successor, George H. W. Bush, continued this approach, notably by sending the first U.S. cabinet member to visit Taiwan and by transferring over $5 billion of advanced jet fighters to Taiwan in a deal that was widely seen to have undermined the understandings reached in the 1982 communiqué with China.

As explained in chapter 5, Sino-American interaction over the issues associated with Taiwan became much more complicated as democracy and a strong movement toward self-determination emerged in Taiwan in the post–Cold War period. The American antipathy to China following the Tiananmen crackdown added to the shift in American attitudes against China and in favor of Taiwan. American attraction to growing democracy in Taiwan overshadowed U.S. attention to the profound implications for China of moves by Taiwan democratic leaders toward greater separation from China. The moves were popular among many Taiwanese people and their supporters in the United States but were fundamentally at odds with China's concerns over sovereignty and nationalism.

The clash of Sino-American interests reached a high point with the military crisis in the Taiwan Strait in 1995–1996 caused by Chinese military reaction to President Clinton's unexpected reversal of U.S. policy in granting Taiwan President Lee Teng-hui a visa in order to visit the United States and give a speech at his alma mater, Cornell University. Following the face-off of U.S. and Chinese forces in the Taiwan area in 1996, China's strong political pressure against Taiwan and its U.S. supporters continued along with concerted Chinese efforts to build up military forces in the Taiwan area designed to coerce Taiwan, prevent its movement toward permanent separation from China, and deter U.S. military efforts to intervene. American policy reflected a complicated mix of efforts to preserve a balance of power favorable to the United States and Taiwan and thereby deter China's coercive pressures on the one hand, while trying to dampen pro-independence initiatives in Taiwan and thereby reassure China regarding U.S. commitment to a one-China policy on the other.

The period from the Lee Teng-hui visit to the United States in 1995 until the end of the administration of Taiwan President Chen Shui-bain in 2008 featured repeated episodes of escalating tensions in U.S.-China relations regarding Taiwan. They usually were prompted by actions by the Taiwan administration, often in reaction to escalating coercive pressure from China, to move in directions seen by China as supporting Taiwan independence. As indicated in chapters 5 and 7, the Bill Clinton and George W. Bush administrations had a hard time in efforts to deter the two sides from provocative actions, to calm tensions when one side or the other took steps that worsened cross-strait relations, and thereby to sustain the broad American interest in preserving peace and stability in the Taiwan area.

The election of Ma Ying-jeou as president of Taiwan in 2008 began a new era in Taiwan-U.S.-China relations that significantly reduced cross-strait tensions and the salience of the Taiwan issue in Sino-American relations. Ma reversed the policies and practices of his immediate predecessors seen by China as moving Taiwan toward independence of China. He put aside the zero-sum competition that had generally prevailed in Taiwan-China relations for sixty

years. He opened Taiwan to much greater interchange with China that made
the Taiwan economy more dependent than ever on close and cooperative
relations with China. China reciprocated with policies and practices designed
to foster closer ties and build closer identity between Taiwan and the mainland. U.S. policy makers in the Bush and Obama administrations warmly
welcomed the moderation of cross-strait tensions.

Near-term prospects for a more cooperative period in U.S.-China relations
over Taiwan seemed good in late 2009. Prevailing trends and interests of the
administrations of Taiwan, China, and the United States supported efforts
to manage differences, foster closer cross-strait interchange, and avoid confrontation and conflict. However, much depended on continued support in
Taiwan for Ma Ying-jeou's cross-strait policies, which were under continued
attack by vocal oppositionists in Taiwan who thus far were unable to garner
majority political support. There also was some debate and uncertainty in
China and the United States regarding the implications of compromises on
cross-strait issues. Meanwhile, China continued to show strong opposition to
sales of U.S. arms to Taiwan that were requested by the Ma Ying-jeou administration despite its growing détente with China.

Determinants and Patterns of Recent
U.S.-China Cooperation over Taiwan

The relevant context of the recent cooperation and easing of tensions over
cross-strait relations is the tumultuous period dating from Taiwan President
Lee Teng-hui's visit to the United States in 1995 to the end of the administration of Taiwan President Chen Shui-bian. Tensions in cross-strait relations
and the perceived danger of conflict in the Taiwan area rose dramatically in
the mid-1990s. Earlier in the decade, China and Taiwan had made some progress in dealing with cross-strait issues during talks carried out by ostensibly
unofficial Taiwan and China organizations, Taiwan's Strait Exchange Foundation (SEF) and China's Association for Relations Across the Taiwan Strait
(ARATS). The two sides seemed to have managed to work around fundamental differences over sovereignty in order to reach agreements on practical
issues. Chinese president and party leader Jiang Zemin made a major policy
statement on Taiwan in 1995 that appeared more moderate and forthcoming
than past Chinese pronouncements.[2]

Against this background, Taiwan President Lee Teng-hui surprised Chinese leaders as he capped recent international activism by gaining permission
from the United States to visit Cornell University in 1995. Lee's actions and
the U.S. role were seen in China as fundamental challenges to Chinese core

interests, and China responded harshly, notably with a series of military exercises in the Taiwan area during a nine-month period leading up to the March 1996 Taiwan presidential election. The U.S. administration of President Bill Clinton became seriously concerned with the need to reassure China of U.S. intentions over Taiwan while deterring China from using force. Prior to the Taiwan presidential election, it sent two aircraft carrier battle groups to the Taiwan area.[3]

Though there were off-again, on-again efforts to improve cross-strait relations, and the U.S. government worked to calm the situation, tensions rose again following Lee Teng-hui's declaration in an international media interview in 1999 that he viewed cross-strait relations as a relationship between two separate states, an implicit challenge to China's "one China" principle with Taiwan being considered part of China. China warned Taiwan voters against choosing the candidate of the Democratic Progressive Party (DPP), Chen Shui-bian, in presidential elections of 2000. Chen and his party had a long record supporting self-determination for Taiwan, an anathema to China. Chen won the election. He made little progress with China, which chose to work with the political opposition of the Kuomintang (KMT) party and its political allies, which controlled the legislature and opposed many of Chen's initiatives.[4]

Chen's reelection campaign in 2003–2004 featured a series of appeals to Taiwan nationalism and identity separate from China that Chinese leaders saw as direct challenges to their national interests and U.S. leaders saw as dangerously provocative.

Chinese officials watched with dismay as cross-strait relations turned for the worse. Even though the Chen government had agreed not to change the country's name (Republic of China), flag, and the few provisions in the constitution that identified Taiwan with China, in the months before the presidential election of March 2004, President Chen and his supporters veered strongly toward greater political independence for Taiwan. They rejected the principle of one China; condemned China's pressure tactics; and pushed hard for broad-ranging legal and institutional reforms in civil service practices, education, cultural support, public information, diplomacy, and other areas. The reforms they sought would have ended past government practices that identified Taiwan with China and reinforced Taiwan's identity as a country permanently separate from China. In this context, they sought major constitutional changes.[5]

Chinese and U.S. officials viewed the reforms as steps toward independence and as making it increasingly unlikely that Taiwan ever would voluntarily agree to be part of China.[6] Chinese officials focused on possible changes in provisions in the constitution that identified Taiwan with China, warning

that removing those provisions and establishing a formal and legally binding status for Taiwan as a country permanently separate from China would
result in China's use of force. Officials from the United States were anxious to
avoid this outcome. Overall, the situation in the Taiwan Strait became tenser.
China's leaders found that their mix of economic incentives, proposals for
talks, military threats, and coercive diplomacy had obviously failed to stop
Taiwan's moves toward greater separation.[7]

While the PRC's long-term objective was reunification, Chinese leaders
for the time being seemed focused on preventing Taiwan from taking further
steps toward permanent separation. Proposals by Deng Xiaoping and Jiang
Zemin, which were supported by current Chinese leaders, stated that Taipei
could have a high degree of autonomy under future arrangements, but insisted Taiwan must recognize itself as part of one China. Although Beijing's
vision of a unified China remained vague, China was clearer on what it would
not tolerate, warning that moves by Taiwan toward greater separation, notably a declaration of independence, would be met with force.[8]

Among the reasons for the Chinese leaders' acute concern over Taiwan's
independence was the fact that Taiwan's status remained a deeply emotional
and nationalistic issue for Chinese leaders and citizens. The CCP leadership
saw its own legitimacy entwined with its ability to show progress toward the
goal of reunifying Taiwan with the mainland. It was reluctant to deviate from
past positions widely accepted in China, sticking to a mix of hard and soft
tactics that—unfortunately for China—seemed at this time to drive Taiwan
further away. Beijing also perceived Taiwan as a security problem; its alignment with the United States and possibly Japan posed a barrier to China's
regional and global influence. Taiwan could serve as a base for subversion in
case of domestic turmoil on the mainland.[9]

In Taiwan, political forces were divided on cross-strait issues. President
Chen Shui-bian, his ruling DPP, and their more radical allies in Lee Teng-
hui's Taiwan Solidarity Union (TSU) party represented the so-called pan-
green camp—one side of the political spectrum that continued to push for
reforms that strengthened Taiwan's status as a country permanently separate
from China. On the other side was the so-called pan-blue camp, made up of
the formerly ruling KMT Party and their ally the People's First Party (PFP),
which generally was more cautious in taking political steps that might antagonize China.[10]

Chinese officials initially reacted with alarm as President Chen pursued his
anti-China and pro-independence initiatives in 2003 and 2004.[11] They viewed
Chen's proposed reforms involving changes in the Taiwan constitution as steps
toward independence and possible cause for war. Seeing the rise of instability
and an increased danger of conflict in the Taiwan area, U.S. officials also were

concerned with Chen's moves and took extraordinary steps to warn against them. Standing alongside Chinese Premier Wen Jiabao, President George W. Bush publicly rebuked Taiwan's president in a meeting with reporters in Washington, D.C., on December 9, 2003. Concerned that popular opinion in Taiwan and pan-blue leaders also were moving toward a tougher stance toward China, Chinese officials urged U.S. and international pressure to rein in the Taiwan leader. They judged that among the few options acceptable to Chinese officials, a strident public Chinese stance probably would be counterproductive for China's purposes. They were concerned that such an approach would likely increase support for Chen in the prevailing atmosphere in Taiwan.[12]

Chen's narrow reelection victory in March 2004 showed Chinese and other observers how far the Taiwan electorate had moved from the 1990s, when pro-independence was a clear liability among the Taiwanese voters. Chinese officials were pleased that U.S. pressure sought to curb Chen's more ambitious reform efforts that flirted with de jure independence, but they pushed for more overt U.S. pressure, including curbs on U.S. arms sales.[13] Officials from the United States continued to press Chen to avoid provocative actions but remained firm in maintaining military support for Taiwan as a means to deter China from using force against Taiwan. They intervened repeatedly in the lead-up to the 2004 legislative elections to highlight differences between U.S. policy and the assertive positions of President Chen and his supporters.[14]

Chinese officials appeared to judge that they were not in a strong position to influence the factors that would curb the Chen administration's push toward greater independence, and at the same time they were not able to tolerate Chen's initiatives. Chen seemed to be driven by election politics, his own and his party's ambitions, and a basic sense in Taiwan that China's military threat was minimal, especially given strong U.S. military support for Taiwan.[15]

The Bush administration by 2003 and 2004 took repeated public and private steps to shake Taiwan assurance of U.S. support and thereby curb provocative pro-independence posturing by the Chen administration. Highlights of such U.S. displays included President Bush's December 9, 2003, public rebuke of President Chen's cross-strait policies; Secretary of State Colin Powell's admonition in October 2004 that the United States did not regard Taiwan as an independent state; and Deputy Secretary of State Richard Armitage's assertion that Taiwan represented a big problem, "a landmine," for U.S. policy. Signs of decline in U.S. support and friction in U.S.-Taiwan relations upset public opinion in Taiwan, prompted pan-blue accusations against the Chen administration, and caused policy reviews within the Chen government.[16]

The Chen administration became more aware that the recent level of U.S. support for Taiwan could decline if Taiwan was seen by Washington as provoking serious tensions with China. Continued U.S. preoccupation with the conflict in Iraq and U.S. reliance on China in dealing with North Korea were seen to restrict U.S. tolerance of Taiwanese reforms or other measures that upset China. Officials in Taiwan also came to worry that the U.S. administration might revert to past U.S. pressure on Taiwan to resume cross-strait dialogues on terms Taiwan was reluctant to accept, or that the United States might seek arrangements to avoid war or other understandings with China that were adverse to Taiwan's interests.[17]

The poor showing of the DPP candidates in the legislative election of December 2004 was seen by President Chen as a public rebuke of his assertive stance, and he and his party reverted for a time to the lower profile on cross-strait issues that he had used prior to 2003. After the dramatic visits of KMT Chairman Lien Chan and PFP leader James Soong to China in the first half of 2005, Chinese President Hu Jintao and other Chinese officials muted China's past insistence on reunification under the "one country–two systems" formula. The formula also was used to govern Hong Kong's return to China and was long rejected by large majorities in Taiwan. He and other Chinese officials and commentators also avoided a discussion of a possible timetable for reunification of Taiwan with the mainland, instead focusing on the need to avoid further steps by Taiwan toward independence and promised various cross-strait economic, cultural, educational, and other benefits for the Taiwanese people. China remained firmly opposed to Taiwan's moves toward independence and notably registered its stance in an anti-secession law passed in 2005.[18]

Amid favorable publicity for the Lien and Soong summits in China, President Chen for a time appeared to vacillate about renewing contacts with China. He soon reverted, however, to positions at odds with China's insistence on one China and curbing moves toward independence. By 2006, President Chen began to renew the kinds of pro-independence, anti-China initiatives that had caused the flare-up of tensions in cross-strait relations and widening differences between the Taiwan and U.S. governments seen in 2003–2004. The president announced in 2006 that the National Unification Council (NUC) would cease to function and that the National Unification Guidelines (NUG) that the NUC created would cease to apply. The continuation of the NUC and NUG, dating back to the early 1990s, were key elements of the status quo that Chen, under pressure from the United States, had pledged not to change as part of his presidential inaugural speech in 2000. The U.S. government pressed Chen to reverse the 2006 initiative, but the results did not fully satisfy the U.S. government and deepened Bush administration suspicion of the Taiwan president.[19]

As the Chen administration wound down its term in office with a reputation for poor governance and rising corruption scandals and as its approval ratings remained low, President Chen carried out a variety of controversial initiatives in pursuing a legacy of developing a national consciousness in Taiwan as a state separate from China. These involved changes in education policies; changes in the naming of government places, organizations, and institutions; constitutional changes; and approaches to the United Nations, related organizations like the World Health Organization, and broader international recognition that emphasized Taiwan's status as a country separate from China. These steps usually were seen as provocative by China and by the Bush administration, with the U.S. government weighing in publicly against measures it saw as upsetting the stability in the Taiwan Strait. The Chen administration's relations with the United States reached a point where U.S. hosting of stopovers for Chen's transits on trips abroad became restrictive and involved locales as far away from Washington as possible.[20]

China duly registered public opposition to Chen's initiatives but placed more emphasis than ever on working in consultation with the Bush administration to deal with Chen's maneuvers. It continued to reinforce the impressive military buildup focused on Taiwan, and to deepen Taiwan's economic interdependence with the mainland. Looking beyond the Chen administration, Chinese officials built on increasingly positive connections they developed with the opposition pan-blue leaders and broader segments of Taiwan business elites and other Taiwan opinion leaders.[21]

In the end, Chen's maneuvers and their negative consequences for cross-strait and Taiwan-U.S. relations, along with the Taiwan president's apparent deep personal involvement in corruption scandals, seemed to undermine the attractiveness of DPP candidates in Taiwan legislative elections in January 2008 and the Taiwan presidential election in March 2008. The result was a landslide victory for KMT candidates. The party gained overwhelming control of the legislature, and new President Ma Ying-jeou had a strong political mandate to pursue policies of reassurance and moderation in cross-strait relations.[22]

Improving Relations

Taiwan President Ma Ying-jeou won the presidential election of March 2008 and came to power in May of that year with an agenda emphasizing improvement in cross-strait relations based on reassurance of China that his government would not move Taiwan toward independence and based on closer economic, social, and other contacts across the strait. President Ma and his colleagues in Taiwan and their counterparts in China have emphasized that progress will be easier in building closer and mutually advantageous economic and social ties while issues of security and sovereignty posed by the growing Chinese military buildup opposite Taiwan and reaching agreement on Taiwan's desired greater international participation will be harder to deal with.[23]

On the whole, the improvements in cross-strait relations have been rapid and impressive. Since March 2008, the security situation in the Taiwan Strait has entered a period of relaxing tensions. Both Beijing and Taipei have emphasized enhancing people-to-people contacts and expanding economic ties. The United States has kept a low public profile as it has joined Beijing and Taipei in welcoming improved cross-strait relations.

Reflecting the difficulty of achieving meaningful progress on security issues, as of late 2009, there were no significant actions on the part of the Chinese administration to reduce its military presence directly opposite Taiwan. However, preceding the March 2008 Taiwan presidential election, PRC rhetoric appeared to signal a greater willingness by Beijing to consider the use of limited force to prevent independence. Such rhetoric and other signs of China's possible use of force declined along with overall tensions between Taiwan and China in the ensuing months.[24]

Chinese president and Communist Party general secretary Hu Jintao has been prominent on the Chinese side in seeking mutually advantageous ties and improved relations across the strait. In a statement after the March election on Taiwan, President Hu proposed that the Mainland and Taiwan "build mutual trust, lay aside disputes, seek consensus and shelve differences, and create a win-win situation" to secure peace and promote the "peaceful development of cross-strait relations." In a signal of his openness to the overture, newly elected Taiwan President Ma referenced Hu's statement during his inaugural address.[25]

Using the momentum of the election victories in 2008, President Ma and his senior colleagues set to work advancing a more positive approach to China. Even before his inaugural address, Ma and his running mate Vincent Siew made clear the incoming Taiwan government would eschew Taiwan independence, increase cross-strait economic and social contacts, try to reach understandings with China on Taiwan's greater participation in international affairs, and endeavor to ease military tensions in the Taiwan Strait. Beijing leaders warmly welcomed the Taiwan initiatives. In April, Hu Jintao met first with Vice President-elect Siew at China's Boao Forum, and later laid out guidelines for managing cross-strait relations in a meeting with KMT Honorary Chairman Lien Chan. The head of the KMT Wu Poh-hsiung visited China and met with Hu Jintao a week after Ma's inauguration. China and Taiwan leaders reached an understanding based on the so-called 1992 consensus that allowed for forward movement in cross-strait relations without explicitly addressing adherence to China's One-China principle, which had impeded progress in the past on account of each side's different views of one China and Taiwan's status. At the same time, the two sides also adhered to an implicit agreement on non-denial; that is, that neither explicitly denied the other's sovereignty.[26]

Against this background, Taiwan's Straits Exchange Foundation (SEF) and China's Association for Relations Across the Taiwan Strait (ARATS) reinstituted semi-official bilateral exchanges in June 2008 after a nine-year hiatus. The first round of dialogue centered on noncontroversial issues: regular direct weekend cross-strait charter flights and increased mainland tourism to Taiwan. The dialogue did not address sensitive political subjects such as sovereignty and Taiwan's international diplomatic representation or participation in international organizations. The SEF Chairperson P. K. Chiang visited China for the talks and agreements. He was received cordially by his Chinese counterparts led by ARATS Chairman Chen Yunlin and also had a friendly meeting with Hu Jintao.

ARATS Chairman Chen visited Taiwan in November 2008 to sign agreements with his SEF counterpart. The visit saw four major agreements on cross-strait relations:

- A shipping agreement that authorized direct shipping between designated ports;
- An air transport agreement that authorized charter flights between an expanded list of cities, authorized limited cargo flights, and approved direct flight routes that no longer had to pass through Hong Kong's airspace;
- A postal agreement authorizing mail to be shipped directly between postal authorities; and
- A food safety agreement providing for direct contacts between food safety and sanitary offices of the two governments.

The last agreement was the result of a recent crisis in cross-strait trade caused by tainted milk products coming to Taiwan from China. The three other agreements effectively achieved the so-called "three links" offered by China as an inducement to Taiwan to improve relations and move toward reunification thirty years earlier.[27]

The ARATS leader had cordial meetings with President Ma and other senior leaders, but the political opposition in Taiwan registered their dissatisfaction in mass demonstrations against the Chinese envoy. At one point, the demonstrators surrounded a Taipei hotel where the envoy was having dinner, preventing his departure for several hours; President Ma had to change arrangements for meeting the envoy in order to outmaneuver the demonstrators.

Many demonstrators and police were injured in the confrontations during the Chinese envoy's visit.

Chinese officials and official media chose to emphasize the positive and play down the significance of the demonstrations. On December 31, 2008, PRC President Hu Jintao gave a speech commemorating the 1979 "Message to Compatriots in Taiwan," in which the PRC abandoned the idea of "armed liberation" in favor of "peaceful liberation." Hu's speech outlined six points that would govern China's approach to future cross-strait relations including cross-strait military confidence-building measures and negotiation of a peace agreement. Since Hu's previous major policy statements on Taiwan had been made to deal with separatist challenges posed by the previous Taiwan administration led by President Chen Shui-bian of the DPP, the December 31 statement set authoritative Chinese guidelines for dealing with the new situation under Taiwan President Ma Ying-jeou.

Hu's remarks duly emphasized China's insistence on the One-China Principle and the necessity of unification, though he noted this should be accomplished with wisdom and patience. Though China was actively participating in resumed SEF-ARATS talks on the basis of the 1992 consensus (which implicitly allowed Taipei to have a different interpretation of one China than Beijing), Hu reaffirmed a standard Chinese stance that on the basis of a "common understanding about one China," all matters can be discussed. In this context he addressed Taiwan's desire for greater international space in the face of strong opposition from China, noting that the issue can be discussed so long as there is no movement toward "two Chinas" or "one China–one Taiwan." He also called for discussion of a comprehensive economic cooperation agreement and the promotion of Chinese culture across the strait in order to strengthen "national consciousness" in Taiwan and the mainland. Generally, the Ma administration in Taiwan viewed Hu's six points positively. Nevertheless, its initial comments reminded China that Taiwan's policy is based on the 1992 consensus allowing for different interpretations of one China and neither side denying the other's sovereignty.[28]

In April 2009, the third round of SEF-ARATS talks produced three new agreements and an understanding to open Taiwan to investors from the mainland. The improvements in cross-strait relations were generally well received in Taiwan. The agreements were an air transport agreement providing for the start of regular scheduled air service, additional direct flights, and expanding passenger and freight service; a financial cooperation agreement creating a framework for negotiating memoranda of understanding on regulation of banking, securities, foreign exchange, and insurance; and an agreement on fighting crime and mutual legal assistance. The understanding on opening Taiwan to mainland investment was followed quickly by administrative actions in both Beijing and Taipei to facilitate mainland Chinese investment in Taiwan.[29]

More controversial in Taiwan was a proposed Economic Cooperation Framework Agreement (ECFA). The Ma administration spoke out in favor of such a comprehensive arrangement to expand cross-strait economic cooperation. Initial discussion focused on the Comprehensive Economic Partnership Agreement similar to the arrangement that China has with Hong Kong, but that proved controversial amid strong opposition from the DPP leaders so the Ma administration shifted to the ECFA, which remains a target of DPP opposition. The DPP opponents see ECFA and the rapid development of cross-strait economic links as compromising Taiwan's economic security and political autonomy.

The ECFA was not on the agenda for the SEF-ARATS meeting in April 2009 though it was discussed by Hu Jintao in May 2009 during the latest in a series of top-level dialogues between Chinese Communist Party (CCP) and Kuomintang (KMT) that began four years earlier with the visit of KMT leader Lien Chan to China. Hu told visiting KMT Chairman Wu Poh-hsiung that the agreement should be of mutual benefit and that the two sides should endeavor to start negotiations on the agreement later in 2009.

The nine SEF-ARATS agreements reached in one year since the start of the Ma Ying-jeou presidency were the highlights of burgeoning face-to-face interaction between Taiwan and China authorities after decades of no direct dealings. The agreements between the ostensibly unofficial Taiwan and China organizations, SEF and ARATS, required officials of the two governments to deal with each other on a host of transportation, food safety, financial regulation, and law enforcement issues. In effect, three channels of communication were now active between the Taiwan and Chinese authorities: the SEF-ARATS exchanges; exchanges between the leaders of the CCP and KMT; and widening government-to-government coordination and cooperation on a variety of cross-strait issues.

Many of the agreements, interactions, and understandings focused on managing the large-scale trade and investment between Taiwan and China. The global economic recession caused cross-strait trade and investment to decline significantly in the latter part of 2008, though the downturn seemed to be slowing by mid-2009 amid Chinese efforts to help Taiwan economically. On the whole, prevailing trends deepened Taiwan's dependence on China for its economic prosperity and well-being.

According to Taiwan administration figures, cross-strait trade in 2008 reached $105 billion, up 3 percent for the year. Taiwan exports were about $74 billion, down slightly from the previous year and Taiwan's imports were about $31 billion, up 12 percent over 2007. As in the past, China's statistics showed higher imports and exports. Two-way trade was $129 billion, up 3.8 percent. China's imports were valued at $103 billion and exports at $25.9 billion. (For comparison, reflecting the large Taiwan investment in the Chinese mainland, China supplanted the United States as Taiwan's largest trade partner in 2003. In 2008, China, including Hong Kong, accounted for over 27 percent of Taiwan's total trade and almost 40 percent of Taiwan's exports. Japan was Taiwan's second-largest trading partner with 13 percent of total trade, including 19 percent of Taiwan's imports. The United States was Taiwan's third-largest trade partner, taking 12 percent of Taiwan's exports and supplying 11 percent of its imports. Taiwan was the United States' twelfth-largest trading partner; Taiwan's two-way trade with the United States amounted to $61.6 billion in 2008.)[30]

Taiwan investment in China has been harder to measure with precision but has long been estimated at over $100 billion with recent estimates much higher. Taiwan official statistics indicate that Taiwan firms had invested about U.S. $75.6 billion in China through 2008, which is more than half of Taiwan's stock of direct foreign investment. According to the U.S. Department of State, many unofficial estimates put the actual value of Taiwan investment in China at over U.S. $300 billion. More than one million Taiwan people are estimated to be residing in China, and more than seventy thousand Taiwan companies have operations there. Taiwan firms are increasingly acting as management centers that take in orders, produce them in Taiwan, the mainland, or Southeast Asia, and then ship the final products to the U.S. and other markets. The recent opening of Taiwan to Chinese tourists saw three hundred thousand Chinese tourists visit the island in the first four months of 2009, equivalent to the number of mainland tourists who visited in 2008.[31]

Meanwhile, the Ma Ying-jeou government achieved an important breakthrough in getting China to allow Taiwan to participate in the annual World Health Assembly (WHA) meeting in May 2009 as an observer using the name "Chinese Taipei." The Taiwan president and his administration focused on the need for China to ease its strong efforts to block Taiwan's participation in this and other international bodies as part of China's broader efforts to isolate Taiwan internationally. Otherwise, it was argued, improved mutual trust in cross-strait relations would be much more difficult to achieve. Taiwan's participation in the WHA meeting had substantial public support in Taiwan, though the DPP criticized the arrangement. How Taipei came to agreement with China over the modalities of Taiwan's participation was not publicly known, suggesting that various channels of communications outside public view are active between the Taipei and Beijing leaderships.[32]

Other evidence of progress in China-Taiwan relations over issues regarding Taiwan's participation in international affairs was the diminishment of what had been strident Taiwan-China competition for international recognition. In recent years, Taiwan had been slowly losing out to China; it retained formal diplomatic relations with twenty-three small governments. The Ma administration proposed a diplomatic truce where each side would halt efforts to win diplomatic recognition from countries at the expense of the other. China seemed to agree, and the truce seemed to hold despite indications that countries like Paraguay, Nicaragua, and others were inclined to shift diplomatic relations from Taipei to Beijing.[33]

U.S. reaction to recent developments in Taiwan has been positive. The Bush administration welcomed the efforts of the Ma government and China's positive response as stabilizing and beneficial for all parties concerned. It turned aside an initiative by President-elect Ma to visit the United States for talks with U.S. officials prior to his inauguration. Ma made no other such requests to the U.S. government; he worked hard to keep his transit stops in the United States discreet in ways that would not complicate U.S. relations with China. High-level contacts occurred between the U.S. and Taiwan government in quiet and private ways that avoided upsetting China, and ongoing U.S. military consultations with and advice to Taiwan's armed forces continued.[34]

The Bush administration delayed until close to the last minute approval of a large arms sales package for Taiwan. The approved package, worth $6.5 billion, was the largest during the tenure of the Bush government. Initial generous offers from the United States were repeatedly delayed and whittled down on account of partisan bickering and funding delays for many years in Taiwan; this was followed by U.S. reluctance to provide arms that would appear to support President Chen Shui-bian's perceived provocative stance toward China. In the end, the package represented about half of what Taiwan said it wanted; and it did not include sixty-six F-16 fighters that Taiwan had been trying for years to get the U.S. government to begin to consider selling to Taiwan. China reacted to the sale with strong criticism and suspension of military contacts with the United States. Those contacts were resumed in mid-2009.[35]

The Ma administration restored mutual trust in Taiwan-American relations that had been damaged during the Chen Shui-bian administration. The incoming Obama government in the United States welcomed the new stability in cross-strait ties. Like the outgoing Bush government, the Obama administration appeared to be relying on President Ma and his team to continue to manage cross-strait ties in positive ways that would not cause the Taiwan "hot spot" to reemerge on the already crowded list of U.S. policy priorities needing urgent attention by the new U.S. leader and his colleagues.[36]

Short-Term Outlook

The likely path of cross-strait relations and implications for U.S.-China relations regarding Taiwan can be addressed by assessing salient costs and benefits for the respective administrations of significant change or continuity in their approaches to cross-strait issues in order to determine their likely approaches and what these approaches mean for their respective relationships. This section will review in this way the approaches of China, Taiwan, and the United States, in order to come to a conclusion about whether the shift toward moderation and cooperation begun in 2008 is likely to be sustained or modified.

China's Costs and Benefits

Developments in cross-strait relations since the advent of the Ma Ying-jeou administration represent a major advance for China over the situation in cross-strait relations prior to Ma's ascension. The improvements in cross-strait relations over the past year seem to work well for Chinese interests. The benefits for China are strong and many. The costs are few. The Chinese appear likely to continue along the current trajectory.[37]

The broad pattern of Chinese policy and practice toward Taiwan shifted from emphasis on military confrontation and liberation of Taiwan in the 1950s and 1960s. By the end of the 1970s, China came to call for rapprochement and reconciliation as Beijing gained international recognition at Taiwan's expense and succeeded in establishing diplomatic relations with the United States, compelling Washington to end all official ties with Taiwan in 1979. Internationally isolated and on the defensive, Taiwan at first rejected China's overtures. However, China's emerging economic reforms in the 1980s proved irresistible to Taiwan traders and investors, and the more democratic Taiwan governments that began to emerge in the 1980s accommodated growing sentiment in Taiwan for closer business ties and other interaction with China.[38]

Chinese leaders showed some confidence that growing cross-strait economic ties and China's international prominence would eventually lead Taiwan to come to terms with China under the rubric of the one country–two systems formula used in China's successful negotiations with Great Britain in 1984 over Hong Kong's return to Chinese sovereignty. The Tiananmen crisis in 1989 and the end of the Cold War undermined China's international prominence. The new developments particularly weakened U.S. willingness to accommodate China's demands regarding U.S. arms sales and other ties with Taiwan for the sake of sustaining close ties with China against the Soviet

Union. Growing democracy in Taiwan also saw the United States pay more positive attention to developments there. China also saw political forces emerge on the island calling for self-determination or permanent separation of Taiwan from China, and those forces seemed to get support from the United States and other foreign governments and interest groups.

With the emergence of serious cross-strait tensions and military confrontations in the period from Lee Teng-hui's visit to the United States in 1995 to the end of the Chen Shui-bian administration in 2008, China settled on policies and practices in cross-strait relations that relied on three major elements to deal with Taiwan. Two were coercive. They involved a major buildup in Chinese military forces opposite Taiwan to provide a warning to Taiwan leaders that moves toward independence would be met with Chinese military force, and a warning to the United States that China would deal with U.S. military intervention in a Taiwan conflict with military force. And they involved an increase in the already intense Chinese competition with Taiwan for international recognition. The latter Chinese effort not only sought to woo from Taiwan those governments that continued to recognize Taipei but also exerted greater pressure against Taiwan's efforts to participate in various governmental and some prominent nongovernmental international organizations and greater pressure to prevent Taiwan officials from traveling to and interacting with foreign government officials. As China rose in economic power and international prominence, it had greater ability to support the military buildup focused on Taiwan; the Chinese defense budget has advanced over 10 percent each year since the early 1990s. China's economic and international importance increased its ability to woo governments previously aligned with Taiwan and to compel international organizations and foreign governments to avoid contacts with Taiwan.

The third element in China's approach to Taiwan was positive. It also relied on China's growing economic and international prominence. On the basis of the burgeoning China market, Chinese officials endeavored to build ever-closer ties with businesspeople and related political and other constituencies in Taiwan interested in profiting from closer economic ties with the Chinese mainland. The rapid growth of Taiwan's trade, investment, business presence, and other interaction with China laid the foundation for strong interests on the island supporting Taiwan policies that would be compatible with Chinese interests, at least to the point of avoiding pro-independence actions that would create serious cross-strait instability adverse to normal business interactions.[39]

The record of Chinese policies and practices in dealing with Taiwan during the often tumultuous developments of 1995–2008 shows periods of considerable uncertainty on the part of Chinese leaders that the three elements of their policies would succeed in preserving China's core commitment to one China and in moving Taiwan eventually to a settlement on reunification acceptable to China. For a time, the Chinese administration supplemented their approach with strong pressure on the Bush administration, in effect relying on the U.S. government to keep Taiwan from moving toward permanent separation from China.[40]

China's response to the policies and practices of the Ma Ying-jeou administration has been to strengthen its positive incentives designed to curb Taiwan's moves toward independence and encourage ever-closer Taiwan interaction and identification with China. China also has continued to strengthen its negative incentives against Taiwan in the form of the continued buildup on Chinese military forces focused on Taiwan. It has made few military concessions despite President Ma's insistence that China reduce its military pressure against Taiwan. Leaders on both sides have mentioned possible confidence-building measures designed to ease military tensions and improve relations, but progress here has been slow.[41]

China has achieved a strong position in efforts to internationally isolate Taiwan. On this basis and in response to the accommodating stance of the Ma Ying-jeou administration, China has offered concessions allowing Taiwan participation in the World Health Assembly and maintaining the diplomatic truce in competition for international recognition.

As the Chinese leadership has endeavored to build positive ties with Taiwan, it has played down past insistence on Taiwan's acceptance of China's view of the One-China Principle and has not denied Taiwan's sovereignty. Also getting less emphasis have been China's past stress on the one country–two systems formula, which has proven to be unpopular in Taiwan, and the need for a formal settlement or resolution of the Taiwan issue. An implication drawn by many in China, Taiwan, and abroad is that China is endeavoring to reciprocate Ma Ying-jeou's initiatives by following a gradual process of reassurance and engagement with Taiwan in the interest of fostering trends on the island opposed to moves toward independence and favorable to closer ties with China.[42]

For now at least, the costs of this more flexible approach for Chinese interests seem small. China has not changed its basic positions on opposition to Taiwan independence or seeking Taiwan reunification with China. The current flexible approach encourages trends in Taiwan to cooperate further with China in ways that appear to work in favor of Chinese goals of curbing pro-independence sentiment in Taiwan and building constituencies favorable to closer Taiwan interaction with China.

Heading the list of manifestations of China strengthening positive incentives encouraging Taiwan to eschew pro-independence moves and deepen engagement and identification with China are the "three links" and other economic, social, and related agreements discussed above which were reached between the two sides as a result of SEF-ARATS negotiations in 2009. They are supported by the expanding Taiwan trade, investment, business presence, and related interaction with China that now includes growing Chinese investment and presence in Taiwan.

Somewhat less prominent but also of considerable importance have been the strong efforts of the Chinese Communist Party–led administration to build closer relations with the KMT party and its pan-blue associates while endeavoring to develop ties with individual DPP leaders. The visit of a prominent DPP leader, Kaohsiung Mayor Chen Chu, to China in May 2009 appeared to be an important milestone in this long-term Chinese effort. Chen sought to promote Chinese interest in attending a major sports event, the 2009 World Games in Kaohsiung. The Chinese outreach effort in welcoming Chen drove home the point that Taiwan politicians, even prominent DPP members, can benefit their constituencies through positive interaction with China. KMT politicians have developed strong party-to-party links that they have used to the benefit of their constituencies and for their personal political benefit. By appealing to individual DPP leaders, China isolates the hard core of the DPP while broadening China's appeal to various Taiwan constituencies. Meanwhile, the CCP-led administration has appealed to important pan-green constituencies in Taiwan by opening segments of the Chinese market to their goods and services. This outreach effort has included Taiwan fruit and vegetable farmers and Taiwan plastic surgeons interested in working in the growing China market for this service.[43]

The web of Taiwan relations with the mainland strengthened with the advance of Hong Kong's relations with Taiwan following the departure of the Chen Shui-bian administration and the advent of the Ma Ying-jeou government. Citing the improved atmosphere in cross-strait relations, the Hong Kong government announced in May 2009 that The Hong Kong Trade Development Council set up an office in Taipei in October 2008, the Hong Kong Tourism Board was planning to open a Taipei office, and "principal officials of the government" will visit Taiwan. It disclosed that prominent KMT leader Jason Hu led a delegation of one hundred members to attend a forum in Hong Kong in April 2009. Hong Kong also relaxed entry arrangements for Taiwan residents visiting Hong Kong and strove to use its Closer Economic Partnership Arrangement (CEPA) with China to benefit Taiwan enterprises in Hong Kong.[44]

The progress China has made in consolidating economic, international, and military influence over Taiwan has not silenced debate, mainly in private discussions, among Chinese officials, specialists, and others about the pace and scope of Chinese concessions toward Taiwan. The main concern relates to the possibility of a return to power of the pan-green leadership as a result of elections in 2012. These leaders are suspected of being likely to use Chinese concessions regarding international space for Taiwan and possible concessions on China's military pressure on Taiwan in order to strengthen their positions as they pursue pro-independence activities. Though plausible, this argument does not seem to take sufficient account for the fact that Chinese concessions toward Taiwan in these sensitive areas remain small and seem easy to reverse if the Taiwan administration began to pursue once again policies adverse to Chinese interests.[45]

Taiwan's Costs and Benefits

The Ma Ying-jeou administration and the KMT-controlled legislature see the improvement in cross-strait relations as serving their interests. The KMT leaders are well aware of the resistance they face in Taiwan from pan-green opponents and the possible risks they run in deepening Taiwan's dependence on China. They seek more concessions from China on international space for Taiwan and on China's military buildup focused on Taiwan. They remain unsatisfied with Chinese concessions but seem unwilling to do much about their frustration. On balance, they seem to judge that Taiwan's recent policies and practices are the best course to pursue.[46]

In the politically divided discourse prevailing in Taiwan, the pan-green camp is strident in its opposition. It sees recent policies compromising Taiwan's sovereignty and increasing to dangerous levels Taiwan's economic, diplomatic, and security dependence on and weakness in the face of rising China.[47] For the time being and maybe longer, the pan-green camp remains in the minority politically and in the view of the Taiwan public. The DPP also remains in considerable disarray as a result of the election losses in 2008 and the arrest and trial of Chen Shui-bian on charges of extensive corruption backed by evidence widely seen as credible. In these circumstances, it appears that the Ma administration will be able and willing to follow existing policies of reassurance and flexibility on cross-strait relations that overall are seen to provide more benefits than costs for the Taiwan government and for majorities in Taiwan.[48]

Nevertheless, the continuing and often strident zero-sum debate between Taiwanese partisans over the recent improvements in cross-strait relations tends to obscure smaller but significant issues that affect the pace and scope of Taiwan's interaction with and reassurance of China in cross-strait relations. For example, the Ma Ying-jeou administration seeks a trade agreement with China but it found the initially proposed Comprehensive Economic Partnership Agreement too controversial in Taiwan domestic politics and instead opted for delay as it reframed the issue under the rubric of the proposed Economic Cooperation Framework Agreement (ECFA). The Ma Ying-jeou government also seeks closer support from the United States in order to shore up Taiwan's position as it deepens dependence on China, but is unwilling to lobby hard in public for sensitive arms transfers (for example, proposed F-16 fighter sales) and other interaction with the United States that would strongly alienate China and complicate Taiwan's efforts to reassure China. The Ma government seeks concessions from China in reductions of Chinese forces targeted at Taiwan but remains reluctant to take steps in building up its own forces or in working militarily more closely with the United States in seeking leverage to compel China to adhere to Taiwan's demands.

At bottom, the Ma government recognized that it has inherited a weak position from which to pressure China for changes desired by Taiwan. It continues to put emphasis on reassurance, diplomacy, and persuasion as the most appropriate means under the circumstances to move China to follow policies compatible with Taiwan's interests. If these policies and practices fail to elicit acceptable Chinese behavior or otherwise seem to run contrary to Taiwan's interests, it is argued by senior Taiwan administration leaders that the policies and practices can be reversed in favor of a more confrontational approach relying on greater Taiwan defense efforts and renewed international diplomatic competition with China.[49]

Pan-green and other strategists in Taiwan and abroad fear that Taiwan will soon become so dependent on China, and China will exert so much influence diplomatically, economically, and militarily over Taiwan, that Taiwan returning to policies and practices of confrontation and competition with China will not work. In their view, Ma is presiding over marked increases in Taiwan's economic dependency on China. Internationally, Ma has reached a point where Taiwan has to ask China's permission as it seeks greater participation in international affairs. Militarily, China's double-digit annual increases over the past two decades have coincided with significant declines both in Taiwan's defense preparedness and in the willingness of Taiwan leaders and people to make the economic and other sacrifices necessary in order to remedy the situation.[50]

U.S. forces remain strong and the United States continues to work closely in supporting reforms of Taiwan's military. But American frustration with comparatively weak Taiwan defense efforts in the face of rising Chinese power raises questions in the United States as to whether America is more committed to the defense of Taiwan than the Taiwan people and leaders. What this frustration will lead to in the realm of U.S. policy or practice is not clear, but the danger of an American shift away from strategic support for Taiwan may rise as the defense asymmetry between China and Taiwan grows and Taiwan efforts to remedy the problem remain inadequate.[51]

U.S. Costs and Benefits

In contrast to the strident public debate in Taiwan and the more restrained private debate in China, there has been little sign of debate in the U.S. government over the pros and cons for the United States regarding the recent improvement in cross-strait relations. U.S. officials responsible for Taiwan have supported recent developments. They also have denied reports that Taiwan's growing ties with China have reduced the influence of the United States over Taiwan. Despite sometimes vocal Chinese objections, U.S. leaders from President Obama on down support U.S. arms sales and defense preparations as means to sustain a "healthy balance" in the Taiwan Strait.[52]

The broader context of the Obama administration's China policy has emphasized continued cooperation. China and the United States have become increasingly interdependent economically and in other ways and need each other's cooperation as the U.S. and Chinese leaders deal with their respective daunting policy agendas. The United States seeks China's assistance in helping to manage adverse consequences of the global economic crisis, new U.S. efforts to deal with climate change, and regional hot spots ranging from Southwest Asia to North Korea. Against this background, the U.S. administration finds its interests best served by supporting the Ma Ying-jeou government's reassurance and engagement with China and avoiding U.S. steps to support Taiwan, such as extraordinary arms sales, that might upset China and complicate the Ma administration's reassurance efforts.[53]

Such debate that exists in the United States takes place mainly among groups of specialists who are not in the government or responsible for making U.S. policy. On the one side are specialists who favor the current Ma Ying-jeou approach and the U.S. administration's support for that approach. Among other things, this approach is seen to provide a significant opportunity to reach agreements easing tensions and supporting peace and stability in cross-strait relations, key goals of U.S. policy toward China and Taiwan for many years.[54]

On the other side are specialists who have a less sanguine view of diplomacy's effect on China's ambitions regarding Taiwan. They argue that the balance of influence and power are critical determinants in China's behavior; U.S. policy and practice need to take account of what they see as a significant change in the balance of power and influence in cross-strait relations being perpetuated by the Ma Ying-jeou policies of reassurance of and engagement with China. Advisers to presidential candidate John McCain argued for a robust buildup of U.S. support for Taiwan in order to counter what they viewed as recent adverse trends toward greater asymmetry between Taiwan and China. Others have argued that the United States should beef up support for Taiwan in order to strengthen the weak hand of the Ma Ying-jeou administration as it seeks concessions from China on China's defense buildup, international participation for Taiwan, and other issues. Still others have warned that American leaders talking of "healthy balance" in the Taiwan Strait are perpetuating a myth as China looms ever more powerful and influential in cross-strait economic, diplomatic, and military affairs. They call for a review of U.S. interests and policy in light of the changing balance of power in the straits that is not likely to be reversed. They worry that the U.S. approach of working with allies and others throughout China's periphery by collaborating in contingency plans for use in case China's rise becomes assertive and disruptive could be put in jeopardy if the Taiwan shifts substantially to China and downgrades the past importance of the United States to Taiwan. Finally, there are those Americans who believe that Taiwan's continued "free-riding" on the United States for defense of the island at a time of massive U.S. defense and economic commitments at home and abroad argues for a fundamental reassessment of the American defense commitment to Taiwan.[55]

Overall, the effect of these arguments on U.S. policy has appeared small in the context of more pragmatic and immediate concerns in Washington as well as in Taiwan regarding fostering positive relations with China and avoiding disruptions in recent reassurance efforts regarding Taiwan.

Conclusion

The tumultuous course of events in U.S.-China-Taiwan relations during the post–Cold War period underlines the current interest of the three administrations to pursue paths of moderation and cooperation. The assessment of the costs and benefits of recent improvement in cross-strait relations for the three main parties involved shows that the improvement is likely to continue.

China appears to gain the most benefit and bear the least cost. The Chinese calculus could change in the event a pan-green candidate wins the 2012 presidential election, but by that time China will have consolidated an even more influential position regarding Taiwan than exists today. China continues to oppose U.S. arms sales to Taiwan and other steps it sees running against Chinese interests in the improving cross-strait relationship.

Continuing policies of reassurance and engagement toward China also appear to offer greater benefits than costs to the Ma Ying-jeou government, though the Taiwan administration faces vocal opposition from the DPP and also faces a series of dilemmas in efforts to establish closer economic ties with China, to build supporting defense and other ties with the United States, and to strengthen Taiwan's own defense efforts. It is unclear at this point how these and other problems faced by the Ma government will be resolved and how they may impact on cross-strait relations.

U.S. policy seems content at least for now to support Ma's reassurance policies toward China as the United States sustains commitments to Taiwan, seeks China's cooperation on some key priorities, and endeavors to avoid trouble with China at a time of U.S. policy preoccupation with other issues. U.S. policy has not explicitly addressed the implications for American interests of Taiwan's ever-greater dependency on China and China's growing economic, diplomatic, and military advantage over Taiwan. For now, those concerns remain on the back burner.

11

Issues of Human Rights in Contemporary U.S.-China Relations

ISSUES OF HUMAN RIGHTS IN U.S.-CHINA RELATIONS reflect a wide range of values dealing with economic, social, political, cultural, and other interests and concerns of groups and individuals. Differences over human rights issues have long characterized Sino-American relations. The differences have their roots in the respective backgrounds of the American and Chinese societies, governments, and peoples. Those backgrounds foster values that are often at odds.[1]

In general, since the opening of Sino-American relations in the early 1970s, the Chinese and American administrations have endeavored to manage these differences in ways that do not block progress in other important areas of Sino-American relations. At times when one side or the other has focused high priority on human rights issues, as the United States did following the Tiananmen crackdown of 1989, U.S.-China relations have tended to stall or retrogress. As U.S. and Chinese leaders more often have devoted only secondary consideration to human rights differences, the obstacles posed by these issues for Sino-American relations have also been less significant.[2]

The importance of human rights differences between the United States and China has also been influenced by changes in policies and practices, especially on the part of China. In a broad sense, the United States has sought to prompt the Chinese administration to adopt policies and practices in line with the international values and norms prevalent in modern developed countries of the West. The review of economic issues in chapter 9 and the examination of security issues in chapter 8 show how Chinese leaders have seen their interests better served by conforming more to international norms in these areas. Economically, China's administration has embraced the norms of the globalized international economy and adapted comprehensively to economic market demands. Significant benchmarks in this process were capped by China's decision to join the WTO with an agreement demanding extensive changes in Chinese economic policies and practices. China's conformity to world norms in the security area has been slower but substantial, especially in areas involving such sensitive issues as the proliferation of weapons of mass destruction.

China's leadership also has endeavored to appear more in line with international norms regarding issues affecting political power and processes in China. Chinese officials have engaged in a broad range of discussions, dialogues, and agreements with various countries and international organizations designed to advance political rights in line with world norms supported by the United States. China has signed international covenants dealing with economic, social, and political rights. Chinese leaders routinely pledge cooperation with other countries in promoting human rights. They have fostered reforms emphasizing the rule of law, greater transparency and accountability, and promoting democracy and democratic decision-making in handling various human rights concerns in China. The progress of Chinese reform in these areas has encouraged some Chinese and foreign specialists to anticipate continued progress leading to the transformation of China's authoritarian one-party political system.[3] However, other specialists in China and abroad see the Chinese leadership as following policies of adaptation and adjustment in the area of political reform and related human rights.[4] The reforms in these areas are seen as not undermining Chinese leadership control of political power in China and the key concern of Chinese leaders to sustain and strengthen one-party rule in China through authoritarian as well as more liberal means.

Changing Importance of Human Rights Issues, 1969–2009

It's hard to imagine two societies and governments with more different sets of values than the United States and Maoist China. The progress made in U.S.-China reconciliation during the initial efforts of normalization begun by President Nixon and Chairman Mao is a testament to the pragmatism of the respective leaderships. Other interests—notably each country's need for support in the face of rising Soviet power and other complications—overrode differences regarding political and other values that divided the United States and China.[5]

President Carter rose to power on a platform pledging to devote more concern to American political values in the conduct of U.S. foreign policy. He pledged to put aside the realpolitik calculations seen as prevalent in the policies of the Nixon and Ford administrations. This shift in policy resulted in divergence and confrontation between the United States and some authoritarian governments, but it had little effect on U.S. relations with China. In the case of China, President Carter and his key aides pursued the pragmatic search for strategic leverage begun by Nixon; they did not allow differences over human rights and values to impede advances in relations, leading to the normalization of diplomatic relations in 1979.[6]

During the first decade of normalization of relations in the 1970s, there were signs of domestic debate and disagreement in both the United States and China over issues involving differences over values and human rights and the tendencies of the respective governments to give little overt attention to these differences in the pursuit of other interests. Leadership debate in China at the end of the Maoist period included disagreements over the alleged corrupting effect American and broader Western values would have on the prevailing authoritarian political order and social and economic structure of China. Removal of the radical Chinese leadership faction known as the Gang of Four following Mao's death in 1976 reduced the debate. Deng Xiaoping's return to power in 1978 coincided with a remarkable demonstration of freer speech in the posting of various proposals for reform, individual freedom, and democracy in Beijing's so-called Democracy Wall. After one year of publicizing proposals for sometimes-radical reform, including some calling for the end of the Communist rule in China, the Chinese leadership closed off this channel of free speech and arrested and imprisoned some prominent reform advocates.[7]

American public and elite opinion supported Nixon's opening to China and gave comparatively small attention to human rights issues in relations with China. A minority of media commentators, specialists, members of Congress, and other influential Americans called attention to President Carter's apparent double standard in pushing human rights issues in relations with various authoritarian governments, but not doing so in his administration's approach to China. The Democracy Wall caught the attention of the American and other foreign media and their audiences. As China opened to greater foreign contact and Chinese intellectuals were able to write about some of the searing experiences of Maoist rule, reporters, academic specialists, and other American and foreign commentators showed greater awareness of the enormous abuses of human rights in China and the wide gap between the United States and China over political and other values.[8]

The disclosures of human rights abuses in Maoist China and the closing of the Democracy Wall and arrests and imprisonment of prominent dissidents had little effect on the forward momentum in U.S.-China relations. Deng Xiaoping's reform programs were widely seen in the United States and elsewhere in the West to be advancing the material well-being of Chinese people while curbing many of the capricious uses of authoritarian administrative power that had prevailed during the Maoist period. Broadly gauged human rights conditions in China were seen to be improving with the post-Mao economic and political reforms and opening to greater international interchange. Some American officials, advocacy groups, and media commentators focused on the negative implications of China's continued Communist rule for imprisoned or otherwise suppressed political dissidents, and for religious and ethnic groups, notably Tibetan followers of the Dalai Lama. U.S. supporters of democracy and self-determination for Taiwan also joined Americans pressing for continued U.S. support for Taiwan's status separate from the control of China's Communist administration. In contrast, President Reagan seemed to capture the generally more optimistic American view about trends in China during his remarks at the time of his official visit to China in 1984. Reagan approved of emerging capitalist economic development in China and tended to soft-pedal criticism of China's authoritarian political system, referring to "so-called communist China," a sharp contrast with his trademark criticism of the "evil empire" seen prevailing in the communist-ruled Soviet Union.[9]

The economic and political reforms in China in the 1980s saw continued Chinese debate over the implications of closer Chinese interchange with the United States and the West. American and broader Western values of individual freedom were widely seen in elite and public opinion in China as a threat to the communist system in China. Conservatives railed against the danger of the so-called "spiritual pollution" from U.S. political values and culture that would undermine and weaken Chinese resiliency and power in the face of international forces, including the United States, that were often seen as unfriendly to China. The conservatives included key leaders in the old guard in the Communist Party hierarchy, and many other senior leaders said to be retired but who actually exerted great influence in Chinese decision-making. The conservatives continued to influence the reformists leading the Chinese Communist administration, forcing them to curb initiatives at home and abroad that might undercut the traditional power and prerogatives of Communist rule in China.[10]

The conservative leaders played a key role in support of the decision to suppress the demonstrators in Tiananmen Square in Beijing and in other Chinese cities in June 1989. Communist Party leaders advocating more moderate treatment of the demonstrators and continued political reform were removed from power. Over time, a Chinese leadership consensus emerged in favor of continued economic reform and outreach to the world for the benefit of Chinese modernization and development on the one hand; and strong efforts on the other hand to sustain authoritarian political rule in China and to resist pressures and other influences coming from U.S. and Western governments and other advocates of political and other change that could lead to the end of Communist Party rule in China. With the demise of the Soviet Union, the main "threat" to China was seen to come from the United States and its allies. The U.S. and other Western governments and a broad array of nongovernmental forces in these countries were seen to be pressing and undermining Communist Party rule and endeavoring to weaken and constrain its influence in Asian and world affairs.[11]

A resumption of more moderate policies of engagement with China by the United States and other governments later in the 1990s helped to reassure Chinese authorities of the intentions of those governments and diminished Chinese concern with the immediate threat of U.S. and other pressure regarding human rights and American values. But the Communist administration remained on guard against U.S. values; it was diligent and generally effective in suppressing political dissidents and perceived deviant religious organizations, ethnic groups, and other nongovernmental organizations and individuals. Those Chinese organizations and individuals sometimes received support from individuals and groups, including some government-sponsored organizations, in the United States or other countries favoring change in China's authoritarian political system in line with American and broader Western values.[12]

The Chinese crackdown on the Tiananmen demonstrators and the emerging consensus in the Chinese leadership regarding the need for a continued hard line against political dissent and unauthorized religious and ethnic movements placed human rights issues in the forefront of American differences with China. For a period after the Tiananmen crackdown, human rights advocates seemed to have the initiative in setting U.S. policy toward China. The George H. W. Bush administration was on the defensive, endeavoring to preserve key elements of the U.S. partnership with China despite the ending of the Cold War and the perceived diminished importance of China as a counterweight to the now sharply declining Soviet Union. Congressional leaders for a few months gave top priority to the often idiosyncratic and inconsistent views of Chinese students in the United States advocating reform in China and punishment for the Chinese authorities suppressing the demonstrators at Tiananmen.[13]

For over a decade, the annual congressional consideration of the president's decision to renew most favored national trade status for China provided an opportunity for American human rights advocates to publicize their criticisms of China and to seek government as well as media and broader public support for their efforts. The human rights advocates were soon joined by other Americans with interests regarding economic and security relations involving China, and advocates for stronger U.S. support for Taiwan, Tibet, and political rights in Hong Kong. As noted in chapter 5, the criticism of Chinese policies and practices in Congress was pervasive, though congressional commitment to a harder line against China often seemed thin. Partisan motives apart from concern with human rights and other differences with China frequently appeared to motivate critics of Chinese policies involved in the annual debates over whether to renew MFN trade treatment for China. When crises emerged in other areas affecting Sino-American interests, as they did during the war over Iraq's invasion of Kuwait in 1990 and the Taiwan Straits crisis of 1995–1996, the congressional criticism of China's human rights policies and practices subsided as American officials pursued pragmatic interaction with the Chinese administration. The Clinton administration succeeded in ending the annual congressional deliberations over China by reaching agreement with China on entry into the WTO and getting Congress to pass related legislation granting China permanent normal trade relations with the United States.[14]

Developments in the current decade have reinforced American tendencies to deal pragmatically with China and to play down differences. The terrorist attack on America in 2001 and the global economic crisis of 2008–2009 prompted U.S. leaders to minimize differences over human rights and related values in pursuit of closer cooperation with China for the sake of other American interests. However, these issues continued to be raised by U.S. leaders in discussions with China. President George W. Bush continued to voice concern with human rights issues, especially freedom of religion in China. He met several times with the Dalai Lama and also met with prominent political dissidents from China.[15]

President Obama seemed to capture the recent balance in the U.S. government's concerns with human rights issues when he spoke to the annual Sino-American leadership dialogue meeting in Washington in July 2009. He advised his Chinese colleagues that the American government did not seek to force China to conform to its view of human rights, but it will nonetheless continue to press China and others to conform to the values of human rights so important to the United States. He said:

> Support for human rights and human dignity is ingrained in America. Our nation is made up of immigrants from every part of the world. We have protected our unity and struggled to perfect our union by extending basic rights to all our people. And those rights include the freedom to speak your mind, to worship your God, and to choose your leaders. They are not things that we seek to impose—this is who we are. It guides our openness to one another and the world.[16]

Chinese leaders for their part highlight the great progress made in advancing economic, social, and other considerations affecting the lives of the vast majority of Chinese people during the post-Mao period. Public opinion in China tends to be supportive of prevailing conditions in the country. Chinese officials also underline China's increasing cooperation with foreign governments and international organizations to promote human rights abroad. They nonetheless draw a line against U.S. and other foreign government and nongovernment efforts to interfere in Chinese internal affairs in ways that would undermine the sovereignty of China and the integrity of its communist institutions. They resist foreign efforts to spotlight Chinese deviations from international norms in international organizations or world media.[17]

At times, these diverging Sino-American approaches have come together in ways that complicate U.S.-China relations. For example, an unanticipated uprising in Tibet in March 2008 saw a strenuous Chinese crackdown against dissent in Tibet. The developments received widespread negative media treatment in the United States and other Western countries. They coincided with an international Olympic Torch Relay that the Chinese administration had organized leading up to the summer Olympic Games in China in 2008. In March the Olympic Torch Relay traveled through several Western countries, including the United States, and was greeted by hostile demonstrators supporting Tibetan rights and condemning Chinese policies. Some Western leaders vacillated on whether to participate in the opening ceremony of the summer games. Chinese official and public resentment against the Western demonstrations, supportive media coverage, and political leaders sympathetic to the Dalai Lama and Tibetan rights was strong. President Bush said firmly that he would attend the summer games in China, easing the tension in Sino-American relations over the episode, but the Tibet issue remained highly sensitive in Chinese interaction with some West European countries and became a focal point of Chinese pressure on the incoming Obama administration.[18]

Contemporary Human Rights Practices and Issues

In the current decade, the Chinese administration has endeavored to deal with public grievances and domestic and foreign calls for redress and reform while suppressing activists who attempt to organize mass protests or create organizations at odds with CCP rule. The results have been some improvements in human rights along with continued serious abuses. On the one hand, China's developing legal system still features corruption and political interference, but it also has provided activists in China with tools with which to promote human rights. Although generally supportive of the status quo, the urban middle class has shown increased willingness to engage in narrowly targeted protests against local government policies. Their activism adds to more widespread social unrest among wage laborers and rural residents demonstrating against local administration policies and practices and other conditions. Despite a massive effort by the Chinese administration to control and censor information available to the public, the Internet and other communications technologies have made it more difficult for the government to clamp down on information as fully as before. On the other hand, the human rights abuses by Chinese authorities include unlawful killings by security forces, torture, unlawful detention, the excessive use of state security laws to imprison political dissidents, coercive family planning policies and practices, state control of information, and religious and ethnic persecution. Tibetan, ethnic Uighur Muslims, and Falun Gong adherents have been singled out for especially harsh treatment.[19]

The United States government duly acknowledges Chinese advances and shortcomings, notably in a series of congressionally supported official reports including the State Department's annual report on human rights conditions in world countries. U.S. government efforts to promote human rights in China include formal criticism of the Chinese government's policies and practices, official bilateral dialogues, public diplomacy, congressionally sponsored legislation, hearings, visits, and research. The U.S. government also provides funding for rule of law, civil society development, participatory government, labor rights, preserving Tibetan culture, Internet access, and other related programs in China. The U.S. government attention to human rights conditions in China is backed by more wide-ranging media coverage of human rights conditions in China and issues in U.S.-China relations and by reports and other publicity from prominent nongovernment groups and individuals in the United States with a strong interest in promoting advancement of human rights conditions in China.[20]

The American activism and pressure on China regarding human rights issues is tempered by an ongoing debate on whether human rights conditions in China have improved or not in recent years. On the negative side are U.S. media, congressional, and other commentators who highlight evidence of increasing Chinese legal restrictions on freedoms and cases of political and religious persecution. The annual State Department reports on human rights conditions in China are said by some to register no major or overall improvements. On the positive side are those who emphasize the expansion of economic and social freedoms in people's lives.[21]

Further complicating the debate has been the efforts of the Chinese administration to become more populist, accountable, and law-based, while rejecting Western democracy and more far-reaching political reforms. Party leader and President Hu Jintao and other senior officials have shown sympathy with segments of the population who have been left behind in the Chinese economic advance. The central leadership also has acknowledged human rights as a concern of the state, continued to develop legal institutions, and implemented limited institutional restraints on the exercise of state power. These steps forward have come amid continuing administrative practices that retain a large degree of arbitrary power for the ruling authorities.[22]

Indeed, the American debate about human rights conditions in China has mirrored a debate among Chinese authorities on where to strike the balance between efforts to improve governance and reduce sources of social and political instability through anti-corruption campaigns and the implementation of political reforms and efforts to check mass pressures for greater change. Some Chinese leaders have expressed fears that China's small but growing civil society, combined with foreign government and nongovernment assistance for advocacy groups in China, could bring about a "color revolution" in China. "Color revolutions" refer to peaceful democratic movements involving mass demonstrations supported by Western governments and nongovernment groups that toppled several post-communist authoritarian administrations in such former Soviet states as Georgia, Ukraine, and Kyrgyzstan. With this kind of fear in mind and with continuing determination to sustain and support Communist Party rule in China, the Chinese administration has enacted legislation aimed at preventing human rights abuses, but without protecting the activities of human rights activists who are subject to apparently arbitrary arrest and detention; it has tolerated protests against official policies, but has arrested protest leaders and organizers; public discourse on a wide variety of topics has become routine, but politically sensitive issues remain off-limits.[23]

Getting the right balance of flexibility and coercion seems especially important as growing economic and social changes have fostered tensions along with growing rights consciousness and social activism. Many efforts by citizens to express grievances and demand redress, having been met by government inaction or opposition, have erupted into large-scale public protests.[24]

The mixed picture of positives and negatives in recent Chinese human rights policies and behavior is well illustrated in the annual State Department reports on conditions in China, which tend to focus on infractions and other negative developments, and assessments by Chinese and foreign specialists highlighting various positive Chinese reforms and advances. Thus, the State Department report in recent years has noted episodes of unlawful or politically motivated killings, including people who died in detention because of torture. Torture seemed to be used commonly against Falun Gong adherents, Tibetans, Uighur Muslims, and other prisoners of conscience as well as criminal suspects. The Re-Education Through Labor system, in which individuals are held in administrative detention for antisocial activity, without formal charges or trial, for a period up to four years, remained a central feature of social and political control in China. Unlawful detention and house arrest remained widespread, particularly against human rights activists, lawyers, and journalists sympathetic to their cause, and leaders of unofficial Christian churches. Thousands of persons were viewed by the State Department as political prisoners, serving jail time for "endangering state security" or the former political crime of "counter-revolution." China's "one child policy" continues with fewer reports of coercive abortions, forced sterilization, and other unlawful government actions against individuals than were more common in earlier decades.[25]

This list of infractions and violations of human rights from the perspective of the American government is balanced by positive developments assisting greater freedom and helping to ensure human rights. Nongovernment organizations are often encouraged by the authorities to remain active in order to improve governance and to allow people to give vent to their frustrations in ways that do not directly oppose one-party rule. Some representatives from these organizations and others outside the Communist Party–controlled system have become more involved in advising regarding government policies and behavior on a variety of topics. Media freedom has been expanded in order to target corruption and other abuses of power. Freedom of worship within the range of government-approved religious organizations and churches remains strong; freedom of movement has been enhanced by government policies that try to accommodate the more than 10 percent of Chinese citizens who have left their rural homesteads to pursue opportunities in the wealthier urban areas.[26]

The purpose and scope of nongovernmental organizations (NGOs) have grown substantially in recent years. There are over three hundred thousand registered NGOs in China and over one million in total, including over two hundred international organizations. Environmental groups have been at the forefront of NGO development in China. Other areas of NGO activity included poverty alleviation, rural development, public health, education, and legal aid. The Chinese administration from time to time tightens restrictions on nongovernment organizations and voices opposition to foreign support for groups pushing reforms not favored by the Chinese administration, but the overall scope and activism of the NGOs continue to grow.[27]

Another area of positive development has been the human rights legislation and reforms enacted by the Chinese administration. In 2006, the government enacted prohibitions of specific acts of torture and requirements that interrogations of suspects of major crimes be recorded. Use of the death penalty, still egregiously high by international standards, has declined markedly under instituted review by the Supreme People's Court. A new Labor Contract Law went into effect in 2008, prompting increases in dispute arbitration cases and lawsuits over wages and benefits. Farmers were provided with new measures in 2008 allowing them more easily to lease, transfer, and sell rights to property allocated to them by the state. Government measures took effect in 2008 to require government institutions, especially local government administrations seen as more prone to corruption than other government bodies, to reveal financial accounts related to land seizures in rural areas. Responding to international criticism of organ transplants for profit from executed prisoners, the government enacted new regulations stipulating that the donation of organs for transplant must be free and voluntary.[28]

Human Rights Issues

A wide range of human rights issues continue to prompt critical attention from American officials in the Congress and the executive branch of government as well as American media, human rights groups, and other groups and individuals with an interest. Some issues—like the status of student demonstrators and others arrested during the Tiananmen crackdown, those suffering as a result of widespread abuses in China's family planning regime, and the status and prospects of pro-democracy advocates in Hong Kong—have subsided with the passage of time and changed circumstances. Others, like the human rights conditions in Tibet and among Uighur Muslims in China's restive Xinjiang region, have become more salient as a result of violence in both Tibet and Xinjiang over the past two years.[29]

Persecution of political dissent. China's state security law is used liberally and often arbitrarily against political dissidents. In 2007, the number of convictions under this law reportedly was 20 percent greater than in 2006, which was double that of 2005. According to the Congressional-Executive Commission on China, more than nine hundred persons in 2008 were serving prison terms for activities related to expression, assembly, spiritual practice, and religious worship. Once charged with crimes such as subversion, the accused are rarely acquitted, while conditions in prison are described as harsh and inhumane. There continue to be numerous reports of torture of human rights activists and other dissidents while in prison. Other activists claim to have been harassed by police or assaulted by unidentified assailants also described as "hired thugs."[30]

State control of information. The state authorities directly control the largest mass media outlets; they pressure other media regarding major or sensitive stories; and they impose severe measures against state critics. However, they exert less control of the media than they did a decade ago. Some scholars characterize state control of the media as evolving from "omnipresence to selective enforcement."[31] The greater volume of news reporting has not translated into significant advances in freedom of expression; and an increase in regulations affecting journalists and other critics has not significantly curbed the flow of information, thanks in large measure to the Internet. In some cases, the government has supported journalistic efforts to expose official corruption and incompetence, particularly at the local level. According to the *Washington Post*, a recent tactic of the central government seems to have been to allow relatively open reporting on such crises as the scandal over tainted baby formula and milk, as long as it assigns blame to economic enterprises or lower-level officials.[32]

The *Washington Post* also reported that Beijing has remained vigilant toward media activities seen challenging Communist Party rule. At the end of 2007, twenty-nine journalists and fifty-one cyber-dissidents were in detention for political reasons, according to the State Department. Reporters Without Borders, an advocacy group for press freedom, stated that twenty-four journalists, cyber-dissidents, and other "free expression activists" were arrested or sentenced to prison terms during the first half of 2008. An advance in media freedom occurred when the central government in October 2008 permanently adopted temporary regulations established for the August 2008 Olympic Games that expanded media freedoms for foreign journalists. According to the U.S.-based advocacy group Human Rights Watch, these freedoms included the ability of foreign journalists to travel within the country and to interview Chinese subjects without official permission.[33]

Scholars outside China pointed out that media freedoms have advanced as increasingly commercialized media outlets negotiate a delicate balance of responding to growing public demand for information while remaining within the bounds of what authorities will allow. Under the economic reform policies of the previous two decades, a vibrant private media industry developed, and market considerations have compelled many newspapers and television stations as well as Internet outlets to push the boundaries of acceptable cultural, social, and even political content. Nearly all media organizations in China rely on sales for support. State media also have had to provide more probing social and political content in order to attract readers, stay competitive, and respond to news and public opinion that appears on the Internet. On the one hand, media commercialization has opened up an unprecedented amount of free flow of information and helped to bolster the media's role as government watchdog. On the other hand, many domestic and foreign media outlets in China have been able to make profits in China without broaching political issues.[34]

According to *The New York Times*, the tug-of-war between society's demand for news and information and the state's attempts to maintain social and political control seemed likely to continue. The Central administration has employed a two-pronged approach, relying on traditional coercive tactics such as intimidation and incarceration of critics, as well as adapting to both society's growing expectations and innovations in communications technologies. Meanwhile, China's media and Internet users have pushed against state restrictions; growing numbers of young Internet users reportedly chafe against information control and express their frustrations online.[35]

As reported by the *Washington Post*, the *Reuters* news agency, and other foreign media, the government closure in 2006 of a politically provocative supplement in the relatively progressive *China Youth Daily* provoked an angry response by Chinese writers, academics, lawyers, and other citizens, especially on the Internet. Two years earlier, foreign media including *The New York Times* reported that the senior editor and other executives of the Guangzhou-based *Southern Weekend*, a weekly known for investigative journalism, were sentenced to prison terms on charges of embezzlement, reportedly provoking an antigovernment petition by dozens of prominent journalists and academics. The real reason for the crackdown, according to foreign media, was the newspaper's reporting of a suspected re-emergence of the SARS virus. The weekly eventually resumed its investigative reporting. In June 2008, it published an extensive article on the Sichuan earthquake and one school's substandard construction. In September, an editor reportedly wrote in his blog that prior to the Opening of the Olympic Games in Beijing, the newspaper received information about tainted milk supplies in China; the blog implied that the state ordered *Southern Weekend* to refrain from investigating the story further.[36]

Religious and ethnic issues. American media and other foreign sources showed that the extent of religious freedom varied widely within China. As noted earlier, participation in officially sanctioned religious activity has increased in recent years. The PRC Constitution protects "normal" religious activities and those that do not "disrupt public order, impair the health of citizens or interfere with the educational system of the state." Chinese regulations enacted in 2005 protect the rights of registered religious groups to publish literature, collect donations, possess property, and train and approve clergy. In 2008, the State Administration for Religious Affairs (SARA) established a new unit to supervise folk religions as well as religions outside the five officially recognized major religions (Buddhism, Protestantism, Roman Catholicism, Daoism, and Islam), including the Eastern Orthodox Church and the Church of Jesus Christ of Latter-Day Saints. The foreign media and other accounts asserted that these laws grant the government continued broad authority in determining what religious groups are lawful and to deny protections to others.[37]

As reported by U.S. government agencies and various U.S. and other foreign media, the religious and religious-ethnic groups that have clashed the most with the state in recent years have been unregistered Protestant and Catholic congregations, Tibetan Buddhists, and the Uighur Muslims in the Xinjiang

Uighur Autonomous Region. The International Religious Freedom Act of 1998 (P.L. 105-292) established the United States Commission on International Religious Freedom to monitor religious freedom around the world and make policy recommendations to the president and Congress. Based largely on Commission reports, the State Department has annually identified China as a "country of particular concern" on account of "particularly severe violations of religious freedom." This designation has subjected China to U.S. sanctions in accordance with provisions of P.L. 105-292, which have involved bans of U.S. exports of crime control and detection instruments and equipment to China. In 2005 the Commission made its first trip to China. It visited significant religious sites and gained much information but complained about the lack of access in their investigations.[38]

Chinese Christians. American-based interest groups, American media, and U.S. government reports disclose that Christians in China find increasing acceptance in Chinese society and, within limits, from the Chinese government. The Chinese leadership has begun to acknowledge the enduring positive roles that Christianity has played and can play in promoting social development and welfare. Yet it remains wary of the Christian church's power as a source of autonomous organization potentially challenging Communist rule. In late 2007, however, the senior Chinese party leaders met to consider religious affairs and were seen by some foreign observers to be more welcoming of the role of Christians and other religions in Chinese development.[39]

By some estimates of foreign specialists and reporters, the number of Christians in China ranges from about forty million to over sixty million, with nearly two thirds gathering in unofficial churches not approved by the Chinese administration. The Chinese government reported that membership in official churches had grown by 50 percent in the decade ending in 2006. Christianity's rise coincided with the rise in other religions; Buddhism, China's largest religion, attracts an estimated 100 million followers. The rise of religious memberships is attributed by foreign reports to the greater freedom and affluence among many Chinese and the need to cope with dramatic social and economic changes.[40]

Many unofficial Protestant churches, also known as "house churches" or "home gatherings" by the government, lack legal protection and remain vulnerable to the often-unchecked authority of local officials. According to reports from American agencies, interest groups, media, and other foreign sources, in some regions and large cities, particularly in southern China, unregistered congregations meet with little or no state interference, while in other areas, notably Henan and Shandong provinces and many rural areas, such independent gatherings experience harassment by local authorities and their leaders have been beaten, detained, and imprisoned.[41]

Many Chinese Protestants reject the official church, known as the Three-Self Patriotic Movement, for political and theological reasons. The government claims it has encouraged unofficial Protestant churches to register with the state but that many of them have been discouraged from doing so by foreign Christian groups. The China Aid Association, a U.S.-based nonprofit organization that monitors religious freedom in China, reported 788 incidents in which house churches were persecuted by the government in 2007, up 18.5 percent from 2006; 693 cases of Chinese Christians detained or arrested in 2007, up 6.6 percent from 2006; and 16 cases of Christians sentenced to prison terms in 2007, down 6 percent from 2006. Most detainees were reported to be released after sessions involving interrogation, intimidation, and sometimes torture by the police.[42] The *Washington Post* reported an upswing in government pressure on unauthorized Christians in the year leading up to the 2008 Olympic Games. The press included tightened restrictions, arrested leaders of house churches, harassed members of congregations, shut down places of worship, and denied visas to foreign missionaries.[43]

China has engaged in dialogue with the Vatican, which broke ties with China in 1951. Both sides express an interest in improved relations. One of the key obstacles to normalization has been China's rejection of the Holy See's authority to appoint bishops. In a 2007 "letter to Chinese Catholics," Pope Benedict conveyed greater flexibility toward Catholic churches that are registered with the government. China was low-key in its response to the letter. In September 2007, the state-sanctioned Catholic Patriotic Association appointed two bishops with the Vatican's blessing. Although government harassment of unregistered Catholic bishops, priests, and laypersons continues, a diminishing dichotomy between the unofficial and official Catholic churches in China has helped to reduce conflicts with the state, according to the 2008 State Department report on International Religious Freedom.[44]

Tibetans. Religious freedom and human rights issues in Tibet have a long history in Sino-American relations. Partly because of past clandestine U.S. support for Tibetan insurgencies against Chinese rule following the escape to India from Chinese rule in Tibet by the Dalai Lama and many thousands of his followers in the late 1950s, the Chinese administration remains wary of American intentions regarding Tibet. Even after the normalization of U.S. diplomatic relations with China, U.S. ambitions to challenge Chinese sovereignty over Tibet have been revealed from time to time as Congress has asserted its view of Tibet as a separate country, though the U.S. administration consistently accepts Chinese sovereignty over Tibet. The intertwined issues of sovereignty, border security, and ethnic and religious freedom make the issue of Tibet difficult to manage in Sino-American relations. Added to the mix is the attraction of many Americans to the Dalai Lama, the leader of

Tibetans abroad who also enjoys a strong but suppressed following among Tibetans in China.[45]

Coming against this background, a series of demonstration on March 10, 2008, began in Lhasa and other Tibetan regions of China to mark the forty-ninth anniversary of an unsuccessful Tibetan uprising against Chinese rule in 1959. The demonstrations appeared to begin peacefully with small groups that were then contained by security forces. But the protests and the response of the PRC authorities escalated in the ensuing days, spreading from the Tibetan Autonomous Region into parts of Sichuan, Gansu, and Qinghai Provinces with Tibetan populations. By March 14, 2008, mobs of angry people were burning and looting establishments in downtown Lhasa. Authorities of the PRC responded by sealing off Tibet and moving in large-scale security forces. The Chinese administration defended its actions as appropriate and necessary to restore civil order and prevent further violence. Media, interest groups, and some officials in the West responded to the Chinese actions by calling for boycotts of the opening ceremonies of the Beijing Olympics and calling on China to hold talks with the Dalai Lama.[46]

The Chinese administration and many Chinese people see China as having provided Tibet with extensive economic assistance and development using money from central government and provincial government coffers, and Chinese officials often seem perplexed at the simmering anger many Tibetans nevertheless retain against them. Despite economic development, Tibetans charge that the PRC interferes with Tibetan culture and religion. They cite as recent examples: Beijing's interference in 1995 in the choice of the Panchen Lama, Tibet's second highest-ranking personage; enactment of a "reincarnation law" in 2007 requiring Buddhist monks who wish to reincarnate to obtain prior approval from Beijing; and China's policy of conducting "patriotic education" campaigns, as well as efforts to foster atheism, among the Tibetan religious community. The PRC defends the campaigns as a tool to help monks become loyal, law-abiding citizens of China.[47]

The Chinese actions have been widely criticized by U.S. media, interest groups supporting Tibetan rights, members of Congress, and, generally more discreetly, U.S. administration officials. Controversy over the role of the Dalai Lama and the impact of PRC control on Tibet's language, culture, and religion have prompted recurring actions by Congress in support of Tibet's traditions—actions routinely denounced by Beijing. Members of Congress responded to the March 2008 demonstrations and crackdowns with legislation requiring U.S. government officials to boycott the Beijing Olympics opening ceremony; proposals condemning the crackdown and asking Beijing to hold talks with the Dalai Lama; and the formation of a new Tibet Caucus in the U.S. Congress.[48]

Many foreign experts judge that there is little hope that China will make significant changes in its Tibet policy, despite foreign pressure and advice. Beijing appears to calculate that it can out-wait the seventy-three-year-old Dalai Lama, and that his passing will result in the fracturing of the Tibetan movement in world politics. Such a Chinese approach seems to open the way to ideological and radical elements of the Tibetan community more inclined to resist Chinese rule with force and violence. While their chances for success seem small, the ability of these radicals to create turmoil and bloody repression seems substantial.[49]

Uighur Muslims. Violent clashes in July 2009 between Uighur and Han Chinese people in Urumchi, the capital city of the Xinjiang Autonomous Region, left almost two hundred dead and hundreds arrested. American leaders, media, and nongovernment organizations supported Chinese administration efforts to separate and arrest the fighters and end the violence, but they also were inclined to place blame on Chinese policies and practices seen to discriminate against and otherwise treat unfairly the Uighur Muslim people.[50]

As in the case of Tibet, Chinese concerns regarding the Uighur Muslims in Xinjiang involve issues of security and sovereignty as well as human rights. Estimates of China's Muslim population range from twenty million to thirty million persons. Many Muslim communities are located in western Chinese provinces, notably Ningxia, Gansu, Qinghai, and Yunnan, and are seen by foreign specialists and media to coexist peacefully with non-Muslims and local authorities under relatively flexible religious and other policies. However, social and political tensions and restrictions on religious practices have long characterized Chinese treatment of the Uighur Muslims in Xinjiang. The vast expanse of the Xinjiang Uighur Autonomous Region is home to over eight million Uighur Muslims who represent 45 percent of the region's population. The Uighurs are by far the largest of several Turkic ethnic groups in the region. The Chinese administration fears Uighur demands for greater religious and cultural freedom, and also is deeply concerned about linkages to Central Asian countries and independent Islamic organizations, including terrorist groups. The East Turkestan Islamic Movement, a Uighur organization with alleged ties to Al Qaeda that advocates the creation of an independent Uighur Islamic state, is a focal point of Chinese suppression. The group is recognized as a terrorist organization by the United States and the United Nations.[51]

Concerns over security and sovereignty, notably pro-independence sentiment and terrorist activities on the part of some Uighurs, have made the Chinese administration monitor and restrict Uighur society more stringently than it does most other religious and ethnic groups. The restrictions often focus on Uighur religious leaders and practices. They include strict governance of the training and duties of imams, use of Uighur and Arabic languages, literature and education, public access to mosques, the celebration of Ramadan, contacts with foreigners, and travel abroad. Uighur children and youth under the age of eighteen are forbidden from entering mosques, and government workers are not allowed to practice Islam. According to Amnesty International, Uighurs were the only known group in China to be sentenced to death for political crimes such as "separatist activities."[52]

The Uighur grievances with Chinese rule go beyond restrictions on religion. The Chinese authorities have long fostered immigration into the region by ethnically Han Chinese people from other parts of China. These migrants are seen to benefit from the economic development in Xinjiang in recent years, while the Uighurs have not. During the clashes between Uighur and Han Chinese people in July 2009, it was widely reported by American media and nongovernment organizations that the Uighurs felt discriminated against and looked down upon by the Chinese settlers.[53]

Falun Gong. Falun Gong is a movement that combines spiritual beliefs with an exercise and meditation regimen derived from traditional Chinese practices known as *qigong*. The movement remained out of the public spotlight as it gained millions of adherents across China in the 1990s. On April 25, 1999, thousands of adherents gathered in Beijing to protest the government's growing restrictions on their activities. The demonstration seemed to take the Chinese leadership by surprise. The ability of the movement to mobilize such an impressive show of support at the seat of Chinese administrative power was viewed as a threat. It reflected infiltration of Falun Gong supporters throughout the police and security forces and other sensitive apparatus of the Chinese administration.[54]

Party leader Jiang Zemin led a major crackdown against the movement that continued for years. The harsh measures against suspected adherents who refused to recant their beliefs and cooperate with the authorities led to widespread reports by the Department of State, U.S.-based and other human rights groups, and foreign media of torture with estimates of adherents who have died in state custody ranging from several hundred to a few thousand. The Chinese government acknowledges that deaths while in custody have occurred but has denied that they were caused by mistreatment. As the Chinese suppression succeeded in wiping out the movement in China, its salience as a human rights issue in U.S.-China relations declined.[55]

Hong Kong. The U.S. government, especially the Congress, took special interest in working to ensure that Hong Kong's transfer to Chinese sovereignty in 1997 under terms of a Sino-British agreement reached in 1984 did not impinge on Hong Kong's autonomy and on the nascent democracy movement in the territory. As time has passed and Chinese rule has caused few major controversies, American interest in Hong Kong as a human rights issue has declined.

More than ten years after the transfer to Chinese sovereignty, the civil liberties of the people in Hong Kong seemed largely intact. Freedom of the press was still strong, though there were widespread reports of self-censorship by media owners reluctant to antagonize China. Economically, Hong Kong sustained an autonomous position, though it saw its interests best served by integrating ever more closely with the Chinese economy. Hong Kong's importance as a "gateway" to China declined as the Chinese economy opened to the world and cities like Shanghai, Beijing, and others allowed for smooth foreign interaction with China. China continued to adhere to the Sino-British agreement and prompted only occasional controversy in its political decisions. The selection of the chief executive continued the nondemocratic practice of the past. Progress in selection of the legislature resulted in more democratic representation. The judiciary remained basically independent, with an occasional intervention from Chinese authorities.[56]

U.S. Government Efforts and China's Reactions Regarding Human Rights in China

Contemporary U.S. government policies and practices regarding human rights issues in relations with China reflect the generally secondary importance of these issues in recent Sino-American relations. The U.S. government has a range of approaches endeavoring to promote democracy, individual rights, and the rule of law in China; their impact has not had a substantial effect on the continuation of one-party authoritarian rule in China. Optimists among American officials, specialists, journalists, and others with an interest in human rights in China tend to argue that U.S. policies and practices of political and economic engagement with China that seek cooperation and avoid confrontation are helping to foster trends in China that create conditions in which progress in democracy and other aspects of human rights has been and will continue to be made. Pessimists among these groups of Americans point out that U.S. policies of engagement and avoiding confrontation have obviously failed to produce political transformation of China's continued authoritarian political system and have not even worked effectively in setting in motion meaningful political change. The pessimists aver that efforts to promote democracy and better human rights conditions through quiet diplomacy and dialogues have been ineffectual; some argue for a much tougher U.S. public stance regarding human rights issues with China.[57]

The George W. Bush administration from time to time, and congressional leaders more frequently, pressured China though public criticism of human rights conditions and calls on Chinese leaders to honor the rights guaranteed under its own constitution, bring its policies and practices into line with international standards, release prisoners of conscience, and undertake major political reforms. President Bush appealed personally to President Hu Jintao to allow more religious freedom; the president met in the White House with Chinese independent Christian leaders, the Dalai Lama, and prominent Chinese political dissidents. The Democratic-led 110th Congress (2007–2008) sponsored around twenty resolutions aimed at promoting improved human rights conditions in China. The U.S. government also provided funding for programs within China that helped strengthen the rule of law, civil society, government accountability, and labor rights. The U.S. government also supported U.S.-based nongovernment organizations and Internet companies that monitored human rights conditions in China and helped enable Chinese Internet users to access Voice of America, Radio Free Asia, and other websites that are frequently blocked by the Chinese government.[58]

The administration of President Barack Obama and the congressional leaders of the 111th Congress generally have followed the practices of the recent past. In public interactions with Chinese leaders, human rights issues have received secondary priority. President Obama went to extraordinary efforts to schedule a meeting with the Dalai Lama after his first trip to China in November 2009. Secretary of State Hillary Clinton and House of Representatives Speaker Nancy Pelosi adopted a generally low profile on human rights issues during their initial visits to China.[59]

The Chinese administration has cooperated with the United States on some programs promoting the rule of law, civil society, village elections, and other programs dealing with aspects of human rights seen as beneficial for China's development; the administration engages in human rights dialogues with the United States and other governments. The Chinese administration remains sensitive to perceived U.S. or other foreign interference in Chinese internal affairs affecting the continuation of authoritarian one-party rule in China. It takes or threatens strong action against perceived infringements on sensitive issues (Chinese officials have been especially sensitive regarding Tibetan matters in recent years). Chinese statements affirm China's commitment to a number of broad principles and practices governing international human rights. They sometimes offer negative commentaries regarding the human rights practices of the United States and other countries that tend to be critical of Chinese human rights policies and practices.[60]

Public U.S. criticism. American officials and other specialists disagree on the utility of strong public U.S. criticism of China over human rights issues. Some argue that the U.S. government should take strong and principled positions against Chinese human rights infractions more frequently and openly, while others believe such methods can undermine human rights efforts in some situations. The Chinese government generally has reacted angrily when the U.S. government has publicly denounced its policies regarding human rights.[61] In some cases, China has made small or token concessions in order to help reduce or avoid open U.S. criticism. A mix of concession and criticism was said to motivate China to restart the U.S.-China human rights dialogue in 2008. Leading up to the Chinese decision, the State Department in 2008 on the one hand excluded China from its annual list of "worst human rights violators," while on the other hand continuing to harshly criticize China's record. In other cases, China has responded to perceived U.S. pressure and insults in a "tit-for-tat" manner. For example, American media and other commentators saw China's denial of a port visit to Hong Kong by the U.S. aircraft carrier *Kitty Hawk* during Thanksgiving in 2007 as a response to U.S. legislation awarding the Congressional Gold Medal to the Dalai Lama during the previous month.[62]

The U.S. government has sponsored resolutions criticizing China's human rights record at the annual meeting of the UN Commission on Human Rights several times in the past decade. The Commission, which was criticized for including some of the world's worst human rights abusers, was terminated in 2006 and replaced by the UN Human Rights Council. The U.S. government, citing a continuation of problems similar to those of the previous Commission, for years refrained from seeking a seat on the Human Rights Council. Since the United States government began sponsoring resolutions critical of Chinese human rights practices in 1991, the Chinese administration has taken often-strenuous efforts to block them by means of "no action" motions by the Commission. Only one, in 1995, was considered by the Commission, but lost by one vote.[63]

Members of Congress have sponsored numerous non-binding resolutions condemning Chinese human rights abuses or calling on the Chinese administration to cease and make improvements regarding various human rights issues. The issues include imprisonment and detention of prominent political, religious, or ethnic figures; persecution of Tibetans and Uighurs; lack of progress in talks between China and the Dalai Lama; the crackdown on political dissent prior to the August 2008 Olympic Games in China; control over the Internet and other mass media; Chinese coercive population control methods; and treatment of North Korean refugees in China. Some proposed legislation restricted U.S.-China trade on account of Chinese human rights abuses and prohibited funding for U.S. officials attending the opening ceremony of the 2008 Olympic Games.[64]

Restrictions and sanctions. Some U.S. sanctions on the PRC in response to the Tiananmen crackdown in 1989 remain in effect. U.S. representatives to international financial institutions regarding loans to China are required to vote no or to abstain except in cases involving programs meeting basic human needs. U.S. representatives to international financial institutions support projects in Tibet only if they do not encourage the migration and settlement of non-Tibetans (majority Han Chinese) into Tibet or the transfer of Tibetan-owned properties to non-Tibetans. Meanwhile, the U.S. government suspended funding for the United Nations Population Fund (UNFPA) from 2002 through 2008 because of the UNFPA's programs in China, where the State Department determined that coercive family planning practices had occurred. In February 2009, the Obama administration announced that it would restore U.S. funding for the UNFPA.[65]

Human rights dialogue. The U.S.-China human rights dialogue was proposed by Presidents Bill Clinton and Jiang Zemin in 1998 but was held only in 2001 and 2002. China formally suspended the dialogue in 2004 after the Bush administration sponsored an unsuccessful UN resolution criticizing China's human rights record. In February 2008, the Chinese government announced that it would resume the human rights dialogue with the United States. The meeting took place in May. Assistant Secretary of State for Democracy, Human Rights, and Labor David Kramer told reporters that the talks included the following topics: prisoners of conscience, freedom of religion, the situation in Tibet, the Muslim population in Xinjiang, and media and Internet freedom. The dialogue prompted continued American debate on how to approach China regarding human rights issues. Some critics argued that while such talks help to create a positive atmosphere in U.S.-China relations, they result in few if any real changes in China. For example, as the bilateral dialogue began in Beijing, a group of Chinese human rights attorneys were detained as they attempted to meet with two visiting members of Congress. Supporters of the dialogue say that even though the discussion may produce limited short-term results, the absence of such dialogue reduces the overall effectiveness of U.S. human rights policies in China.[66]

U.S. support for rule of law and civil society programs. In recent years, the U.S. government foreign operations appropriations have supported democracy-related programs in China, particularly those focused on developing the rule of law. There also has been support for Tibetan communities. The funding grew from $10 million in fiscal year 2002 to $23 million in fiscal year 2008. Major programs include legal training, legal aid, criminal defense, labor rights, civil society development, media reform, participatory government, and preserving Tibetan culture. Financial support has also been provided to support U.S. educational institutions for exchange programs with Chinese universities in these areas.[67]

The National Endowment for Democracy is a private, nonprofit organization created in 1983 and funded by the U.S. government to promote democracy around the world. The U.S. General Accounting Office found in 2004 that NED programs constituted over one-third of all U.S. democracy funding in China during 1999–2003. The Endowment's programs in China have involved legal aid, labor rights, investigative reporting, HIV/AIDS awareness, and training of nongovernment activists. The Endowment also funds several U.S.-based organizations that monitor human rights conditions in China, including Tibet and Xinjiang, research and publish newsletters and journals on democracy-related topics, and disseminate political works from China.[68]

Public diplomacy. The U.S. government strives to influence progressive-minded, Chinese-educated elites through its public diplomacy programs. According to the State Department, nearly half of all Chinese citizens participating in U.S. government supported educational and cultural exchanges in the United States are engaged in activities related to democracy, religious freedom, and other human rights issues. The U.S.-funded Fulbright Scholarship and Humphrey Fellowship exchange programs devote significant resources for rule of law studies. The U.S. International Visitor Leadership Program sponsors U.S. speakers to travel to China to discuss rule of law issues and brings PRC counterparts to the United States. In 2007, 398 U.S. citizens and 552 PRC citizens participated in U.S. government educational and cultural exchange programs with China.[69]

Internet freedom. The U.S. government has funded programs to help circumvent Chinese government Internet censorship. The government also has called upon U.S. Internet providers that have entered the Chinese market to promote human rights. The U.S. government's International Broadcasting Bureau funds anti-jamming technologies (approximately $1 million per year) to help Internet users in China, Iran, and other countries to access Voice of America and other censored U.S. government and nongovernment websites, and to receive Voice of America e-mail newsletters. The Consolidated Appropriations Act for fiscal year 2008 (P.L. 110-161) appropriated $15 million for an Internet freedom initiative to "expand access and information in closed societies." The funds are to be used to develop software to broaden access in countries where the web is heavily censored, particularly China and Iran. The $15 million is part of the "Human Rights and Democracy Fund" which was allocated $164 million in 2008.[70]

In May 2008, congressional hearings saw representatives from Google, Yahoo, and Cisco Systems testify regarding their operations in China. They were accused of either cooperating with PRC censorship systems or supplying China with censorship technology. In August 2008, Google, Yahoo, and Microsoft reached an agreement in principle on a voluntary code of conduct for their activities in China as well as other countries that restrict Internet use.[71]

Labor rights. The U.S. government has promoted PRC adherence to international labor standards. U.S. officials monitor PRC compliance with the 1992 U.S.-China Memorandum of Understanding and 1994 Statement of Cooperation on the issue of prison labor. In 2000, the measure granting permanent normal trade relations (PNTR) status to China (P.L. 106-286) authorized the Department of Labor to establish a program to promote worker rights and related rule of law training. The United States and China have conducted exchanges on coal mine safety, dispute resolution, occupational safety and health, wage and hour (payroll) administration, and pension programs.[72]

Congressional-Executive Commission on China. Among the provisions of P.L. 106-286, the measure granting permanent normal trade relations (PNTR) treatment to China, was one establishing the Congressional-Executive Commission on China (CECC) to monitor human rights and the rule of law in China and to submit an annual report with recommendations to the president and Congress. The body consists of nine senators, nine members of the House of Representatives, five senior administration officials appointed by the president, and a staff of ten. On its website, the Commission provides human rights-related news and analysis, keeps track of pertinent PRC laws and regulations, and maintains a database of political prisoners. The CECC has held 80 public hearings and roundtables on rights-related topics, including rule of law development, social unrest, religious freedom, ethnic minorities, political reform, labor conditions, mass media, property rights, and the Internet in China. It has an annual operating budget of approximately $2 million.[73]

12

Outlook:
Continued Positive Equilibrium
amid Differences and Suspicions

THE COURSE OF SINO-AMERICAN RELATIONS ONE YEAR AFTER THE ELECTION of Senator Barack Obama to be the president of the United States generally was smooth. There was a notable absence of debate in the United States over China policy during both the U.S. presidential election campaign and the initial months of the Obama presidency. This stands in contrast to the last three transfers of U.S. presidential power from one party to the other: from Jimmy Carter to Ronald Reagan; from George H. W. Bush to Bill Clinton; and from Bill Clinton to George W. Bush. Those major turning points in American politics saw issues in U.S. China policy figure prominently in the election campaigns and in the early years of each incoming U.S. government. The changes in presidential power were accompanied by contentious U.S. debates and U.S. government positions strongly at odds with those of China over U.S. relations with Taiwan (especially from Carter to Reagan), human rights, trade practices, and Taiwan (Bush to Clinton), and the security threat posed to the United States, Taiwan and U.S. allies in Asia by rising Chinese economic, political, and especially military power (Clinton to Bush).[1]

Well aware of this historical record and of the many differences and leadership suspicions that continue to divide China and the United States, Chinese and U.S. advocates of close U.S. engagement with China were initially wary of the incoming Democratic president.[2] During the campaign, Senator Obama and Senator Hillary Clinton, his main opponent in the Democratic Party presidential primaries and his choice as Secretary of State, had at times voiced strong views on protecting American jobs from unfair Chinese and other international competition. They also were close to Democratic Party leaders in the Congress, House Speaker Nancy Pelosi and Senate Majority Leader Harry Reid, who had long records strongly opposing Chinese policies and practices over human rights, trade, Tibet, and support for so-called rogue regimes like Sudan, Iran, Zimbabwe, Myanmar, and North Korea.[3]

As noted in chapter 7, after coming to power, the Obama government took steps to reassure Chinese leaders, notably during Secretary of State Clinton's initial visit to China in February and during President Obama's initial meeting with Chinese President Hu Jintao at the sidelines of the G-20 summit on the international economic crisis in London in April. Over the course of a few months, U.S. and Chinese leaders reached agreement on positive terms like "constructive" and "cooperative" that they then used consistently to characterize their relationship. They began top-level exchanges between U.S. and Chinese leaders at international meetings and planned Sino-American summits in China and the United States. A more comprehensive dialogue between top economic and international affairs leaders of both countries was established, and the initial set of meetings was conducted smoothly in July. Military exchanges, suspended by China on account of a U.S. announcement of a large sale of arms to Taiwan in 2008, were resumed. The two governments were in agreement on the need to address salient issues like the global economic crisis, climate change, and energy issues, and a variety of regional hot spots in Asia ranging from North Korea to Southwest Asia and the Middle East.[4]

Differences and Suspicions

The prevailing positive interaction between U.S. and Chinese leaders in these months failed to hide assessments by many U.S. and Chinese officials, specialists, and other observers about important differences and concerns that continued to hamper improvement in U.S.-China relations. The differences seen in 2009 often were rooted in the conflicting interests and values of the two governments and societies that were examined in earlier chapters. They not only served as a drag on forward movement in relations, but they also were seen as capable of prompting a crisis or decline in relations under possible circumstances.[5]

Security issues. China's rising military power seemed to be moving beyond a strategy designed to thwart or delay the intervention of U.S. forces in a possible military conflict between China and Taiwan. The advent of the Taiwan administration of President Ma Ying-jeou in 2008 abruptly changed Taiwan's approach to China from confrontation to reassurance. The change greatly eased tensions in cross-strait relations. Whether by design or coincidence, Chinese government surface ships and submarines at this juncture became more active in challenging U.S. Navy surveillance activities in international waters near China but distant from Taiwan. The result was a number of incidents and confrontations between Chinese and U.S. ships in the South China Sea and the Yellow Sea. The actions of Chinese ships confronting and harassing the U.S. surveillance ships, and the accompanying Chinese official commentary labeling the U.S. patrols as illegal and unjustified, indicated to many observers heightened Chinese resolve to challenge U.S. access to and control of the seas near China, something the U.S. government has pursued as a primary interest of the United States since the end of World War II.[6]

Concerning Southwest Asia, the Obama government came to power with new emphasis on pursing the conflict in Afghanistan and dealing with violence and internal instability in Pakistan. Seeking international support for these efforts, high-level U.S. officials pressed China to do more to support the U.S.-led military efforts against the Taliban in Afghanistan and to support improved governance in Pakistan. The Americans were privately disappointed with China's reluctance to work closely with the United States in these areas. The Chinese arguments against more active and substantive support for the American-led efforts varied. They included Chinese worry about the viability of U.S. strategy and what a failed American effort in Afghanistan and Pakistan theater would mean for China, a neighbor of both countries. There also were Chinese concerns that, if successful in Afghanistan, the United States might broaden its presence in Central Asia along China's periphery, an outcome long opposed by China. And Chinese concerns also focused on disadvantages for China in identifying closely with the U.S.-led assistance effort to Pakistan which could reduce China's ability to interact with various forces, including those opposed to the United States, in this neighboring state of great strategic importance for China.[7]

Regarding North Korea, the Obama government entered office poised to use the Six-Party Talks and bilateral discussions with North Korea in seeking progress in getting Pyongyang to fulfill its obligations under agreements reached in the talks during the previous U.S. administration. As described in chapter 7, North Korea's escalating provocations created a major international crisis in 2009 that forced the Obama government to change priorities and give top-level attention to dealing with Pyongyang. Escalating North Korean provocations and the Pyongyang regime's strident defiance of UN Security Council resolutions and international condemnation compelled a U.S. policy review. The Obama government's close consultations with China and other powers assured a firm response from the UN Security Council in June that imposed sanctions in addition to those imposed after North Korea's first nuclear test in 2006, and called for inspections of suspected weapons shipments to and from North Korea. The United States also planned its own unilateral sanctions in order to pressure Pyongyang to halt the provocations and return to negotiations.

The common ground between the United States and China as a result of ongoing Sino-American and other consultations in dealing with the crisis seemed substantial. Nevertheless, differences continued between the United States and China over such issues as the utility of international pressure against North Korea. For example, China continued to be wary of change involving North Korea that would consolidate U.S. power on the Korean peninsula. Moreover, there was no assurance in either Washington or Beijing that negative and positive incentives from the United States, China, and other concerned powers would ease the crisis. Pyongyang appeared to moderate its stance on some issues following former U.S. President Clinton's mission to North Korea in August 2009 to gain release of U.S. journalists captured by the North Korea authorities intruding into North Korea. However, the standoff on North Korea's nuclear weapons development continued. Further North Korea provocations, especially North Korean moves to transfer nuclear capabilities to terrorists abroad, were seen likely to provoke strong use of force by the United States at odds with China's concern with preserving stability in the neighboring country.[8]

Climate change. The shift in the U.S. government's policies and practices on climate change has had important and possibly negative implications for China. The Obama government and the 111th Congress have been much more committed than the previous U.S. government of President George W. Bush to take meaningful steps to address global warming and to cooperate with international measures to address aspects affecting the world environment and climate change. The government of President Obama began to take concrete measures long supported by U.S. and international environmental activists who had been thwarted by and strongly opposed to the George W. Bush administration and its approach to climate change and the environment. Against this background, China's position as the world's largest emitter of greenhouse gases and its otherwise poor to mediocre record in protecting the environment loomed larger than in the past in the calculations and debate of U.S. and international environmental activists, associated media and international governmental discussion and negotiations. In the United States, the Obama government and congressional leaders pressed China to join in cooperative ways the new U.S. efforts. Chinese support for and cooperation with these U.S. efforts were deemed important by U.S. leaders in order to convince skeptics in the U.S. Congress and others in the United States to support American legislation and other binding U.S. commitments on greenhouse gas emissions and other environmental issues. If China did not join and "do its part" in these environmental efforts, the skeptics argued, U.S. industry would

be at a further economic disadvantage in competing with Chinese manufacturers at a time of continued massive U.S. trade deficits with China that
were seen by many of these Americans to result from various unfair trading
practices by China.[9]

At bottom, the new U.S. policies and practices on climate change ran the
risk for the Chinese administration that China would have to take substantial
action on greenhouse gas emissions and other environmental issues. Such actions could pose a serious drag on Chinese economic growth—a key priority
of Chinese leaders concerned with sustaining healthy employment and improved living standards for the Chinese people. The costs of changing Chinese
energy use, notably inefficient and wasteful when compared with developed
countries including the United States, could be enormous. Yet the costs
of being seen as an outlier in the broad international discussion of climate
change seemed substantial as well. China in recent years has undertaken significant efforts to improve energy efficiency and to reduce the level of growth
of its greenhouse gas emissions, but the results have not come very close to
meeting the ambitious goals. The Barack Obama and Hu Jintao governments
chose to deal with environmental issues mainly through constructive and
usually private dialogues between senior officials. This allowed differences
to be managed in private and reduced the danger of a public split between
the two governments. But the danger of such a split seemed real and could
emerge as a result of U.S. frustration with what it might view as lack of substantive cooperation on China's part, or Chinese frustration with perceived
unreasonable demands by the United States, or other factors.[10]

Economic crisis. Dealing with the global economic crisis and recession of
2008–2009 topped the priority list of both the U.S. and Chinese governments.
Though much was said in world media about China playing a role second
to the United States in dealing with the international aspects of the crisis,
Chinese leaders were careful to lower expectations about what China was
prepared to do, apart from the major efforts of the Chinese administration
to stimulate and revive economic growth in China that would have indirect
benefit for the world economy. Chinese leaders were prominent and active
in meetings in world capitals dealing with the crisis, but their commitments
that involved substantial costs to the Chinese economy were limited. Chinese
leaders sometimes discussed alternatives to the U.S. dollar for international
financial transactions, engaged in some swap arrangements with Asian neighbors, and promised modest amounts of aid to countries along China's periphery. The net effect of such steps had little immediate impact on Chinese and
international trade.[11]

Chinese traders continued to rely on the U.S. dollar for international transactions; Chinese merchants and traders in other export-oriented economies

in Asia and the world encouraged the United States and European leaders to revive their economies and their demand for imports from abroad. Even with diminished foreign trade, China continued to run a trade surplus, continued to seek foreign investment from the United States and other developed countries, and continued to invest the bulk of its foreign exchange holdings in U.S. government securities. Discussion in China and abroad about the Chinese currency, renminbi or yuan, becoming a significant international currency seemed pushed into the future despite some initial Chinese steps with some countries to use the Chinese currency for their transactions.[12]

Chinese complaints about U.S. stewardship of international markets and the negative effect possible U.S. inflation would have on the large Chinese holdings of U.S. securities appeared in official Chinese and other media. Nevertheless, senior Chinese leaders continued to see China's interests better served by cooperation with the United States than by confrontation over these and other issues. One change in Chinese behavior that appeared to have a greater impact on the world stage involved substantive and significant Chinese purchases of resources important for China's own economic growth. Notably, as Chinese leaders continued to accumulate more foreign exchange reserves as a result of continuing foreign trade surpluses and foreign investment inflows, they took steps to take advantage of low-commodity prices in order to conclude long-term, multi-billion-dollar arrangements guaranteeing supplies of energy and other raw materials for China's development for many years.

In sum, the danger in this situation for U.S.-China relations related particularly to expectations and suspected manipulation. The incoming U.S. government might be inclined to call upon China to use its massive foreign exchange reserves in ways that would benefit the world economy without an immediate tangible benefit for China, something the Chinese administration has been reluctant to do, at least up to this point. Meanwhile, Chinese leaders have already seen their stake in U.S. government securities lose value with swings in the value of the U.S. dollar. As the Obama government's dramatic stimulus plan creates a massive increase in U.S. government debt, there is an obvious choice for U.S. policy makers to use inflation and a resulting decline in the value of the U.S. dollar, in order to pay back this debt more advantageously. For Chinese holders of U.S. dollar securities, such a turn of events would pose a disaster.[13]

China's "core" interests: Taiwan, Tibet, Xinjiang. Taiwan continues to represent what Chinese officials consistently say is the most important issue in U.S.-China relations. Chinese sensitivity did appear to decline somewhat, presumably reflecting the thaw in tensions in cross-strait relations as a result of the reassurance policies directed at China over the past year by the new Taiwan president, Ma Ying-jeou. Notably, Chinese refusal to hold U.S.-China military dialogues on account of the U.S. agreement in 2008 to transfer a large package of arms to Taiwan ended in 2009 with China agreeing to a very active schedule of meetings between military leaders of the two countries. Nevertheless, Chinese officials and other specialists persist in warning of dire consequences for U.S.-China relations if the Obama government sold arms to Taiwan in the near future or took other measures that substantially increased U.S. support for Taiwan.[14] The sixtieth anniversary of the People's Republic of China on October 1, 2009, was seen by some Chinese officials and other observers as a focal point of nationalistic Chinese sentiment, similar to the Olympic Games in China in August 2008. The Chinese specialists advised that U.S. arms sales to Taiwan in the lead-up to the October celebration would be particularly difficult for Chinese leaders to handle in ways that did not seriously damage U.S.-China relations.

Tibet is an issue that recently has topped Taiwan as a concern by Chinese officials and specialists. The salience of the issue rose dramatically because of 2008 riots in Tibet and the suppression of Tibetan dissent by Chinese authorities, widespread criticism of the Chinese suppression in West European countries and the United States, and meetings of Germany's and France's leaders with the Dalai Lama that led to crises in Chinese relations with those governments.[15] In this context, Chinese officials and specialists warned, a meeting by President Obama or other senior U.S. leaders with the Dalai Lama might lead to Chinese reaction similar to the harsh Chinese treatment of Germany's and France's leaders after they met with the Tibetan leader in recent years.

The July 5 riot and mass killings in the Chinese city of Urumchi renewed U.S. and other international attention to Chinese firm determination and frequent harsh tactics in dealing with dissent and disturbance among the minority peoples in the strategically important and resource-rich border region of Xinjiang. Like Taiwan and Tibet, the Xinjiang Uighur Autonomous Region is a "core" concern of the Chinese administration. Perceived U.S. interference in the issue, even in the form of criticism from American leaders of China's policies and practices in the region, could lead to nationalistic Chinese backlash negatively affecting U.S.-China relations.

Mutual suspicions. Kenneth Lieberthal, a prominent American China specialist with frequent and close contact with high-level American and Chinese policy makers, has been notable in his writings in assessing how U.S. and Chinese decision makers remain privately wary and distrustful of one another despite the numerous Sino-American dialogues and positive public discourse between the leaders of the two countries. He advises that there has been little improvement in the mutual suspicion between the two leaderships in recent years.[16] Chinese and American officials and other specialists privately confirm this observation, noting the concerns of each side over differences on salient issues, especially those discussed above.

Reasons for Optimism: Enduring Sino-American Pragmatism

Though Sino-American divergence over sensitive issues and mutual suspicions underline continued fragility in Sino-American relations, enduring patterns of pragmatic decision-making among the Chinese and American leaders amid important converging interests argue that the positive equilibrium that has prevailed recently in U.S.-China relations is likely to continue into the first years of the Obama government and possibly longer.

The Chinese administration of Hu Jintao will remain in power until 2012–2013. It has set a central foreign and domestic policy goal for the next decade focused on China fostering a continuation of the prevailing international situation seen as generally advantageous for China in order to allow for expeditious domestic economic and other modernization in China. Exploiting this period of perceived "strategic opportunity" in international affairs requires keeping U.S.-China relations and most other important Chinese international relationships on a course of stable development and moving in positive directions. The Hu Jintao administration worked hard in fostering businesslike and constructive relations with the George W. Bush administration. China's pragmatic approach to the United States played an important role in shifting the Bush government from a posture of suspicion and confrontation with China to one of close positive engagement.[17]

Against this background, if change is to come in the U.S.-China relationship, it may be more likely to emerge from the U.S. side, notably from the new U.S. government of President Obama. However, the initial moves of the U.S. president and his administration indicate that they are unlikely to deviate from the positive engagement with China that characterized the latter years of the Bush administration. The U.S. government remains in a strong leadership position in Asia, where engagement with China adds to U.S. beneficial relationships throughout the region. What changes the new U.S. government will adopt in Asian affairs seem to be in secondary areas, involving probably greater U.S. policy attention to Southeast Asia, or in areas where the United States has been confronted and provoked, as in the case of the recent crisis with North Korea. Meanwhile, American preoccupation with a variety of other policy priorities at home and abroad seems likely to continue to place a premium on keeping Sino-American relations moving in a positive direction despite differences, suspicions, and possible difficulties.

In effect, the dynamics underlining the recent positive equilibrium in U.S.-China relations noted in chapter 7 are strong and likely to continue. The positive features of the relationship tend to outweigh the negatives because:

- Both governments gain from cooperative engagement—the gains include beneficial economic ties, as well as cooperation over North Korea, the war on terrorism, Pakistan, and even Taiwan. It also includes smaller progress on Iran and even less on Sudan and Myanmar/Burma.
- Both governments recognize that, because of ever-closer U.S.-China interdependence, focusing on negative aspects in U.S.-China relations would be counter productive to their interests.
- Both governments recognize that, because of other major policy preoccupations they both have, focusing on negative aspects in U.S.-China relations would be counterproductive to their interests.

As noted in chapter 7, the recent U.S. relationship with China continues to rest upon a common commitment to avoid conflict, cooperate in areas of common interest, and prevent disputes from shaking the overall relationship.[18] Against this background, the Obama government seems most likely to advance relations with China in small ways. It probably will show sufficient resolve to avoid major conflict with China over trade, currency, environmental, security, Taiwan, Tibet, human rights, and other issues that appear counterproductive for what seem to be more important U.S. interests in preserving a collaborative relationship with China and avoiding frictions with such an important economy at a time when international economic cooperation seems of utmost importance.[19]

Those in the United States who seek to give greater prominence to differences with China seem of less importance, particularly given the salience of the global economic crisis and the perceived U.S. need to be seen to cooperate with China in restoring international economic confidence.[20] Events in China or U.S.-China relations could bring their issues to the fore, as they did in the 2008 Chinese crackdown on dissent and violence in Tibet. But such spikes in American criticism of China in recent years have not had lasting impact on the overall positive interactions between the Chinese and American governments.

Meanwhile, those prominent Americans who recently have called for a closer Sino-American condominium, a "G-2," in managing Asian and world affairs have received tepid endorsement and outright rejection from Chinese commentators and strong criticism and some ridicule from a wide range of American specialists.[21] The differing goals, interests, and values of the United States and China appear to make such close cooperation an unrealistic expectation. More mainstream commentary in both countries calls for continued pragmatic "management" of the Sino-American relationship, differences as well as points of convergence, in the years ahead.[22]

The broader historical perspective seen in this book offers a view of often negative and troubled interaction between the United States and China. The last four decades have seen sometimes-surprising improvement in relations but also feature on-again/off-again cooperation between the two governments because of important common interests dependent on international and domestic circumstances. Against this background, it seems important to assess what might happen to the Sino-American relationship should the circumstances prompting the current pragmatic cooperation in U.S.-China relations change. The collapse of the Soviet Union and the end of the Cold War twenty years ago destroyed the common interest that bound the United States and China together in the 1970s and the 1980s. As the tide of Cold War conflict ebbed, it exposed the many layers of differences between the two countries, differences that were exacerbated by China's crackdown on demonstrators in Tiananmen Square.

One can argue that a similar decline in the current circumstances causing U.S.-China leaders to persist in pragmatic interchange with one another could prompt serious retrogression in relations like that seen in the 1990s. Fortunately for the future course of Sino-American relations, those circumstances today are multifaceted and often deeply rooted. They are not dependent on one or two dimensions, as was the case with U.S.-China relations in the 1970s and 1980s that relied heavily on common opposition to Soviet expansionism.

The interdependence between the U.S. and Chinese economies recently has become truly massive and seems poised to continue to grow. How that interdependence can unravel without enormous negative consequences for both the United States and China is very hard to imagine. The consequences of Sino-American military conflict over Taiwan or other flash points could have devastating effects on both societies and destroy the nation-building agendas of both the American and Chinese administrations. Meanwhile the webs of relationships between people, institutions, businesses, and other elements in the U.S. and Chinese societies are many times denser than those prevailing at the end of the cold war. The relationships continue to grow rapidly. They do not always lead to friendship and close collaborations, but they do lead to greater realism and better understanding among broader segments in both societies about the strengths and weaknesses of Sino-American relations and the utility of avoiding drastic or extreme solutions to prevailing problems and difficulties.[23]

Some thinkers in international affairs of the realist school of International Relations argue that a major turning point in Sino-American relations will come when rising China reaches a point of power and influence at which it will supersede America as the leading power in Asia and compromise and undermine the range of strategic, economic, and other interests that the United States has long sought to protect through a leading position in Asia. How that power transition is managed will be extremely difficult and full of tension with potential for conflict, in their view.[24] Others argue that the transition may be a gradual one that will allow for pragmatic adjustments that lead to a new situation in Asia broadly compatible with the respective U.S. and Chinese interests.[25] A third group of specialists, including this writer, judge that we have seen several times in the past predictions of U.S. decline in the face of challenges from rising powers in Asia. Those predictions proved wrong because they underestimated the weaknesses and limitations of the rising power, and they underestimated the resiliency and strengths of the United States. This group of specialists sees predictions of China superseding the United States as Asia's leading power falling into the same faulty pattern of such past predictions.[26]

In conclusion, this book is cautiously optimistic that Sino-American relations will continue modest improvement amid many differences and mutual wariness in the years ahead. The record of U.S.-China relations and an examination of the salient issues driving the two nations together and apart presented here show that it is unrealistic to expect dramatic breakthroughs or close convergence between the two powers. They also show that dramatic decline and reversal of gains achieved thus far is unlikely.

Notes

Chapter 1: Introduction and Overview

1. Wang Jisi, "Trends in the Development of U.S.-China Relations and Deep-Seated Reasons," (Beijing) *Danddai Yatai* June 20, 2009, 4–20; Aaron Friedberg, "Is China a Military Threat?—Menace," *The National Interest*, September-October 2009, 19–25, 31–32; Robert Ross, "Is China a Military Threat?—Myth," *The National Interest*, September–October 2009, 19, 25–31, 33–34.

2. Kenneth Liberthal, "The China-U.S. Relationship Goes Global," *Current History* 108:719 (September 2009): 243–246; "China-U.S. Dialogue Successful—Vice Premier," *China Daily* July 29, 2009, 1; Hillary Clinton and Timothy Geithner, "A New Strategic and Economic Dialogue with China," *Wall Street Journal*, July 27, 2009, www.wsj.org (accessed September 7, 2009).

3. Prominent Americans identified with this view include Zbigniew Brzezinski, Robert Zoellick, and C. Fred Bergsten. For critical response see, Elizabeth Economy and Adam Segal, "The G-2 Mirage," *Foreign Affairs* 88:3 (May–June 2009): 56–72.

4. See contrasting views of various differences in China-U.S. relations in Bates Gill, *Rising Star* (Washington, DC: Brookings Institution, 2007) and Susan Shirk, *China: Fragile Superpower* (New York: Oxford, 2007).

5. Kerry Dumbaugh, *China-U.S. Relations: Current Issues and Implications for U.S. Policy* (Washington, DC: Congressional Research Service of the Library of Congress Report RL33877, February 10, 2009).

Chapter 2: Patterns of American-
Chinese Relations Prior to World War II

1. John K. Fairbank, *Trade and Diplomacy on the China Coast: the Opening of the Treaty Ports, 1842–1854* (Cambridge, MA: Harvard University Press, 1953); Li Changjiu and Shi Lujia, *Zhongmei guanxi liangbainian* [Two hundred years of Sino-American relations] (Peking: Xinhua Publishing House, 1984).

2. Warren Cohen, *America's Response to China: A History of Sino-American Relations* (New York: Columbia University Press, 2000, 7–25); Michael Hunt, *The Making of a Special Relationship: The United States and China to 1914* (New York: Columbia University Press, 1983).

3. Daniel Bays, ed., *Christianity in China* (Stanford, CA: Stanford University Press, 1996).

4. Michael Hunt, *Frontier Defense and the Open Door: Manchuria in Chinese-American Relations, 1895–1911* (New Haven, CT: Yale University Press, 1973); Michael Schaller, *The United States and China: Into the Twenty–First Century* (New York: Oxford University Press, 2002), 26–48.

5. Akira Iriye, *After Imperialism: the Search for a New Order in the Far East, 1921–1931* (Cambridge, MA: Harvard University Press, 1965); Dorothy Borg, *The United States and the Far Eastern Crisis of 1933–1938* (Cambridge, MA: Harvard University Press, 1964).

6. John K. Fairbank, *The United States and China* (Cambridge, MA: Harvard University Press, 1983); Cohen, *America's Response to China*; Schaller, *The United States and China.*

7. Ernest R. May and John K. Fairbank, eds., *America's China Trade in Historical Perspective: the Chinese and American Performance* (Cambridge, MA: Harvard University Press, 1986).

8. John Fairbank and Suzanne W. Barnett, eds., *Christianity in China* (Cambridge, MA: Harvard University Press, 1985).

9. Walter LaFeber, *The New Empire: an Interpretation of American Expansion, 1860–1898* (Ithaca, NY: Cornell University Press, 1963).

10. Cohen, *America's Response to China*, 26–81.

11. John Fairbank, Edwin Reischauer, and Albert Craig, *East Asia: Tradition and Transformation* (Boston: Houghton Mifflin, 1973), 593–595, 766.

12. Ronald Takaki, *Strangers from a Different Shore: A History of Asian America* (Boston: Little, Brown, 1998).

13. Hunt, *Making of a Special Relationship*; Li Changjiu and Shi Lujia, *Zhongmei guanxi liangbainian* [Two hundred years of Sino-American relations] (Peking: Xinhua Publishing House, 1984).

14. Cohen, *America's Response to China*, 7–54.

15. Paul Cohen, *China and Christianity: The Missionary Movement and the Growth of Chinese Antiforeignism, 1860–1870* (Cambridge: Harvard University Press, 1963).

16. Delber McKee, *Chinese Exclusion Versus the Open Door Policy, 1900–1906* (Detroit, MI: Wayne State University Press, 1977).

17. Li Tien-yi. *Woodrow Wilson's China Policy, 1913–1917* (New York: Twayne, 1952).

18. Dorothy Borg, *American Policy and the Chinese Revolution, 1925–1928* (New York: Macmillan, 1947); Dorothy Borg, *The United States and the Far Eastern Crisis of 1933–1938* ; Akira Iriye and Warren I. Cohen, eds., *American, Chinese, and Japanese Perspectives on Wartime Asia, 1939–1949* (Wilmington, DE: Scholarly Resources, 1990).

19. Jonathan Goldstein, *Philadelphia and the China Trade* (University Park, PA: Pennsylvania State University Press, 1978).

20. Cohen, *America's Response to China*, 4.

21. Peter Ward Fay, *Opium War, 1840–1842* (Chapel Hill, NC: University of North Carolina Press, 1997).

22. Fairbank, *Trade and Diplomacy on the China Coast.*

23. Edward Gulick, *Peter Parker and the Opening of China* (Cambridge, MA: Harvard University Press, 1973).

24. Eugene Boardman, *Christian Influence upon the Ideology of the Taiping Rebellion 1850–1864* (Madison, WI: University of Wisconsin Press, 1952).

25. David Anderson, *Imperialism and Idealism: American Diplomats in China, 1861–1898* (Bloomington, IN: University of Indiana Press, 1985); Cohen, *America's Response to China*, 22

26. Fairbank, Reischauer, Craig, *East Asia: Tradition and Transformation*, 558–596.

27. Immanuel C. Y. Hsu, *The Rise of Modern China* (New York: Oxford University Press, 2000, 297–299).

28. Schaller, *The United States and China*, 18–24.

29. Fairbank, Reischauer, Craig, *East Asia: Tradition and Transformation*, 570–575.

30. Anderson, *Imperialism and Idealism*, 154–170.

31. Tyler Dennett, *Americans in Eastern Asia: a Critical Study of the Policy of the United States with Reference to China, Japan, and Korea in the 19th Century* (New York: Macmillan, 1922), 485–504; Hunt, *The Making of a Special Relationship*; Cohen, *America's Response to China*, 32–34.

32. Robert Sutter, *Historical Dictionary of United States–China Relations* (Lanham, MD: Scarecrow Press, 2006), 108.

33. Marilyn Young, *The Rhetoric of Empire: American China Policy, 1895–1901* (Cambridge, MA: Harvard University Press, 1968).

34. Cohen, *America's Response to China*, 26–81; Schaller, *The United States and China*, 26–48.

35. John Fairbank, Edwin Reischauer, and Albert Craig, *East Asia: The Modern Transformation* (Boston: Houghton Mifflin, 1965), 476–477.

36. Joseph Esherick, *The Origins of the Boxer Uprising* (Berkeley, CA: University of California Press, 1987).

37. Cohen, *America's Response to China*, 39–53.

38. Hunt, Michael H. Frontier Defense and the Open Door. Cohen, *America's Response to China*, 50–53.

39. Sutter, *Historical Dictionary*, 25–26.

40. Cohen, *America's Response to China*, 59–60.

41. Sutter, *Historical Dictionary*, 25–26.

42. Edward Rhodes, *China's Republican Revolution: The Case of Kwangtung 1895–1913* (Cambridge, MA: Harvard University Press, 1975), 176–181.

43. Hunt, *Frontier Defense and the Open Door*.

44. Sutter, *Historical Dictionary*, 192.

45. Cohen, *America's Response to China*, 61–63.

46. Hunt, *Frontier Defense and the Open Door*.

47. Li, *Woodrow Wilson's China policy*; Fairbank, Reischauer, Craig, *East Asia: The Modern Transformation*, 571, 645, 665.

48. Iriye, *After Imperialism*; Fairbank, Reischauer, Craig, *East Asia: The Modern Transformation*, 674–676.

49. James Sheridan, *China in Disintegration: the Republican Era in Chinese History, 1912–1949* (New York: The Free Press, 1975).

50. Fairbank, Reischauer, Craig, *East Asia: The Modern Transformation*, 685.

51. Benjamin Schwartz, *Chinese Communism and the Rise of Mao* (Cambridge, MA: Harvard University Press, 1958).

52. Cohen, *America's Response to China*, 99–101; *Fairbank*, Reischauer, Craig, *East Asia: The Modern Transformation*, 688–691.

53. Schaller, *The United States and China*, 42–43.

54. Borg, *The United States and the Far Eastern Crisis*; Cohen, *America's Response to China*, 115–116.

55. Schaller, *The United States and China*, 51.

56. Sutter, *Historical Dictionary*, 78–79.

57. Fairbank, Reischauer, Craig, *East Asia: The Modern Transformation*, 608–612.

58. Schaller, *The United States and China*, 54, 63.

59. Cohen, *America's Response to China*, 123–125.

60. Neils, Patricia. *China Images in the Life and Times of Henry Luce* (Lanham, MD: Rowman & Littlefield, 1990); Peck, Graham, *Two Kinds of Time* (Boston: Houghton Mifflin, 1967).

61. Thomson, James C. Jr. *While China Faced West: American Reformers in Nationalist China, 1928–1937* (Cambridge, MA: Harvard University Press, 1968).

62. Fairbank, Reischauer, Craig, *East Asia: The Modern Transformation*, 701–706.

Chapter 3: Relations during World War II, Civil War, Cold War

1. Michael Schaller, *The US Crusade in China, 1938–1945* (New York: Columbia University Press, 1979); Herbert Feis, *The China Tangle: the American Effort in China from Pearl Harbor to the Marshall Mission* (Princeton, N.J.: Princeton University Press, 1953); Barbara Tuchman, *Stilwell and the American Experience in China, 1911–1945* (New York: Macmillan, 1971); Tsou Tang. *America's Failure in China, 1941–1950* (Chicago: University of Chicago Press, 1963); Jay Taylor, *The Generalissimo: Chiang Kai-shek and the Struggle for Modern China* (Cambridge, MA: Harvard University

Press, 2009); Wang Taiping, ed., *Xin Zhongguo waijiao wushinian* [50 years of diplomacy of the new China] (Beijing: Beijing Chubanshe, 1999).

2. Feis, *The China Tangle.*

3. Russell Buhite, *Patrick J. Hurley and American Foreign Policy* (Ithaca, NY: Cornell University Press, 1973).

4. Dorothy Borg and Waldo Heinrichs, eds., *Uncertain Years: Chinese-American Relations, 1947–1950* (New York: Columbia University Press, 1980).

5. Taylor, *The Generalissimo*; Schaller, *The U.S. Crusade in China, 1938–1945.*

6. Buhite, *Patrick Hurley and American Foreign Policy*; John Beal, *Marshall in China* (Garden City, NY: Doubleday, 1970).

7. Warren Cohen, "The Development of Chinese Communist Policy Toward the United States, 1922–1938," *Orbis* II (1967): 219–37.

8. James Reardon-Anderson, *Yenan and the Great Powers: the Origins of Chinese Communist Foreign Policy, 1944–1946* (New York: Columbia University Press, 1980).

9. Odd Arne Westad, *Brothers in Arms: the Rise and Fall of the Sino-Soviet Alliance, 1945–1963* (Stanford, CA: Stanford University Press, 1998).

10. Borg and Heinrichs, *Uncertain Years*; Zi, Zhongyun. *Meiguo duihua zhengce de yuanqi he fazhan, 1945–1950* [The Origins and Development of American Policy toward China, 1945–1950] (Chongqing: Chongqing, 1987).

11. Tsou, *America's Failure in China.*

12. Charles Romanus and Riley Sunderland, *Time Runs Out on CBI* (Washington, DC: Department of the Army, 1959).

13. Charles Romanus and Riley Sunderland, *Stilwell's Command Problems* (Washington, DC: Department of the Army, 1956).

14. Tuchman, *Stilwell and the American Experience in China, 1911–1945.*

15. Michael Schaller, *The United States and China: Into the Twenty-First Century* (New York: Oxford University Press, 2002), 59–61.

16. Schaller, *The United States and China*, 72; Warren Cohen, *America's Response to China: A History of Sino-American Relations* (New York: Columbia University Press, 2000), 126.

17. Tuchman, *Stilwell and the American Experience in China, 1911–1945.*

18. Kenneth Shewmaker, *Americans and the Chinese Communists, 1927–1945: A Persuading Encounter* (Ithaca, NY: Cornell University Press, 1971).

19. Robert Sutter, *China Watch: Toward Sino-American Reconciliation* (Baltimore: John Hopkins University Press, 1978), 12–14.

20. Sutter, *China Watch*, 14–18.

21. Immanuel C. Y. Hsu, *The Rise of Modern China* (New York: Oxford University Press, 2000), 603–604.

22. Sutter, *China Watch*, 18–23.

23. Hsu, *The Rise of Modern China*, 604–605.

24. Buhite, *Patrick J. Hurley and American Foreign Policy.*

25. Schaller, *The United States and China*, 94–96.

26. Cohen, *America's Response to China*, 151.

27. Robert Sutter, *Historical Dictionary of United States–China Relations* (Lanham, MD: Scarecrow Press, 2006), 57–58.

28. Schaller, *The United States and China*, 99–102.

29. Cohen, *America's Response to China*, 174–176.

30. John Fairbank, Edwin Reischauer, Albert Craig, *East Asia: The Modern Transformation* (Boston: Houghton Mifflin, 1965), 858–859.

31. Schaller, *The United States and China*, 115.

32. Nancy Bernkopf Tucker, *Strait Talk: United States-Taiwan Relations and the Crisis with China* (Cambridge, MA: Harvard University Press, 2009), 13.

33. Schaller, *The United States and China*, 116–117; Zi, *Meiguo duihua zhengce de yuanqi he fazhan.*

34. Yu-ming Shaw, *An American Missionary in China: John Leighton Stuart and Chinese-American Relations* (Cambridge, MA: Harvard University Press, 1992).

35. Tucker, *Strait Talk* 13; Sutter, *China Watch*, 31–34.

36. Chen Jian, *China's Road to the Korean War* (New York: Columbia University Press, 1994); Westad, *Brothers in Arms*; Zi Zhongyun and He Di, eds., *Meitai Guanxi Sishinian* [Forty years of US-Taiwan relations] (Beijing: People's Press, 1991).

37. Allen Whiting, *The Chinese Calculus of Deterrence: India and Indochina* (Ann Arbor, MI: University of Michigan Press, 1975); Robert S. Ross and Jiang Changbin, *Re-examining the Cold War: U.S.-China Diplomacy 1954–1973* (Cambridge, MA: Harvard University Press, 2001).

38. Chen Jian, *Mao's China and the Cold War* (Chapel Hill, NC: University of North Carolina Press, 2001); Thomas Christensen, *Useful Adversaries: Grand Strategy, Domestic Mobilization, and Sino-American Conflicts, 1949–1958* (Princeton, NJ: Princeton University Press, 1996).

39. Richard Wich, *Sino-Soviet Crisis Politics* (Cambridge MA: Harvard University Press, 1980).

40. Ralph Clough, *Island China* (Cambridge, MA: Harvard University Press, 1978), 5–10.

41. Tucker, *Strait Talk*, 13–26.

42. Robert Blum, *Drawing the Line: the Origins of the American Containment Policy in East Asia* (New York: W.W. Norton, 1982).

43. Schaller, *The United States and China*, 152–162.

44. Bruce Cumings, *The Origins of the Korean War* (Princeton, NJ: Princeton University Press, 1990).

45. Cohen, *America's Response to China*, 169–172.

46. Schaller, *The United States and China*, 129–135.

47. Rosemary Foot, *A Substitute for Victory: The Politics of Peacemaking and the Korean Armistice Talks* (Ithaca, NY: Cornell University Press, 1990).

48. Barry Naughton, *The Chinese Economy* (Cambridge, MA: MIT Press, 2007), 55–83.

49. Chen, *Mao's China and the Cold War.*

50. Christensen, *Useful Adversaries.*

51. Schaller, *The United States and China*, 144–146.

52. Ross Koen, *The China Lobby in American Politics* (New York: Harper and Row, 1974).

53. Tucker, *Strait Talk* 13–15.

54. Clough, *Island China*, 10–14.

55. Sutter, *China Watch*, 34–46.

56. Zhang Baijia and Jia Qingguo, "Steering Wheel, Shock Absorber, and Diplomatic Probe in Confrontation: Sino-American Ambassadorial Talks Seen from the Chinese Perspective," in Ross and Jiang, eds., *Re-examining the Cold War*, 173–199; Sutter, *China Watch*, 34–46.

57. Sutter, *Historical Dictionary of United States–China Relations*, 4.

58. Steven Goldstein, "Dialogue of the Deaf?: The Sino-American Ambassadorial-Level Talks, 1955-1970," in Ross and Jiang, eds., *Re-examinng the Cold War*, 200–237.

59. Tucker, *Strait Talk*, 14–17.

60. Chen, *Mao's China and the Cold War*.

61. Schaller, *The United States and China*, 152–156.

62. Tucker, *Strait Talk*, 17–21.

63. Cohen, *America's Response to China*, 190–194; Goldstein, "Dialogue of the Deaf?" 229–237.

64. Tony Saich, *Governance and Politics of China* (New York: Palgrave Macmillan, 2004), 44–56.

65. Hsu, *The Rise of Modern China*, 689–702.

66. Roderick MacFarquhar and Michael Schoenhals, *Mao's Last Revolution* (Harvard 2006).

67. Sutter, *China Watch*, 65–67.

68. Van Ness, Peter. *Revolution and Chinese Foreign Policy* (Berkeley: University of California, 1970).

69. Jisen Ma, *The Cultural Revolution in the Foreign Ministry of China* (Hong Kong: Chinese University Press, 2004).

70. Schaller, *The United States and China*, 156–162.

71. Tucker, *Strait Talk*, 21–26.

Chapter 4: Rapprochement and Normalization

1. Doak Barnett, *A New U.S. Policy toward China* (Washington, DC: The Brookings Institution, 1971); Rosemary Foot, *The Practice of Power: US Relations with China Since 1949* (New York: Oxford University Press, 1997); Evelyn Goh, *Constructing the U.S. Rapprochement with China, 1961–1974* (New York: Cambridge University Press, 2005); Gong Li, *Kuayue: 1969–1979 nian Zhong-Mei guanxi de yanbian* [Across the Chasm: The Evolution of Relations between China and the United States, 1969–1979] (Zhengzhou: Henan renmin chubanshe, 1992).

2. Chen Jian, *Mao's China and the Cold War* (Chapel Hill, NC: University of North Carolina Press, 2001).

3. Foot, *The Practice of Power*; Goh, *Constructing the U.S. Rapprochement with China*.

4. Robert Ross, *Negotiating Cooperation: the United States and China, 1969–1989* (Stanford, CA: Stanford University Press, 1995); Robert Sutter, *China Watch: Toward Sino-American Reconciliation* (Baltimore: Johns Hopkins University Press, 1978),

83–102; Thomas Gottlieb, *Chinese Foreign Policy Factionalism and the Origins of the Strategic Triangle* (Santa Monica, CA: RAND, 1977); John Garver, *China's Decision for Rapprochement with the United States, 1968–1971* (Boulder, CO: Westview Press, 1982). Wang Zhongchun, "The Soviet Factor in Sino-American Normalization, 1969–1979," in William Kirby, Robert Ross, and Gong Li, eds., *Normalization of U.S.-China Relations* (Cambridge, MA: Harvard University Press, 2005).

5. James Mann, *About Face: a History of America's Curious Relationship with China, from Nixon to Clinton* (New York: Knopf, 1999).

6. Sutter, *China Watch*, 1–62.

7. The developments in the United States during 1968 noted here and below are covered in *American History Online—Facts on File* (www.fofweb.com) and *CQ Almanac 1968* (Washington, DC: Congressional Quarterly News Features [1968]).

8. Mann, *About Face*, 13–25.

9. Li Jie, "China's Domestic Politics and the Normalization of Sino-U.S. Relations, 1969–1979," in Kirby, Ross, and Li, eds., *Normalization of U.S.-China Relations*, 56–89; Philip Bridgham, "Mao's Cultural Revolution: The Struggle to Seize Power," *The China Quarterly* 41 (1970): 1–25.

10. Gottlieb, *Chinese Foreign Policy Factionalism and the Origins of the Strategic Triangle*; Roderick MacFarquhar and Michael Schoenhals, *Mao's Last Revolution* (Cambridge, MA: Harvard University Press, 2006).

11. Harlan Jencks, *From Muskets to Missiles: Politics and Professionalism in the Chinese Army, 1945–1981* (Boulder, CO: Westview Press, 1982).

12. Thomas Robinson, "The Sino-Soviet Border Dispute: Background, Development and the March 1969 Clashes," *American Political Science Review* lxvi: 4 (December 1972): 1175–78.

13. John Garver, *Foreign Relations of the People's Republic of China* (Englewood Cliffs, NJ: Prentice Hall, 1993), 304–320.

14. Gottleib, *Chinese Foreign Policy Factionalism*.

15. Sutter, *China Watch*, 72–75.

16. Sutter, *China Watch*, 75–78.

17. Garver, *Foreign Relations of the People's Republic of China*, 306–310.

18. Sutter, *China Watch*, 78–102.

19. Michael Schaller, *The United States and China: Into the Twenty-First Century* (New York: Oxford University Press, 2002), 170.

20. Ross, *Negotiating Cooperation*, 28, 34–35.

21. Immanuel C. Y. Hsu, *The Rise of Modern China* (New York: Oxford University Press, 2000), 711–14, 822.

22. Sutter, *Historical Dictionary of United States–China Relations* (Lanham, MD: Scarecrow Press, 2006), 190–191.

23. Hsu, *The Rise of Modern China*, 710–714; 820–23.

24. Nancy Bernkopf Tucker, *Strait Talk: United States-Taiwan Relations and the Crisis with China* (Cambridge, MA: Harvard University Press, 2009), 35–40.

25. Tucker, *Strait Talk*, 52, 68; Mann, *About Face*, 51–52.

26. The most recent authoritative account of the U.S.-China opening is Tucker, *Strait Talk*.

27. Tucker, *Strait Talk* 52.

28. U.S. Congress. House. Committee on Foreign Affairs. *Executive-Legislative Consultations over China Policy, 1978–1979* (Washington, DC: US Government Printing Office, 1980).

29. Schaller, *The United States and China*, 178–184; Tucker, *Strait Talk*, 29–68; Ross, *Negotiating Cooperation*, 17–54.

30. Warren Cohen, *America's Response to China: A History of Sino-American Relations* (New York: Columbia University Press, 2000), 198–200.

31. Hsu, *The Rise of Modern China*, 763–773.

32. John K. Fairbank and Merle Goldman, *China: A New History* (Cambridge, MA: Harvard University Press, 1999), 404–405.

33. Hsu, *The Rise of Modern China*, 817–23.

34. Fairbank and Goldman, *China: A New History*, 406–410.

35. Nayan Chanda, *Brother Enemy: The War after the War* (New York: Harcourt Brace Jovanovich, 1986).

36. Garver, *The Foreign Relations of the People's Republic of China*, 166–177, 310–11.

37. Cohen, *America's Response to China*, 201.

38. Mann, *About Face*, 82–92.

39. Tucker, *Strait Talk*, 101–115.

40. Harry Harding, *A Fragile Relationship: The United States and China Since 1972* (Washington, DC: The Brookings Institution, 1992), 80–81.

41. Ross, *Negotiating Cooperation*, 125–126; Mann, *About Face*, 98–100.

42. House. Committee on Foreign Affairs. *Executive-Legislative Consultations over China Policy, 1978–1979*.

43. Harding, *Fragile Relationship*, 86–87.

44. Schaller, *The United States and China*, 193–196.

45. Tucker, *Strait Talk*, 129–152.

46. Schaller, *The United States and China*, 177.

47. On the costs, see Tucker, *Strait Talk*, 52, 68, 153; Ross, *Negotiating Cooperation*, 163–245; Mann, *About Face*, 125–136; Schaller, *The United States and China*, 177; House: Committee on Foreign Affairs, *Executive-Legislative Consultations on China Policy, 1978–1979*.

48. See discussion of congressional debates on China policy in chapter 5, below.

49. Tucker, *Strait Talk*, 153–160.

50. Harding, *A Fragile Relationship*; Ross, *Negotiating Cooperation*; Mann, *About Face*. Major works covering later developments are Tucker, *Strait Talk*; David Michael Lampton, *Same Bed Different Dreams* (Berkeley, CA: University of California Press, 2001); Robert Suettinger, *Beyond Tiananmen* (Washington, DC: Brookings Institution, 2003); Jean Garrison, *Making China Policy: From Nixon to G.W. Bush* (Boulder, CO: Lynne Rienner Publishers, 2005). Garrison's analysis (80–85) identifies two competing groups of U.S. decision-makers regarding China policy in the early 1980s as the "China-first" group and the "pan-Asian" group. The analysis in this book builds on the Garrison analysis.

51. Ross, *Negotiating Cooperation*, 170–245; Mann, *About Face*, 119–136; Garrison, *Making China Policy*, 79–106; Tucker, *Strait Talk*, 153–160.

52. Harding, *Fragile Relationship*, 131–145. David Shambaugh, "Patterns of Interaction in Sino-American Relations," in Thomas Robinson and David Shambaugh, eds., *Chinese Foreign Policy: Theory and Practice* (New York: Oxford University Press, 1994), 203–205.

53. Garver, *The Foreign Relations of the People's Republic of China*, 310–319.

54. Robert Sutter, *Chinese Foreign Relations: Developments after Mao* (New York: Praeger, 1986), 18–96.

55. Garver, *The Foreign Relations of the People's Republic of China*, 98–103, 317–319.

56. Ross, *Negotiating Cooperation*, 164–174.

57. Sutter, *Chinese Foreign Relations: Developments after Mao*, 182.

58. Sutter, *Chinese Foreign Relations: Developments after Mao*, 178.

59. Garver, *The Foreign Relations of the People's Republic of China*, 98–103; Ross, *Negotiating Cooperation*, 170–200.

60. Tucker, *Strait Talk*, 153–160; Mann, *About Face*, 128–133.

61. Sutter, *Chinese Foreign Relations: Developments after Mao*, 178.

62. Richard Nations, "A Tilt Towards Tokyo," *Far Eastern Economic Review* April 21, 1983, 36; Ross, *Negotiating Cooperation*, 228–233.

63. Sutter, *Chinese Foreign Relations: Developments after Mao*, 178–179.

64. Ibid.

65. Ross, *Negotiating Cooperation*, 233–245; Tucker, *Strait Talk*, 160–161.

66. Sutter, *Chinese Foreign Relations: Developments after Mao*, 180–181.

67. Ross, *Negotiating Cooperation*, 233–244; Sutter, *Chinese Foreign Relations: Developments after Mao*, 181–182.

68. Tucker, *Strait Talk*, 155–160.

69. Gerald Segal, *Sino-Soviet Relations after Mao*, Adelphi Papers, no. 202 (London: International Institute for Strategic Studies, 1985.

70. The review of Sino-Soviet relations in the remainder of this section is adapted from Sutter, *Chinese Foreign Relations: Developments after Mao*, 182–186. See also Segal, *Sino-Soviet Relations after Mao*.

Chapter 5: Tiananmen, Taiwan, and Post–Cold War Realities, 1989–2000

1. Tony Saich, *Governance and Politics of China* (New York: Palgrave Macmillan 2004, 70–74).

2. Jean Garrison, *Making China Policy: From Nixon to G.W. Bush* (Boulder, CO: Lynne Rienner, 2005), 210–217; Steven Mufson, "Coverage of China in the American Press," in *China in the American Political Imagination*, ed. Carola McGiffert (Washington, DC: CSIS Press, 2003); David Michael Lampton, *Same Bed, Different Dreams: Managing U.S.-China Relations, 1989–2000* (Berkeley, CA: University of California Press, 2001), 276–278; Kenneth Lieberthal, "Why U.S. Malaise over China?" *Yaleglobal online*, January 19, 2006, www.yaleglobal.yale.edu (accessed September 27, 2009).

3. Lampton, *Same Bed, Different Dreams*, 17–55.

4. Barry Naughton, *The Chinese Economy* (Cambridge, MA: MIT Press, 2007), 98–100.

5. Carola McGiffert, ed., *Chinese Images of the United States* (Washington, DC: CSIS Press, 2006).

6. Kenneth Lieberthal, "China: How Domestic Forces Shape the PRC's Grand Strategy and International Impact," in *Strategic Asia 2007–2008*, eds. Ashley Tellis, and Michael Wills (Seattle: National Bureau of Asian Research, 2007), 63.

7. Garrison, *Making China Policy*, 182–183; Michael Swaine, *Reverse Course? The Fragile Turnabout in U.S.-China Relations* Policy Brief 22 (Washington, DC: Carnegie Endowment, February 2003).

8. Warren Cohen, *America's Response to China* (New York: Columbia University Press, 2000). 229.

9. Michael Schaller, *The United States and China: Into the Twenty-First Century* (New York: Oxford University Press, 211–214.

10. John Garver, *Face-off* (Seattle: University of Washington Press, 1997).

11. Lampton, *Same Bed, Different Dreams*, 55–63.

12. Suettinger, *Beyond Tiananmen*, 358–409.

13. Robert Sutter, *U.S. Policy Toward China: An Introduction to the Role of Interest Groups* (Lanham, MD: Rowman & Littlefield, 1998).

14. Harry Harding, *Public Engagement in American Foreign Policy* (New York: The American Assembly, Columbia University, February 23–25, 1995), 8–9.

15. Charlotte Preece and Robert Sutter, *Foreign Policy Debate in America* (Washington, DC Congressional Research Service, Library of Congress, Report 91–833F, November 27, 1991).

16. Sutter, *U.S. Policy Toward China: An Introduction to the Role of Interest Groups*, 12.

17. "Ross Perot on the Issues," *On the Issues*, http://www.issues2000.org/Ross_Perot.htm (accessed September 21, 2009).

18. Sutter, *U.S. Policy Toward China: An Introduction to the Role of Interest Groups*, 13–14. Joseph Nye, *Bound to Lead* (Cambridge, MA: Harvard University Press, 1992).

19. Sutter, *U.S. Policy Toward China: An Introduction to the Role of Interest Groups*, 14–15; Lampton, *Same Bed, Different Dreams*, 17–63.

20. "John McCain on the Issues, *On the Issues*, http://www.issues2000.org/John_McCain.htm (accessed September 21, 2009).

21. Lampton, *Same Bed, Different Dreams*, 332–335, 338–339.

22. Kerry Dumbaugh, "Interest Groups: Growing Influence," in *Making China Policy: Lessons from the Bush and Clinton Administrations*, eds. Ramon Myers, Michel Oksenberg, and David Shambaugh (Lanham, MD: Rowman & Littlefield, 2001), 113–178.

23. Sutter, *U.S. Policy Toward China: An Introduction to the Role of Interest Groups*, 16.

24. Kent Wong, "The AFL-CIO and China," UCLA Asian American Studies Center, *U.S.-China Media Brief*, 2008, www.aasc.ucla.edu/uschina/ee_aflciochina.shtml (accessed September 21, 2009).

25. Dumbaugh, "Interest Groups: Growing Influence," 150, 158–159, 161, 162, 170–171.

26. Sutter, *U.S. Policy Toward China: An Introduction to the Role of Interest Groups,* 16–17.

27. Nancy Bernkopf Tucker, *Strait Talk* (Cambridge, MA: Harvard University Press, 2009).

28. Suettinger, *Beyond Tiananmen,* 294, 330.

29. The four crises are identified and reviewed in Lampton, *Same Bed, Different Dreams,* 17–63. See also Suettinger, *Beyond Tiananmen.*

30. Schaller, *The United States and China,* 204–205.

31. Sutter, *U.S. Policy Toward China: An Introduction to the Role of Interest Groups,* 26–44.

32. Mann, *About Face,* 274–278.

33. Cohen, *America's Response to China,* 229–231.

34. Schaller, *The United States and China,* 214–219.

35. Cohen, *America's Response to China,* 234–239.

36. For this and the next two paragraphs, see Robert Sutter, *Historical Dictionary of United States–China Relations* (Lanham, MD: Rowman & Littlefield, 2006), lxix–lxx.

37. Schaller, *The United States and China,* 219–227.

38. Cohen, *America's Response to China,* 235–236.

39. Tucker, *Strait Talk,* 217–218, 231–243.

40. Sutter, *Historical Dictionary of United States–China Relations,* lxxi.

41. Suettinger, *Beyond Tiananmen,* 369–377.

42. Tucker, *Strait Talk,* 239–244.

43. Lampton, *Same Bed, Different Dreams,* 95–97.

44. Garrison, *Making China Policy,* 148–152.

45. Garrison, *Making China Policy,* 165–182; Robert Sutter, "The Democratic-Led 110th Congress: Implications for Asia," *Asia Policy* 3 (January 2007): 125–150.

46. The following analysis summarizes points made at greater length in Robert Sutter, "U.S. Domestic Debate over Policy toward mainland China and Taiwan: Key findings, outlook, and lessons," *The American Journal of Chinese Studies* VIII/2 (October 2001): 133–144; and Robert Sutter, "The Bush Administration and U.S. China Policy Debate," *Issues and Studies* 38:2 (June 2002): 14–22.

47. Tucker, *Strait Talk*; Myers, Oksenberg, Shambaugh, eds., *Making China Policy*; Lampton, *Same Bed-Different Dreams*; Mann, *About Face*: Sutter, *U.S. Policy Toward China.* Robert Sutter, *The China Quandary* (Boulder, CO: Westview Press, 1983).

48. Tucker, *Strait Talk,* 29–52.

49. Reviewed in Tucker, *Strait Talk,* 116–128; Sutter, *The China Quandary,* 5, 19, 85, and 146.

50. U.S. House of Representatives, Committee on Foreign Affairs. *Executive-Legislative Consultations over China Policy, 1978–1979* (Washington DC: U.S. Government Printing Office, 1980).

51. Dumbaugh, "Interest Groups: Growing Influence," James Mann, "Congress and Taiwan," and Robert Sutter, "The U.S. Congress: Personal, Partisan, Political," in Myers, Oksenberg, and Shambaugh, eds., *Making China Policy,* 79–222.

52. Sutter, "U.S. Domestic Debate over Policy toward mainland China and Taiwan: Key Findings, Outlook, and Lessons," 137.

53. Bill Gertz and Rowan Scarborough, "Inside the Ring," *Washington Times*, March 22, 2002 (Internet version); Murray Hiebert and Susan Lawrence, "Crossing Red Lines," *Far Eastern Economic Review*, April 4, 2002 (Internet version).

54. Sutter, "The Bush Administration and U.S. China Policy Debate," 16.

55. Lampton, *Same Bed, Different Dreams*; Chu Shulong, "Quanmian jianshe xiaokang shehui shiqi de zhongguo waijiao zhan-lue," *Shijie Jingji yu Zhengzhi* 8 (August 2003); Fu Hao and Li Tongcheng, eds., *Lusi shui shou? Zhongguo Waijiaoguan zai Meiguo* [Who Will Win the Game? Chinese Diplomats in the United States] (Beijing: Hauqiao chubanshe, 1998).

56. Song Qiang, Zhang Changchang, and Qiao Bian. Zhongguo keyi shuo bu: Lengzhanhou shidai de zhengzhi yu qinggan jueze [China Can Say No: The Decision Between Politics and Sentiment in the Post–Cold War] (Beijing: Zhonghua Gongshang Lianhe Chubanshe, 1996).

57. Robert Sutter, *Chinese Policy Priorities and Their Implications for the United States* (Lanham, MD: Rowman & Littlefield, 2000), 40–41; Wang Jisi, *China's Changing Role in Asia* (Washington, DC: The Atlantic Council of the United States, January 2004), 1–5, 16–17; Qian Qichen, "Adjustment of the United States National Security Strategy and International Relations in the Early New Century," (Beijing) *Foreign Affairs Journal* 71 (March 2004): 1–7; Wang Jisi, "Xinxingshi de Zhuyao Tedian he Zhongguo Waijiao" (Beijing) *Xiabdai Guoji Guanxi* 4 (April 2003): 1–3; Yuan Peng, "Bumpy road ahead for sustainable Sino-U.S. ties," *China Daily*, May 8, 2007, 11; Kenneth Lieberthal, "Why the U.S. Malaise over China?"; Fu Mengzi "Sino-U.S. Relations," (Beijing) *Xiandai guoji guanxi* 17 (January 2007): 32–46.

58. Suettinger, *Beyond Tiananmen*, 340–351; Schaller, *The United States and China*, 223–224.

59. Sutter, *Chinese Policy Priorities*, 41–42.

60. "Experts Appraise Sino-U.S. Relations," *Jeifang Junbao* (June 1995), 5; Wang Jisi, "Deepening Mutual Understanding and Expanding Strategic Consensus," *Renmin Ribao* (June 16, 1998), 6; "Questions and Answers at Qian Qichen's Small-Scale Briefing," (Hong Kong) *Wen Wei Pao* (November 4, 1997), A6; Sutter, *Chinese Policy Priorities*, 42.

61. Lampton, *Same Bed, Different Dreams*, 39–45; Sutter, *U.S. Policy toward China*, 47–65.

62. David Michael Lampton, "America's China Policy in the Age of the Finance Minister: Clinton Ends Linkage," *China Quarterly* 139 (September 1994): 597–621.

63. Sutter, *Chinese Policy Priorities*, 43–44.

64. Lampton, *Same Bed, Different Dreams*, 45.

65. Sutter, *Chinese Policy Priorities*, 52; Garver, *Face-Off*. See also, Su Ge. *Meiguo: Dui hua Zhengce yu Taiwan wenti* [America: China Policy and the Taiwan Issue]. Beijing: Shijie Zhishi Chubanshe, 1998.

66. *U.S. News and World Report*, October 23, 1995, 72.

67. Suettinger, *Beyond Tiananmen*, 264–357.

68. Sutter, *Chinese Policy Priorities*, 57–58.

69. Susan Shirk, *China: Fragile Superpower* (New York: Oxford University Press, 2007), 220.

70. Robert Sutter, *China's Rise in Asia* (Lanham, MD: Rowman & Littlefield, 2005), 12–13.

Chapter 6: U.S.-China Policy Priorities and Implications for Relations in the Twenty-First Century

1. Kenneth Lieberthal, "Behind the Crawford Summit," *Pac Net 44*, October 24, 2002.

2. Michael Swaine, *Reverse Course: The Fragile Turnabout in US-China Relations.* Policy Brief 22 (Washington, DC: Carnegie Endowment for International Peace, February 2003).

3. Hugo Restall, "Tough Love for China," *Wall Street Journal*, October 21, 2002, A14.

4. Kerry Dumbaugh, *China-U.S. Relations: Current Issues and Implications for U.S. Policy* (Washington, DC: The Congressional Research Service of The Library of Congress CRS Report RL33877, May 25, 2007).

5. David M. Lampton, *Same Bed, Different Dreams: Managing US-China Relations, 1989–2000,* (Berkeley, CA: University of California Press, 2001).

6. Ramon Myers, Michael Oksenberg, David Shambaugh, eds., *Forging a Consensus: Making China Policy in the Bush and Clinton Administrations* (New York: Rowman & Littlefield, 2001).

7. Jean Garrison, *Making China Policy: From Nixon to G. W. Bush* (Boulder, CO: Lynne Reinner Publishers, 2005).

8. Kerry Dumbaugh, *China-US Relations* (Washington, DC, The Library of Congress, IB 98018, updated July 17, 2001); Swaine, *Reverse Course.*

9. Sutter, *US Policy Toward China*, 94.

10. Bates Gill. *Meeting the Challenges and Opportunities of China's Rise* (Washington, DC: Center for Strategic and International Studies, October 2006), 6–12.

11. As noted in footnotes below, the following discussion relies on reports on China-US relations done by the Congressional Research Service of the Library of Congress. Other sources include *Congressional Quarterly Weekly Report, CQ Weekly, Congressional Quarterly Almanac,* and *CQ Almanac.*

12. Tony Saich, *Governance and Politics of China* (New York: Palgrave, 2004), 83.

13. Dumbaugh, *China-US Relations*, IB 98018, updated July 17, 2001, 5.

14. Kerry Dumbaugh, *China and the 105th Congress: Policy Issues and Legislation, 1997–1998,* (Washington, DC: The Library of Congress, CRS Report RL 30220, June 8, 1999).

15. Larry Q. Nowels, *US International Population Assistance: Issues for Congress* (Washington, DC, The Library of Congress, CRS IB 96026, June 15, 2001).

16. "Religion in China: When Opium Can Be Benign," *The Economist*, February 1, 2007, www.economist.com (accessed November 9, 2007).

17. Erica Werner, "US Lawmakers Criticize Yahoo Officials," *Washington Post*, November 6, 2007, A1.

18. Testimony of CIA Director George Tenet to the Senate Armed Services Committee, March 20, 2002, www.cia.gov (accessed March 25, 2002).

19. Kerry Dumbaugh, *China-US Relations in the 109th Congress* (Washington, DC: Congressional Research Service of the Library of Congress, Report RL32804, December 31, 2006), 20.

20. Shirley Kan, et al., *China: Suspected Acquisition of US Nuclear Weapons Data* (Washington, DC, The Library of Congress, CRS Report RL 30143, 1999).

21. Amy Argetsinger, "Spy Case Dismissed for Misconduct," *Washington Post*, January 7, 2005, A-4; Steve Lohr, "State Department Yields on PC's from China, *New York Times*, May 22, 2006, www.nytimes.com (accessed November 9, 2007).

22. Wayne Morrison, *China-US Trade Issues* (Washington, DC, The Library of Congress, CRS Report RL 33536, April 23, 2007).

23. Dumbaugh, *China-US Relations in the 109th Congress*, 19.

24. Morrison, *China-US Trade Issues*.

25. Ibid.

26. Dumbaugh, *China-US Relations in the 109th Congress*, 4.

27. Dumbaugh, *China-US Relations in the 109th Congress*, 27.

28. Bonnie Glaser, "Mid-air Collision Cripples Sino-US Relations," *Comparative Connections*, Honolulu, CSIS/Pacific Forum, April-June 2001, http://www.csis.org/pacfor.

29. Dumbaugh, *China-US Relations in the 109th Congress*, 8.

30. Dumbaugh, *China-US Relations*, 10–11.

31. Peter Grier, "Why Bush Risks China's Ire to Honor Dalai Lama," *Christian Science Monitor*, October 17, 2007, 1.

32. Thomas Friedman, "Will Congress View China as Scapegoat or Sputnik?" *New York Times*, November 10, 2006 (accessed www.taiwansecurity.org November 13, 2006).

33. The analysis in and sources for this section are reviewed in Robert Sutter, "The Democratic-Led 110th Congress: Implications for Asia," *Asia Policy 3* (January 2007): 125–150; and Robert Sutter, "The Democratic Victory in Congress: Implications for Asia," *Brookings Northeast Asian Commentary* No. 4, December 2006.

34. *New Study Reveals Most Americans Remain Committed To Steady Internationalism Despite Frustration Over Iraq War*, Chicago Council on Global Affairs Media Advisory, October 11, 2006.

35. Robin Toner, "After Many Years, Now It's His Turn at the Helm," *New York Times* January 8, 2007 A1. Carl Hulse, "Leadership Tries to Restrain Fiefs in New Congress," *New York Times*, January 7, 2007, www.nytimes.com (accessed September 27, 2009).

36. For sources and examples, see Robert Sutter, *Chinese Foreign Relations: Power and Policy Since the Cold War* (Lanham, MD: Rowman & Littlefield 2008), 2.

37. David Shambaugh, "China's 17th Party Congress: Maintaining Delicate Balances," *Brookings Northeast Asia Commentary*, November 2007, www.brookings.edu (accessed November 11, 2007).

38. Denny Roy, *China's Foreign Relations* (New York: Rowman & Littlefield, 1998).

39. Robert Sutter, *Chinese Policy Priorities and Their Implications for the United States* (Lanham, MD: Rowman & Littlefield, 2000), 18. See review of this period in Barry Naughton, *The Chinese Economy* (Cambridge, MA: MIT Press, 2007), and Tony Saich, *Governance and Politics of China* (London: Palgrave, 2004).

40. Kerry Dumbaugh, *China's 17th Party Congress, October 15–21, 2007*, Congressional Research Service Memorandum, October 23, 2007.

41. Maureen Fan, "China's Party Leadership Declares New Priority: 'Harmonious Society,'" *Washington Post*, October 12, 2006, A18.

42. These developments and determinants are reviewed in Sutter, *Chinese Foreign Relations*, 2–3.

43. Bates Gill, *Rising Star* (Washington, DC: Brookings Institution, 2007); Susan Shirk, *China: Fragile Superpower* (New York: Oxford University Press, 2007).

44. Reviewed in Sutter, *Chinese Foreign Relations*, 3–4.

45. People's Republic of China State Council Information Office, "China's Peaceful Development Road," *People's Daily Online*, December 22, 2005 (accessed July 7, 2006).

46. Zhang Yunling and Tang Shiping, "China's Regional Strategy," in David Shambaugh, ed., *Power Shift* (Berkeley, CA: University of California Press, 2005), 48–70.

47. Institute for International and Strategic Studies (IISS), *China's Grand Strategy: A Kinder, Gentler Turn* (London: IISS, November 2004).

48. Thomas Christensen, "China," in Richard Ellings and Aaron Friedberg, eds., *Strategic Asia, 2001–2002* (Seattle, WA: National Bureau of Asian Research, 2001), 27–70.

49. Condoleezza Rice, "Remarks at Sophia University," Tokyo, March 19, 2005, www.state.gov (accessed March 27, 2005).

50. Robert B. Zoellick, "Whither China: From Membership to Responsibility?" Remarks to National Committee on U.S.-China Relations, New York City, September 21, 2005. www.state.gov (accessed September 29, 2005); "Gates: China Not a Strategic Adversary," *China Daily*, March 8, 2007, 1.

51. Reviewed in Sutter, *Chinese Foreign Relations* 8–12.

52. Richard Bush, *Untying the Knot* (Washington, DC: Brookings Institution, 2005).

53. Bates Gill, "China's Evolving Regional Security Strategy," in Shambaugh, ed., *Power Shift*, 247–265; Jonathan Pollack, "The Transformation of the Asian Security Order: Assessing China's Impact," in Shambaugh, ed., *Power Shift*, 329–346.

54. Aaron Friedberg, "The Future of US-China Relations: Is Conflict Inevitable?," *International Security* 30:2 (2005): 7–45.

Chapter 7: An Emerging U.S.-China Equilibrium in the Twenty-First Century

1. This dualism and respective Gulliver strategies are discussed in Robert Sutter, "China and U.S. Security and Economic Interests: Opportunities and Challenges," in Robert Ross and Oystein Tunsjo, eds., *U.S.-China-EU Relations: Managing The New World Order* (London: Routledge, 2010).

2. Avery Goldstein, *Rising to the Challenge: China's Grand Strategy and International Security* (Stanford, CA: Stanford University Press, 2005).

3. Evan Medeiros and R. Taylor Fravel, "China's New Diplomacy," *Foreign Affairs* 82:6 (November-December 2003): 22–35.

4. Susan Shirk, *China: Fragile Superpower* (New York: Oxford University Press, 2007).

5. Robert Sutter, *Chinese Foreign Relations: Power and Policy since the Cold War* (Lanham, MD: Rowman & Littlefield 2008), 3–12.

6. Phillip Saunders, *China's Global Activism: Strategy, Drivers, and Tools* (Washington, DC: National Defense University Press Institute for National Strategic Studies Occasional Paper, 4 June 2006), 8–9.

7. Murray Hiebert, *The Bush Presidency: Implications for Asia* (New York: The Asia Society: Asian Update, January 2001), 5–9.

8. Robert Sutter, *Grading Bush's China Policy* (Honolulu: CSIS Pacific Forum PACNET 10: March 8, 2002).

9. James Shinn, ed., *Weaving the Net: Conditional Engagement with China* (New York: Council on Foreign Relations Press, 1996).

10. Bonnie Glaser, "Bilateral Relations on Reasonably Sound Footing," *Comparative Connections* (Honolulu: CSIS Pacific Forum, January 2001), www.csis.org/pacfor.

11. Bonnie Glaser, "First Contact: Qian Qichen Engages in Wide-ranging, Constructive Talks," *Comparative Connections* April 2001 www.csis.org/pacfor.

12. John Keefe, *Anatomy of the EP-3 Incident*, (Alexandria, VA: Center for Naval Analysis, January 2002).

13. Nick Cummings-Bruce, "Powell Will Explain Bush's Asia Policy," *Wall Street Journal*, July 23, 2001, A 11. Alternative explanations for the improvement of China-U.S. relations at this time are noted in chapter 6.

14. "Concern over U.S. plans for war on terror dominate Jiang tour," *Reuters*, April 7, 2002 www.taiwansecurity.org (accessed April 9, 2002); Willy Wo-Lap Lam, "U.S., Taiwan Catch Jiang off-guard," *CNN.com* March 19, 2002.

15. Bonnie Glaser, "Playing up the Positive on the Eve of the Crawford Summit," *Comparative Connections* October 2002, www.csis.org/pacfor

16. "U.S. Says China Regulations Should Free Up Soybean Exports," *Statement* Office of the U.S. Trade Representative, October 18, 2002, http://usinfo.state.gov; "Mainland Offers Taiwan Goodwill Gesture," *China Daily*, October 18, 2002, www.taiwansecurity.org (accessed October 20, 2002); "China Tightens Rules on Military Exports," *Reuters*, October 21, 2002 www.taiwansecurity.org (accessed October 23, 2002); Ashcroft to Open China FBI Office," *Reuters*, October 22, 2002, www.taiwansecurity.org (accessed October 24, 2002); "U.S. and China Seal Billion Dollar Deals," *BBC*, October 22, 2002, www.taiwansecurity.org (accessed October 24, 2002); "U.S. and China Set New Rights Talks," *Washington Post*, October 24, 2002 www.taiwansecurity.org (accessed October 26, 2002).

17. Lu Zhenya, "Jiang Zemin, Bush agree to maintain high-level strategic dialogue," Beijing *Zhongguo Xinwen She*, October 26, 2002 www.taiwansecurity.org (accessed October 30, 2002)

18. Bonnie Glaser, "Sustaining Cooperation," *Comparative Connections,* January 2003, www.csis.org/pacfor.

19. "Bush, Kerry Square Off in 1st Debate," *Japan Today* October 1, 2004, www.japantoday.com/jp/news/313422/all (accessed March 21, 2008).

20. Robert Sutter, "The Taiwan Problem in the Second George W. Bush Administration—U.S. Officials' Views and Their Implications for U.S. Policy," *Journal of Contemporary China* 15:48 (August 2006): 417–442.

21. Secretary of State Condoleezza Rice, *Remarks at Sophia University,* Tokyo Japan, March 19, 2005, http://www.state.gov/secretary/rm/2005/43655.htm (accessed March 21, 2008).

22. Rosemary Foot, "Chinese Strategies in a U.S.-Dominated Global Order," *International Affairs* 82, no. 1 (2006): 77–94.

23. Off-the-record interviews with U.S. officials reviewed in Robert Sutter, "Dealing with a Rising China: U.S. Strategy and Policy," in Zhang Yunlin, ed., *Making New Partnership: A Rising China and Its Neighbors* (Beijing: Social Sciences Academic Press, 2008), 370–374.

24. Among published sources see U.S.-China Economic and Security Review Commission *2005 Report to Congress* (Washington, DC: U.S. Government Printing Office, 2005), 143–190.

25. Remarks of Deputy Secretary of State Robert Zoellick, "Wither China? From Membership to Responsibility," New York, National Committee for U.S.-China Relations, September 21, 2005, http://usinfo.state.gov/eap/Archive/2005/Sep/22-290478.html.

26. Victor Cha, "Winning Asia: Washington's Untold Success Story," *Foreign Affairs* 86: 6 (November–December 2007): 98–113; Robert Sutter, *The United States in Asia* (Lanham, MD: Rowman & Littlefield, 2008), 270–276, 281–283.

27. See reviews of Chinese leaders' priorities following the major party and government meetings in the Jamestown Foundation's weekly publication *China Brief,* www.jamestown.org/index.php and the quarterly publication *China Leadership Monitor,* www.hoover.org/publications/clm/.

28. Testimony on U.S.-China relations before the House Foreign Affairs Committee of Deputy Secretary of State John Negroponte, May 1, 2007 www.state.gov (accessed May 5, 2007). Victor Cha, "Winning Asia."

29. See contrasting views of China's recent approach to the United States and of various differences in China-U.S. relations in Bates Gill, *Rising Star* (Washington, DC: Brookings Institution, 2007); Shirk, *China: Fragile Superpower,* and Sutter, *Chinese Foreign Relations.*

30. Kerry Dumbaugh, *China-U.S. Relations: Current Issues and Implications for U.S. Policy* (Washington, DC: The Congressional Research Service of the Library of Congress Report RL33877, February 10, 2009).

31. In addition to reviewing published sources on Congress and political projections, this author benefited from consultation with three leading political lobbyists in Washington, DC, during 2008.

32. Wayne Morrison, *China-U.S. Trade Issues* (Washington, DC: The Congressional Research Service of the Library of Congress Report RL33536, March 4, 2009).

33. Council on Foreign Relations *U.S. Election 2008* www.cfr.org (accessed June 23, 2008).

34. Morrison, *China-U.S. Trade Issues.*

35. Kenneth Lieberthal and David Sandalow, *Overcoming Obstacles to U.S.-China Cooperation on Climate Change* (Washington, DC: Brookings Institution, John Thornton China Center Monograph 1, January 2009), 2, 8–9.

36. Joanna I. Lewis, "China's Strategic Priorities in International Climate Change Negotiations," *Washington Quarterly* 31:1 (Winter 2007–2008): 155–174.

37. Shirley Kan, *Taiwan: Major U.S. Arms Sales Since 1990* (Washington, DC: The Congressional Research Service of the Library of Congress Report RL30957, February 11, 2009).

38. Dumbaugh, *China-U.S. Relations*

39. USC U.S.-China Institute, *Survey: Most Americans now have an unfavorable Impression of China* March 5, 2008 http://china.usc.edu/Default.aspx (accessed March 21, 2008). Gallup, "Canada Remains Americans' Most Favored Nation," February 19, 2009 www.gallup.com (accessed March 30, 2009).

40. Edmund Andrew, "Report Projects A Worldwide Economic Slide," *New York Times,* March 9, 2009, B1; Robert Sutter, "The Obama Administration and U.S. Policy in Asia," *Contemporary Southeast Asia* 31:2 (2009): 189–216; Robert Sutter, "The Obama Administration and China: Positive but Fragile Equilibrium," *Asian Perspective* 33:3 (2009): 81–106.

41. Kenneth Katzman, *Afghanistan: Post Taliban Governance, Security, and U.S. Policy* (Washington DC: Congressional Research Service, Library of Congress, February 9, 2009).

42. *America's Role in the World: Foreign Policy Choices for the Next President* (Washington, DC: Institute for the Study of Diplomacy, School of Foreign Service, Georgetown University, 2008).

43. Victor Cha, "What Do They Really Want: Obama's North Korea Conundrum," *Washington Quarterly* 32:4 (2009): 119–138.

44. Donald Zagoria, *Cross-Strait Relations: Cautious Optimism,* Report of Conference on Prospects for Relations Across the Taiwan Strait, National Committee on American Foreign Policy, New York, 13–14 January 2009.

45. Kenneth Lieberthal and David Sandalow, "Overcoming Obstacles to U.S.-China Cooperation on Climate Change" Brookings Institution John L. Thornton China Center Monograph Series Number 1 (January 2009).

46. Morton Abramowitz and Stephen Bosworth, *Chasing the Sun* (New York: Century Foundation, 2006).

47. David Shambaugh, "China Engages Asia: Reshaping the Regional Order," *International Security* 29, no 3 (Winter 2004/2005): 64–99; Joshua Kurlantzick, *Charm Offensive: How China's Soft Power is Transforming the World* (New Haven, CT: Yale University Press, 2007); David Kang, *China Rising: Peace, Power and Order in East Asia* (New York: Columbia University Press, 2007).

48. Robert Sutter, "Assessing China's Rise and U.S. Leadership in Asia—Growing Maturity and Balance," Honolulu: Pacific Forum/CSIS *PacNet 6,* January 29, 2009, www.csis.org/pacfor.

49. Victor Cha, "Winning Asia: America's Untold Success Story," *Foreign Affairs*, November/December 2007, www.foreignaffairs.org.

50. Evelyn Goh, "Southeast Asia: Strategic Diversification in the 'Asian Century,'" in *Strategic Asia 2008–2009*, eds. Ashley Tellis, Mercy Kuo, and Andrew Marble (Seattle: National Bureau of Asian Research, 2008), 261–296.

51. These factors are explained in detail in Robert Sutter, *The United States in Asia* (Lanham, MD: Rowman & Littlefield, 2009). For alternative perspectives, see among others, David Shambaugh and Michael Yahuda, eds., *International Relations of Asia* (Lanham, MD: Rowman & Littlefield, 2008).

52. "We Should Join Hands: Chinese Premier Interviewed," *Newsweek*, October 6, 2008, www.newsweek.com.

53. Evan Medeiros, *Pacific Currents: The Responses of U.S. Allies and Security Partners in East Asia to China's Rise* (Santa Monica, CA: RAND Corporation, 2008).

54. Kerry Dumbaugh, *China-U.S. Relations: Current Issues and Implications for U.S. Policy* (Washington, DC: Congressional Research Service, Library of Congress, Report 33877, December 8, 2008).

55. Evan Medeiros, "Strategic Hedging and the Future of Asia-Pacific Stability," *The Washington Quarterly* 29:1 (2005–2006): 145–167; Rosemary Foot, "Chinese Strategies in a U.S.-Hegemonic Global Order: Accommodating and Hedging," *International Affairs* 82: 1 (2006): 77–94.

56. *China's National Defense in 2008* (Beijing: Information Office of the State Council of the People's Republic of China, January 2009). Briefing by delegation from the Chinese Academy of Military Science, Georgetown University, Washington DC, October 2, 2008.

57. Edward Gresser and Daniel Twining, "Shock of the New: Congress and Asia in 2009," *NBR Analysis*, February 2009, 21.

58. C. Fred Bergsten, "A Partnership of Equals: How Washington Should Respond to China's Economic Challenge," *Foreign Affairs*, July–August 2008, www.foreignaffairs.org.

Chapter 8: Security Issues in Contemporary U.S.-China Relations

1. In addition to sources noted in chapter 4, see Wang Zhongchun, "The Soviet Factor in Sino-American Normalization, 1969–1979," in William Kirby, Robert Ross, and Gong Li, eds. *Normalization of U.S.-China Relations* (Cambridge, MA: Harvard University Press 2005).

2. John Garver, *Foreign Relations of the People's Republic of China* (Englewood Cliffs, NJ: Prentice Hall, 1993), 166–177, 310–311.

3. James Mann, *About Face* (New York: Knopf, 1999), 33–35.

4. Garver, *Foreign Relations of the People's Republic of China*, 166–173; Harry Harding, *A Fragile Relationship* (Washington, DC.: Brookings Institution, 1992), 119–122, 332–333.

5. U.S. Congress, House, Committee on Foreign Affairs, Subcommittee on Asian and Pacific Affairs, *Playing the China Card: Implications for United States-Soviet*

Union-Chinese Relations (Washington, DC: U.S. Government Printing Office, 1979).

6. Robert Sutter, *The China Quandary: Domestic Determinants of U.S. China Policy, 1972–1982* (Boulder, CO: Westview Press, 1983), 99–100, 111–126.

7. Mann, *About Face*, 98–100, 109–114; Yitzhak Shichor, "The Great Wall of Steel: Military and Strategy in Xinjiang," in S. Frederick Starr, ed., *Xinjiang: China's Muslim Borderland*, Armonk, (New York: M.E. Sharpe, 2004), 148–150.

8. Harry Harding, *Fragile Relationship* (Washington, DC: Brookings Institution, 1992), 224–234.

9. David Michael Lampton, *Same Bed Different Dreams* (Berkeley, CA: University of California Press, 2001), 39–63; Jean Garrison, *Making China Policy: From Nixon to G.W. Bush* (Boulder, CO: Lynne Rienner Publishers, 2005), 165–172.

10. Shirley Kan, *U.S.-China Military Contacts: Issue for Congress* (Washington, DC: Congressional Research Service of the Library of Congress, Report RL32496 April 15, 2009), 6–11.

11. Lampton, *Same Bed, Different Dreams*, 71–110.

12. The Chinese reactions and motivations concerning these developments are reviewed in Lampton, *Same Bed, Different Dreams*, and Robert Suettinger, *Beyond Tiananmen* (Washington, DC: Brookings Institution, 2003).

13. U.S. Department of Defense, *Annual Report on the Military Power of the People's Republic of China, 2009* (www.defenselink.mil, accessed October 26, 2009); Roy Kamphausen, David Lai, and Andrew Scobell eds. *Beyond the Strait: PLA Missions Other Than Taiwan* (Carlisle Barracks, PA: Strategic Studies Institute, U.S. Army War College 2009).

14. Robert S. Ross, "The Geography of Peace: East Asia in the Twenty-First Century," *International Security* 23:4 (Spring 1999): 81–118.

15. Aaron Friedberg, "Is China a Military Threat?" *The National Interest* 103 (September/October 2009): 19–25.

16. Kan, *China-U.S. Military Contacts*.

17. Evan Medeiros, *Reluctant Restraint: The Evolution of China's Nonproliferation Policies and Practices, 1980–2004* (Stanford, CA: Stanford University Press, 2007).

18. Bonnie S. Glaser, "China's Policy in the Wake of the Second DPRK Nuclear Test," *China Security*, www.chinasecurity.us/index.php?option=com_content&view=article&id=287&Itemid= =zh (accessed October 26, 2009).

19. Evan Medeiros, *China's International Behavior: Activism, Opportunism, and Diversification* (Santa Monica, CA: RAND Corporation 2009), 96–101.

20. Institute for International Studies (IISS), *China's Grand Strategy: A Kinder Gentler Turn* (London: IISS, November 2004).

21. Medeiros, China's International Behavior, 48–53.

22. Bonnie Glaser and Evan Medeiros, "The Ecology of Foreign Policy Decision-making in China: The Ascension and Demise of the Theory of Peaceful Rise," *China Quarterly* 190 (June 2007): 291–310.

23. Robert Sutter, *China's Rise in Asia* (Lanham, MD: Rowman & Littlefield, 2005), 265–276.

24. Avery Goldstein, *Rising to the Challenge: China's Grand Strategy and International Security* (Stanford, CA: Stanford University Press, 2005).

25. Robert Sutter, *Chinese Foreign Relations: Power and Policy Since the Cold War* (Lanham, MD: Rowman & Littlefield, 2008), 177.

26. Sutter, *Chinese Foreign Relations* 178.

27. David Michael Lampton, *The Three Faces of Chinese Power: Might, Money, and Minds* (Berkeley, CA: University of California Press, 2008), 27.

28. Susan Shirk, *China: Fragile Superpower* (New York: Oxford University Press, 2007).

29. Sutter, *Chinese Foreign Relations*, 178.

30. U.S.-China Security Review Commission, *Report to Congress 2008*, www.uscc.gov.

31. Sutter, *China's Rise in Asia*, 272–273.

32. People's Republic of China State Council Information Office, "China's Peaceful Development Road," *People's Daily Online*, December 22, 2005 (accessed July 7, 2006).

33. Interview, Chinese Foreign Ministry, Beijing, May 30, 2006.

34. Briefings, Academy of Military Science, Beijing, June 2008; briefings by senior representatives of the Academy at a public meeting at Georgetown University, Washington, DC, on October 2, 2008.

35. Deputy Secretary of States James Steinberg publicly called on China to reassure the United States over these and other concerns in a speech on September 23, 2009. *East Asia and the Pacific: Administration's Vision of the U.S.-China Relationship* Keynote Address at the Center for a New American Security, September 24, 2009.

36. People's Republic of China State Council Information Office, "China's National Defense in 2004" (Beijing, December 27, 2004); People's Republic of China State Council Information Office, "China's National Defense in 2006" (Beijing, December 29, 2006). People's Republic of China State Council Information Office, "China's National Defense in 2008" (Beijing, January 2009).

37. Paul Godwin, "China as a Major Asian Power: The Implications of Its Military Modernization (A View from the United States)," in *China, the United States, and Southeast Asia: Contending perspectives on politics, security, and economics*, eds. Evelyn Goh and Sheldon Simon (New York: Routledge, 2008), 145–166.

38. Chu Shulong and Lin Xinzhu, "It Is Not the Objective of Chinese Military Power to Catch Up and Overtake the United States," *Beijing Huanqiu Shibao*, June 26, 2008, 11.

39. United States Department of Defense, *Annual Report on the Military Power of the People's Republic of China, 2009* (Washington, DC: U.S. Department of Defense, March 2009).

40. "China's National Defense in 2004," 2–4.

41. Andrew Scobell and Larry M. Wortzel, eds., *Shaping China's Security Environment: The Role of the PLA* (Carlisle, PA: Strategic Studies Institute, U.S. Army War College, 2006), 2.

42. Briefings, Beijing June 2008, Georgetown University, Washington DC, October 2, 2008.

43. Hu Xiao, "Japan and U.S. Told, Hands Off Taiwan," *China Daily*, March 7, 2005, 1.

44. "China-Southeast Asia Relations," *Comparative Connections* 9:3 (October 2007): 75.

45. "China-Southeast Asia Relations," *Comparative Connections* 10:4 (January 2009): 76.

46. Evan Medeiros, "Strategic Hedging and the Future of Asia-Pacific Stability," *Washington Quarterly* 29:1 (Winter 2005–2006): 145–167.

47. Richard Bush and Michael O'Hanlon, *A War Like No Other: The Truth about China's Challenge to America* (Hoboken, NJ: John Wiley), 2007

48. Paul Godwin, "China as a Major Asian Power," 145–166; Kamphausen et al., eds., *Beyond the Strait.*

49. Michael Swaine, "China's Regional Military Posture," in *Power Shift: China and Asia's New Dynamics*, ed. David Shambaugh (Berkeley: University of California Press, 2005), 266. David Michael Lampton, The *Three Faces of Chinese Power* (Berkeley: University of California Press, 2008) 40–42.

50. Bates Gill, *Rising Star: China's New Security Diplomacy* (Washington, DC: Brookings Institution, 2007).

51. The discussion in the following several paragraphs is adapted from Michael Swaine, "China's Regional Military Posture," in *Power Shift: China and Asia's New Dynamics*, ed. David Shambaugh (Berkeley: University of California Press, 2005), 268–72.

52. John Garver, *Foreign Relations of the People's Republic of China* (Englewood Cliffs, NJ: Prentice Hall, 1993), 249–64.

53. Robert Suettinger, *Beyond Tiananmen* (Washington, DC: Brookings, 2003), 200–63.

54. David Shambaugh and Michael Yahuda, eds., *International Relations of Asia* (Lanham, MD: Rowman & Littlefield, 2008).

55. See explanations in Robert Sutter, *The United States in Asia* (Lanham, MD: Rowman & Littlefield, 2009), 149–168.

56. For full discussion see Sutter, *The United States and Asia*, and the alternative perspectives reviewed in Shambaugh and Yahuda, eds., *International Relations of Asia.*

Chapter 9: Economic and Environmental
Issues in Contemporary U.S.-China Relations

1. Barry Naughton, *The Chinese Economy: Transitions and Growth* (Cambridge, MA: MIT Press 2007); David Michael Lampton, *The Three Faces of Chinese Power* (Berkeley: University of California Press, 2008), 78–116; C. Fred Bergsten, Charles Freeman, Nicholas Lardy, Derek Mitchell *China's Rise: Challenges and Opportunities*, 105–137;

Wayne Morrison, *China's Economic Conditions* (Washington, DC: The Congressional Research Service of the Library of Congress Report RL 33534, March 5, 2009); Wang Jisi, "Trends on the Development of U.S.-China Relations and Deep-Seated Reasons," Lecture delivered by Wang Jisi, Dean, School of International Studies, Beijing University, at the Chinese Academy of Social Science Asia Pacific Institute Beijing *Dangdai Yatai,* June 20, 2009, 4–20.

2. Bergsten *China's Rise* 9–32; C. Fred Bergsten, Bates Gill, Nicholas Lardy, Derek Mitchell, *China: A Balance Sheet* New York: Public Affairs, 2006, 73–117; Wayne Morrison, *China-U.S. Trade Issues* (Washington, DC: The Congressional Research Service of the Library of Congress Report RL33536 March 31, 2009).

3. Kenneth Lieberthal, "How Domestic Forces Shape the PRC's Grand Strategy and International Impact," in *Strategic Asia 2007–2008,* eds. Ashley Tellis and Michael Wills (Seattle: National Bureau of Asian Research, 2007), 29–68; Lampton, *Three Faces of Chinese Power,* 207–251; Naughton, *The Chinese Economy,* 377–424.

4. Robert Suettinger, *Beyond Tiananmen* (Washington, DC: The Brookings Institution, 2003), 358–409.

5. Yuan Peng, "China, U.S. should find common ground in strategic dialogue," *China Daily,* July 27, 2009, 4; "Round and Round it Goes: America Buys Chinese exports, China buys American Treasuries. Can it continue?" *The Economist,* October 22, 2009, www.economist.com (accessed October 27, 2009); Robert Samuelson, "The China Conundrum: Using Tires to Send a Message" *Newsweek,* September 28, 2009 www.newsweek.com (accessed September 20, 2009).

6. Morrison, *China-U.S. Trade Issues*; "Congress Assesses U.S.-China Strategic and Economic Dialogue," *U.S. Asia Pacific Council Washington Report* 3 (September 2009): 1, 3, 9

7. Bergsten, *China's Rise,* 5–6, 105–136.

8. Wayne Morrison, *China's Economic Conditions* (Washington, DC: Library of Congress, Congressional Research Service, Report 33534, November 20, 2008), 8.

9. Lampton, *Three Faces of Chinese Power,* 88–101.

10. Liu Yantang, "Political Bureau Study Session: Seizing Initiative in International Competition" (Beijing) *Liaowang* (June 6, 2005): 12–15; "China's Reforms: The Second Long March," *The Economist,* December 11, 2008 www.economist.com. Trade figures taken from United Nations COMTRADE Database http://comtrade.un.org/db/.

11. Diao Ying, "Firms Urged to Diversify Export Markets," *China Daily,* December 24, 2008, 1. Morrison, *China's Economic Conditions* March 5, 2009, 1.

12. Wayne Morrison, *China-U.S. Trade Issues* (Washington, DC: The Congressional Research Service of the Library of Congress, Issue Brief IB 91121 May 15, 2006), 1.

13. "Foreign Firms Dominate China's Exports," *China Business,* June 30, 2006, www.taiwansecurity.org (accessed July 3, 2006); "Investment Overseas and Imports a Priority," *China Daily,* December 8, 2006, 1.

14. Australian Parliamentary Library Research Service, *Directions in China's Foreign Relations: Implications for East Asia and Australia* (Canberra: Parliamentary Library Research Brief 9: 2005–2006, December 5, 2005), 6–10.

15. Trade figures used in this section are from United Nations COMTRADE Database http://comtrade.un.org/db/.

16. Thomas Lum, Coordinator, *Comparing Global Influence: China's and the U.S. Diplomacy, Foreign Aid, Trade, and Investment in the Developing World* (Washington, DC: Library of Congress, Congressional Research Service Report RL34620 August 15, 2008), 46–47.

17. "China's Reforms: The Second Long March," *The Economist*, December 11, 2008 www.economist.com.

18. Lum, *Comparing Global Influence*, 46–47.

19. Diao Ying, "Firms Urged to Diversify Export Markets,"

20. Randall Morck, Bernard Yeung, Minyuan Zhao, *Perspectives on China's Outward Foreign Direct Investment* (Washington, DC: International Monetary Fund Working Paper, August 2007).

21. People's Republic of China, Ministry of Commerce, *2006 Statistical Bulletin of China's Outward Foreign Investment* (2007), 51.

22. Lum, *Comparing Global Influence*, 59.

23. Fu Jing, "Be bold in expanding overseas, firms told," *China Daily*, December 23, 2008, 1.

24. Carol Lancaster, The Chinese Aid System (Washington, DC: Center for Global Development, June 2007).

25. Lum, *Comparing Global Influence* 33–34.

26. Robert Sutter, *Chinese Foreign Relations: Power and Policy Since the Cold War* (Lanham, MD: Rowman & Littlefield, 2010), 84, 93, 293, 311.

27. Morrison, *China's Economic Conditions*, March 5, 2009, 17–19.

28. "China-Southeast Asia: Economic Concerns Begin to Hit Home," *Comparative Connections* 10:4 (January 2009) www.csis.org/pacfor.

29. Wang Xu, "Currency Crosses Borders," *China Daily*, December 25, 2008, 1; "China Rolls Out Aid Package," *Xinhua*, April 12, 2009 www.xinhuanet.com (accessed April 15, 2009).

30. "Round and Round it Goes," *The Economist*.

31. Wayne Morrison, *China-U.S. Trade Issues* (2009), 1.

32. Chris Buckley and Doug Palmer, "U.S. Slaps Duty on Chinese Tyres: China Says Move Signals Protectionism," *Reuters*, September 14, 2009, www.reuters.com (accessed November 2, 2009).

33. Morrison, *China-U.S. Trade Issues* (2009): 6.

34. Morrison, *China-U.S. Trade Issues* (2009): 7.

35. Kerry Dumbaugh, *China-U.S. Relations: Current Issues and Implications for U.S. Policy* (Washington, DC: The Congressional Research Service of the Library of Congress Report R40457 March 17, 2009), 4.

36. Morrison, *China-U.S. Trade Issues* (2009): 9.

37. Bergsten, *China's Rise*, 18–19.

38. Wayne Morrison and Marc Labonte, *China's Holding of U.S. Securities: Implications for the U.S. Economy*, Congressional Research Service of the Library of Congress Report RL34314, November 20, 2008, 10–11.

39. Morrison and Labonte, 11.

40. Bergsten, *China's Rise*, 18–19.

41. Morrison and Labonte, 12.

42. Li Yanping, "China 'Super Currency' Call May Signal Dollar Concern," *Bloomberg*, March 25, 2009, www.bloomberg.com (accessed November 2, 2009).

43. Dumbaugh, *China-U.S. Relations* (2009): 6–10; Bergsten, *China's Rise*, 9–21.

44. Dumbaugh, *China-U.S.* Relations (2009): 9–10.

45. "Consumer Product Safety Commission to Create Beijing Office to Oversee Safety of Chinese Exports," August 6, 2009 www.standardusers.org (accessed November 2, 2009).

46. Morrison, *China-U.S. Trade Issues* (2009): 10–11.

47. Morrison, *China-U.S. Trade Issues* (2009): 11.

48. Margaret Mikyung Lee, *Consumer Product Safety Improvement Act of 2008: P.L. 110–314* (Washington, DC: Congressional Research Service of the Library of Congress Report 34684, January 15, 2009).

49. Tina Wang, "Olympics Led to Milk Scandal Hush-Up, Some Say," *Forbes*, September 17, 2008, www.forbes.com (accessed November 2, 2009).

50. Wayne Morrison, *China's Currency: A Summary of the Economic Issues* (Washington, DC: Congressional Research Service of the Library of Congress Report RS 21625, May 8, 2008).

51. Bergsten, *China's Rise*, 14.

52. Morrison, *China-U.S. Trade Issues* (2009): 13.

53. Wayne Morrison and Marc Labonte, *China's Currency: Economic Issues and Option for U.S. Trade Policy* (Washington, DC: Congressional Research Service of the Library of Congress, Report RL32165, January 9, 2008), 6

54. Dumbaugh, *China-U.S. Relations* (2009): 8.

55. Bergsten, *China's Rise*, 18–19.

56. Robert Sutter, *Chinese Foreign Relations: Power and Policy Since the Cold War* (Lanham, MD: Rowman & Littlefield, 2008), 97.

57. Deepak Bhattasali, Shantong Li, and Will Martin, eds., *China and the WTO* (Washington, DC: The World Bank, 2004).

58. David Barboza, "Trade Surplus Tripled in '05, China Says," *New York Times*, January 12, 2006, www.nytimes.com (accessed January 12, 2006).

59. Sutter, *Chinese Foreign Relations* (2008), 98.

60. Kerry Dumbaugh, *China-U.S. Relations: Current Issues and Implications for U.S. Policy* (Washington, DC: Library of Congress, Congressional Research Service Report RL33877, December 9, 2008) 7–9.

61. U.S. Special Trade Representative (USTR) *2008 Report to Congress on China's WTO Compliance* December 23, 2008, www.ustr.gov (accessed November 2, 2009).

62. This summary is taken from Morrison, *China-U.S. Trade Issues* (2009), 16.

63. Robert Sutter *Chinese Policy Priorities and Their Implications for the United States* (Lanham, MD: Rowman & Littlefield, 2000), 11, 46, 53.

64. Sutter, *Chinese Foreign Relations*, 2008, 99.

65. Morrison, *China-U.S. Trade Issues* (2006): 13–14; Morrison, *China-U.S. Trade Issues* (2009): 20.

66. U.S. Special Trade Representative *"Special 301" annual report*, April 25, 2008, http://www.ustr.gov/sites/default/files/asset_upload_file558_14870.pdf (accessed November 3, 2009).

67. Morrison, *China-U.S. Trade Issues* (2009): 20–21.

68. Bergsten, *China's Rise*, 78–81.

69. Morrison, *China-U.S. Trade Issues* (2009): 22–23.

70. Kerry Dumbaugh, *China-U.S. Relations for the 110th Congress: Issues and Implications for U.S. Policy* (Washington, DC: Congressional Research Service of the Library of Congress Report RL33877 February 10, 2009), 18–20; Dumbaugh, *China-U.S. Relations* (2009), 6–10.

71. "Commerce Applies Anti-subsidy Law to China," *Press Release* U.S. Department of Commerce March 30, 2007, www.commerce.gov (accessed November 3, 2009).

72. Morrison, *China-U.S. Trade Issues* (2009): 24.

73. Jonathan Weisman, "U.S. to Impose Tariff on Chinese Tires," *Wall Street Journal*, September 13, 2009 www.wsj.com (accessed November 3, 2009).

74. *George W. Bush on Environment*, Issues 2000, http://www.issues2000.org/George_W__Bush_Environment.htm (accessed November 3, 2009).

75. Bergsten, *China's Rise*, 137–168; Sutter, *Chinese Foreign Relations: Power and Policy Since the Cold War* (2010), 97–99.

76. Kenneth Lieberthal and David Sandalow, *Overcoming Obstacles to U.S.-China Cooperation on Climate Change* (Washington DC: Brookings Institution John L. Thornton China Center Monograph Series Number 1, January 2009).

77. Dumbaugh, *China-U.S. Relations: Current Issues and Implications for U.S. Policy*, 18–19.

78. Elizabeth Economy and Adam Segal, "The G-2 Mirage," *Foreign Affairs* 88:3 (May-June 2009): 14–23.

79. Joanna I. Lewis, "China's Strategic Priorities in International Climate Change Negotiations," *Washington Quarterly* 31:1 (Winter 2007-2008): 155–174.

80. Jane Leggett, Jeffrey Logan, Anna Mackey, *China's Greenhouse Gas Emissions and Mitigation Policies* (Washington, DC Congressional Research Service of the Library of Congress Report 34659, September 10, 2008).

81. Sutter, *Chinese Policy Priorities*, 188.

82. Elizabeth Economy, "China's Environmental Challenge," *Current History* (September 2005): 278–79; Sutter, *Chinese Policy Priorities*, 189.

83. Bergsten, *China's Rise*, 144–146, 152–153, 161–162.

84. Te Kan, "Past Successes and New Goal," *China Daily*, December 26, 2005–January 1, 2006, Supplement, 9.

85. Sutter, *Chinese Foreign Relations: Power and Policy Since the Cold War* (2010), 98.

86. Zhou Shijun, "Green Future," *China Daily*, January 9–15, 2006, Supplement, 1.

87. Economy, "China: A Rise That's Not So 'Win-Win'"; Lieberthal and Sandalow, *Overcoming Obstacles to U.S.-China Cooperation on Climate Change.*

88. Hua Jianmin, "Strengthen Cooperation for Clean Development," Chinese Foreign Ministry Statement, January 12, 2006, www.fmprc.gov.cn/eng (accessed January 30, 2006).

89. Lewis, "China's Strategic Priorities in International Climate Change Negotiations."

90. Fu Jing, "Meeting Plan Target 'Difficult,'" *China Daily*, December 25, 2008, 1.

Chapter 10: Taiwan Issues in Contemporary U.S.-China Relations

1. Nancy Bernkopf Tucker, *Strait Talk* (Cambridge, MA: Harvard University Press, 2009); Su Ge, *Meiguo: Dui hua Zhengce yu Taiwan wenti* [America: China Policy and the Taiwan Issue] (Beijing: Shijie Zhishi Chubanshe, 1998); Zi Zhongyun and He Di, eds., *Meitai Guanxi Sishinian* [Forty Years of U.S.-Taiwan Relations] (Beijing: People's Press, 1991).

2. See the authoritative reviews of this period in Richard Bush, *Untying the Knot: Making Peace in the Taiwan Strait* (Washington DC: Brookings Institution, 2005) and Tucker, *Strait Talk*.

3. Bush, *Untying the Knot*, 22–57; Denny Roy, *Taiwan: A Political History* (Ithaca, NY: Cornell University Press, 2003), 146–50, 195–202, 212–22, 235–40; T. Y. Wang, "Taiwan's Foreign Relations under Lee Teng-hui's Rule, 1988–2000," in *Sayonara to the Lee Teng-hui Era*, ed. Wei-chin Lee and T. Y. Wang (Lanham, MD: University Press of America, 2003), 250–60; Dennis Van Vranken Hickey, *Foreign Policy Making in Taiwan* (New York: Routledge, 2007).

4. Bush, *Untying the Knot*, 57–71; Steven Goldstein and Julian Chang, eds., *Presidential Politics in Taiwan: The Administration of Chen Shui-bian* (Norwalk, CT: East-Bridge, 2008).

5. Philip Yang, "Cross-strait Relations under the First Chen Administration," in *Presidential Politics in Taiwan*, eds. Goldstein and Chang, 211–222.

6. Consultations with twenty U.S. officials with responsibility for assessing Taiwan-China relations and their implications for U.S. interests, Washington DC, October–November 2004; consultations and interviews with U.S. officials responsible for Taiwan affairs, Washington, DC, March-May 2005; interviews with Chinese officials and specialists Vail, Colorado, October 2003; Beijing and Shanghai, May-June 2004; Washington, DC, August-November 2004; David Brown, "China-Taiwan Relations: Campaign Fallout" *Comparative Connections* (January 2005): www.csis.org/pacfor; Shi Yinhong, "Beijing's Lack of Sufficient Deterrence to Taiwan Leaves a Major Danger," (Hong Kong) *Ta Kung Pao*, June 23, 2004.

7. David Brown, "China-Taiwan Relations: Campaign Fallout" *Comparative Connections* (January 2005) www.csis.org/pacfor.

8. China's Anti-Secession Law of March 2005 was among the PRC pronouncements that displayed firmness against Taiwan's moves toward independence mixed with signs of flexibility on cross-strait issues. Notably, Chinese President Hu Jintao was said to have moved away from considering a timetable for Taiwan's reunification with China, which had been discussed during the leadership of Jiang Zemin (who left the last of his major leadership posts in 2004). Interviews with Chinese officials and specialists and U.S. government officials and specialists, Washington DC, March–June 2005.

9. Thomas Christensen, "China," in *Strategic Asia 2001–2002*, eds., Richard Ellings and Aaron Friedberg (Seattle: National Bureau of Asian Research, 2001), 47–51; International Crisis Group, *Taiwan Strait I: What's Left of 'One China'?* (Brussels: International Crisis Group Asia Report 53, June 6, 2003), 17–22; Alan Wachman, *Why Taiwan?: Geostrategic Rationales for China's Territorial Integrity* (Stanford, CA: Stanford University Press, 2007).

10. Consultations with thirty Taiwanese government officials and specialists in Taiwan in May–June 2004, with twenty such officials and specialists visiting the United States in 2004–2005, and with twenty such officials and specialists in Taipei in May–June 2005.

11. Interviews with Chinese government officials and specialists, Vail, Colorado, Washington, DC, October–December 2003.

12. David Brown, "China-Taiwan Relations: Strains over Cross-Strait Relations" *Comparative Connections* (January 2004) www.csis.org/pacfor; interviews with Chinese government officials and specialists, Washington, DC, January–March 2004.

13. Interviews, Beijing and Shanghai, May 2004.

14. See discussion, below. At this time, Taiwan media reported that George Bush had used an epithet to refer to Chen Shui-bian (Brown, "China-Taiwan Relations: Campaign Fallout").

15. International Crisis Group, *China-Taiwan: Uneasy Détente* (Brussels: International Crisis Group Asia Briefing No. 42, September 21, 2005).

16. Interviews with U.S. government specialists on Taiwan, March–May 2005; interviews with Taiwan and U.S. government and nongovernment specialists, Taiwan, May–June 2005.

17. Interviews with U.S. government specialists on Taiwan, March–May 2005; interviews with Taiwan and U.S. government and nongovernment specialists, Taiwan, May–June 2005.

18. The Chinese proposals and DPP calculations are reviewed in *China-Taiwan: Uneasy Détente.*

19. Michael Swaine, "Managing Relations with the United States," in *Presidential Politics in Taiwan,* eds. Goldstein and Chang, 197–198.

20. Steven Goldstein, "Postscript: Chen Shui-bian and the Political Transition in Taiwan," *Presidential Politics in Taiwan,* eds. Goldstein and Chang, 296–298.

21. Goldstein, "Postscript," 299–304.

22. David Brown, "Taiwan Voters Set a New Course," *Comparative Connections* 10:1 (April 2008): 75.

23. Dennis Hickey, "Beijing's Evolving Policy toward Taipei: Engagement or Entrapment," *Issues and Studies* 45:1 (March 2009): 31–70; Alan Romberg, "Cross Strait Relations: 'Ascend the Heights and Take a Long-term Perspective,'" *China Leadership Monitor* No. 27 (Winter 2009): www.chinaleadershipmonitor.org; author's interviews and consultations with Taiwan national security and international affairs officials, Taipei, May, July, August, and December 2008, April 2009.

24. U.S. Department of Defense. *The Military Power of the People's Republic of China* 2009, http://www.defenselink.mil/pubs/pdfs/China_Military_Power_Report_2009.pdf.

25. Ibid.

26. David Brown, "Dialogue Resumes in Relaxed Atmosphere," *Comparative Connections* 10:2 (July 2008) 83–86; for discussion of 1992 Consensus, see Yang, "Cross Strait Relations Under the First Chen administration," 208–209.

27. David Brown, "Progress in the Face of Headwinds," *Comparative Connections* 10:3 (October 2008): 73–74.

28. "Join Hands to Promote Peaceful Development of Cross Strait Relations," speech by Hu Jintao, *Xinhua*, December 31, 2008, People's Republic of China State Council Information Office, "China's National Defense in 2008" (Beijing, January 2009); David Brown, "More Progress; Stronger Headwinds," *Comparative Connections* 10:4 (January 2009). www.csis.org/pacfor; David Brown, "New Economic Challenges," *Comparative Connections* 11:1 (April 2009) www.csis.org/pacfor.

29. For data on the following paragraphs, see David Brown, "Moving Relations toward a New Level," Comparative Connections 11:2 (July 2009): www.csis.org/pacfor.

30. Brown, "New Economic Challenges"; U.S. Department of States *Background Note: Taiwan* (April 2009) www.state.gov.

31. *Background Note: Taiwan.*

32. Jacques deLisle "Taiwan in the World Health Assembly: A Victory with Limits," *Brookings Northeast Asia Commentary* (July 19, 2009), www.brookings.edu.

33. "Ma Defends Diplomatic Truce," *Straits Times* April 22, 2009, www.straits times.com.

34. Interviews and consultations with Taiwan national security and international affairs officials, Taipei, May, July, August, and December 2008, and April 2009.

35. Shirley Kan, *Taiwan: Major U.S. Arms Sales since 1990* (Washington, DC: Library of Congress, Congressional Research Service Report RL 30957, October 8, 2008); Kathrin Hille and Demetri Sevastopulo "U.S. and China Set to Resume Military Talks," *Financial Times*, June 21, 2009 www.ft.com.

36. Interviews and consultations, Taiwan, December 2008, April 2009.

37. Donald Zagoria, *Cross-Strait Relations: Cautious Optimism*, Report of Conference on Prospects for Relations Across the Taiwan Strait, National Committee on American Foreign Policy, New York, 13–14 January 2009. The findings in this section also are based in part on the author's presentations at and participation in off-the-record conferences with Chinese and American officials and nongovernment specialists dealing with issues in contemporary U.S.-China relations including the situation in the Taiwan Strait. The conferences took place in April 2009 (Washington, DC), May 2009 (Shanghai, Washington, Beijing), June 2009 (Shanghai, Washington), July 2009 (Washington).

38. Hickey "Beijing's Evolving Policy Toward Taiwan"; Bush, *Untying the Knot*, 22–57.

39. Tucker, *Strait Talk*, 193–272.

40. Reviewed in Robert Sutter, *Chinese Foreign Relations: Power and Policy Since the Cold War* (Lanham, MD: Rowman & Littlefield, 2010), 153–172.

41. For background, see Robert Ross, "Taiwan's Fading Independence Movement," *Foreign Affairs* 85:2 (March/April 2006): 141–148; Yun-han Chu and Andrew Nathan, "Seizing the Opportunity for Change in the Taiwan Strait," *Washington Quarterly* 31:1 (Winter 2007–2008): 77–91.

42. Zhang Nianchi, "The Current Status, Problems, and Prospects of Cross-strait Relations," in *Making Peace in the Taiwan Strait* (New York: The National Committee on American Foreign Policy, May 2009) 44–48; see also quarterly assessments by David Brown in *Comparative Connections* (www.csis.org/pacfor) and Alan Romberg *in China Leadership Monitor* (http://www.hoover.org/publications/clm/).

43. "Mayor of Kaohsiung Starts 'Ice Breaking' Visit to Beijing," *China Daily*, May 22, 2009, www.chinadaily.com.cn. Consultations, Washington, DC, May 24, 2009.

44. Hong Kong Government Secretariat Press Office (Constitutional and Mainland Affairs) May 11, 2009. Response to Media serial No. GIS200905110240.

45. Consultations noted in footnote 36. Meetings with Chinese officials concerned with Taiwan, Washington, DC, May 14, June 11, June 23, 2009. Donald Zagoria, "National Committee on American Foreign Policy Trip to Taiwan, Beijing and Shanghai, April 12–22, 2009," in *Making Peace in the Taiwan Strait*, 26–29.

46. Wu Ray-Kuo, "Cross-Strait Relations and Domestic Politics since May 2008," in *Making Peace in the Taiwan Strait*, 34–42.

47. Bi-khim Hsiao, "A DPP Perspective on Domestic and Cross-Strait Challenges for Taiwan," in *Making Peace in the Taiwan Strait*, 29–34.

48. On Taiwan developments during Ma Ying-jeou administration, review quarterly assessments by David Brown in *Comparative Connections* (www.csis.org/pacfor) and Alan Romberg in *China Leadership Monitor* (http://www.hoover.org/publications/clm/). See also Thomas Gold, "Taiwan in 2008," *Asian Survey* 49:1 (January–February 2009): 88–97; Shelley Rigger, "Needed: A Newish U.S. Policy for a Newish Taiwan Strait," Foreign Policy Research Institute *E Notes* (March 2009), www.fpri.org.

49. Consultations, Taiwan, 2008–2009.

50. Rigger, "Needed: A Newish U.S. Policy for a Newish Taiwan Strait"; Hsiao, "A DPP Perspective on Domestic and Cross-Strait Challenges for Taiwan."

51. Bernard Cole, Testimony before the U.S.-China Economic and Security Review Commission, March 29, 2007, www.uscc.gov; Lyle Goldstein, "A Rapidly Changing Military Balance: A National Security Perspective on Richard Bush's *Untying the Knot*," *Asia Policy* (July 2006): 123–124; Justin Logan and Ted Galen Carpenter *Taiwan's Defense Budget: How Taipei's Free Riding Risks War*, Washington, DC: Cato Institute (September 13, 2007); William S. Murray "Revisiting Taiwan's Defense Strategy," *Naval War College Review* (Summer 2008), 13–38; Andrew Erickson and David Yang, "On the Verge of a Game-Changer," *Proceedings Magazine* 135 (May 2009).

52. Peter Enav, "U.S. dedicates new diplomatic office in Taiwan," *Associated Press*, June 22, 2009, www.ap.com. "Ties Not Competing with Cross-Strait Relations, Outgoing AIT Chief," *The China Post*, July 3, 2009, www.chinapost.com.tw. "Roundtable: Defining a Healthy Balance Across the Taiwan Strait," *Asia Policy* 6 (July 2009): 1–46.

53. Edward Gresser and Daniel Twining, "Shock of the New: Congress and Asia in 2009," *NBR Analysis*, February 2009; Kerry Dumbaugh, *China-U.S. Relations: Current Issues and Implications for U.S. Policy* (Washington, DC: Congressional Research Service, Library of Congress, Report 40457, March 17, 2009).

54. Richard Bush and Alan Romberg, "Cross Strait Moderation and the United States—A Response to Robert Sutter," PacNet Newsletter 17A March 12, 2009, www.csis.org/pacfor.

55. Dan Blumenthal and Randall Schriver, *Strengthening Freedom in Asia: A Twenty-First-Century Agenda for the U.S.-Taiwan Partnership* (Washington, DC: American Enterprise Institute, 2008); Rigger, "Needed: A Newish U.S. Policy"; Robert Sutter "Cross-Strait Moderation and the United States—Policy Adjustments needed,"

PacNet Newsletter, 17 March 5, 2009, www.csis.org/pacfor; Logan and Carpenter, *Taiwan's Defense Budget*; Kerry Dumbaugh, *Taiwan-U.S. Relations: Developments and Policy Implications* (Washington, DC: Congressional Research Service, Library of Congress, Report 40493, April 2, 2009).

Chapter 11: Issues of Human Rights
in Contemporary U.S.-China Relations

1. For historical treatment of these differences, see John K. Fairbank, *The United States and China* (Cambridge, MA: Harvard University Press, 1983).

2. See discussion of human rights issues in Harry Harding, *A Fragile Relationship* (Washington, DC: Brookings Institution, 1992); James Mann, *About Face* (New York: Knopf, 1999); David Michael Lampton, *Same Bed Different Dreams* (Berkeley: University of California Press, 2001); and Ming Wan *Human Rights in Chinese Foreign Relations: Defining and Defending National Interests* (Philadelphia: University of Pennsylvania Press, 2001). See also People's Republic of China State Council Information Office National Human Rights Action Plan of China (2009–2010), April 13, 2009 http://www.china.org.cn/archive/2009-04/13/content_17595407.htm (accessed November 8, 2009).

3. Yu Keping, "Ideological Change and Incremental Democracy in Reform-Era China," in *China's Changing Political Landscape: Prospects for Democracy*, ed. Cheng Li (Washington, DC: The Brookings Institution, 2008), 44–60.

4. Jacques deLisle, "Legalization without Democratization in China under Hu Jintao," in *China's Changing Political Landscape: Prospects for Democracy*, ed. Cheng Li (Washington, DC: The Brookings Institution, 2008), 185–211.

5. Gong Li. "The Difficult Path to Diplomatic Relations: China's U.S. Policy, 1972–1978," in *Normalization of U.S.-China Relations: An International History*, eds. William Kirby, Robert Ross, and Gong Li (Cambridge, MA: Harvard University Press, 2005).

6. Harding, *Fragile Relationship*, 198–199; Warren Cohen, *America's Response to China* (New York: Columbia University Press, 2000), 213.

7. Cohen, *America's Response to China*, 212–213.

8. Harding, *Fragile Relationship*, 198–206; Mann, *About Face*, 100–109.

9. Michael Schaller, *The United States and China Into the Twenty-First Century* (New York: Oxford University Press, 2002), 197.

10. John K. Fairbank and Merle Goldman, *China: A New History* (Cambridge, MA: Harvard University Press, 1999), 419–426.

11. Lampton, *Same Bed, Different Dreams*, 130–153.

12. Song Qiang, Zhang Changchang, and Qiao Bian. *Zhongguo keyi shuo bu: Lengzhanhou shidai de zhengzhi yu qinggan jueze* [China Can Say No: The Decision Between Politics and Sentiment in the Post-Cold War] (Beijing: Zhonghua Gongshang Lianhe Chubanshe, 1996).

13. Mann, *About Face*, 200–201.

14. Lampton, *Same Bed: Different Dreams*, 15–63.

15. Sheryl Gay Stolberg, "Bush Meets 5 Dissidents form China before Games," *New York Times*, July 30, 2008, www.nytimes.com (accessed November 7, 2009).

16. "Remarks by the President at the U.S./China Strategic and Economic Dialogue," The White House, Office of the Press Secretary, July 27, 2009, www.whitehouse.gov (accessed November 7, 2009).

17. C. Fred Bergsten, Bates Gill, Nicholas Lardy, and Derek Mitchell, *China: The Balance Sheet* (New York: Public Affairs, 2006), 62–72.

18. Kerry Dumbaugh, *Tibet: Problems, Prospects, and U.S. Policy* (Washington, DC: Congressional Research Service, Library of Congress Report RL34445, July 30, 2008); John Pomfert, "Obama's Meeting with Dalai Lama is Delayed," *The Washington Post*, October 5, 2009, www.washingtonpost.com (accessed November 8, 2009).

19. Bergsten, *China: The Balance Sheet*, 62–72; Cheng Li, "Will China's 'Lost Generation' Find a Path to Democracy? in *China's Changing Political Landscape*, 98–120; Joseph Fewsmith, "Staying in Power: What Does the Chinese Communist Party Have to Do?" in *China's Changing Political Landscape*, 212–228.

20. U.S. Department of State, *2008 Country Reports on Human Rights Practices* February 25, 2009, www.state.gov; Congressional-Executive Commission on China, *Annual Report 2009* October 10, 2009, www.cecc.gov; U.S. Commission on International Religious Freedom, *Annual Report of the U.S. Commission on International Human Rights* May 1, 2009, www.uscirf.gov; Amnesty International, www.amnesty.org; Human Rights Watch, www.hrw.com.

21. Thomas Lum and Hannah Fischer, *Human Rights in China: Trends and Policy Implications* (Washington, DC: Congressional Research Service, Library of Congress Report RL34729, July 17, 2009), 1.

22. Andrew Nathan, "China's Political Trajectory: What Are the Chinese Saying?" in *China's Changing Political Landscape*, 25–43. People's Republic of China State Council Information Office National Human Rights Action Plan of China (2009–2010), April 13, 2009, http://www.china.org.cn/archive/2009-04/13/content_17595407.htm (accessed November 8, 2009).

23. Bergsten, *China: The Balance Sheet*, 62–64; Thomas Lum and Hannah Fischer, *Human Rights in China: Trends and Policy Implications* (Washington, DC: Congressional Research Service, Library of Congress Report RL34729, October 31, 2008), 2. As seen from source notes, below, this report, along with some other reports from the Congressional Research Service of the Library of Congress, provide comprehensive, up-to-date and balanced coverage of human rights issues in China of great use to researchers and specialists.

24. Bergsten, *China's Rise*, 96–97.

25. This summary of the findings of the State Department report is taken from Lum and Fischer, *Human Rights in China: Trends and Policy Implications* (2008), 3–4.

26. Yu Keping, *Democracy is a Good Thing* (Washington, DC: Brookings Institution, 2008); Bergsten, *China's Rise*, 38.

27. Paul Mooney, "How to Deal with NGOs—Part 1, China," *Yaleglobal Online*, August 1, 2006, www.yaleglobal.yale.edu.

28. Lum and Fischer, *Human Rights in China* (2008), 5–7.

29. Kerry Dumbaugh, *China-U.S. Relations in the 110th Congress: Issues and Implications for U.S. Policy* (Washington, DC: Congressional Research Service, Library of Congress Report RL33877, February 10, 2009); Kerry Dumbaugh, *China-U.S. Relations: Current Issues and Implications for U.S. Policy* (Washington, DC: Congressional Research Service, Library of Congress Report R40457, March 17, 2009); Bonnie Glaser, "U.S.-China Relations," *Comparative Connections* 11:3 (October 2009): 36–37.

30. Congressional-Executive Commission on China, *Annual Report 2007*, October 11, 2007, www.cecc.gov, cited in Lum and Fischer *Human Rights in China* (2008), 11–12.

31. Hongying Wang and Xueyi Chen, "Globalization and the Changing State-Media Relations in China," Paper Prepared for Presentation at the 2008 Annual Conference of the American Political Science Association, August 28–31, 2008.

32. Ariana Eunjung Cha, "Public Anger over Milk Scandal Forces China's Hand," *Washington Post*, September 19, 2008, www.washingtonpost.com.

33. Lum and Fischer *Human Rights in China* (2008), 12.

34. Wang and Chen, "Globalization and the Changing State-Market Relations in China"; Brady, *Marketing Dictatorship*, 175–202.

35. Howard French, "Great Firewall of China Faces Online Rebels," *New York Times*, February 4, 2008, www.nytimes.com.

36. Lum and Fischer, *Human Rights in China* (2009), 12–13.

37. Lum and Fischer, *Human Rights in China* (2008), 14

38. United States Commission on International Religious Freedom, "Frequently Asked Questions," www.uscirf.gov/index.php?option=com_content&task=view&id=337&Itemid=1 (accessed November 8, 2009).

39. Lum and Fischer, *Human Rights in China* (2009), 13.

40. "Poll Shows 300M in China 'Religious,'" *South China Morning Post*, February 7, 2007, www.scmp.com ; "Survey Finds 300M China Believers," *BBC News* February 7, 2007, www.bbcworldnews.com.

41. *2008 Country Reports on Human Rights Practices*, cited in Lum and Fischer, *Human Rights in China* (2009), 14.

42. China Aid Association USA, *Annual Report of Persecution by the Government on Christian House Churches within Mainland China, January 2007–December 2007*, February 2008, 5, www.chinaaid.org (accessed November 9, 2009).

43. Maureen Fan, "Beijing Curbs Rights it Says Citizens Have to Worship," *Washington Post*, August 1, 2008, www.washingtonpost.com.

44. U.S. Department of State, *International Religious Freedom Report, 2008*, cited in Lum and Fischer, *Human Rights in China* (2008), 16.

45. Melvyn Goldstein, Tashi Tsering, and William Siebenschuh, *The Struggle for Modern Tibet* (Armonk, NY: M.E. Sharpe, 2000); Warren Smith, *China's Tibet: Autonomy or Assimilation* (Lanham, MD: Rowman & Littlefield, 2009); Kerry Dumbaugh, *Tibet: Problems, Prospects, and U.S. Policy* Congressional Research Service, Library of Congress Report RL34445, July 30, 2008.

46. Warren Smith, *Tibet's Last Stand? The Tibetan Uprising of 2008 and China's Response* (Lanham, MD: Rowman & Littlefield, 2009).

47. Dumbaugh, *Tibet: Problems, Prospects, and U.S. Policy*, 6–9.

48. Dumbaugh, *Tibet: Problems, Prospects, and U.S. Policy*, 20–21.

49. Smith, *Tibet's Last Stand?*

50. Hugo Restall, "The Urumqi Effect," *Wall Street Journal*, July 10, 2008, www.wsj.com; Nicholas Bequelin, "Behind the Violence in Xinjiang," *New York Times*, July 10, 2008, www.nytimes.com.

51. James Millward, *Eurasian Crossroads: A History of Xinjiang* (New York: Columbia University Press, 2007); Lum and Fischer, *Human Rights in China* (2009), 16.

52. *Amnesty International Report 2008*, May 5, 2008, cited in Lum and Fischer, *Human Rights in China* (2008), 18.

53. Edward Wong, "Violence Dashes Uighurs' Dreams," *International Herald Tribune*, July 14, 2009, www.iht.com.

54. Maria Hsia Chang, *Falun Gong: The End of Days* (New Haven, CT: Yale University Press, 2004).

55. Thomas Lum, *China and Falun Gong* (Washington, DC: Congressional Research Service, Library of Congress Report 33437, May 25, 2006).

56. Michael Martin, *Hong Kong: Ten Years After the Handover* (Washington, DC: Congressional Research Service, Library of Congress Report RL34071, June 29, 2007).

57. James Mann, *The China Fantasy* (New York: Viking, 2007); David Michael Lampton and James Mann, "*The China Fantasy*, Fantasy," *The China Quarterly* 191 (September 2007): 745–754.

58. Lum and Fischer, *Human Rights in China* (2008), 27–28.

59. John Pomfert, "Obama Postpones Dalai Lama meeting," *Washington Post*, October 5, 2009, www.washingtonpost.com; Ariana Eunjung Cha and Glenn Kessler, "Pelosi, Like Clinton, Plays Down Human Rights before China Trip," *Washington Post* May 24, 2009, www.washingtonpost.com.

60. People's Republic of China State Council Information Office National Human Rights Action Plan of China (2009–2010); "China Hits Back with Report on U.S. Human Rights Record," *People's Daily Online* February 26, 2009, http://english.people.com.cn/90001/90776/90883/6602049.html (accessed November 9, 2009).

61. Michael Wines, "China Says U.S. Distorts Facts in Report on Rights," *New York Times*, February 26, 2009 www.nytimes.com.

62. Lum and Fischer, *Human Rights in China* (2009), 28.

63. Lum and Fischer, *Human Rights in China* (2008), 28.

64. Dumbaugh, *China-U.S. Relations in the 110th Congress*, 33–36; Dumbaugh, *China-U.S. Relations: Current Issues and Implications for U.S. Policy*, 23–27.

65. Dianne Rennack, *China: Economic Sanctions* (Washington, DC: Congressional Research Service, Library of Congress Report RL31910, February 1, 2006); Steven Ertelt, "Obama Admin sends UN Population Fund $50 Million," *Lifenews.com*, March 18, 2009, www.lifenews.com.

66. Lum and Fischer, *Human Rights in China* (2009), 29–30.

67. Thomas Lum, *U.S.-Funded Assistance Programs in China* (Washington, DC: Congressional Research Service, Library of Congress Report RS22663, April 24, 2009).

68. Lum, *U.S.-Funded Assistance Programs in China*, 10.

69. U.S. Department of State, Bureau of Democracy, Human Rights, and Labor, *Advancing Freedom and Democracy Reports—2008: China (Includes Tibet)*, May 23, 2008, cited in Lum and Fischer, *Human Rights in China* (2008), 30.

70. "State Department Gets Funds to Fight Internet Censorship," *Federal Times*, January 14, 2008, www.federaltimes.com.

71. Lum and Fischer, *Human Rights in China* (2008), 31–32.

72. *Advancing Freedom and Democracy Reports—2008: China (Includes Tibet)*, May 23, 2008.

73. Lum and Fischer, *Human Rights in China* (2009), 33.

Chapter 12: Outlook: Continued Positive Equilibrium amid Differences and Suspicions

1. As noted in earlier chapters, changes in U.S. China policy are reviewed in, James Mann, *About Face* (New York: Knopf, 1999), Harry Harding, *A Fragile Relationship* (Washington, DC: Brookings Institution 1992), Robert S. Ross, *Negotiating Cooperation* (Stanford, CA: Stanford University Press, 1995), David Michael Lampton, *Same Bed Different Dreams* (Berkeley, CA: University of California Press, 2001), Robert Suettinger, *Beyond Tiananmen* (Washington, DC: Brookings Institution, 2003), Jean Garrison, *Making China Policy* (Boulder, CO: Lynne Rienner 2005); Nancy Bernkopf Tucker, *Strait Talk: United States-Taiwan Relations and the Crisis with China* (Cambridge, MA: Harvard University Press, 2009).

2. The findings of this section are based on the author's presentations and participation in seven daylong conferences with groups of Chinese and American government and nongovernment specialists on the status and outlook of U.S.-China relations under the Obama administration which took place in Washington DC (April 2009), Shanghai, Washington DC, Beijing (May 2009), Shanghai, and Washington DC (June 2009), and Washington DC (July 2009). An average of 25 U.S. and Chinese specialists participated in each of the conferences.

3. Jacques deLisle, *China Policy Under Obama* Foreign Policy Research Institute *E-Notes* February 15, 2009; David Shambaugh, "Early Prospects of the Obama Administration's Strategic Agenda with China," Foreign Policy Research Institute *E-Notes* April 2009; Joshua Pollack, "Emerging Dilemmas in U.S.-Chinese relations," *Bulletin of the Atomic Scientists* (July–August 2009), 53–63; Evan Medeiros, "Is Beijing Ready for Global Leadership," *Current History* 108:719 (September 2009): 250–254; Avery Goldstein, "Prolonging East Asia's Surprising Peace—Can It Be Managed?" Foreign Policy Research Institute *E-Notes*, August 14, 2009.

4. Bonnie Glaser, "Laying the Groundwork for Greater Cooperation," *Comparative Connections* 11:2 (July 2009): 27–34.

5. In addition to sources noted, these findings come from the discussions at the seven conferences cited in note 3.

6. Scot Marciel, Deputy Assistant Secretary of State, testimony before the Senate Foreign Relations Committee, July 15, 2009, www.state.gov.

7. Andrew Small, "China's Af-Pak Moment," *Policy Brief* German Marshall Fund of the United States, May 20, 2009, http://209.200.80.89//doc/Small_Af-Pak_Brief_0509_final.pdf (accessed September 7, 2009).

8. Victor Cha, "All North Korea, All the Time," *Comparative Connections* 11:2 (July 2009): 39–44.

9. David Pierson and Jim Tankersley, "U.S., China Try to Reach Accord on Green House Gas Emissions," *Los Angeles Times* July 15, 2009, www.latimes.com; Linda Jacobson, "China and Climate Change Negotiations," *theworldtoday.org*, May 2009, 4–7.

10. Kenneth Lieberthal and David Sandalow, *Overcoming Obstacles to U.S.-China Cooperation on Climate* Change, Brookings Institution, John L. Thornton China Center Monograph Series Number 1 (January 2009); Elizabeth Economy and Adam Segal, "The G-2 Mirage," *Foreign Affairs* 88:3 (May–June 2009): 56–72.

11. Medeiros, "Is Beijing Ready for Global Leadership?"

12. Wayne Morrison, *China-U.S. Trade Issues* (Washington, DC: Congressional Research Service, Library of Congress, Report 33536, June 3, 2009).

13. Wayne Morrison, *China's Economic Conditions* (Washington DC: Congressional Research Service of the Library of Congress Report RL 33534, March 5, 2009); Economy and Segal, "The G-2 Mirage."

14. Kerry Dumbaugh, *Taiwan-U.S. Relations: Developments and Policy Implications* (Washington DC: Congressional Research Service of the Library of Congress Report R40493, April 2, 2009).

15. Kerry Dumbaugh, *Tibet: Problems, Prospects, and U.S. Policy* Washington DC: Congressional Research Service of the Library of Congress Report RL34445, July 30, 2009; Kerry Dumbaugh, *China U.S. Relations: Current Issues and Implications for U.S. Policy* Washington DC: Congressional Research Service. Library of Congress, R40457 March 17, 2009.

16. Kenneth Lieberthal, "How Domestic Forces Shape the PRC's Grand Strategy and International Impact," in Ashley Tellis and Michael Wills, eds., *Strategic Asia 2007–2008* (Seattle, WA: National Bureau of Asian Research, 2007), 63; Lieberthal and Sandalow, *Overcoming Obstacles to U.S.-China Cooperation on Climate Change*, ix.

17. David Michael Lampton, *The Three Faces of Chinese Power* (Berkeley, CA: University of California Press 2008), 1–2.

18. Edward Gresser and Daniel Twining, "Shock of the New: Congress and Asia in 2009," *NBR Analysis*, February 2009, 21.

19. C. Fred Bergsten, "A Partnership of Equals: How Washington Should Respond to China's Economic Challenge," *Foreign Affairs*, July–August 2008, www.foreignaffairs.org.

20. "Clinton: Chinese Human Rights Can't Interfere with Other Crises," *CNN*, February 21, 2009 www.cnn.com.

21. "China Wants Closer U.S. Relations but Not G-2—Official," *Reuters* May 1, 2009, http://www.reuters.com/article/companyNewsAndPR/idUSN0140788620090501 (accessed September 7, 2009); Christopher Clarke, "U.S.-China Duopoly Is a Pipedream," *YaleGlobal Online*, August 6, 2009 http://yaleglobal.yale.edu/content/us-china-duopoly-pipedream (accessed September 7, 2009).

22. Goldstein, "Prolonging East Asia's Surprising Peace—Can It Be Managed?"

23. Morrison, *China-U.S. Trade Issues*; Dumbaugh, *China-U.S. Relations*; Morrison, *China's Economic Conditions*; Lampton, *Three Faces of Chinese Power*, 252–74.

24. Aaron Friedberg, "Is China a Military Threat?—Menace," *The National Interest* (September–October 2009), 19–25, 31–32.

25. Hugh White, "The geo-strategic implications of China's growth," in Ross Garnaut, Ligang Song, and Wing Thye Woo, eds., *China's New Place in a World in Crisis* (Canberra: Australian National University, 2009), 89–102.

26. Robert Sutter, *The United States in Asia* (Lanham, MD: Rowman & Littlefield, 2009), 281–283.

Selected Bibliography

Accinelli, Robert. *Crisis and Commitment: United States Policy toward Taiwan, 1950–1955.* Chapel Hill, NC: University of North Carolina Press, 1996.

Bachrack, Stanley D. *The Committee of One Million: "China Lobby" Politics, 1953–1971.* New York: Columbia University Press, 1976.

Barnett, A. Doak. *China and the Major Powers in East Asia.* Washington, DC: Brookings Institution, 1977.

———. *U.S.-China Relations: Time for a New Beginning—Again.* Washington, DC: Johns Hopkins University, School for Advanced International Studies, 1994.

Bays, Daniel H. ed. *Christianity in China.* Stanford, CA: Stanford University Press, 1996.

Beal, John R. *Marshall in China.* Garden City, NY: Doubleday, 1970.

Bernstein, Richard, and Ross H. Munro. *Coming Conflict with China.* New York: Knopf, 1998.

Borg, Dorothy. *American Policy and the Chinese Revolution, 1925–1928.* New York: Macmillan, 1947.

———. *The United States and the Far Eastern Crisis of 1933–1938.* Cambridge, MA: Harvard University Press, 1964.

Borg, Dorothy, and Waldo Heinrichs, eds. *Uncertain Years: Chinese-American Relations, 1947–1950.* New York: Columbia University Press, 1980.

Buhite, Russell D. *Patrick J. Hurley and American Foreign Policy.* Ithaca, NY: Cornell University Press, 1973.

Bush, Richard. *At Cross Purposes: US-Taiwan Relations since 1942.* Armonk, NY: M.E. Sharpe, 2004.

———. *Untying the Knot* Washington, DC: Brookings Institution, 2005.

Chang, Gordon. *Friends and Enemies: the United States, China, and the Soviet Union, 1948–1972.* Stanford, CA: Stanford University Press, 1990.

Chen Jian. *Mao's China and the Cold War*. Chapel Hill, NC: University of North Carolina Press, 2001.

Christensen, Thomas. *Useful Adversaries: Grand Strategy, Domestic Mobilization, and Sino-American Conflicts, 1949–1958*. Princeton, NJ: Princeton University Press, 1996.

Cohen, Warren I. *America's Response to China: a History of Sino-American Relations*. New York: Columbia University Press, 2000.

Dennett, Tyler. *Americans in Eastern Asia: a Critical Study of the Policy of the United States with Reference to China, Japan, and Korea in the 19th Century*. New York: Macmillan, 1922.

Dong Mei, ed. *Zhong-Mei guanxi ziliao xuanbian* [Selected Materials on Sino-American Relations]. Beijing: Shishi chubanshe 1982.

Dulles, Foster Rhea. *American Policy Toward Communist China, 1949–1969*. New York: Thomas Y. Crowell, 1972.

Fairbank, John K. *The United States and China*. Cambridge, MA: Harvard University Press, 1983.

Fairbank, John K. and Suzanne W. Barnett, eds. *Christianity in China*. Cambridge, MA: Harvard University Press, 1985.

Foot, Rosemary. *The Practice of Power: US Relations with China Since 1949*. New York: Oxford University Press, 1997.

Fu Hao and Li Tongcheng, eds. *Lusi shui shou? Zhongguo waijiaoguan zai Meiguo* [Who Will Win the Game? Chinese Diplomats in the United States]. Beijing: Hauqiao chubanshe, 1998.

Garrison, Jean. *Making China Policy*. Boulder, CO: Lynne Rienner, 2005.

Garver, John W. *China's Decision for Rapprochement with the United States, 1968–1971*. Boulder, CO: Westview Press, 1982.

———. *Face Off: China, the United States, and Taiwan's Democratization*. Seattle, WA: University of Washington, 1997.

———. *The Sino-American Alliance: Nationalist China and American Cold War Strategy in Asia*. Armonk, NY: M.E. Sharpe, 1997.

Goh, Evelyn. *Constructing The US Rapprochement with China, 1961–1974*. New York: Cambridge University Press, 2005.

Gong Li. *Kuayue: 1969–1979 nian Zhong Mei guanxi de yanbian* [Across the Chasm: The Evolution of China-US Relations, 1969–1979]. Henan: Henan People's Press, 1992.

Gong Li, William Kirby and Robert Ross, eds. *Zong jiedong zouxiang jianjiao: Zhong Mei guanxi zhengchanghua jincheng zai tantuo* [From thaw to normalization: a re-examination of the normalization of US-China relations]. Beijing: Zhongyang wenxian chubanshe, 2004.

Griswold, A. Whitney *The Far Eastern Policy of the United States*. New York: Harcourt Brace, 1938.

Han Nianlong and Xue Mouhong, eds. *Dangdai Zhongguo waijiao* [Contemporary Chinese Diplomacy]. Beijing: Zhongguo shehui kexue chubanshe, 1990.

Harding, Harry. *A Fragile Relationship: the US and China Since 1972*. Washington, DC: Brookings Institution, 1992.

Harding, Harry, and Yuan Ming, eds. *Sino-American Relations, 1945–1955.* Wilmington, DE: Scholarly Resources, 1989.

Hu Sheng, ed. *Zhongguo gongchandang de qishi nian* [Seventy Years of the Chinese Communist Party]. Beijing: Zhonggong Dangshi Chubanshe, 1991.

Hunt, Michael H. *The Making of a Special Relationship: The United States and China to 1914.* New York: Columbia University Press, 1983.

Iriye, Akira. *Across the Pacific: An Inner History of American–East Asian Relations.* New York: Harcort, Brace and World, 1967.

Iriye, Akira, and Warren I. Cohen, eds. *American, Chinese, and Japanese Perspectives on Wartime Asia, 1939–1949.* Wilmington, DE: Scholarly Resources, 1990.

Issacs, Harold R. *Scratches on Our Minds: American Images of China and India.* New York: John Day, 1958.

Jacoby, Neil H. *US Aid to Taiwan.* New York: Praeger, 1966.

Jespersen, T. Christopher. *American Images of China, 1931–1949.* Stanford, CA: Stanford University Press, 1996.

Jia Qingguo, *Wei Shixian de Hejie: Zhongmei Guanxi de Gehe yu Weiji* [The unmaterialized rapprochement: Estrangement and crisis in Sino-American talks in retrospect]. Beijing: Shijie Zhishi Chubanshe, 1985.

Jiang Changbin and Robert S. Ross, eds. *1955–1971 Nian de Zhong Mei Guanxi— Huanhe Zhigian: Lengzhan Chongtu yu Keshi de Cai Tantao* [US-China Relations 1955–1971—Before Détente: An Examination of Cold War Conflict and Restraint]. Beijing: Shijie Zhishi Chubanshe, 1998.

———. *Cong Duizhi zouxiang Huanhe: Lengzhan Shiqi Zhong Mei Guanxi zai Tantao* [From Confrontation Toward Détente: A Reexamination of US-China Relations During the Cold War]. Beijing: Shijie Zhishi Chubanshe, 2000.

Kirby, William, Robert Ross, and Gong Li, eds. *Normalization of US-China Relations.* Cambridge, MA: Harvard University Press, 2005

Koen, Ross Y. *The China Lobby in American Politics.* New York: Harper and Row, 1974.

Lampton, David M. *Same Bed, Different Dreams: Managing US-China Relations, 1989–2000.* Berkeley, CA: University of California, 2001.

Latourette, Kenneth S. *The History of Early Relations Between the United States and China, 1784–1844.* New Haven, CT: Yale University Press, 1917.

Li Changjiu and Shi Lujia, *Zhongmei guanxi liangbainian* (Two hundred years of Sino-American relations) Peking: Xinhua Publishing House, 1984.

Lin Qing. *Zhou Enlai zaixiang shengya* [the Career of Prime Minister Zhou Enlai]. Hong Kong: Changcheng Wenhua Chubanshe, 1991.

Liu Xiaoyuan. *A Partnership for Disorder: China, the United States, and Their Policies for the Postwar Disposition of the Japanese Empire.* New York: Cambridge University Press, 1996.

MacMillian, Margaret, *Nixon in China.* Toronto: Viking Canada, 2006.

Mann, James. *About Face: A History of America's Curious Relationship with China, from Nixon to Clinton.* New York: Knopf, 1999.

———. *China Fantasy.* New York: Viking 2007.

May, Ernest R. *The Truman Administration and China, 1945–1949.* New York: Lippincott, 1975.

May, Ernest R., and John K. Fairbank, eds. *America's China Trade in Historical Perspective: the Chinese and American Performance.* Cambridge, MA: Harvard University Press, 1986.

Miller, Stuart Creighton. *The Unwelcome Immigrant: the American Image of the Chinese, 1785–1882.* Berkeley, CA: University of California Press, 1969.

Myers, Ramon, ed. *A Unique Relationship: the United States and the Republic of China Under the Taiwan Relations Act.* Stanford, CA: Hoover Institution, 1989.

Myers, Ramon, Michel Oksenberg, and David Shambaugh, eds. *Making China Policy.* Lanham, MD: Rowman & Littlefield, 2001.

Neils, Patricia, *United States Attitudes Toward China: the Impact of American Missionaries.* Armonk, NY: M.E. Sharpe, 1990.

Peck, Graham. *Two Kinds of Time.* Boston: Houghton Mifflin, 1967.

Pei Jianzhang. *Yanjiu Zhou Enlai: Waijiao sixiang yu shijian* [Researching Zhou Enlai: Diplomatic Thought and Practice]. Beijing: Shijie Zhishi Chubanshe, 1989.

———. *Zhonghua renmin gongheguo waijiao shi, 1949–1956* [A Diplomatic History of the People's Republic of China, 1949–1956]. Beijing: Shijie Zhishi, 1994.

Qian Qichen. *Ten Episodes in China's Diplomacy.* New York: HarperCollins, 2005.

Romberg, Alan. *Rein in at the Brink of the Precipice.* Washington, DC: Henry Stimson Center, 2003.

Ross, Robert S. *Negotiating Cooperation: the United States and China, 1969–1989.* Stanford, CA: Stanford University Press, 1995.

Ross, Robert S., and Jiang Changbin, eds. *Reexamining the Cold War.* Cambridge, MA: Harvard University Press, 2001.

Schaller, Michael. *The United States and China: Into the Twenty-First Century.* New York: Oxford University Press, 2002.

———. *The US Crusade in China, 1938–1945.* New York: Columbia University Press. 1979.

Shambaugh, David. *Beautiful Imperialist: China Perceives America, 1972–1980.* Princeton, NJ: Princeton University Press, 1991.

Shaw, Yu-ming. *An American Missionary in China: John Leighton Stuart and Chinese-American Relations.* Cambridge, MA: Harvard University Press, 1992.

Shewmaker, Kenneth E. *Americans and the Chinese Communists, 1927–1945: A Persuading Encounter.* Ithaca, NY: Cornell University Press, 1971.

Shinn, James, ed., *Weaving the Net: Conditional Engagement with China.* New York: Council on Foreign Relations, 1996.

Snow, Edgar. *Red Star over China.* New York: Random House, 1938.

Solomon, Richard H. *The China Factor: Sino-American Relations and the Global Scene.* Englewood Cliffs, NJ: Prentice Hall, 1982.

Song Qiang, Zhang Changchang, and Qiao Bian. *Zhongguo keyi shuo bu: Lengzhanhou shidai de zhengzhi yu qinggan jueze* [China Can Say No: The Decision Between Politics and Sentiment in the Post-Cold War]. Beijing: Zhonghua Gongshang Lianhe Chubanshe, 1996.

Su Ge. *Meiguo: Dui hua Zhengce yu Taiwan wenti* [America: China policy and the Taiwan issue]. Beijing: Shijie Zhishi Chubanshe, 1998.

Suettinger, Robert L. *Beyond Tiananmen: the Politics of US-China Relations, 1989–2000*. Washington, DC: Brookings Institution, 2003.

Sutter, Robert G. *US Policy Toward China: an Introduction to the Role of Interest Groups*. Lanham, MD: Rowman & Littlefield, 1998.

Swaine, Michael and Zhang Tuosheng, eds. *Managing Sino-American Crises*. Washington, DC: Carnegie Endowment for International Peace, 2006.

Tao Wenzhao, *Zhong Mei guanxi shi*. Shanghai: Renmin Chubanshe, 2004.

Taylor, Jay. *The Generalissimo*. Cambridge, MA: Harvard University Press, 2009.

Thomson, James C. Jr. *While China Faced West: American Reformers in Nationalist China, 1928–1937*. Cambridge, MA: Harvard University Press, 1968.

Tian Zengpei, ed. *Gaige kaifang yilai de Zhongguo waijiao* [Chinese Diplomacy Since Reform and Opening]. Beijing: Shijie Zhishi Chubanshe, 1993.

Tsou, Tang. *America's Failure in China, 1941–1950*. Chicago: University of Chicago Press, 1963.

Tuchman, Barbara. *Stilwell and the American Experience in China, 1911–1945*. New York: Macmillan, 1971.

Tucker, Nancy B. *China Confidential: American Diplomats and Sino-American Relations, 1945–1996*. New York: Columbia University Press, 2001.

———. *Strait Talk: United States–Taiwan Relations and the Crisis with China*. Cambridge, MA: Harvard University Press, 2009.

US Congress. House. Committee on Foreign Affairs. *Executive-Legislative Consultations over China Policy, 1978–1979*. Washington, DC: US Government Printing Office, 1980.

Varg, Paul A. *The Making of a Myth: the United States and China, 1897–1912*. East Lansing, Mich.: Michigan State University Press, 1968.

———. *Missionaries, Chinese and Diplomats: The American Protestant Missionary Movement in China, 1890–1952*. Princeton, NJ: Princeton University Press, 1958.

Wachman, Alan M. *Taiwan: National Identity and Democratization*. Armonk, NY: M.E. Sharpe, 1994

———. *Why Taiwan?* Stanford, CA: Stanford University Press, 2007

Wang, Bingnan. *Zhongmei huitan jiunian huigu* [Nine Years of Sino-American Ambassadorial Talks]. Beijing: Shijie Zhishi, 1985.

Wang Taiping, ed. *Xin Zhongguo waijiao wushinian* (Fifty years of diplomacy of the new China) Beijing: Beijing Chubanshe 1999.

Xie Xide and Ni Shixiong. *Quzhe de licheng: Zhong Mei jianji ershi nian* [From normalization to renormalization: Twenty years of Sino-U.S. relations]. Shanghai: Fudan Daxue Chubanshe, 1999.

Xue Mouhong and Pei Jianhang, eds. *Danggai Zhongguo waijiao* [The diplomacy of contemporary China]. Beijing : Zhongguo shehui kexue chubanshe, 1987

Yan Xuetong. *Zhongguo guojia liyi fenxi* [The Analysis of China's National Interest]. Tianjin: Tianjin Renmin Chubanshe, 1996

Yan Xuetong, Wang Zaibang, Li Zhongcheng, and Hou Roushi. *Zhongguo jueqi: Guoji huanjing pinggu* [International Environment for China's Rise]. Tianjin: Renmin Chubanshe, 1998

Young, Kenneth T. *Negotiating With the Chinese Communists: The United States Experience, 1953–1967*. New York: McGraw Hill, 1968.

Young, Marilyn B. *The Rhetoric of Empire: American China Policy, 1895–1901*. Cambridge, MA: Harvard University Press, 1968.

Zhang, Shuguang. *Deterrence and Strategic Culture: Chinese-American Conflicts, 1949–1959*. Ithaca, NY: Cornell University Press, 1992.

Zhang Yunling., ed. *Hezou haishi duikang: Lengzhanhou de Zhongguo, Meiguo he Riben* [Cooperation or Confrontation: China, the United States, and Japan After the Cold War]. Beijing: Zhongguo Shehui Kexue Chubanshe, 1997

Zi, Zhongyun. *Meiguo duihua zhengce de yuanqi he fazhan, 1945–1950* [The Origins and Development of American Policy toward China, 1945–1950]. Chongqing: Chongqing, 1987.

Zi Zhongyun and He Di, eds. *Meitai Guanxi Sishinian* [Forty years of US-Taiwan relations]. Beijing: People's Press, 1991.

Zou Jing-wen. *Li Denghui Zhizheng Gaobai Shilu* [Record of revelations on Lee Tenghui's administration]. Taipei: INK, 2001.

Index

About the Author

Robert G. Sutter has been visiting professor of Asian Studies at the School of Foreign Service, Georgetown University, since 2001. Prior to taking this full-time position, Sutter specialized in Asian and Pacific Affairs and U.S. foreign policy in a U.S. government career of thirty-three years involving the Congressional Research Service of the Library of Congress, the Central Intelligence Agency, the Department of State, and the Senate Foreign Relations Committee. He was for many years the Senior Specialist and Director of the Foreign Affairs and National Defense Division of the Congressional Research Service. He also was the National Intelligence Officer for East Asia and the Pacific at the U.S. Government's National Intelligence Council, and the China Division Director at the Department of State's Bureau of Intelligence and Research. A Ph.D. graduate in History and East Asian Languages from Harvard University, Sutter taught part-time for over thirty years at Georgetown, George Washington, and Johns Hopkins Universities, and the University of Virginia. He has published seventeen books, over one hundred articles, and several hundred government reports dealing with contemporary East Asian and Pacific countries and their relations with the United States. His most recent books are *The United States in Asia* (2008) and *Chinese Foreign Relations: Power and Policy since the Cold War* (second edition, 2010).

Lightning Source UK Ltd.
Milton Keynes UK
03 March 2011
168627UK00001B/25/P

ML

2-12